Gordian Knot

OXFORD STUDIES IN INTERNATIONAL HISTORY

JAMES J. SHEEHAN, SERIES ADVISOR

The Wilsonian Moment:
Self-Determination and the International Origins of Anticolonial Nationalism
Erez Manela

In War's Wake:
Europe's Displaced Persons in the Postwar Order
Gerard Daniel Cohen

Grounds of Judgment:
Extraterritoriality and Imperial Power in Nineteenth-Century China and Japan
Pär Kristoffer Cassel

The Acadian Diaspora:
An Eighteenth-Century History
Christopher Hodson

Gordian Knot:
Apartheid and the Unmaking of the Liberal World Order
Ryan M. Irwin

Gordian Knot

Apartheid and the Unmaking
of the Liberal World Order

RYAN M. IRWIN

OXFORD
UNIVERSITY PRESS

OXFORD
UNIVERSITY PRESS

Oxford University Press is a department of the University of Oxford.
It furthers the University's objective of excellence in research,
scholarship, and education by publishing worldwide.

Oxford   New York
Auckland   Cape Town   Dar es Salaam   Hong Kong   Karachi
Kuala Lumpur   Madrid   Melbourne   Mexico City   Nairobi
New Delhi   Shanghai   Taipei   Toronto

With offices in
Argentina   Austria   Brazil   Chile   Czech Republic   France   Greece
Guatemala   Hungary   Italy   Japan   Poland   Portugal   Singapore
South Korea   Switzerland   Thailand   Turkey   Ukraine   Vietnam

Oxford is a registered trade mark of Oxford University Press
in the UK and certain other countries.

Published in the United States of America by
Oxford University Press
198 Madison Avenue, New York, NY 10016

Library of Congress Cataloging-in-Publication Data
Irwin, Ryan M.
Gordian knot : apartheid and the unmaking of the liberal world order / Ryan M. Irwin.
p.   cm.—(Oxford studies in international history)
Includes bibliographical references and index.
ISBN 978-0-19-985561-2 (hardcover : alk. paper)
1. South Africa—Politics and government—1961–1978.
2. Apartheid—Political aspects—South Africa.
3. Self-determination, National—South Africa.
4. Decolonization—South Africa.
5. South Africa—Foreign relations. I. Title.
II. Series: Oxford studies in international history.
DT1945.I79   2012
968.06—dc23   2012003122

1 3 5 7 9 8 6 4 2

Printed in the United States of America
on acid-free paper

For Amy

Turn him to any cause of policy,
The Gordian Knot of it he will unloose . . .
    —William Shakespeare, *Henry V*, Act 1, Scene 1, 45–46

CONTENTS

PREFACE AND ACKNOWLEDGMENTS

Every piece of writing is partly autobiographical. For me, this book started the first time I was hit over the head with a police baton. It was in Amsterdam in early 2002, and I was a junior in college, studying abroad in London. I was in Amsterdam for the same reason twenty-somethings everywhere go to Amsterdam when they're in their twenties and, admittedly, the story of how exactly I found myself at the receiving end of that particular nightstick is of little relevance to this book. What matters is that I happened to be in the middle of an anti-American riot, perpetuated by a group of individuals dissatisfied with both the George W. Bush administration's most recent policy decisions in the Middle East and the Dutch government's recent immigration policies toward people of Middle Eastern descent living in Amsterdam. I understood none of this at the time. Frankly, as I sat with my hand on my head on that particular street, watching vaguely as events swirled around me, my thoughts were limited pretty much to two things: (1) That officer, whoever he was, was a lot stronger than he looked; and (2) life in Amsterdam was *much* different than I had imagined from the confines of my college town in upstate New York.

For a long time, the experience was just something that happened. It took some Advil, a bit of self-reflection, and several years for me to see that it underscored, probably better than any class I had taken as an undergraduate, the central lesson of a liberal arts education. Perspective matters. This book is about perspective. It emerges from an attempt to better understand the contradictions of our current world. Why did people in Amsterdam care so much about U.S. foreign policy? What was the relationship between Bush's Middle East policies and European immigrant experiences? How could the son of a middle-class American family afford to travel abroad while so many others lived in such obvious poverty? Why do "they" hate "us"? It is difficult to conceptualize answers to such questions without untangling the knotted historical relationship between globalization, decolonization, and the United States. Ideas about our world have evolved alongside an assortment of political pathways—entwined with competing narratives about the past, present, and future, and contested in ways that reveal much about the complex marriage of empire and power to autonomy and identity. At its most basic level, this book strives to make sense of this messy process. It examines a particularly controversial issue in a fluid moment of world history: when Europe relinquished formal control of much of the global south and new leaders stepped onto the international stage for the first time. My aim is to shed light on the political impact of decolonization and highlight the way perspective shaped perception in the second half of the twentieth century. In doing so, I hope to explain some of the antecedents and paradoxes of our world today.

My debts—material and intellectual—are numerous. The archival research for this project was conducted in Africa, Europe, and North America with the support of International Security Studies (ISS) at Yale University, the Society for Historians of American Foreign Relations (SHAFR), the George C. Marshall Foundation, the Kirwan Center for the Study of Race and Ethnicity, the Mershon Center for International Security Studies at Ohio State University, and the History Department at Ohio State University. My project would never have gotten off the ground without this institutional support. I am grateful especially to Joby Abernathy for her assistance at Ohio State, as well as Susan Hennigan and Kathleen Murphy for the help they provided at Yale. During my final years as a Ph.D. candidate, I attained full-year fellowships from Yale and SHAFR, which gave me an unparalleled opportunity to step away from teaching and write this manuscript in New Haven, Connecticut.

Many people helped nurture the ideas developed in this manuscript. At Ohio State, Peter Hahn, Robert McMahon, Carole Fink, Mitch Lerner, Kevin Boyle, and Judy Wu provided support on many levels. I also benefited from the feedback and criticism of my fellow graduate students, most especially Paul Chamberlin, Alex Poster, and Chapin Rydingsward. At Yale, Paul Kennedy and John Gaddis have been mentors and advocates. Like many others, I have been humbled by their generosity. Adam Tooze challenged several of my conclusions in helpful ways, and I received valuable feedback from many of the young scholars who have passed through ISS's doors in recent years, including Jeff Byrne, James Cameron, Chris Dietrich, Jeremy Friedman, Sulmaan Khan, Nathan Kurz, Charlie Laderman, Chris Miller, Victor McFarland, Lien-Hang Nguyen, and Sarah Snyder. Tim Borstelmann, Frederick Cooper, Nick Cullather, Richard Hull, Miguel Jerónimo, Fredrik Logevall, Wm. Roger Louis, Jason Parker, Jeremi Suri, and Marilyn Young provided generous feedback on different parts of this manuscript at workshops in Bloomington, Boston, Madison, New York, Potsdam, and Washington, DC. I am also grateful to this project's anonymous reviewers for their essential critiques, as well as to the editors of *Diplomatic History* and *International History Review*, who gave me permission to incorporate aspects of my earlier work—specifically articles published in 2009 and 2010—into this book. My Oxford editor, Susan Ferber, shepherded this manuscript through the publication process with tremendous skill.

In South Africa, Anna-Mart and Johann van Wyk, as well as Tilman Dedering, opened their homes and provided companionship, as well as assistance and critical feedback on this project. Christopher Saunders, Geoffrey Allen, Jan Picard, Neels Muller, and Mosoabuli Maamoe were also welcoming and helpful. My research experiences abroad would have been much different without their assistance. At a different stage, Sue Onslow offered valuable guidance about research in South Africa. Scott Cappuzzo, Seth and Emily Art, Brian Nordell, Adam and Rachael Gloo, Jason and Kate Behan, and Scott and Pat Clark provided irony and places to stay in New York, Washington, and Boston. My parents, grandparents, and in-laws gave sage advice and encouragement from afar; my brother passed along invaluable information on the importance of Florida sea grass to the apartheid debate of the 1960s. I remain deeply grateful to everyone.

My biggest debt, however, is to Amy. For over a decade she has sat at the center of my life. From that vantage point, she has pushed me incessantly to be a better version of myself, forced me to laugh at my excesses, and patiently provided feedback on every single word I have written. Without her toleration, my routine sojourns would be impossible. Without her curiosity, my unanswerable questions would remain uninterrogated. Without her love, this manuscript would be incomplete. This work is hers.

Gordian Knot

Introduction

Opening the Curtain

A racial consciousness, evoked by the attitudes and practices of the West, had slowly blended with a defensive religious feeling; here, in Bandung, the two had combined into one: a racial and religious system of identification manifesting itself in an emotional nationalism which was now leaping state boundaries and melting and merging, one into the other.

—Richard Wright, *The Color Curtain* (1956)

One needs to appreciate the sense of possibility of these years and to understand what ensued not as an imminent logic of colonial history but as a dynamic process with a tragic end.

—Frederick Cooper, *Colonialism in Question* (2006)

Bandung teemed with energy in April 1955. Nestled at the heart of the sprawling Citarum river basin on the island of Java, the city was one of independent Indonesia's most cosmopolitan and culturally diverse urban centers. Diplomats from twenty-nine decolonized countries, as well as dozens of activists from sub-Saharan Africa and over 650 reporters, had converged on the city to participate in the first official gathering of decolonized peoples from the global south. This six-day "Asian-African" summit began on April 18 at the architectural crown jewel of Bandung, the newly renovated Gedung Merdeka building. The center's colonial origins—it had been built by the Dutch in 1895 and used throughout the first half of the twentieth century to celebrate European art, culture, and social privilege—mattered little to the representatives assembled in its spacious main hall. "Every religion under the sun" was present, novelist Richard Wright wrote as he watched the opening proceedings from the press gallery. "Almost every race on earth, every shade of political opinion, and one and a half billion people from 12,606,938 square miles of the earth's surface were represented here."[1] For the participants, the gathering embodied both the shared possibilities and the political optimism of decolonization.

The first speaker, Indonesia's President Sukarno, was a man, in Wright's view, "who knew words and how to use them." Speaking fluently in English, the president explained that the people assembled in Bandung had spent the past generation "voiceless" and "unregarded" in the world—united in humiliation and burdened by European domination. That era had come now to its official end. Although still threatened by the hydrogen bomb and the hubris of the superpowers, the rising peoples of the so-called Third World shared a moral commitment to refocus the world's attention on the true banes of human civilization—colonial rule and white racism. These mutually constitutive threats, not American-led capitalism or Soviet-inspired communism, were the greatest dangers to lasting peace and prosperity in the second half of the twentieth century. In tethering this assertion to contemporary events, Indonesia's Prime Minister Ali Sastroamidjojo, the event's second speaker and principal organizer, gravitated toward a seemingly obvious example. "How often had the timid attempts" to fight "color bars [been] outweighed by measures of ruthless discrimination?" he queried. "Is not Apartheid policy a form of absolute intolerance more befitting the Dark Ages than this modern world?" As the speeches continued through the morning, delegates continued to hearken on the specter of South Africa. The most "typical example of outworn colonial polic[ies]" in the world could be found in Pretoria, Thailand's Prince Wan argued, "where color prejudice and superiority of the white man" had resulted in "discrimination against Indians and natives, and to the segregation of the so-called colored people." If the free people of the decolonized world failed to mobilize against this disease of discrimination, the assumptions that buttressed life in South Africa would surely seep out into the world and contaminate the intellectual well of postcolonial freedom.[2]

The Bandung conference was the opening act of a momentous time in world history. The decade following the Second World War had been shaped largely by events in the northern hemisphere. The United States had successfully systemized its intellectual, economic, and political authority through a series of new global institutions, trade agreements, and military bases, establishing an unprecedented alliance system that stretched across the rim of Eurasia and enshrined America's burgeoning "preponderance of power" on the global stage.[3] Opposite this expanding network sat Josef Stalin's Union of Soviet Socialist Republics—devastated by World War II yet determined to protect its flank in Europe and extend its control at home—and Mao Zedong's newly formed People's Republic of China, ascendant after an epic struggle against Japanese invaders and a long, brutal civil war against Washington's Nationalist ally, Chiang Kai-shek.[4] These trends had merged most violently on the Korean peninsula in the early 1950s.[5] By 1955, however, it seemed increasingly apparent that the second decade of the postwar era would be shaped by events along the so-called periphery. Decolonization was on the rise and, as the Bandung meeting made clear, the emerging leaders of Africa and Asia had little enthusiasm for the turgid East-West binary that pitted Moscow against Washington and divided the world into warring ideological camps. The world-view of these leaders, to the extent that it existed coherently, flowed not from Cold War maxims but from a sense of frustration with the pan-European world's historic attempt to cast the colonized world as its racial "other." Divided on many questions, representatives at Bandung shared a common desire to destroy the epistemology of colonialism and erect in its place an intellectual edifice that treated territorial independence, economic development, and racial equality as universal rights.[6]

South Africa's role as the foil to this emerging vision was not insignificant. The program of apartheid—designed to control the movement, residential rights, and work opportunities of non-Europeans in South Africa—challenged many of the arguments that emanated from the Bandung conference. As Asian and African leaders cast off colonial stereotypes and trumpeted the importance of postcolonial viewpoints, Pretoria moved defiantly in the opposite direction by embracing racial segregation and colonial-style paternalism. South Africa, as such, was a lodestar. The country's policies sharpened opinions in ways that attached specific, shared meaning to amorphous words like freedom, justice, and equality, and encouraged a diverse cross-section of influence makers—politicized intellectuals and intellectual politicians alike—to think more thoroughly about their views on the past, present, and future of the international world. Just as anticommunism animated Washington's Cold War and anticapitalism oriented Moscow's stance abroad, the fight against apartheid gave form to the political project known as the Third World.

This book tells the story of the apartheid debate in the years that surrounded African decolonization. It attempts to answer one of the twentieth century's fundamental questions: How did the rapid growth of small, non-European nation-states at midcentury affect the international community? Located at the meeting point of the African, Atlantic, and Indian worlds, South Africa provides an answer. With a violent history and a multiethnic population, the country was a physical and imaginative borderland of the postcolonial Cold War.[7] It embodied the contradictions of modernity, showcasing the material possibilities of economic progress as well as the burdensome legacies of racial discrimination, forced labor, and imperial conquest. *Gordian Knot* examines the conversation about South Africa during the 1960s—a period bracketed by feelings of intense optimism and pessimism toward the decolonization project. Apartheid was not the most important issue of the postcolonial decade, but it highlighted well the agency of and the differences between actors in the pan-European and non-European worlds, and it explains much about deeper trajectories that remade international affairs during the late twentieth century.

Several groups tried to legitimize their views about apartheid during this period. In the early Cold War, global criticism of South Africa had come primarily
from South Asian politicians and North American liberals. After the 1955 Bandung meeting, the fight against South Africa's policies was sharpened, elaborated,
and expanded by the growth of African nationalism. Although independence in
West and East Africa emerged from a heterogeneous set of local conflicts, African nationalism was a potent global movement in the heady years that surrounded decolonization's apex. Three principles tended to unite Africa's new
leaders: racial inequality was intellectually bankrupt, Africans were better
equipped than Europeans to deliver economic progress in Africa, and legitimacy
was tied directly to political control of a territory and membership in the United
Nations. The apartheid system was controversial because it not only offended
the conscience of leaders in the decolonized world, but because it also challenged the conceptual scaffolding of these claims. By suggesting that economic
progress and territorial autonomy could be accomplished without racial equality,
South Africa's domestic race policies undermined the intellectual rationale of
the postcolonial nation itself.

African nationalists adopted a distinct strategy to confront apartheid as they
stepped into the international arena. Throughout the 1960s, African diplomats
used their numerical advantage at the U.N. General Assembly to push the Security Council to impose diplomatic and economic sanctions against the South
African government. These efforts turned on whether the so-called African
Group—a lobbying entity formed in 1958 to coordinate African diplomacy in
New York—could convince the great powers to accept that racial discrimination
was a clear threat to international peace and security. Such a move would give
the Security Council authorization to act and buttress racial equality as a core
tenet of national sovereignty. The apartheid question was only one of many issues that reached the Security Council in these years, but it was unique in highlighting how global forums built by European internationalists after World War
II were transformed in the postcolonial decade by the imperatives of African
decolonization. By laying claim to Western institutions, African elites aimed
literally to institutionalize support for their broader worldview.

The South African government was initially caught off guard by the African
Group's offensive. Although criticized at the United Nations during the 1950s,
Pretoria had been consistently shielded by Washington and London from Secu-
rity Council sanctions. At the height of the Algerian war in the mid-1950s, South
Africa's leaders were so confident of their status that they temporarily left the
United Nations under the assumption that the West would rather punish their
critics than let the Union of South Africa permanently turn away from the inter-
national community. This perception of strength came from the ubiquity of the
Cold War in the decade after World War II, which united the Western bloc and

helped rationalize South Africa's internal problems as an outgrowth of communist subversion. The argument lost sway in the years after the Bandung conference. As the General Assembly became more diverse and criticism of apartheid more pointed, the support of the United States and the United Kingdom grew steadily less unconditional. By 1960, the South African government was vulnerable in the international arena. In the emerging decolonized world, apartheid was a propaganda liability that undermined the West's ability to project its influence in independent Africa.

Afrikaner leaders responded to these changes with a targeted campaign of political suasion in North America and Western Europe. Government officials—especially within the Afrikaans-oriented National Party—worked to circumvent the burgeoning authority of African nationalists at the U.N. General Assembly by appealing directly to media elites, investors, and policymakers in the United States and Great Britain. Legitimacy, for Pretoria, emerged not from international organizations like the United Nations, but from a diffuse network of powerbrokers in New York, Washington, and London. As National Party leaders implemented this counteroffensive, they challenged negative perceptions of apartheid by wrapping South Africa's domestic policies in the languages of modernization theory and territorial nationalism. These efforts were not entirely successful, but they showcased how some elites in North America, Western Europe, and South Africa squared their longstanding racial paternalism with the new discourse of modernization. Pretoria's initiatives also underscored the global context of the apartheid idea. Although designed to alleviate white anxieties at home, the language of apartheid was married to an international debate about the meaning of territoriality, race, and progress after World War II.

Policymakers in Washington, and to a lesser extent London, were reluctant referees in this contest. As South Africa's principal patrons and important players at the Security Council, the United States and Great Britain had the ability to either punish South Africa for apartheid or protect it from African nationalist criticism. Reconciling these two extremes was not easy. On the one hand, Washington and London shared deep and longstanding material investments in the Union. South Africa was not only a major source of uranium and gold for the Western bloc, but it also provided American and British capitalists with millions of dollars in trade each year and gave homes to a U.S. tracking station and a British military base. On the other hand, the United States and Great Britain shared a commitment to the legitimacy of the United Nations, and as the organization's membership changed dramatically in the early 1960s, faith in liberal internationalism and collective security began to buckle under the weight of calls for racial justice and economic progress. Policymakers in Washington and London understood that the apartheid issue was symbolically important to newly independent nations. A stand against South Africa, in theory, would shore up support for the

West, prevent Africa's alignment with the Soviet Union, and demonstrate that the United Nations could respond to controversial problems in this new postcolonial era of international affairs.

The Western bloc reconciled its dilemma in two distinct phases. In the years between 1960 and 1965, events pushed the United States and Great Britain into a confrontation with South Africa. Not only was the African Group successful in expanding its power at the United Nations, but the American civil rights movement also infused apartheid issues with additional authority. These trends were buttressed by bureaucratic changes within the U.S. State Department, as the newly formed African Bureau became a supporter of sanctions and diplomatic intervention in southern Africa. Although the British government remained reluctant to support these changes, it nonetheless partnered with Washington in the wake of Rhodesia's unilateral declaration of independence in 1965, establishing a united front against Pretoria in 1966. However, the momentum for action began to fracture in the late 1960s. With the Americanization of the Vietnam War, U.S. policy became the target of heightened criticism at the United Nations, subtly creating a backlash within Washington against officials who put precedence on Third World viewpoints and political initiatives. Even more, the clarity of the U.S. civil rights movement declined as the movement went north, just as a series of military coups removed the most prominent African nationalists from power in West Africa. The result was a dramatic shift in American policy. By the end of the 1960s, Washington and London not only supported the legitimacy of the apartheid state, they also embraced the wholesale containment of Third World political campaigns.

By the end of the decade, too, African nationalist diplomats—who enjoyed enormous prestige in the immediate wake of decolonization—had been discredited widely, and liberation organizations throughout southern Africa were building relationships with groups beyond Africa, supplanting the ideological bonds of postcolonial nationalism with broader discourses that emphasized human rights, Third Worldism, and Marxist internationalism. The African National Congress (ANC) helped drive this transformation. Isolated by African nationalists throughout the early and mid-1960s, the organization helped reframe the apartheid question during the early 1970s, positioning both itself and South Africa's problems at the center of an emerging community of stateless activists in the global north and south. The South African government also experienced a revival of sorts on the international stage in these years. As Washington began to alter its stance toward postcolonial demands, Afrikaner elites implemented an outreach program in Africa north of the Zambezi River that culminated in a series of trade relationships in West and East Africa. Even as anti-apartheid sentiment grew more widespread in the 1970s, these concrete state-to-state bonds insulated and strengthened the National Party, ensuring apartheid's paradoxical survival into the 1990s.

By situating the apartheid debate in its global context, *Gordian Knot* contributes to scholarship about the end of European imperialism and the ascendancy of U.S. global power. It seeks to establish a bridge between African and American international history. For decades, Africanists have sought to make sense of South Africa's awkward place in African history. While adept at explaining social and cultural negotiations between colonial bureaucrats and indigenous peoples, especially within local settings, the field has provided fewer insights about international affairs and rarely ventured into the postindependence period. Despite the sophisticated nature of work about colonial hybridity and peasant identity, decolonization—a process with immense transnational importance—has been treated as a fragmented and theorized phenomenon, and topics relating to African geopolitics, postcolonial nationalism, and the apartheid debate have garnered little scholarly attention. The resulting blind spots have made it difficult to fully understand how and why the optimism of the immediate postcolonial years, widespread in so many intellectual circles, gave way to the pessimistic environment of the 1970s.[8]

This book approaches the apartheid debate by looking at the politics of identification. It explicates how a cross-section of governmental and nongovernmental elites employed discourse to build alliances, identify enemies, and lay claims on the international stage. The result is a portrait of contestation, tethered to a global canvas and relevant to historians of the African continent, which lingers not on the heroism of anti-apartheid activists but on the way universalisms became plural as different groups competed to define the meaning of the world they inhabited. Although certain terminologies—freedom, justice, equality—persisted over long periods of time, the reference points that oriented these concepts changed as the fortunes of these groups ebbed and flowed on the international stage. Looking carefully at their gains and setbacks provides insight about how and why particular trajectories developed (and others did not) during the twentieth century.[9]

Gordian Knot's first principal argument flows from this framework: Africa's independence marked one of the twentieth century's seminal ruptures. The continent's global importance predated the 1960s. Long before U.S. policymakers embraced modernization theory as the West's response to Soviet-style industrial planning, Europeans had popularized the language of development to justify their presence in Africa. This turn globalized the development idea after World War II and launched a contentious two-way conversation about the nature of territoriality, race, and economic progress—a conversation that reshaped the imaginative terrain of the mid-twentieth century. This debate was neither straightforward nor monolithic: some African activists, eager to gain access to the provisions of the European welfare state, tried to use developmental imperialism to gain citizenship rights within shared Afro-European polities; others

sought to replace foreign rule with a continental nation in the image of the
United States or the Soviet Union; still others embraced communism and proletarian revolution. Decolonization's ultimate form—independence and General
Assembly membership for nearly forty new nation-states between 1957 and
1967—resulted from a messy give-and-take process between people with different expectations and objectives.[10]

This process did not end in 1960; it merely evolved as Africans moved from
imperial frameworks into the international community. Beneath the surface of
the apartheid debate in these years sat a question that defined diplomacy in the
decolonized age: What was the postcolonial nation? Over the course of the 1960s,
empire—celebrated once as a vehicle of cosmopolitanism and globalization—
reemerged as the nation's imagined antipode and as an agent of economic exploitation and racial supremacy. Self-determination, a concept that Woodrow Wilson
used to manage the disintegration of the Ottoman Empire, grew into the panacea
of economic underdevelopment. Sovereignty evolved from a layered notion of
self-government, fully consonant with membership within an imperial polity, into
the prerequisite of material progress and cultural autonomy. African decolonization, in short, was a watershed. It marked a moment when old arguments gained
new currency by moving from informal spaces—union halls, classrooms, and
community centers—into formal arenas such as the United Nations.

As a political outlier, the apartheid debate shaped the trajectory of this
process. The fight against Afrikaner nationalism hardened how African leaders
talked about territoriality, development, and race, and empowered the brand of
nationalism associated with such postcolonial figures as Kwame Nkrumah,
Nnamdi Azikiwe, and Jomo Kenyatta. By providing the Third World project
with a real-time foil, the apartheid debate helped unite African nationalists
with their Asian, Middle Eastern, and, eventually, Latin American counterparts. The victories of this coalition—namely the delegitimization of racial discrimination and the creation of a new discourse of autonomy—*are* the victories
of decolonization. The setbacks this group experienced, especially its inability
to topple apartheid through U.N. sanctions, underscored that decolonization
had only replaced one system of unequal power with another—a realization
that encouraged the Third World's collective turn away from the United Nations and toward the economic nationalism and dependency theories of the
early 1970s.

Africa's decolonization altered the international community and remade
America's role therein, a process that U.S. international historians are well positioned to explain. A crop of American historians now incorporate perspectives
from the non-European world—moving beyond the tendency to analyze every
aspect of this history through the lens of the East-West superpower contest—but
the field has clustered toward camps that either embrace the motif of imperial

continuity or subsume diplomatic exchange within macroprocesses such as cultural transfer, disease control, and population management.[11] Neither approach captures the possibility and uncertainty that characterized American foreign relations in the decade after Africa's independence. Looking at the United States from the outside in—through the lens of apartheid debate—underscores the unusual nature of American power during the mid-twentieth century. For many observers along the periphery, the Cold War was a contest that pitted an especially powerful Eurasian empire against a hegemon with unprecedented political, economic, and intellectual authority in the world. Cognizant of the Soviet Union's limited influence beyond the Eurasian rim, African and Afrikaner nationalists brought their arguments to American-backed forums and molded their rhetoric deliberately to appeal to American powerbrokers. Neither group saw the United States as an empire at the outset of the 1960s; attitudes changed only as the limitations of the nation-state system (and advocacy at the United Nations) became clear. Even if the United States wanted to downplay the combustible issues at the heart of the apartheid debate, its political, economic, and intellectual authority placed it always at the center of international politics.[12]

Gordian Knot's second argument flows from this framework: Washington's approach toward the rest of the world—its stance toward global governance—changed fundamentally during the 1960s. Containment shaped America's foreign policy throughout the Cold War, but containment interacted with older ideas about civilization and evolved as decolonization swept through the international arena.[13] The postwar years saw the United States try to establish a Pax Americana that enshrined U.S. supremacy without using the tactics and tropes of imperial Europe. In the parlance of contemporary political science, Washington sought to create a form of legitimate hegemony. Base agreements, covert interventions, and bilateral trade arrangements projected U.S. influence into the rim of Eurasia and halted the growth of the Soviet empire, but America's grand strategy purposely went beyond the traditional markers of hard power. The initial decades of the Cold War saw Washington invest enormous resources in liberal institutions such as the United Nations, International Monetary Fund (IMF), World Bank, and International Court of Justice—institutions that not only promoted interdependence and collective security, but also formed the scaffolding of a new type of geopolitical system. Shaped by American thinkers and U.S. interests, this system normalized American ideas and political goals on a global scale.[14]

By the early 1960s, the United States had reason to view its efforts as a success. Moscow had grown adept at using its Security Council veto to frustrate some U.S. goals, but the great powers had avoided a third world war, and Washington still shaped the agenda of the General Assembly, the International Court, and the various economic agencies of the Bretton Woods system. African decolonization changed everything. The sudden emergence of almost forty non-European states constituted both the realization of America's postimperial vision of the world and a direct threat to Washington's continued hegemony. By placing questions of race squarely at the center of world affairs, African states exposed the prejudices that quietly underpinned America's liberal world order. For many U.S. leaders, the black Atlantic was a uniquely uncivilized and troubled place—devoid of the cultural heritage that characterized the Levant, South and East Asia, or Latin America. The African Group's energetic diplomacy at the General Assembly challenged this perception directly, and it did so just as America's civil rights movement exposed the depth of America's own race problem. On a level far deeper than Moscow's strategic intrigues or Asia's independence, African decolonization challenged the intellectual edifice of Washington's worldview. It marked the moment when small, non-European states took formal control of the agenda of the international community.

Because it focused the energy of African nationalists, the apartheid debate influenced the trajectory of U.S. thinking. American liberals initially believed that they could preserve U.S. authority through a combination of racial reforms at home, symbolic declarations abroad, and economic modernization programs. In theory, U.N. membership would bracket the sovereignty debate and encourage African leaders to accept interdependence on Washington's terms. Apartheid proved this assumption wrong. Just as African diplomats grew frustrated by America's refusal to recognize the merits of their struggle, the United States became increasingly exasperated by the African Group's insistence on reinterpreting the U.N. Charter and reframing the General Assembly agenda. As U.S. policymakers lost confidence that institutions could bring about pro-American consensus, their support for the larger idea of liberal internationalism eroded, eventually leading to new attitudes toward organizations like the United Nations, World Bank, and IMF. This process not only laid the seeds of detente; it also marked the unmaking of America's liberal world order.

By the end of the 1960s, decolonization's contradictions were thrown into sharp relief. The growth of non-European nation-states opened discursive opportunities for Third World actors and facilitated the partial transformation of international norms—with the United Nations serving as a forum to project new questions into the international public sphere. But success as defined by these nationalists did not materialize. South Africa's opponents failed to pass sanctions against Pretoria, primarily because their political goals differed from the priorities of American policymakers. More important, however, was the shifting nature of political space. As non-Western diplomats at the General Assembly grew more adept at using their numbers to shape the agenda of the United Nations, U.S. leaders pulled away from the organization and the idea that it could be a bulwark of American global power. This shift—and the underlying attitudes that supported it—altered the influence of new states at the international level and played into the hands of South Africa's initiatives abroad. With disappointment on the rise throughout the Third World, political momentum within southern Africa (as well as the Middle East and Southeast Asia) shifted definitively to leaders in the nongovernmental realm, just as Washington began to initiate its slow, halting rapprochement with Pretoria. The results were profound. By the end of the 1960s, the United States—once heralded as a supporter of the decolonization process—was being recast everywhere as the world's cynical "New Empire."

Ultimately this book studies how multiple international actors—large and small—interacted in a moment of rapid and profound change. It highlights how politics and narratives pulled people together and pushed them apart in the 1960s, and it shows how knowledge was policed and challenged on different stages in the global arena. The debate over South Africa showcases why certain issues became controversial while others faded into the background, and it exposes the way America's approach toward global governance changed in the wake of decolonization. In a world defined today by material integration yet divided through competing prisms of local reality—where consciousness of the chasm between ideology and material power has never been wider and the challenges of leadership never more unwieldy—the story of the global apartheid debate offers a window to consider events of the late twentieth century. Singular moral lessons do not do justice to the complexity of today's world. But process-oriented histories—told on global and local canvases with an eye for ambiguity and contestation—are, perhaps, a tentative step in a positive direction.

PART ONE

WINDS OF CHANGE

Architects and Earthquakes

Behold, they are one people, and they have all one language; and this is
only the beginning of what they will do; and nothing that they propose
to do will be impossible to them.

—Genesis 11:5

1961. Listen: "Let us waste no time in sterile litanies and nauseating
mimicry. Leave this Europe where they are never done talking of Man,
yet murder men everywhere they find them, at the corner of every one
of their own streets, in all the corners of the globe. For centuries they
have stifled almost the whole of humanity in the name of a so-called
spiritual experience." The tone is new. Who dares speak thus?
—Jean-Paul Sartre in Frantz Fanon, *The Wretched of the Earth* (1961)

On January 17, 1960, British Prime Minister Harold Macmillan stood in the
lobby of Johannesburg's Jan Smuts International Airport—gateway to the South
African nation—with a self-consciousness that few expected from one of the
leading political figures in the Western world. Having lost his footing as he
entered the airport's reception area, the prime minister had pirouetted awk-
wardly in front of the cameras and nearly fallen to the ground. It was a slip rife
with symbolism. Commenting on the scene several decades later, Johannesburg's the *Star* said that Macmillan's misstep foreshadowed an "entire decade
that seemed to get off on the wrong foot" for South Africa.[1]

The Union of South Africa was the last stop on Macmillan's tour of Africa in
early 1960. The prime minister had just led the British Conservative Party to its
first general election victory on his watch. His trip provided a brief reprieve from
the demands of domestic politics and gave him an opportunity to reassert his
government's flagging authority on the world stage. Under his leadership, Great
Britain had accelerated the liquidation of its global empire and, as Macmillan traveled abroad that January, he trumpeted continually both the legitimacy of African
nationalist movements and the importance of continued Commonwealth membership. With Nigeria and Tanganyika on the verge of political independence, the

prime minister wanted to project the message that Great Britain could be a trusted partner in world affairs.

Macmillan's stop in South Africa highlighted the difficulties he faced as he built support for this position. As many observers acknowledged in the days before his visit, Britain's ties to the Union were economically deep but politically problematic. Beyond the tensions among English and Afrikaans speakers over the legacy of the Anglo-Boer War, the Union's racial policies sat in juxtaposition to the trends spreading through West and East Africa. Apartheid was premised on the illegitimacy of black enfranchisement and majority rule. This divergence put Great Britain in a difficult position. So long as material and moral aid continued to flow toward South Africa, Whitehall's overtures to Ghana, Nigeria, Tanganyika, and the rest of Africa would be viewed with suspicion. As one newspaper commented, South Africa had become the British government's "African albatross."[2]

A week after arriving in South Africa, the British prime minister sat down to discuss the political landscape with the Union's two most influential politicians, Prime Minister Hendrik Verwoerd and Foreign Minister Eric Louw. The conversation highlighted the growing chasm between the Western bloc and South Africa. Drawing immediately on the vocabulary of interwar colonialism, Verwoerd explained that South Africa was the "resident representative of European civilization in Africa." In his mind, "If the United Kingdom and the United States could show greater confidence in what the Union Government [was] trying to do to further the Western cause," the Union would repay them by bringing more influence "to bear on the other African states."[3] Macmillan remained deferential, but Verwoerd's approach was out of sync with his own attitudes toward postcolonial questions. Africans were capable of modernization on their own terms, in his mind, and their support—given freely without intimidation—was essential to the West's future success in the Cold War.

Macmillan made this point directly in a public speech on February 3 at a special joint session of South Africa's Parliament. Arguing that a "wind of change" was blowing through Africa, he told his audience that whether they liked it or not, "the growth of [African] national consciousness [was] a political fact. We must all accept it as a fact. Our national policies must take account of it." In clear language, Macmillan connected this nationalist sentiment to the European project of development, lauding those who wanted to push the frontiers of knowledge, put science in the service of human needs, expand food production and communication, and spread education. The great issue of the second half of the twentieth century was not how the West would reinvigorate colonialism, but whether supporters of African nationalism would swing toward the East or to the West. Turning subtly to face Verwoerd, Macmillan declared that Great Britain supported societies "in which individual merit, and individual merit alone,

[was] the criterion for a man's advancements, whether political or economic." The Commonwealth would continue to respect each member's "sovereignty in matters of internal policy." However, he closed with the ominous warning that it was time for South Africa to "recognize that, in this shrinking world in which we live today, the internal policies of one nation may have effects outside it."[4]

South Africa's political leaders were stunned. As Verwoerd listened to Macmillan's speech, his face "grew slowly more pale and tense" and he stared "stonily ahead," refusing to make eye contact with those around him.[5] At the end of the address, the South African prime minister walked slowly to the podium. Clearly angered, he stammered that the Union had enough problems "without [Macmillan] coming to add to them," and declared that black nationalism was only possible because of European civilization. As the "only true Western state in Africa," his government was entitled to "just treatment" abroad. Drawing on the familiar maxims of apartheid, he lamented that his government alone could provide "a full future to the Black man in [its] midst."[6]

His words were met with applause, but they failed to stem the effects of Macmillan's speech outside South Africa's Assembly Hall. Having anticipated a collegial address on the Union's continued importance to the West, many white South Africans were genuinely shaken by the earnestness of the British prime minister's words. "We cannot hand over any part of Africa for which we are responsible," Cape Town's *Die Burger* contended. "The state of emergency we have been plunged into by this Western panic can only be fought with united forces. It is a struggle for civilization."[7] Other writers responded with angst, admitting, "Circumstances are changing. The protection of the great imperial powers is disappearing. Our spiritual place in the world is disappearing."[8] Newspapers and commentators forwarded an array of arguments in the weeks that followed, but few challenged the underlying premise of Macmillan's address—global trends were isolating the Union of South Africa.

The "winds of change" speech captured an important moment in the twentieth century. Delivered in the midst of African decolonization, it framed the challenges facing not only South Africa but also the broader international community in the 1960s. If the ideological fight between the United States and the Soviet Union had shaped the parameters of world conflict in the immediate postwar years—reproducing certain Eurocentric, hierarchical assumptions about power and order—Macmillan's words underscored that African decolonization was shifting the intellectual terrain of global politics, not only opening new opportunities for cold warriors but also expanding the appeal of Third World nationalism and universalizing the tenets of Western development theory. In this new environment, a variety of actors jockeyed to shape the terms of international legitimacy. For leaders like Macmillan, it was incumbent upon the West to redouble its support for nonracial democracy, self-determination, and economic progress, rationalizing its power not through political domination but through multilateral collaboration. Only such an effort would establish equilibrium between postcolonial goals and Cold War norms.

South Africa challenged this formula on a very deep level. The architects of apartheid were committed intellectually and entrenched politically, with a worldview based on the full rejection of both Western liberalism and Third World nationalism. This chapter explores how the Union of South Africa became the outlier in this fast-changing, postcolonial world. It frames the origins of the apartheid story, looking first at the evolution of the apartheid system itself. Born of the country's unique domestic landscape, the concept of racial stratification emerged in response to the contradictions of minority rule in the Union during the interwar period. It was a contested idea and multiple interest groups strove to define it, but by the end of the 1950s a particular vision of apartheid—championed by Hendrik Verwoerd—had achieved bureaucratic supremacy within the National Party and widespread currency among white South Africans. This ideology drew a sharp line between the Union and the world community, embracing South African exceptionalism and a static view of global affairs.

However, this push toward racial stratification did not unfold in a vacuum. Throughout South Africa, nonwhite groups, organized in unions, classrooms, and religious settings, confronted the logic and instruments of apartheid in the interwar and postwar periods. These efforts were hardly monolithic—debates existed over the proper balance between black unity and multiracial equality, and tensions persisted between certain nonwhite political organizations—but by the end of the 1950s, a particular vision of African nationalism commanded widespread support in many corners of the country. Inspired by events in West Africa and South Asia, this ideological framework collapsed the distinctions between the Union and the rest of the African continent and positioned South Africa at the imaginative vanguard of the decolonization struggle.

In the moment before 1960, these dual movements created the boundaries of what would become the postcolonial apartheid debate. Conflict was inevitable. On philosophical and political levels, the architects of white power and their opponents envisioned two different futures for the Union and embraced incompatible arguments about the country's place in the world beyond South Africa's borders. Their differences foreshadowed many of the themes that would shape global politics in the decade after African or second-wave decolonization. Through its theoretical sophistication, the apartheid system pushed a pair of abstract, often unspoken queries to the surface of international relations: Who defined the rules of global politics? And what was the full significance of decolonization? By the time Macmillan put forward his own answer in February 1960, responses to these questions presaged not only the lines of the apartheid debate but also the fault lines of the coming postcolonial decade.

Citadel of Whiteness

It is impossible to understand the origins of the apartheid debate without examining the unique context of South Africa's national development. The idea of
creating a single, unified state in southern Africa emerged during the early twentieth century. The rationale was tied closely to economic concerns. Southern
Africa had been a loosely organized backwater of the British Empire through
much of the 1600s and 1700s. The discovery of diamonds in the 1860s and gold
in the 1870s amplified the region's international importance. Located in the in-
terior of the continent, mining towns like Kimberly and Johannesburg created
new incentives for a host of settlers from the United Kingdom, Australia, and the
United States to flock to the territory in the late 1800s, giving the colonial government in Cape Town a concrete reason to expand its borders northward
toward the Zambezi River.[9] In the case of Kimberly, British expansion was accomplished with relatively little opposition. Farther north, however, in the gold-
fields surrounding Johannesburg, Dutch farmers—those who had left the Cape
region in the 1830s and 1840s to establish an independent South African Republic, away from British influence—posed a more serious challenge to the Cape
Colony's goals. These Dutch *voortrekkers*, known as Afrikaners, had worked hard
to establish a foothold among African pastoralists and few wanted to cede their
autonomy to British officials.[10] As capitalist interests expanded in the Cape, the
mining region around Johannesburg grew steadily more important, culminating
in a series of British-led military campaigns against the Zulu and Swazi kingdoms in the Natal region and eventually open conflict between British soldiers
and Afrikaner farmers from the South African Republic. The resulting Anglo-
Boer Wars (1880–81, 1899–1902) gave Great Britain control over the mineral
resources in the Transvaal, and established the outlines of the state that would
become South Africa.[11]

The British government's first task was to reinforce its authority over the
former South African Republic. Under the guidance of Governor General Alfred
Milner, the colonial government moved from Cape Town to Johannesburg and
assembled a group of Oxford- and Cambridge-educated engineers to create bureaucratic institutions to govern the territory. The goal of British policy was to
establish an industrial nation with a unified public culture. This approach mirrored the stance taken in the empire's other dominion territories and put precedence on forming a unified state with authority over everyone, wherein all laws
applied equally to every individual.[12] Milner and his surrogates worked assiduously toward this end in the early twentieth century, establishing a modern tax
system, a host of new government agencies, an elaborate police force, and a
European judicial system. In the process, they Anglicized South African civil

society and opened the door for further investment in the mining industry. By the time Milner departed Johannesburg to accept a cabinet position in London in 1905, the outlines of the South African nation were established. European in its orientation, the country united several previously autonomous states and ostensibly embodied the tenets of nineteenth-century liberal capitalism.[13]

In practice, however, Milner's vision ran into problems. First, urbanization in Africa was much different than urbanization in Europe. The mining industry relied heavily on inexpensive African labor and, rather than treating nonwhites as equals within the Anglo system of law, Milner opted to establish a reserve system to segregate and destabilize the black work force, forcing Africans to reside in separate townships and migrate for employment on a seasonal basis. In his words, "If aboriginal natives [were] to come and go in large numbers in search of labour and to reside for considerable periods in the midst of a white community . . . the place [would] be in pandemonium."[14] Milner's decision to force Africans to carry identification cards helped the government monitor their movements, but it also racialized capitalist development in South Africa and planted the seeds of significant social unrest.[15]

At the same time, Afrikaner farmers in the Transvaal remained resentful of the outcome of the Anglo-Boer Wars. Having grown accustomed to a feudal system of governance that valued local autonomy and ethnic solidarity, few Afrikaners accepted the legitimacy of Milner's postwar drive for industrial capitalism, government intervention, and cultural homogenization. This rift manifested along urban-rural lines and fueled an intense backlash that came to center on educational standards and language requirements. Although British officials hoped their policies would foster unity between the country's two white ethnic groups, many Afrikaners instead embraced conservative Christianity and xenophobia as an alternative to British cosmopolitanism and Western liberalism.[16]

These parallel axes of conflict deepened after South Africa became an independent Union in 1910. The new government, under the leadership of Louis Botha and Jan Smuts, tried to maintain social stability and ameliorate Anglo-Afrikaner tensions without abandoning Milner's vision of liberal capitalism. As urbanization among blacks and Afrikaners increased, however, new debates emerged over the proper role of Europeans and nonwhites in the workplace, leading to a series of strikes and racial outbursts in the years surrounding World War I. In the wake of these conflicts, J.B.M. Hertzog of the National Party came to power. Promising to reverse the Anglicization of civil society and expand racial segregation, his government spent much of the 1920s promoting bilingualism and land redistribution in urban centers and rural communities. When the economy began to buckle in the early 1930s, South Africa's political terrain again shifted, resulting in another round of labor upheavals and a coalition government under the dual leadership of Hertzog and Smuts.[17] By the mid-twentieth century, South Africa had become a paradoxical nation of extremes. Fractured deeply along lines of wealth and race, the country struggled under the weight of its own contradictions, balancing its economic ambitions and Lockean political ideals with strident racism and Anglo-Afrikaner animosity. At best, Milner's vision of a unified, liberal South Africa was unfulfilled at the outset of the Second World War.

The concept of apartheid emerged as an alternative to racial capitalism in the midst of this turmoil. Propagated by the first generation of Afrikaners who came of age in Milner's South Africa, it addressed the complexities of the new South Africa in ways that directly challenged the "Anglo worldview." Apartheid's intellectual founders—Hendrik Verwoerd, Werner Eiselen, Geoffrey Cronje, and Nico Diederichs, among many others—met in university classrooms, union halls, and coffee shops during the 1930s to engage in debates on the nature of urban poverty and social unrest in their country. In their minds, racial capitalism was an unsustainable system. So long as the mining industry relied heavily on African laborers—nearly 322,000 of 360,000 mineworkers were black in 1939—South Africa's cities would continue to be plagued by strife. The reason was embedded in the hypocrisy of British nation-building efforts; beneath the government's public espousal of universality was a system that deliberately exploited laborers in pursuit of economic greed. This common diagnosis, couched often in nationalist language and laced with anti-British invective, created the basis for a vibrant cultural revival among young, urban Afrikaners.[18]

Members of this movement talked about apartheid in alternative ways. For northerners like Nico Diederichs, Milner's attempts at social engineering were immoral because they violated God's plan for South Africa. Framing his argument around the biblical analogy of Babel, he claimed that each of God's nations contained its own intrinsic "spirituality" and required a separate "sphere of sovereignty." South Africa had grown unstable because it had disregarded these natural boundaries in pursuit of capitalist profits. Therefore, only strict race separation would ameliorate the country's problems.[19]

Intellectuals from Stellenbosch and Cape Town arrived at a similar conclusion from a different direction. Geoffrey Cronje, for instance, claimed that as long as the Union was dependent on black mining labor, whites would continue to oppress Africans as a matter of economic sustenance and demographic survival. The moral solution was not racially segregated capitalism, but complete separation of whites and blacks so that each group could develop along its own lines. Such an approach would not only open space for the growth of an independent Afrikaner working class; it would also dampen the uncertainties of urbanity and create a foundation for long-term workplace stability.[20] Without advocating a reversal of industrial development, Afrikaner activists revised the central premise of Milner's vision of modernization by reimagining South Africa as a plural, vertically stratified society rather than a singular, horizontally unified nation-state.

Layered on top of these points were competing economic interests within the broader white community. While urban workers and their allies—concerned principally with wages, urban plight, and white autonomy at the local level—tended to support the full extraction of blacks from "white" cities, Afrikaner businessmen and large-scale farmers, reliant in different ways on cheap black labor, preferred flexible alternatives that expanded government control over nonwhite communities. These competing interests caused a rift between apartheid "theorists" and "pragmatists."[21] They also meant that early disagreements over apartheid were overwhelmingly domestic in their orientation and often framed around the question of whether labor reform could deliver both economic growth and Afrikaner security. The inward nature of this discussion defined the nationalist vision of the South African state. Resentful of European cultural arrogance and suspicious of the United Party's close connections with Great Britain, Afrikaner leaders rallied around the conclusion that South Africa's role in the world was secondary to issues facing white farmers, workers, and intellectuals at home.[22]

The conversation about apartheid expanded with the formation of an Afrikaans-speaking public sphere removed from British influence. Politically, the first step was the reinvigoration of Hertzog's defunct National Party. Under the leadership of Daniel Malan, Party elites refashioned their message and positioned themselves in opposition to the Hertzog-Smuts coalition. Their efforts were supported by an impressive organizational infrastructure at the grassroots level, anchored by the Broederbond (Brotherhood)—a secret society for intellectuals and public leaders to circulate ideas and discuss political strategy—and buttressed by an assortment of subsidiary groups like the Federasie van Afrikaanse Kultuurverenigings (Federation of Afrikaans Cultural Organizations), the Instituut vir CNO (Institute for Christian National Education), Reddingsdaadbond, and the White Workers Protection Association.[23] These organizations built political support for the National Party. They also pushed Afrikaners to boycott stores that did not serve their customers in Afrikaans or advertise in multiple languages. In 1938, the Broederbond even orchestrated a four-month long reenactment of the so-called Great Trek from the Cape Colony to the Transvaal, which culminated in a massive celebration in Pretoria and the commencement of construction of the Voortrekker Monument.[24]

Afrikaner elites also developed their own newspapers, magazines, and journals to broadcast their positions to Afrikaans-speaking audiences throughout the country. *Die Burger*, for instance, was created explicitly to "inquire about the wishes and rights of [Afrikaner] land and people and not the wishes and instructions of

Johannesburg and elsewhere."[25] Along with *Transvaler* and *Volksblad*, the paper functioned as a mouthpiece for the National Party, stoking resentment of Anglo cultural superiority and editorializing about the benefits of apartheid. Journals like *Koers* coordinated intellectual activities between the Broederbond and university campuses, and magazines such as *Huisgenoot* and *Burger Boekhandel* worked methodically to reinforce Afrikaner cultural solidarity.[26] This top-down mobilization effort proved very effective. Apartheid was not in the mainstream at the onset of World War II, but it was attached inexorably to nationalist Afrikaner sentiment.

Three events coalesced to expand support for the National Party in the mid-1940s. First, the United Party split over the question of whether to bring the Union into the Second World War, with Smuts pushing for entry and Hertzog advocating neutrality. When Hertzog dissolved the government and called for a general election to solve the conflict, British Governor General Patrick Duncan unilaterally appointed Smuts prime minister, provoking widespread anxiety about Great Britain's influence over internal South African affairs.[27] Second, the Allied wartime demand for munitions, vehicles, equipment, and food created an industrial boom that heightened the need for workers and expanded trends toward urbanization in the Union. With Africans comprising nearly 85 percent of this expanded working class, Smuts's government initiated a series of stabilization reforms that relaxed some travel restrictions, raised African wages, extended pensions to some nonwhites, and trained blacks for skilled and semi-skilled jobs. These changes—defensive in their orientation—provoked further anxiety among whites who resented competition with Africans and feared the long-term implications of uncontrolled black urbanization.[28] In addition to these domestic intrigues sat the propaganda dimensions of the Allied campaign against Nazi Germany. By casting the war as a fight for universal self-determination, freer trade, and New Deal-style social provisions, Anglo-American leaders propagated a new language of liberal internationalism that piqued white South African fears about majoritarian rule and nonracial reform in their own country. When some African labor groups began using the Atlantic Charter to justify their own calls for universal adult suffrage and black collective bargaining rights, white apprehension grew dramatically.[29]

Against the backdrop of these events, the National Party experienced a groundswell of support and defeated the United Party in 1948. Once in power, Malan focused principally on inter-white politics at home. Having achieved only a slim majority in the Assembly, his government needed to navigate the fault lines that had plagued previous administrations—balancing the concrete labor demands of industrial capitalists with tensions among white farmers at the local level—while bolstering the National Party's political power on the national stage. The new prime minister, relying on a tentative alliance among the Afrikaner intelligentsia, white farmers, and white urban workers, achieved this goal by expanding the economic security of his constituents. The National Party secured jobs for poor urban Afrikaners in the railway system and civil service; expanded the Afrikaner education system, investing state resources in schools, colleges, and universities; and established an Afrikaans radio network that furthered cultural solidarity.[30] These programs expanded the organization networks of the previous decade, while establishing concrete lines of patronage that solidified the National Party's popularity among Afrikaners. Malan was an apartheid pragmatist, concerned more with replacing British dominance with Afrikaner political primacy than with implementing a pure vision of race separation in South Africa.

The new government's policies toward nonwhites reflected these tendencies. In 1947, Malan asked his close confidant, Paul Sauer, to develop a blueprint for the implementation of apartheid in South Africa. The subsequent report underscored the difficulties of creating a society based on complete racial stratification. On one level, it reiterated ideas popularized in the interwar years, explaining that God favored separation between racial groups and suggesting that labor upheavals were caused by racial proximity.[31] The solution, for Sauer, was the establishment of separate "fatherlands" that removed nonwhites from urban environments. However, when outlining concrete workplace reforms, the report hedged, admitting that whites would have to rely on black labor for "many years." Social stratification was appealing in the abstract, but National Party leaders feared it would undercut South Africa's mining economy if implemented. As historian Hermann Giliomee argues, "The whole thrust of the Sauer report [was] the elimination of 'surplus' black labor, not black labor, and the channeling of sufficient labor to mines, farms and industry."[32] This distinction shaped the Malan government's policy toward blacks in the late 1940s and early 1950s. Rather than dismantling Milner's system of racial capitalism, the National Party worked simply to undo those stabilization reforms that had accelerated black urbanization and had given African workers better jobs, higher wages, and more social mobility during World War II.

In implementing this goal, the Nationalist government turned to the Department of Native Affairs. Wrapping their actions in the mantra of "orderly urbanization," department officials marshaled state resources to dismantle new nonwhite communities in cities like Johannesburg, Cape Town, Durban, and Port Elizabeth. In the process, they destroyed homes and forcibly relocated residents to areas beyond white urban nodes. Within these townships, government officials worked deliberately to curtail further urbanization by removing unemployed nonwhites and imposing strict population control measures. Those individuals without specific jobs in the white economy were relocated again, this time to ethnic reserves or homelands in the South African countryside.[33] This cumbersome and violent process exacerbated discontent among nonwhites, leading the Nationalist government to expand its power to confront those who opposed strict racial segregation in South Africa. Blaming all forms of unrest on communist infiltration, Malan's surrogates initially felt they could curtail resistance by banning white groups that supported socialism, cosmopolitanism, or majoritarian democracy. However, as nonwhite protest expanded in the early 1950s and the multiracial African National Congress grew into a formidable political opponent, the National Party broadened its tactics. Using its slim majority in the Assembly, the government passed legislation that redefined the parameters of public safety, criminalized labor activism, and gave officials the ability to curtail communication between townships and homelands, and detain nonwhite labor organizers.[34] Highly oppressive and innately inhumane, these programs embraced a form of demographic fatalism that flattened the complexities of African society. As one National Party official explained succinctly, "Our policy is one of survival. Without it we will be swallowed by the Bantu."[35] By the end of Malan's tenure in 1953, apartheid was little more than a blunt tool to address white fears about black urbanization.

Hendrik Verwoerd is often credited as the principal architect of early apartheid. Born in the Netherlands but raised in Milner's South Africa, Verwoerd had worked as a professor of psychology through the 1930s, playing a pivotal role in early discussions of racial stratification as the editor of *Die Transvaaler* before becoming the minister of Native Affairs in 1950. While Malan and others had few qualms framing the National Party's policies as a return to prewar segregation, Verwoerd remained adamant that his department's efforts were best interpreted as the first step in an evolutionary plan called "separate development." The meaning of this term remained fluid in his first years in office. Although Verwoerd never relinquished the premise that nonwhites would advance on their own terms within racially specific territories, he rarely discussed how his short-term proposals connected with any long-term strategic plan. In a speech to an African audience in 1957, he framed his worldview in colloquial terms:

> When I went to Europe there was always a desire in my heart to return to my own country and my own coast. I could not become a Frenchman, or Italian or anything else because I am an Afrikaner . . . Should it not be the same with the Bantu? Should his children there in Cape Town, Port Elizabeth and East London not always hanker after their Chiefs, Authorities, and own people? . . . Every child that is lost [to the urban areas] is like a branch broken from a tree.[36]

Like many other apartheid theorists, Verwoerd's perspective was built around the idea that South Africa contained a series of culturally distinct ethnic groups with fixed value systems. This worldview rested on an imagined, ahistorical

vision of Africa and Africans—common in the interwar colonial context—
that reified categories of tradition and tribalism and ignored the existence of
"nontribal" Africans who traversed the boundaries between rural reserves and
urban townships and spoke eloquently in the language of Western liberalism.[37]
However, Verwoerd refused to adjust his logic—because all Africans viewed
the world in "tribal" terms, Africans in the "cities [were] not distinct from the
Bantu in the Native Reserves."[38] As such, the central task of his department—
which he renamed the Department of Bantu Affairs to underscore the permanence of whites in South Africa—was to create the conditions necessary for
the eventual reversal of black urbanization. By the mid-1950s, Verwoerd was
coupling his policies of slum destruction and labor suppression with programs
that gave him control of black education, providing a leverage point to institutionalize the premise that African culture was fundamentally at odds with
European social norms.[39] His goal was nothing less than complete ideological
hegemony over nonwhite people.

Verwoerd's ambition and methods made him a controversial figure in South
Africa, but by 1958 he had secured enough support within the National Party to
become prime minister. His ascension was a blow to apartheid pragmatists and
announced a series of new premises, objectives, and ideological tenets.[40] Verwoerd's legislative agenda in 1959—often termed "grand apartheid"—had three
components. First, he eliminated the last vestiges of black political representation outside the rural homelands, handing control of urban Africans over to
elites from the reserves who were partly beholden to the National Party. Second,
he expanded resources for black education, establishing universities and colleges
in reserves to bifurcate society further and reaffirm the intrinsic differences
between racial groups in South Africa. Third, the prime minister established
mechanisms to funnel money from multinational corporations to black homelands for economic development, so he could claim that viable economic alternatives existed for blacks outside urban centers like Johannesburg, Cape Town,
Port Elizabeth, and Durban.[41]

When taken together, these initiatives marked an important moment in the
apartheid story. Verwoerd's policies not only further eroded African residential
rights, but they also replaced local authorities with Afrikaner government officials, closed loopholes that facilitated black travel in South Africa, and expanded
the slum clearance programs he had pioneered as minister of Bantu Affairs. Even
more, his actions started a process that mechanized industrial jobs dominated by
Africans and began moving labor-intensive industries away from "white" areas.
According to Verwoerd, these policies would create a system that required only
six million urban Africans and four million black farm workers. All other Africans would be relocated to the homelands.[42] For the new prime minister, the
time had arrived to contain fully black population growth and curtail economic

integration across racial lines. By the eve of Macmillan's visit, this vision had become a formidable ideological framework, affecting nearly every aspect of South African life.

Language of Dissent

Verwoerd's approach to apartheid was partly an outgrowth of his personal convictions and partly a defensive response to the changed nature of black protest in the late 1950s. For over five decades, the dominant nonwhite political organization in the Union of South Africa was the South African Native National Congress (SANNC), renamed the African National Congress (ANC) in 1923. Established in the early twentieth century by a group of moderate black educators, newspaper editors, lawyers, and court translators, the organization drew its support overwhelmingly from nonwhites in urban environments—those individuals who did not fit into Verwoerd's mental map of South Africa. Like Afrikaner intellectuals, Congress members—who included John Dube, Pixley Ka Isaka Seme, and Solomon Plaathe—tended to diagnose the Union's instability as an outgrowth of British hypocrisy. But the problem was not the philosophical underpinnings of Milner's worldview so much as the government's unwillingness to practice the universalism it espoused at the rhetorical level.[43]

Positioned at the interface between white officials and black urbanites, the SANNC envisioned a nation of racial equality and argued that all Africans would fully assimilate into white society if they were given enough time. In framing this position, the organization's first president, John Dube, drew implicitly on the language of European colonialism: "Onward! Upward! Into the higher places of civilization and Christianity—not backward into the slump of darkness nor downward into the abyss of antiquated tribal systems."[44] When the SANNC formed its constitution in 1912, it wrapped its goals in vague and nonconfrontational terms, calling for "unity and mutual co-operation between the Government and the Abantu Races of South Africa" and encouraging "better understanding between the white and black inhabitants of South Africa."[45] The organization, in other words, did not seek a black version of apartheid. Educated within the Western tradition, SANNC members were products of the colonial world and they wanted full membership within Milner's liberal state.[46]

Unlike Afrikaner intellectuals who focused primarily on their domestic grievances, SANNC members tended to define themselves in reference to events abroad. In 1918, for instance, the organization petitioned the British king to request an intervention in South Africa to eliminate racial discrimination. They cast their arguments in the language of colonial sacrifice, focusing on the 17,000 black South Africans who fought in East Africa during World War I and the

25,000 who served in the trenches and docks in France.[47] When the British government turned its back on the Congress delegation, the SANNC traveled to the Versailles peace conference. Like countless other intellectuals and activists from Asia and beyond, they embraced Wilsonianism and called for the extension of self-determination to non-Europeans, even as they were denied access to the actual conference proceedings.[48] John Dube acknowledged at the time that the organization's efforts centered primarily on moral suasion at the international level, based on the hope that "the sense of common justice and love of freedom so innate in the British character" would result in concrete pressure to end racial segregation in South Africa.[49] As racial discrimination expanded under Hertzog's tenure in the 1920s, however, it became clear that the SANNC's strategy was unfounded. The Empire's supposed cosmopolitanism lacked the persuasive power or political tools to reverse trends toward racial capitalism, and South Africa's membership in the international community was not enough to rationalize meaningful change at home.

The only alternative for Congress members was to mobilize at home. The black community's heterogeneity made this task extremely difficult. In the countryside, rural peasants tended to experience European rule through taxes and levies. Concerned primarily with land and labor autonomy, their resistance was spontaneous, broad-based and visceral, but rarely informed by ideology or long-term vision.[50] Migrant laborers, in contrast, often experienced colonialism through urban plight and workplace discrimination. Their proximity to each other theoretically facilitated sustained organizational efforts, but workers often moved between rural homelands and city environments and drew on notions of ethnic identity—not class status—to navigate the complexities of urban life.[51] Even more, nine linguistic groups divided Africans. Although Congress politicians tried to create a public sphere through newspapers and political rallies, distribution remained low and attendance was sporadic.[52] Their message of cosmopolitan liberalism—transmitted in English—simply did not resonate with the vast majority of black South Africans.

Through the interwar period, political resistance to government policies tended to reflect these fault lines. The Industrial and Commercial Worker's Union in South Africa (ICU), a labor group sustained by dockworkers and railway laborers, experienced an influx of support early in the 1920s by adapting its message to local complaints and ethnic concerns, but persistent attacks by white officials and inherent regional differences fragmented the organization as it moved to foment national resistance.[53] Similarly, while charismatic church leaders and youth groups like Amalaita proliferated in the interwar period, providing a host of concrete social and psychological services to their supporters, neither group was able to mobilize on a truly national level.[54] The structural problems facing organizers were compounded by the actions of government surrogates in nonwhite communities. In the countryside, African "headmen" actively used Union resources to maintain stability and put down peasant unrest, while "boss boys" and black policemen deliberately subverted black labor protests in South African cities. Even more, government leaders built positive relationships with many traditional African authorities in the homelands, augmenting the power of chiefs through stipends and other rewards, thereby transforming some indigenous African leaders into surrogates of the state. These policies, part of a broad "retribalization" effort by Union officials, fragmented African resistance throughout the first half of the twentieth century.[55] African political movements were unorganized, ineffectual, and overwhelmed by government counterinitiatives.

The dynamics began to change during World War II. As the Smuts government used stabilization reforms to deal with African urbanization and South African labor needs, a new generation of ANC members moved to reinvigorate their defunct organization. This group—which included Anton Lembede, Nelson Mandela, Peter Mda, Jordan Ngubane, Walter Sisulu, and Oliver Tambo—formed the Congress Youth League (CYL) in 1944. Their message differed from the old guard of the African National Congress. In its founding manifesto, the Youth League took an oppositional stance toward colonialism. Redemption in South Africa would occur not through assimilation with European culture, but through resistance to Western modes of thinking. Their argument was built on an important philosophical binary:

> The White man regards the Universe as a gigantic machine hurtling through time and space to its final destruction: individuals in it are but tiny organisms with private lives and private deaths: personal power, success and fame are the absolute measures of values; the things to live for ... The African, on his side, regards the Universe as one composite whole; an organic entity, progressively driving towards greater harmony and unity whose individual parts exist merely as interdependent aspects of one whole realising their fullest life in the corporate life where communal contentment is the absolute measure of values.[56]

For Youth League members, these differences enlivened the African freedom struggle. In their "Basic Policy Document," issued in 1948, the group skimmed over the questions consuming their white contemporaries—urbanization, labor protest, and uncontrolled residential growth—and focused instead on the new international context of South African problems. For the Congress Youth League, unrest in the Union was tied inextricably to the worldwide problem of racial discrimination. "African people in South Africa ... suffer national oppression in common with thousands and millions of oppressed Colonial peoples in other parts of the world."[57] Only "true democracy"—in South Africa and the rest of the African continent—would establish lasting peace and security. In defining this term, Youth League leaders forwarded a vision of South Africa that contrasted sharply with apartheid. Their policy proposals emphasized the singular nature of economic development. They pushed for scientific farm practices, land reclamation initiatives, and water conservation projects in the countryside, as well as safer work environments, nondiscriminatory labor practices, and black union rights in urban centers. Although the CYL's boldest initiative involved the redistribution of farmland to reflect better South Africa's demographic realities, most of its proposals centered on education. Hoping to achieve 100 percent literacy among blacks, the organization embraced a system of free, nonracial compulsory education that aimed to open doors of possibility for all Africans in the Union. South Africa's future lay not in racial stratification, according to the CYL, but in universal nonracial economic progress.[58]

The Youth League's policy proposals reflected an emerging ideological framework that sat in juxtaposition to apartheid—African nationalism. The intellectual engine of the group, Anton Lembede, was keenly aware of intellectual trends at the international level. Having earned degrees at Adams College and the University of South Africa, he had taught in Natal and the Orange Free State before becoming a political activist in Johannesburg during World War II. A voracious reader well versed in European philosophy, Lembede drew not only on the work of Western thinkers, such as Jean Jacques Rousseau and Giuseppe Mazzini, but also South Asian intellectuals like Jawaharlal Nehru and Mahatmas Gandhi.[59] He was not alone in this endeavor. A broad constellation of Western-educated Africans engaged in a similar process of intellectual synthesis in the period after the First World War.[60] Their efforts brought long-standing notions of pan-Africanism—nurtured by the black diaspora and anchored in cities like New York, London, and Paris—into dialogue with the emerging lessons of independence struggles in India, Indonesia, Egypt, and beyond. This fusion created the basis for an exciting, transnational conversation about race and politics. Nationalism, for many, was the antidote to colonial exploitation, with the power to mobilize disparate groups into a unified, nonviolent mass that could topple imperial governments throughout Asia and Africa.[61]

At the international level, three premises tended to undergird African nationalist thought in the 1940s. The first centered on anticolonialism. Having come of age in the contentious interwar years—when European governments expanded their economic presence in Africa and moved away from the language of universalism—few African elites viewed Europe's civilizing mission with anything other than disdain. For Kwame Nkrumah, George Padmore, Nnamdi Azikiwe, Tom Mboya, Léopold Senghor, and countless others, colonialism was exploitative and racist, bent on fracturing African society through unfair labor practices, land seizures, and military domination.[62] This vision of colonial power often flattened the diverse, fragmented hegemonic processes that actually constituted European rule and reinforced binaries of power/resistance and whiteness/blackness that simplified the diverse ways Africans experienced and engaged colonial networks.[63] However, for many nationalist elites, that was the point. Anticolonialism provided its champions with a powerful epistemological tool to explain indigenous discontent as an outgrowth of non-African social interventions. Nationalists, not surprisingly, augmented this thesis frequently with information on precolonial African kingdoms, suggesting that Africa's natural, linear social and political growth toward national power had been interrupted unjustly by Europe's economic greed and demagogy. The implications were self-evident. Freedom from colonialism would reestablish a natural balance in Africa and redress the continent's many labor and land related discontents. Framed in the language of territoriality—ubiquitous in Europe and elsewhere after World War I—this premise cast political control of African land as the first step toward true freedom.[64]

A second, common component of African nationalism was pan-Africanism. Grounded in the long-standing contributions of the black diaspora, this concept developed in the nineteenth century in response to assertions that Western values had innate appeal among nonwhites.[65] Countless strands of pan-Africanism proliferated in the mid-twentieth century—clustered broadly around complementary notions of négritude and African personality—but nationalists agreed generally that blacks were naturally more communal and egalitarian than Europeans and inclined to view the world as a unified, harmonious social network rather than a disjointed, antagonistic political battlefield. The traits associated with pan-African identity—peacefulness, tolerance, and interpersonal flexibility—were cast generally in static terms and tied to the idea that precolonial African societies had been classless utopias where these values reigned and conflict was ameliorated through discussion.[66] Historians of Africa have complicated greatly this idyllic portrait.[67] However, in the context of the period, the narrative of pan-Africanism was an instrumental means to a political end, dovetailing well with the message of anticolonialism. As Alex Quaison-Sackey, Ghana's foreign minister, explained, pan-Africanism was not "a simple reaction to the colonial past" so much as "a complex and positive reaction to—indeed, a recreation of—the distant past, too."[68] The goal, in other words, was to use pan-African identity to unite blacks and give meaning to Africa's shared fight against European rule.

A third theme of African nationalism was nonracial, economic development. As economic progress became a more salient feature of colonial discourse in the postwar years, many African leaders articulated the thesis that their familiarity with local conditions equipped them better to deliver the promises of material uplift in Africa. This premise evolved, especially in West and East Africa, as

European planners implemented stabilization reforms to address wartime domestic unrest, but it formed an important linchpin of African nationalism.[69] For black intellectuals, economic growth was universal and linear—if Africans pursued appropriate agricultural and labor policies their societies would naturally experience growth analogous to Western nation-states. The main barrier to progress, in their minds, was the mutually constitutive problems of racism and greed, born from Europe's tendency to view blacks as backward and see the colonies as a source of unshared wealth.[70] The goal of nationalism was not to return Africa to precolonial conditions but to fuse African values with development planning and deliver a form of modernity in line with the continent's ideological proclivities.

Lembede's writing embraced all of these themes. White racism, in his mind, drove all decision-making by the Union government. In South Africa, he explained, "more than in any other country in the World, the colour of man's skin is worshipped, idolised and adopted as an essential mark or criterion of human superiority and inferiority."[71] This "colour ideology" was a "menace to the existence and survival of Africans as a race" and responsible for high infant mortality, tuberculosis, venereal disease, moral decay, physical deterioration, crime, violence, illiteracy, and poverty among Africans.[72] In his words, political independence would be the "panacea of all the ills" in South Africa.[73] It would allow Africans, who were "naturally socialistic" because of "their social practices and customs," to establish a society that was peaceful and unified, in harmony with other African states. Although Lembede acknowledged the utility of occasional cooperation with other non-European groups in the Union, he urged fellow African nationalists to achieve freedom on their own terms so that the new South Africa would reflect their values and priorities. In his mind, these values were best understood in terms of economic development.[74] Pushing back against Afrikaner nationalism, he drew a line between racial supremacy and modernity. Although white civilization "as understood by the Whites in Africa" had no future in the Union, "Western Culture and civilisation in the form of science, art, philosophy" was "the common property of humanity as a whole."[75] It was important, therefore, that the black nationalist movement stand for social, educational, cultural, moral, economic, and political reform.

The relationship between African nationalism and European decolonization has been much debated. In the immediate aftermath of decolonization, disagreements tended to focus on whether African activists or European elites deserved more credit for the decision to end colonialism in Africa—with newly ascendant nationalist leaders and European bureaucrats clustered predictably on opposite ends of the interpretive spectrum. Recent examinations of African laborers, peasants, women, and subalterns have provided less polemical, more ambiguous interpretations of decolonization.[76] In locales throughout Africa, discontent toward colonial rule was heterogeneous, tied not to latent nationalist yearnings but to local frustrations over Europe's wartime labor policies. Great Britain and France responded to these upheavals with reforms that recast colonialism in developmental terms and established labor relations boards similar to those found in Western Europe and North America.[77] The goal of colonial planners was to extend and legitimize colonialism through soft power, but nationalist activists—Kwame Nkrumah, Sekou Touré, Léopold Senghor, Jomo Kenyatta, and countless others—seized this moment to insert their own definitions of self-government, citizenship, and development into policymaking conversations.[78] The pattern was set in the Gold Coast in the 1950s, when Nkrumah used his clout among urban laborers to push British officials toward political independence, then turned to the language of nationalism to build support among cocoa farmers, subalterns, and traditional elites outside Accra.[79] This process, repeated in various contexts in subsequent years, was messy and contentious but it served two overlapping purposes, both coding African political demands in terms familiar to European historical narratives and downplaying the diverse economic, political, and social fault lines within African societies.

On one level, the Youth League's efforts mirrored this global pattern. Drawing heavily on the teachings of Lembede, who died unexpectedly in 1947, the organization published a "Programme of Action" in 1949, encouraging laborers to engage in boycotts, work stoppages, strikes, and civil disobedience. Like other nationalist organizations, the League's support was grounded mostly in urban communities, even though it framed its actions as an outgrowth of deeply held nationalist yearnings among all black South Africans. When these efforts did not result in government reform, members of the Youth League turned to a "defiance campaign" in the early 1950s, which used Gandhi-style nonviolent methods to violate segregation laws and fill the Union's jails. However, the Nationalist government still refused to open a dialogue with African leaders.[80]

The League's problems were twofold. Most obvious, the Afrikaner regime, unlike colonial governments in West and East Africa, continued to publicly repudiate the idea that blacks could exist outside their "tribal cages," thereby eliminating the possibility of dialogue so essential to the success of African leaders elsewhere. Simultaneously, the League faced important difficulties in the nonwhite community. Lembede's suggestion that "non-European unity [was] a fantastic dream [with] no foundation in reality" clashed directly with the ANC's traditional mantra of cosmopolitan inclusion.[81] Because blacks were never the only oppressed group in South Africa—Indians and Coloreds also lost their citizenship rights in the 1950s, and the Communist Party was banned shortly after the election of 1948—the ideological milieu within the Union was more complex than elsewhere on the continent. Many members of the Congress Youth League—including Mandela, Tambo, and Sisulu—moderated their views and partnered with other nonwhites in the 1950s. However, certain deep-seated conceptual questions continued to plague the anti-apartheid struggle in South Africa: Could pan-Africanism be squared with nonracial liberalism? What place did communists have in the South African resistance movement? And how could the Nationalist government be pushed to ameliorate its racial policies?

The strategy of inclusion gained currency after the defiance campaign's collapse in 1953. In August, a group of older ANC leaders declared their intention to draft a broad "Freedom Charter" that brought Africans, Indians, Coloreds, communists, and liberals under a common political banner. The organizations that represented each group—the African National Congress, the South African Indian Congress, the South African Coloured People's Organization, the South African Congress of Trade Unions, and the South African Congress of Democrats, among many others—were asked to share their viewpoints and political demands, which were then synthesized by a committee and presented at the widely publicized Congress of the People conference in 1955. The result was a markedly different philosophical assault on apartheid. The Charter was predictably eclectic, blending a collection of Western-style liberal rights—equality before the law, freedom of movement, the right to vote, and equal pay for equal work—with socialist demands on the redistribution of land and industrial wealth in South Africa, but it enshrined the notion that resistance to apartheid must be multiracial.[82]

In the minds of its authors, the Charter reflected the complex realities within the Union. The document still embraced themes of anticolonialism and economic development—common through much of the Third World in the years surrounding the 1955 Bandung conference in Indonesia—but it downplayed the conceptual importance of pan-African identity, putting emphasis instead on the idea that South Africa belonged "to all who live in it, black and white."[83] In the minds of many activists, joined under the banner of a newly formed Congress Alliance, this approach would reinvigorate and broaden the movement started by the Youth League and convince the National Party finally to open a dialogue with nonwhite leaders.

The Alliance's approach toward the Union government reflected its preference for peaceful negotiation. Although the coalition organized occasional boycotts, there were few efforts on the scale of the defiance campaign, and public statements by African elites grew more conciliatory. "We are not callous to the situation of the white man in this country, who entertains certain fears [that] he may be swamped and may lose his racial identity because of our numerical superiority," the new head of the African National Congress, Chief Albert Luthuli, stated diplomatically in the mid-1950s. "The question is not the preservation of one group or another, but to preserve the values which have been developed over generations."[84] The Nationalist government, however, continued to view the Freedom Charter through the lens of apartheid doctrine. Premised on the idea that nonwhites deserved equality in a Milner-style South Africa, the document challenged the intellectual and moral scaffolding of the apartheid idea. In September 1955, the police searched the homes of over 150 Congress Alliance members, eventually charging dozens—including Luthuli, Tambo, Sisulu, and Mandela—with treason against the government.[85] By the end of the 1950s, it was clear that the South African government was not going to adhere to the pattern set by its contemporaries in East and West Africa.

Against this backdrop, African nationalism experienced a revival. Africanists from the township of Orlando, in particular, did not hesitate to express their displeasure with the ANC's embrace of multiracialism. Using the *Africanist* as their mouthpiece, they questioned the assumptions of the Freedom Charter and the tactics of the Congress Alliance, and broke eventually from the African National Congress in 1959 to establish the Pan Africanist Congress (PAC). According to Robert Sobukwe, the first president of the organization, African nationalism was "the only liberatory creed" that could "weld the illiterate and semi-literate masses . . . into a solid, disciplined and united fighting force; provide them with a loyalty higher than that of the tribe, and give formal expression to their desire to be a nation."[86] As the Pan Africanist Congress stepped on to the national scene, it advanced two interlocking arguments both geared toward revitalizing pan-Africanism. The first posited that because "Africans [were] the true and rightful owners of Africa,"[87] other South Africans needed to coalesce behind black leadership. "No sane man can come to your house and claim as his the chamber or room you are not occupying," one PAC leader explained. "The non-Africans are guests of the Africans . . . [and] have to adjust themselves to the interests of Africa."[88]

Second, the Pan Africanist Congress argued that South Africa's freedom struggle was tied directly to events elsewhere in Africa. First-wave decolonization was important, but the independence of Ghana in 1957 formed the symbolic rallying point for the organization. The event legitimized the original tenets of African nationalism while spreading Nkrumah's unique phraseology through black intellectual circles in Johannesburg and elsewhere. By the end of the 1950s, the *Africanist* and other periodicals were openly appropriating common Nkrumah idioms and claiming that the Pan Africanist Congress would lead the African masses "into the greater family of a United States of Africa."[89] Sobukwe spoke often of the illegitimacy of the "doctrine of South African exceptionalism," and suggested the Union's future lay in a "unitary, centrally-controlled" organization of African nations.[90] South Africa, in his mind, could not escape the larger freedom movement reshaping the continent's political landscape.[91]

Many Youth League veterans refused to join the Pan Africanist Congress. On an organizational level, the group was hampered by meager resources and interpersonal rivalries.[92] However, its membership nonetheless grew substantially in 1959, in part because of the intellectual ferment of African or second-wave decolonization. In one of his first public speeches, Sobukwe announced that his organization would initiate a campaign against the pass system—which forced black Africans to carry identification cards whenever they left their designated "homeland" territories—and promised to lead all black South Africans to freedom by 1963, a date chosen for the end of European rule at Accra's All African People's Conference in 1958.[93] For those angered by Verwoerd's grand apartheid legislation but uninspired by the ANC's Freedom Charter, this message resonated as an inspirational alternative to multiracialism.

The Pan Africanist Congress spent nine months laying the foundation for its anti-pass campaign. Emulating the strategy of the defiance campaign of the early 1950s, the plan was to have Africans converge on police stations and demand to be arrested for not carrying their required identification cards—when prisons overflowed the National Party would be forced into a state of crisis and Africans would take control of the government. As months wore on, however, the organization continued to postpone its launch date, worried that it did not yet have sufficient domestic support. It ultimately took criticism from the African National Congress to push Sobukwe into action.[94] At a conference in December 1959, ANC leaders declared that it was "treacherous for a liberation movement to embark on a campaign" that it did not "properly prepare for, and which has no reasonable prospects of success," and they announced their own intention to start an anti-pass campaign on March 31, 1960.[95] Pushed into a corner, the Pan Africanist Congress countered by setting its start date for March 21.

By the time Macmillan arrived in Cape Town in February 1960 to deliver his "winds of change" address, the fault lines of the apartheid debate were set. On an ideological level, Afrikaner nationalists and African nationalists viewed the world through diametrically opposed lenses. National Party elites, led by Prime Minister Verwoerd and others in the 1950s, used domestic events as their frame of reference—concerned with British elitism and the demographic challenges of white rule, their policies sought to redistribute resources to Afrikaners, control urban environments, and reduce the need for migrant laborers. In their minds, blacks existed in essentialist tribal cages, making them innately prone to violent behavior and emotionalism, and it was the responsibility of whites to act as "trustees" for the country, providing blacks the space to develop along their own lines and the resources to pursue local development.

African nationalists like Anton Lembede and Robert Sobukwe defined nationalism in very different terms. They focused on the symmetry between their struggle and the fight against European exploitation elsewhere in Africa and viewed political freedom, not racial assimilation, as the gateway to economic progress in the Union. To them, Africa's value system was defined through collaboration and unity, not tribalism and division, and because blacks were not individualistic or greedy they had the ability to implement a form of development that overcame Europe's natural weaknesses. Points of continuity existed between these two worldviews—neither framework fully acknowledged the fluidity or intellectual hybridity of South Africa, and both tended to view power in terms of race consciousness and territorial autonomy—but their differences made conflict nearly inevitable. Verwoerd's domestic programs and Sobukwe's call to action, implemented at nearly the same moment in South African history, reflected deeper ideological patterns and foreshadowed the fault lines of the global apartheid debate of the subsequent decade.

Several events coalesced to amplify and crystallize this fight in early 1960. The first was Harold Macmillan's speech in February. Widely covered by the international press, the British prime minister's decision to praise African nationalism—in the Cape Town Assembly Hall—subtly legitimized one side of this nascent debate and announced that apartheid was out of step with modern history. The effect was semantic but powerful, establishing a mental map that linked the inevitability of decolonization to the moral inequity of Afrikaner racialism. This sentiment gained additional power when over a dozen African nations gained political independence in the early months of 1960. Decolonization not only infused the ideology of African nationalism with more legitimacy; it transformed the complexion and composition of the U.N. General Assembly, giving African nationalists abroad a powerful forum to legitimize, extend, and elaborate their views to the world community.

Finally, there was the implementation of the PAC's anti-pass campaign. On Friday, March 18, after promising that the "African people" would conduct themselves "in a spirit of absolute nonviolence," Sobukwe commented presciently that if "the other side so desires," they would have an opportunity in the coming days "to demonstrate to the world how brutal they can be."[96] If the police had not taken him up on this offer, the events of March 21 would likely have been remembered as one more abortive campaign in the history of nonwhite protest in South Africa.[97] Indeed, in Vereeniging, Evaton, and Vanderbijlpark, government authorities quietly suppressed PAC protest with minimal violence. However, at the township of Sharpeville, and later in Langa and Nyanga, officers used tear gas to break up the protesters, provoking a series of confrontations that eventually left sixty-seven Africans dead and nearly two hundred people injured. Eyewitness accounts of the Sharpeville Massacre vary to this day, but, in the weeks that followed, upheavals spread throughout the Union as Africans revolted against the white government and the South African military took unprecedented steps to quell domestic unrest.[98] The wind of change finally blew onto the shores of South Africa. Even Prime Minister Verwoerd admitted that events now deserved to "be seen against the background . . . of similar occurrences in the whole of Africa, and around the world."[99]

Nineteen sixty marked the internationalization of the apartheid dilemma. Although pathways began to close for African nationalists in South Africa in the wake of the Sharpeville Massacre, new networks proliferated at the global level in the early 1960s. As the Pan Africanist Congress and African National Congress established missions abroad, their message fused with the imperatives of an emerging bloc of nations at the U.N. General Assembly called the African Group. Committed to isolating the Union and controlling knowledge about South Africa, this constellation of nation-states dominated the international apartheid debate in the coming years, providing patronage to South African exiles and solidarity in the anti-apartheid struggle.

Surprised by this turn of events, National Party officials began to wrestle with their intellectual and political isolation from the West. While subjected to criticism by South Asian nations and Western liberals through the 1950s, few Afrikaner nationalists expected that elites in Europe and North America would ever turn their backs on the Union. By mid-1960, however, global capitalists were fleeing the country in huge numbers and South Africa was being hailed widely as the next Algeria. This crisis triggered a new stage in the South African story, propelling the apartheid question to the center of a larger conversation about the Cold War and decolonization in the postcolonial decade.

2

Defining the Debate

We have come to a stage in this world which, on the one had, has become so shrunken, and on the other hand is conscious of such wide implications, that it is a world at once larger and smaller that we inhabit. And in these circumstances—in the words of Abraham Lincoln—we cannot have a world that is half enslaved and half free.
—Krishna Menon, *U.N. General Assembly (1961)*

South Africa has become the "whipping boy" of the world.
—Eric Louw, *House of Assembly (1961)*

Oliver Tambo was not where he expected to be in 1964. For four years he had labored as the exile leader of the African National Congress, tasked with the job of gaining international political support for his organization and establishing the building blocks for the liberation of South Africa—a challenging assignment by any standard. Writing from Dar-es-Salaam, Tanzania, to a colleague at the United Nations, he candidly revealed his mindset, lamenting, "rightly or wrongly, the African States started off with strong demands." Now, four years into their anti-apartheid campaign, it would "be a mistake to demand less, for if South Africa persist[ed] and the big powers in the West continue[d] to resist action, a stepping down on demands [would] be the beginning of a complete withdrawal, ending in the disbandment of the Afro-Asian forces as far as this issue is concerned."[1] Not only was the fight against South Africa at risk, the cohesion of the Third World alliance was at stake.

Fifteen hundred miles to the south, the situation looked equally dire for very different reasons. In a policy memorandum just months before Tambo's letter to New York, South African officials acknowledged that the government's position abroad had grown contingent on the tacit support of the West. The problem with this arrangement was self-evident: "The United Nations continues to be used and to be recognized as a major instrument of the United States," a policy-maker summarized in 1963. "Because this is so, and because the nature of the

41

United Nations itself has undergone such a major transformation in the last few years, the United States is obliged to take account ... of the strength of feeling in that organization against [South Africa] and the influence exercised in terms of votes by the Afro-Asian/Communist line-up." This structural reality meant that the Nationalist government needed to redouble its efforts "to convince the American Administration that economic, social and political stability and progress at the southern end of the African Continent ... [could] only be secured on the basis of *white* rule."[2] Failure would result in the end of Afrikaner preeminence in South Africa.

Tambo's letter and the National Party's report captured the two ends of the international apartheid debate in the early 1960s. On one side sat South African liberation groups and their international patrons, empowered by second-wave decolonization but unsure exactly how to expand support for their message beyond the global south. Opposite them were South African politicians, convinced that a cohort of black radicals and irrational humanitarians had manufactured the apartheid crisis for personal gain. Although the conceptual chasm between these rival camps was wide, their shared assumptions gave their contest an element of coherence in the early 1960s. For both African and Afrikaner nationalists, the United Nations was the central battlefield of the apartheid debate. Neither group denied that the growth of the General Assembly's membership had altered the terrain of global politics, opening space and giving tools to states concerned with colonialism, economic exploitation, and racial discrimination. Equally important, both groups accepted that the great powers, with their military strength, economic influence, and Security Council authority, were the arbiters of South Africa's fate, with the power to either punish the Union for its policies or insulate it from international criticism. By 1964, the apartheid debate was as much a contest over Western policy toward South Africa as a fight about white racism in South Africa.

This chapter narrates how African nationalists and the Nationalist government arrived at this complex impasse. Focused on the period between 1960 and 1964, it evaluates the strategies, tactical initiatives, and methods of persuasion adopted by each side as they built support for their respective positions. For African nationalists, the early 1960s marked a high point, as a broad constellation of elites from West and East Africa joined together and framed their ascendance as a triumph of non-Western ideas over European colonialism. Although inevitable contradictions appeared during these years, the apartheid question provided a common reference point in African politics that reified and popularized binaries of power/resistance and whiteness/blackness. African leaders shared a common cause in the fight against South Africa and coordinated their fight against the Nationalist government at forums like the United Nations and British Commonwealth. Their goal was to build support for economic sanctions, compensating for Africa's military and economic weaknesses through activism at global institutions.

Two closely related impulses drove these efforts. On one hand, many African leaders felt genuine affinity for black South Africans and real outrage at the National Party's domestic policies. They hoped that international pressure would modulate Pretoria's approach and eventually bring black Africans to power in the Union. At the same time, others recognized that apartheid, through its theoretical sophistication and political intransigence, represented a direct rebuttal of the rationale and legitimacy of African nationalism. So long as apartheid existed at the southern end of the continent, the authority of Africa's nascent message would remain incomplete. These overlapping mindsets reinforced each other and created a powerful incentive for confrontation in the early 1960s. Africans quickly became vocal players in the international arena, using their numerical power to push a difficult choice on the Western powers: join the fight against apartheid or lose the support of the Third World.

South Africa's response to the African bloc's campaign evolved over time. Although criticism of its policies was hardly new, the events of 1960 undeniably changed the calculus of the apartheid question, putting the moral, political, and economic support of Washington and London in serious jeopardy for the first time. For more than a decade, Nationalist leaders had confronted their perceived enemies—Western liberals and Indian nationalists—on the familiar grounds of the United Nations and British Commonwealth. They engaged their enemies directly, labeling them hypocrites and liars, and wrapped South Africa's views in doctrines of nonintervention and anticommunism.

By 1961, with American and British officials apparently pulling away from the Union, it was clear that this approach had faltered. The South African government responded by repackaging the apartheid ideology, shifting attention away from global institutions and building quiet support among powerbrokers and nonstate organizations in North America and Western Europe. Faced with the futility of public debate, South African officials tried to shift the conversation and appeal to the economic and security interests of individuals in the business and defense communities. At the same moment that African elites were presenting Western leaders with a Manichean choice between postcolonial justice and neocolonial oppression, Nationalist diplomats were reworking their message to specific actors in Washington, New York, and London. Their argument—that African immaturity had undermined the utility of multilateral cooperation—aimed subtly to shift the terrain of the apartheid conversation.

These dueling approaches shaped the international apartheid debate in the early 1960s. On one level, the contest raised several basic questions: What was the nature of Afro-Asian collaboration? How could the African states actually implement a U.N. sanctions regime against South Africa? Under what conditions would the Security Council support sanctions? Just under the surface, however, sat equally important but abstract queries: Where did international norms come from? Who got to define the scope and direction of the United Nations' agenda? And what was the relationship between politics and ideas in the postimperial age? The apartheid debate captured how policymakers and politicians answered both sets of questions at a unique moment in world history, when possibilities seemed limitless and multiple actors strove to shape the meaning of international legitimacy. When viewed from this vantage point, the debate about South Africa becomes a microcosm of the postcolonial moment. It reveals why deep fissures separated First World politicians from Third World ones, and how certain groups traversed the slippery boundary between older forms of colonial paternalism and the new discourse of universal development.

Confronting the Citadel

The ideology of African nationalism animated the anti-apartheid movement in the early 1960s. From the perspective of the Pan Africanist Congress, the struggle against apartheid was only one part of a unified fight against colonialism everywhere in Africa. According to historian Gail Gerhart, the organization tended to view second-wave decolonization in the late 1950s as the realization of "Lembede's predictions about the destiny of Africa."[3] Robert Sobukwe, the PAC's first president, often explained current events in the language of well-known nationalists. In his opening address at the PAC's inaugural convention in April 1959, Sobukwe quoted George Padmore directly: "There is a growing feeling among politically conscious Africans throughout the continent that their destiny is one, that what happens in one part of Afrika [sic] to Africans must affect Africans living in other parts." Drawing on themes of territorial freedom and pan-Africanism, he claimed that Africans would join together in a unified state, spanning from Cape Town to Cairo in the postcolonial era: "The days of small, independent countries are gone . . . America and Russia cover huge tracts of land territorially and number hundreds of millions in population."[4] In the "Manifesto of the Africanist Movement" published that year, the organization went even further, defining "freedom" as pan-African in its orientation, tied inexorably to black land ownership, bound by an "Africanistic socialist democratic social order," and contingent on the formation of a singular African nation-state.[5] These linkages formed the scaffolding of African nationalist thought.

In grounding such sentiment, PAC leaders drew unabashedly on the symbolism of Nkrumah's Ghana. The organization's flag—a black image of Africa set against a green backdrop—featured a golden star shining outward from Ghana, underscoring the organization's intellectual and political affinity for Nkrumah's brand of African nationalism.[6] This ideology, which was a "third social force in the world" distinct from communism or liberal capitalism, had "become a concrete reality when the African nationalists from all over the continent met in Accra" for the All-Africa People's Conference in December 1958—a meeting designed explicitly to "match Bandung on an African scale with Asians as observers."[7] The Pan Africanist Congress drew often and explicitly on the declarations of the All-Africa People's Conference, claiming that complete African independence would arrive in 1963, after which Nkrumah and other established leaders would "probably act as Big Brother to the younger States."[8] Once annexed into a singular country, nationalist leaders would then cut waste "through systematic [state] planning" and "bring about the most rapid development to every part of the State."[9] Within a generation, Africa would stand on even ground with the superpowers.

This particular conceptual vision did not go uncontested within the Union. African nationalism competed with the parallel tradition of multiracialism in the late 1950s, embodied by the African National Congress. At the All-Africa People's Conference in 1958, ANC representatives openly noted their apprehension regarding Nkrumah's ideas and claimed that any effort to impose "a common ideology and philosophy [would] only lend the Conference into difficulties and unpleasantness."[10] The statement foreshadowed the sometimes visceral conflict between the African National Congress and Pan Africanist Congress. On the one hand, ANC critics lambasted Sobukwe's nationalist reading of South African history. Joe Matthews, an ANC activist with strong ties to Nelson Mandela and Oliver Tambo, claimed in an opinion piece in July 1959 that Sobukwe's conceptual map—specifically his assertion that pan-Africanism formed an alternative to communism and liberal capitalism—was naïve and arrogant. Opting for a Marxist reading of history, Matthews asserted that South Africa's experiences were better viewed in material terms and lamented the PAC's suggestion that the Soviet Union was an enemy of Africa. "The whole world is marching to socialism," he claimed, "and the only argument now is how to carry out the re-organisation of society on the basis of socialism."[11] For others, specifically Z. K. Matthews, who taught many of South Africa's postwar leaders while working as a professor at the University of Fort Hare, PAC's assault on South African exceptionalism was disconcerting. "South Africa differs from other territories in Africa such as Ghana," he argued in mid-1959. "In addition to the African we have settled here significant numbers of other groups—Europeans, Asians, and Colored—and therefore the country must frankly be recognized as a multi-racial country with all that that implies."[12] It was better, in his mind, to foster inclusive class-consciousness than exclusive, race-based nationalism.

The Sharpeville Massacre put the African National Congress on the defensive. As Nelson Mandela later admitted, "In just one day, [the Pan Africanist Congress] moved to the front lines of the struggle, and Robert Sobukwe was being hailed inside and outside the country as the savior of the liberation movement. We in the ANC had to make rapid adjustments to this new situation."[13] The organization's mindset was clearly revealed in its first statement after the killings, when it asked for "all the peoples and Governments of the whole world" to help the South African people in its struggle and requested that the United Nations "quarantine the racialist Verwoerd Government by imposing full economic sanctions against the Union."[14] With the ANC's leadership arrested or forced underground by the Nationalist government in late March,[15] renewed action in the global arena represented a logical avenue forward. However, building partnerships with political patrons abroad was extremely difficult. The ANC's international wing—led by Deputy President-General Oliver Tambo—encountered skepticism immediately from Africanists who were apathetic about the ANC's multiracial orientation and support of nonviolence.[16] For many observers, Algeria appeared to be the harbinger of things to come. In visits to East, North, and West Africa in early 1960, Tambo struggled to connect with prominent African leaders and found himself dismissed as a lackluster speaker with an anachronistic message. In the words of ANC activist Aziz Pahad, "With its slogan of 'Africa for the Africans' the PAC captured the mood."[17]

Indeed, the PAC's path abroad was much easier after the Sharpeville Massacre. Its foreign mission—headed ostensibly by Nana Mahomo and Peter Molotsi—was already in Ghana on a goodwill mission when Sobukwe implemented the anti-pass campaign in March 1960. According to Molotsi, he and Mahomo were greeted in Accra, the "Mecca of Pan Africanism," with the words, "*Akwaba*! Welcome Home!"[18] In an account reliant mostly on unpublished interviews with participants, historian Luli Callinicos suggests that Nkrumah actively pushed the African National Congress into discussions with the Pan Africanist Congress in Ghana, flying Tambo and his entourage from North Africa to Accra that April. "Nkrumah was keenly interested to hear about recent events in South Africa, but expressed concern that there had been a split in the liberation movement," she explains. According to the Ghanaian president, "A union of the two liberation movements . . . was both necessary to achieve success at home and appropriate for Pan-Africanism in the region."[19] Although archival records of this meeting have yet to surface, the Pan Africanist Congress, African National Congress, and several liberation groups from South West Africa did form an organization called the United Front (UF) in London in May 1960.[20] Announcing itself that year as a "coordinating body of the main nationalist liberatory movements in South Africa,"[21] the alliance allowed the Pan Africanist Congress and African National Congress to pool their human and financial resources, and gave politicians from both organizations a platform to speak with greater authority about South African issues at the international level.

Rhetorically, some of the differences between the two organizations blurred in the months that followed. "The beginning of the end of an era has begun," the ANC's *Congress Voice* declared in an article on global affairs in November 1960. "The day for which the oppressed and exploited people throughout the world have yearned and struggled so long has at long last arrived."[22] Two years earlier, the African National Congress had framed international events very differently, claiming that while it was "naturally pleas[ing] to know that the world is with us" no one "imagine[d] for a moment" that liberation would come from abroad.[23] In a subtle yet meaningful shift, the organization's propagandists began downplaying such sentiment after Sharpeville and focused instead on the relationship between the "vast empires of the 19th and 20th centuries" and the "lofty and noble declarations of the United Nations." Even more, the African National Congress tentatively embraced the idea that African nationalism was pushing these two systems into confrontation. "With the recent accession of thirteen new independent African states" global politics had changed, the *Congress Voice* admitted. "The United Nations Organisation, which was up to the middle of 1960, a stronghold of the big imperialists and colonial powers, has now become the stronghold of the anti-colonial forces, and [if] properly used, it could help in furthering the struggle for national independence and for equality and freedom."[24]

The shift was semantic but important. Although personality differences and ideological considerations made genuine unity between the African National Congress and Pan Africanist Congress difficult to sustain in South Africa, the two organizations shared the view that the United Nations could meaningfully influence events in the Union.[25] In an interview in May 1960, Tambo went so far as to claim that a "solution [could] only come from the outside."[26] The United Front's principal task in 1960, therefore, was to form a common strategy to push the United Nations toward action. In a memorandum entitled "Boycott and Economic Sanctions," prepared in London that year, UF leaders noted that the situation in South Africa could no longer be "settled by persuasion, a change of heart, or even a condemnation of apartheid in the strongest possible terms." It needed to be "seen for what it [was]: a serious threat to peace and security, calling for forceful and resolution matters." Against this backdrop, the "economic isolation of South Africa, through the boycott of South African goods and the enforcement of economic sanctions by the United Nations, [was] essential to a peaceful solution of the growing crisis in South Africa."[27] By isolating the Nationalist government economically, the United Front would create the conditions for political change at home.

Implementing this strategy was a difficult task. There were essentially two pathways to U.N. sanctions. Support could be built for action through the U.N. General Assembly. While article 2(7) of the U.N. Charter explicitly forbade the organization from "interven[ing] in matters which are essentially within the domestic jurisdiction of any state," article 14 gave the General Assembly the ability to "recommend measures for the peaceful adjustment of any situation . . . it deems likely to impair the general welfare or friendly relations between nations." If the United Front could convince enough member-nations to endorse a resolution that cast apartheid as a "clear threat to international peace and security," article 2(7) would be moot and the Security Council would be permitted to take action under the provisions of chapter VII, which outlined the Council's role in dealing with member-state aggression.[28] So long as the General Assembly resolution framed apartheid as a "clear threat to international peace and security," the argument could be made that South African issues were transnational in nature and required an international solution.

Alternatively, the United Front could focus its efforts on the South African government's tentative legal claims in South West Africa. For UF leaders, the termination of South Africa's World War I-era Mandate over its northern neighbor was a "matter of urgency," necessitated both by the "crying demand of the people of South West Africa" and the "will of the countries and peoples of the world."[29] By 1960, the International Court of Justice (ICJ) had already issued a series of advisory opinions that condemned the Union's refusal to place its Mandate under the recently expanded U.N. Trusteeship program. Further action would require a formal, contentious ICJ case and a binding judgment at The Hague. If the Court ruled against the Union, the Security Council would be obliged to take action under article 94 of the U.N. Charter, which outlined the Council's role in enforcing the Court's decisions. In this scenario, not only were sanctions possible, but UF leaders could also argue for an armed intervention in South West Africa if the National Party refused to accept the Court's authority.

The United Front lacked the political tools to pursue either of these strategies on its own. With offices in Accra, Cairo, and London, the organization's initial efforts focused mostly on staffing and communication issues.[30] Its first true political test came in June 1960 at the Second Conference of Independent African States in Addis Ababa, where members presented a short paper on South Africa and listened to the proposals of African representatives from Ghana, Guinea, Liberia, Egypt, Morocco, Tunisia, and Libya. The resolution passed by the African states that month, in many ways, formed the tactical blueprint for African action against the Nationalist government in the early 1960s. The document focused on concrete issues—it called on independent African states to sever diplomatic relations with the Union, close African ports to South African vessels, boycott all South African goods, and close African air space to South African aircraft; it also invited British Commonwealth states to expel South Africa from the Commonwealth.[31] Equally important, the African states announced that Liberia and Ethiopia would challenge the legality of South Africa's Mandate in contentious proceedings at the International Court of Justice.[32] Speaking before the Assembly on June 14, Ethiopian Emperor Haile Selassie explained, "We must resolutely unite as fearless and determined advocates for our South African brothers." In his words, "The task that remains to be accomplished in the political field is certainly a considerable one, but we trust that, united in our determination to see the complete independence of every African people, we shall succeed in our endeavors."[33] The UF's agenda, for Selassie and many other African leaders, was Africa's cause.

In addition to this excursion, Tambo and other ANC members worked to cultivate support among liberal organizations in London. In the 1950s, clergymen such as Canon John Collins, Trevor Huddleston, and Michael Scott had established the International Defence and Aid Fund and African Bureau, which funneled donations to the Congress Alliance and lobbied Labor and Liberal leaders to denounce South Africa in the British Parliament. Groups of communists, college students, and trade unions were beginning to take public stands against apartheid.[34] Collins, in particular, held an extremely powerful position within the Anglican Church and, with the royal family, several Labor politicians, and a handful of journalists in his congregation, he possessed unmatched fundraising skills in London and beyond. Determined to take advantage of this situation, the ANC's Tennyson Makiwane moved to Britain in late 1959 and helped organize a month-long boycott of South African goods in February–March 1960, which laid the foundation for the British Anti-Apartheid Movement.[35] Tambo joined him in mid-1960 and worked to expand the UF's network of political patrons, putting pressure on prominent British politicians like Barbara Castle, Hugh Gaitskell, Jeremy Thorpe, and Lord Altringham to support U.N. sanctions.[36] Tambo further worked to build relations with Swedish activists like Per Wästberg, who, like Collins and Huddleston, had previously raised funds for the African National Congress and lobbied government leaders on behalf of the Congress Alliance.[37] In Tambo's first trip to Scandinavia in May, he framed the "enemies of Africa" as "those devoted friends of apartheid and racial discrimination— the governments, countries or concerns—which have trade agreements with South Africa" and argued that South African goods were made inexpensive by the "forced labour of the Africans."[38] By casting apartheid in the language of labor exploitation, the ANC's deputy president-general subtly broadened the UF's message beyond pan-Africanism and cemented its support among liberal Christians, labor activists, and communists in Western Europe.

This dual strategy—directed simultaneously toward nation-states in Africa and liberals in Europe—highlighted the fault lines of the anti-apartheid struggle in the early 1960s and presaged the United Front's eventual dissolution in 1962. For the African National Congress, beholden doctrinally to the Congress Alliance's Freedom Charter, gaining the moral and financial help of Europeans was a logical step toward isolating the South African government. Indeed, ANC members spent most of their time in London in 1960 and 1961.[39] The Pan Africanist Congress, in contradistinction, tended not only to center its efforts on Ghana but also to trumpet the inherent supremacy of African viewpoints and political allies. When the African National Congress began pushing for the inclusion of Indians and communists in the United Front in late 1960, the Pan Africanist Congress immediately denounced the suggestion as political blasphemy—because apartheid was an African problem, it followed that only black leaders in Africa could legitimately challenge the Nationalist government's policies. Unlike the African National Congress, the PAC's goal was never simply to gain independence for nonwhites, but to do so in a manner that established a unified pan-African nation free from European influences.

This philosophical disjuncture led to political conflict between the two organizations in 1961. According to historian Sifiso Mxoisi Ndlovu, by October, the Pan Africanist Congress was using *Voice of Africa*, a monthly magazine published by the Ghanaian Bureau of African Affairs, to suggest that the African National Congress was a "moribund and indeed defunct" organization with ties to "white communist racial supremacists."[40] The South African Communist Party (SACP), which did coordinate closely with ANC leaders in London and South Africa, summarized the effects of these attacks in its annual review the following year: "Members returning from both official and unofficial visits abroad—and especially in Africa—have reported that generally, among African people and leaders, our policy of multi-racial democratic alliance ... is not understood or supported." For many African elites, the ANC's approach "concealed a form of white leadership of the African national movement, [that] they deduce" to be "liberalistic, moderate, timid and compromising."[41] When the ANC's Nelson Mandela attended a conference in East Africa in early 1962, he too lamented in his diary that African leaders had turned against the "concept of partnership between black and white."[42] The "nature of the [counter] accusations we make against the PAC makes them sort of heroes," Mandela opined during his trip. "It does not discredit any African politician to be called a racialist or anti-white."[43]

This impasse helped accelerate the ANC's shift to strategic violence in South Africa. While Mandela later framed the 1961 decision to form Umkhonto we Sizwe (MK)—the armed wing of the African National Congress—in purely personal terms, his first task was not to train a domestic guerilla army but to travel abroad to "arrange political and economic support," gain "military training for our men," and "boost our reputation in the rest of Africa."[44] In private meetings that year, with African leaders such as Julius Nyerere, Kenneth Kaunda, William Tubman, Sékou Touré, Leopold Senghor, and London newspaper editors, Mandela challenged directly the PAC's international image, arguing that MK's existence made the African National Congress the legitimate liberation movement of South Africa.[45] This move, which met with skepticism in many cases, pushed the Pan Africanist Congress into a defensive posture in 1962.[46] Because Robert Sobukwe was imprisoned for instigating the Sharpeville Massacre, it fell to Potlako Leballo, the PAC's controversial but de facto leader in Basutoland, to show that his organization was still functional. In March 1963, Leballo not only publicly challenged South African Defense Minister John Vorster to "face me, as I have assumed the leadership of the PAC" but also released plans for an insurrection that would supposedly begin among vigilantes in the Cape Province and Transkei on April 8, 1963.[47] Regardless of the wisdom of these decisions, both the African National Congress and Pan Africanist Congress developed these policies with African audiences in mind. Liberal Europeans may have possessed influence in some corners of the world, but only African nation-states had the institutional authority and political inclination to pass U.N. sanctions against South Africa. Both organizations understood that their long-term survival was contingent partly on their credibility among Africa's nationalist leaders.[48]

This seemed like a reasonable assumption in the early 1960s. The period after second-wave decolonization was undoubtedly the high point of African nationalist sentiment, and the fate of South Africa dominated political discussions throughout the continent. The Sharpeville Massacre occurred the same year that seventeen African states stepped onto the global stage, and while India had long criticized the Union's treatment of nonwhites at the U.N. General Assembly, the proliferation of African nation-states immediately changed the tone of the apartheid conversation.[49] In a subtle swipe at older, non-African arguments, one representative at the United Nations claimed in 1960 that the "policy of racial discrimination and segregation is much more than the denial of human rights . . . It is the prelude to the most hateful kind of war: a war between races."[50] Hyperbole or not, African leaders mostly agreed that apartheid was an affront to the idea of black liberation—apartheid questioned the meaning of African independence and dismissed the conceptual marriage of territorial freedom, pan-Africanism, and development. Not all African leaders adhered to Nkrumah's particular brand of nationalism in these years—indeed sharp disagreements emerged almost immediately over Ghana's political unity plan, and states clustered into rival blocs during the Congo crisis in 1960—but most black elites framed Africa's political relevance in similar terms and embraced a common coda to explain the continent's role in the world. The Ghanaian foreign minister's assertion that "colonialism is the source of *all* the troubles which afflict mankind in our age" was widely accepted among African leaders, and it ensured that the anti-apartheid cause would be at the forefront of global politics for years to come.[51]

Apartheid's conceptual importance to African nationalists was on display at the United Nations in 1960. In a prominent speech to the General Assembly in

September, Kwame Nkrumah—introduced by W. E. B. Du Bois as "the undisputed voice of Africa"—reiterated the sentiment that "the United Nations [was] the only organization that [held] out any hope for the future of mankind." He noted that while "the flowing tide of African nationalism" had the potential to "sweep away" everything in its path, new African nations wanted only one thing—the elimination of white racism from their continent. Referring specifically to South Africa, the Ghanaian president argued, "The interest of humanity compels every nation to take steps against such inhuman policy and barbarity and to act in concert to eliminate it from the world."[52] The events at Sharpeville were tragic, but they provided evidence that the "wall of intense hate" that protected South Africa was beginning to crumble. Apartheid—framed as the epitome of white colonial racism—was untenable in Nkrumah's view. Guinea's foreign minister further captured this sentiment, commenting, "The 'wind of change' which has been referred to recently by Prime Minister Macmillan, threatens to soon become a hurricane . . . Guns and bayonets can no longer prevail in the face of the strong conscience of the populations of Africa which are determined to put an end to colonialism."[53]

In many ways, this sentiment predated the United Front's overtures at the Second Conference of Independent African States in Addis Ababa. According to Ghana's U.N. Ambassador Alex Quaison-Sackey, "It was at the Accra Conference [in 1958] that [African] delegates first agreed upon the need for . . . consultation and cooperation, and decided" that collaboration at the United Nations was "the best means" of achieving their goals. The result was the formation of "an informal but permanent machinery of African states at the United Nations—referred to as the African Group."[54] The group operated as the political nerve center of African nationalism. Its members, committed to protecting and expanding the terms of African sovereignty, pledged to fulfill the promise of the "Charter of the United Nations, the Universal Declaration of Human Rights, and the principles enunciated at the Afro-Asian Conference held in Bandung."[55] Officially, the African Group termed itself the "Informal Permanent Machinery." It consisted of a rotating four-member coordinating body and a secretariat elected to a one-year term. At least once a month, members would meet in New York to exchange information, study the U.N. agenda, and discuss strategy; and they followed a meticulous set of procedures to ensure internal consensus. Because most African countries lacked the financial resources to establish embassies abroad, these meetings served a vital purpose, making it possible for African leaders to communicate about African issues, systemize their views on current events, and maximize their impact at the General Assembly. The Informal Permanent Machinery was the institutional form that African nationalism took in the postcolonial world.[56]

As Africa's numbers swelled from nine to twenty-two states in 1960, the Group first set itself to passing General Assembly Resolution 1514 (XV), entitled the

"Declaration of Independence to Colonial Peoples and Territories." The document—which received broad support despite the resistance of several prominent West European countries—asserted both that colonialism was an impediment to social, cultural, and economic development, and that friendly relations between nations could flow only from universal equality and self-determination. Such pronouncements encoded a particular conceptual map of global affairs that linked human rights with racial equality and equated freedom with territorial autonomy.[57] The distinctions were important, because as Quaison-Sackey explained, "What prompted the Declaration of 1960 was the so-called 'Sharpeville incident.'"[58] South Africa's system of apartheid—associated widely with explicit race hierarchy, separate development, and territorial segregation—formed the conceptual antithesis of African nationalism, united African nation-states politically, and gave direction to their efforts in the global arena.

Almost immediately, the African Group began work to pass sanctions against South Africa. Even before Ethiopia and Liberia challenged the South African government's Mandate in South West Africa at the International Court of Justice in June 1960, the possibility of concrete U.N. action seemed tantalizingly real. In April, under pressure from the General Assembly, the Security Council considered the apartheid question for the first time. During the meeting, the United States—having hardened its formal stance toward apartheid issues at the General Assembly only a year earlier—threw support behind a resolution that "deplored" South Africa's actions at Sharpeville and recognized "the situation in the Union" as "one that has led to international friction and if continued might endanger international peace and security."[59] In April 1961, African leaders tried to cut through this word play with a General Assembly resolution that both declared South Africa a "clear threat to international peace and security" and labeled apartheid "inconsistent with the U.N. Charter and the Declaration of Human Rights" and "incompatible with membership in the United Nations."[60] The document's specific proposals closely mirrored the resolution passed in Addis Ababa in June 1960. As Quaison-Sackey explained during the General Assembly debate, "We in all the twenty-five African States . . . are all with one voice appealing to the Assembly to consider sanctions. To us the sanctions would serve as the sword of Damocles over the head of the Union of South Africa."[61]

Not every member of the Afro-Asian bloc agreed with this sentiment. The Republic of India—which had spearheaded its own brand of U.N. anti-apartheid criticism during the 1950s—balked as Africa's political campaign came into focus in 1961. Indian leaders had genuine reservations about the tactical wisdom of the African Group's proposals. In their minds, it was better to pass widely supported moderate resolutions than a divisive, partially supported punitive measure. "We do not want any resolution in this Assembly this time to receive even a single vote less than last year," India's U.N. ambassador explained at the General Assembly.[62] Indian leaders also expressed deeper reservations about the tone and implications of African nationalism. Sanctions were "not child's play," India's representative said during the Political Committee debate, and the United Nations should not be tempted by "remedies which do not lie entirely within the four corners of the Charter." Referring to the specific declarations of the African resolution, he went on, "We feel we would not be right in our relations with other countries to say that they must break off diplomatic relations, that they must close their ports, that they must enact legislation, that they must boycott South African goods, that they must refuse landing facilities and so on."[63] India, disconnected from the intellectual currents of pan-Africanism and perhaps self-conscious of its internal problems, disagreed ultimately with the premise that apartheid was a clear threat to international peace and security. In New Delhi's mind, article 2(7) of the Charter trumped transnational racial solidarity. In 1961, the majority of nations from Latin America and Asia agreed, throwing the General Assembly's support behind India's comparatively weak resolution, which called vaguely on states to "consider taking such separate and collective action" that would "bring about the abandonment of [apartheid] policies."[64]

However, the setback did not halt the African Group's political advance. The Nationalist government's expulsion from the British Commonwealth in 1961 marked a crucial, if occasionally misunderstood, moment in the global apartheid story. In the months preceding South Africa's transition from a Union to a fully independent Republic, Verwoerd worked diligently to secure support for his country's reentry into the Commonwealth, hoping to follow the precedents set by India, Canada, and Ghana. When the prime minister applied for reentry to the Commonwealth on March 23, however, several African member-states established preconditions that made South Africa's readmission contingent on domestic political reform. According to Ghana, Nigeria, and Tanganyika, the Commonwealth could only be "effective" if the "racial policies of the member-governments [were] consistent with the multiracial character" of the organization.[65] The stance took the South African prime minister by surprise. "South Africa is one of the senior members of the Commonwealth," Verwoerd said during a prime ministers' meeting in London that month. "No self-respecting member of any voluntary organization could ... be expected to retain membership in what is now becoming a pressure group."[66] The Republic's subsequent withdrawal marked the first time a nation was forcibly removed from an intergovernmental institution in the postwar era.

It would not be the last. At the annual conference of the International Labor Organization (ILO) in June 1961, African diplomats used their numbers to pass a resolution that declared apartheid "incompatible" with the organization's founding documents and called upon the Republic to leave the organization immediately.[67]

Later that month, when South Africa's foreign minister gave a speech at the General Assembly that questioned the African Group's understanding of article 2(7)—reiterating themes that had animated South African addresses throughout much of the 1950s—the representative from Liberia motioned to delete his comments from the U.N. records. The unprecedented gesture sent shockwaves through the Assembly. While the motion was rejected on the grounds of the precedent it would set, the African delegates nonetheless gained enough political support to formally censure South Africa's comments by a vote of sixty-seven to one, with twenty abstentions.[68] In explaining the move to the General Assembly in October, the Nigerian delegate commented:

> I want to warn South Africa once more. We have managed to get it out of the Commonwealth. If South Africa persists in this behavior we may have to get it outside this world . . . We are opposed to everything that the present South African Government stands for.[69]

The African Group's actions put the rest of the nonaligned world in a difficult position. While apartheid provided Third World diplomats and politicians with a rhetorical foil at the international level, many states outside Africa were initially aloof toward the Group's actions against the South African government. For large nations like India, the United Nations was an organization of consensus, one that complemented national power without overriding the principle of national sovereignty.[70] The African Group, however, took a different approach, treating the United Nations as a mechanism to reshape international norms. Working from a position of acute economic and military weakness, African leaders embraced the anti-apartheid cause not simply because of the plight of black South Africans; they hoped also to delegitimize and demonize the intellectual scaffolding of white supremacy and, in the process, gain power by universalizing their own understandings of race, development, and territoriality. By using their numbers to determine literally "correct" opinions at the General Assembly, African leaders were laying claim to the terms of legitimacy in the nation-state system. "Our power comes from history," Nkrumah explained in late 1960. And history had coalesced, in his mind, behind the African nationalist vision of the postimperial world.[71] By the end of 1962, as it grew increasingly obvious that Africans would not back down from the apartheid fight, nations outside Africa confronted a difficult choice: they could either turn actively against the Group's efforts, thereby eroding the basis of the larger intellectual and political project known as the Third World, or recalibrate their stance toward South African issues.

This impasse resolved itself at the General Assembly in 1962. In November, the African Group resubmitted its controversial resolution on apartheid. "If you find it impossible to go with us, I beg you, in the name of humanity, not to vote against this draft resolution," Nigeria's representative said during the Political Committee debate on November 7.[72] The Ugandan diplomat followed suit, explaining, "We, the people of Africa . . . are not going to rest until our people in that country are set free." He continued, "The Government of South Africa is engaged actively in torturing—that is the word—the majority of its citizens. If there is one spot on this globe which is pregnant with the dynamic [of] an international time bomb, it is surely the Republic of South Africa."[73] Colombia, Mexico, Guatemala, and Great Britain all attempted to remove controversial aspects of the African resolution, but support from India pushed it through the Special Political Committees in its entirety. Resolution 1761 (XVII) passed ultimately by a vote of sixty-seven to sixteen, with twenty-three abstentions. The result was a formal U.N. declaration that apartheid "seriously endanger[ed] international peace and security" and an official call for member-states to break their economic, diplomatic, and cultural ties with the Republic and to establish a permanent U.N. oversight committee to monitor the situation in South Africa.[74]

The African Group's victory made it difficult for the Security Council to ignore the apartheid question in 1963. African efforts in the subsequent months unfolded along two parallel lines. First, in late May 1963, African heads of state assembled again at Addis Ababa, this time to establish the Organization of African Unity (OAU). While disagreements proliferated over the best formula for African unification, colonial questions dominated most of the meetings, providing a common cause that transcended regional differences among Africans and gave particular, shared meaning to discussions about equality, development, and territorial integrity. After passing a broad resolution on decolonization, OAU delegates turned their attention to another, more controversial resolution entitled "Apartheid and Decolonization." Rather than focusing exclusively on South Africa, the discussion provocatively highlighted the commonalities between anti-apartheid unrest in the Republic and events in Birmingham, Alabama, where the local police had recently attacked American civil rights protestors led by Martin Luther King Jr. "Nothing is more paradoxical than that these events should take place . . . at a time when [the United States] is anxious to project its image before the world screen as the archetype of democracy and the champion of freedom," Uganda's Prime Minister Milton Obote commented.[75] The African Group placed direct diplomatic pressure on the most powerful actor at the Security Council—the United States—by declaring that the "intolerable mal-practices" of Jim Crow would "seriously deteriorate" Africa's relationship with America and foregrounding such sentiment in a resolution on apartheid.[76] The resolution aimed to pressure U.S. officials into taking a strong position against South Africa at the United Nations.[77]

Simultaneously, the African Group worked to systemize the case against South Africa through the newly formed U.N. Special Committee on Apartheid.

Chaired by Diallo Telli of Guinea, the committee—whose members hailed almost exclusively from the decolonized world—published a series of reports in 1963, free from "hatred or partiality," that provided information on land ownership in the Republic, narrated the evolution of South Africa's political system, and highlighted the repressive results of apartheid.[78] Framing this information as the official word of the United Nations, the African Group concluded that "the problem of *apartheid* is not an aspect of the Cold War."[79] It existed along a separate, more important, axis that pitted the "protagonists of racial domination" against "the advocates of racial equality."[80] According to Telli, South Africa was "a microcosm of the world." And the Nationalist government's unwillingness to promote "amity, on the basis of racial equality" violated article 2(7) because so many member-states shared "close kinship" with people in the Republic, making apartheid "a source of international friction and a threat to the peace and security in Africa and the world."[81] To strengthen this argument, the Special Committee opened its doors to South Africa's freedom fighters and American civil rights activists, all of whom endorsed the committee's findings. "I cannot believe that this world body . . . could stand by, calmly watching what I submit is genocide masquerading under the guise of a civilized dispensation of justice," Oliver Tambo declared famously to the committee in 1963.[82] Strategically, the African Group hoped for a breakthrough at the Security Council by framing apartheid as the symbolic epicenter of the worldwide struggle against white domination.

When the issue went finally to the Security Council in August 1963, African diplomats received the jolt of support they had hoped for. U.S. representative Adlai Stevenson adopted a stronger than expected line against apartheid. Referring subtly to the pronouncements of the 1963 Addis Ababa conference, he admitted that the United States suffered from "the disease of discrimination in various forms." Whereas Washington and most other governments in the modern world acknowledged racism as "a disfiguring blight," National Party leaders stood alone, set on "prescribing for the malady of racism the bitter toxic of apartheid." Stevenson went on to contextualize his comments firmly in U.S. domestic politics, asserting that "just as the United States was determined to wipe out discrimination" at home, it would "support efforts to bring about a change in South Africa." Acknowledging that apartheid was preventing the full independence of Africa, the declaration was accompanied by a U.S. pledge that the Security Council would help end the sale of all military equipment to the Republic by the end of the calendar year.[83] It was the strongest condemnation of South Africa ever made by a Western government.

However, to the disappointment of the African Group, the American plan ignored Resolution 1761 (XVII) and said nothing of economic sanctions. African nationalists responded by amplifying their position at the General Assembly. "In discussing apartheid, some have called it racial discrimination, on the principle of separate existence," Nigeria's ambassador said on October 11. "We, the African States, do not accept this at all. Apartheid as interpreted and practiced in South Africa spells only one word: slavery." As such, article 2(7) could no longer be used to insulate the Republic from concrete international action. "Is slavery essentially within the domestic jurisdiction of any State? My answer is no. South Africa is a slave state. This is Africa's position."[84] The Group passed another General Assembly measure on apartheid that November but coupled it with Resolution 1904 (XVIII), entitled the "Declaration on the Elimination of All Forms of Racial Discrimination." Complementing Resolution 1514 (XV) in tone and scope, the document outlined eleven "universal and effective" measures that, among other things, declared the incongruity of race discrimination with the U.N. Charter and called on every member-state to pass domestic laws and policies that remedied the wrongs of racial discrimination.[85] For the African Group, the resolution raised the stakes of the fight by making racism—defined in reference to apartheid—the moral bane of the United Nations. In Telli's words, South Africa's domestic policies "not only raise[d] questions of principle and morality, but also directly jeopardize[d] the very basis of our Organization—its real influence, its practical efficiency and, in a word, indeed, its very *raison d'être*."[86] The African Group's intention, quite literally, was to make sanctions the barometer of the United Nation's effectiveness in the postcolonial era.

The move worked. In late November, the Nordic countries stepped into the fray with a proposal that tried to accommodate African demands. Denmark's U.N. ambassador explained, "Constructive progress can only result from a dialogue between on the one hand the countries—primarily the African States—which have special interests and special responsibilities and naturally advocate an unconditional policy of pressure and, on the other hand, the major trading partners of South Africa, which will eventually have to carry the main burden of such a policy."[87] Norway, Sweden, and Denmark marshaled support that month for the creation of a "Group of Experts"—composed of Alva Myrdal of Sweden, Sir Edward Asafu-Adjaye of Ghana, Sir Hugh Foot of Great Britain, and Ahmed De Ould Sidi Baba of Mauritania—who were empowered to formulate a uniform international approach toward South Africa. Much to the chagrin of Western nations, when the experts presented their report to the Security Council in April 1964 their conclusions buttressed the African Group's position—the United Nations needed to consider sanctions. The experts implored South Africa to hold a national convention to establish a plan for nonracial democracy and declared that if the Republic refused such action, the Security Council should respond with "economic and strategic" action "beyond the arms embargo" that compelled a new stance toward racial discrimination.[88]

The decision triggered "expressions of joy" among Africa's diplomats.[89] Having worked for four years to pass sanctions through the General Assembly, it seemed as if they had finally forced the Security Council's hand. Even more, the expert group's conclusions tacitly affirmed the moral righteousness, even the epistemological validity, of the African Group's stance on South Africa. Justice hinged on racial equality, majoritarian democracy prefigured economic development, and the U.N. agenda belonged to the new nations of Africa. Having used General Assembly resolutions to present these positions in universal terms, African leaders had succeeded in securing support elsewhere in the international community. After a brief round of political wrangling that spring, the Security Council reconvened in June 1964 and agreed to establish another committee of experts to study the logistical prerequisites and economic implications of U.N. sanctions.[90] In response, the African Group agreed to hold its diplomatic offensive in abeyance. With the International Court of Justice scheduled to deliver its ruling on the legality of the South West Africa Mandate in mid-1965 and the expert committee's report scheduled for release at approximately the same time, sanctions appeared to many to be inevitable. Either through article 94 or chapter VII, the African Group would bring its international campaign against South Africa to a crescendo in 1965.

(Re)Selling Apartheid

The Nationalist government did not sit idly on the sidelines during this four-year diplomatic assault. Nor did it dismiss the African Group's attacks as unimportant. This "goes deeper than a 'publicity problem with political overtones,'" Willem Naude, South Africa's ambassador to the United States, explained after the 1960 General Assembly session. These attacks "have become a full scale international political problem affecting the *survival* of South Africa itself." The country was "confronted by an exceptional situation"—and only "extraordinary measures" would keep it from being engulfed by the political tempest of African nationalism.[91]

For many officials in Pretoria, the storm clouds had been on the horizon for some time. Throughout the 1940s and 1950s, the Union engaged in political skirmishes along two distinct fronts. On the one side were Western liberals who expressed negative opinions about Afrikaner nationalism. Throughout his tenure as foreign minister, the mercurial Eric Louw—who dominated politics and policymaking within South Africa's Department of External Affairs in the early Cold War—used both domestic radio addresses and speeches abroad to attack liberalism in the United States and Great Britain.[92] The minister's comments followed a familiar pattern. "'Fundamental Human Rights and Freedoms' is today a popular cry," he declared in 1957. "Let us be careful that it does not become a cliché, or develop into a political slogan."[93] In a 1959 National Party report, he argued that "irrational humanitarianism" was "no less dangerous than its Russian-communist prototype." In fact, it was "perhaps even more [dangerous] in that it [was] not so clearly defined and operate[d] in ways which [did] not easily allow its being identified and exposed."[94] For South African officials, criticism that emanated from liberals could be traced to "the ranks of these social revolutionaries, possibly in combination with repressed communist plotters but not necessarily so."[95] This convoluted, conspiratorial logic shaped the National Party's engagement with world politics in the years before Sharpeville and molded the government's assumptions about apartheid's enemies abroad.

At the same time, South Africa faced a persistent political adversary in the so-called Bandung voting bloc at the United Nations. In 1946, India submitted the first U.N. complaint about the Union's policies toward South Asians and in 1952 it supported a joint resolution that broadly condemned the policy of apartheid. Pretoria tried to parry these complaints by wrapping its international identity in the doctrine of nonintervention, enshrined in article 2(7) of the U.N. Charter, but the resolutions continued to accumulate through the 1950s. Returning from New York in 1956, Louw commented that the United Nations was becoming "less of a forum . . . for dealing with and discussing matters affecting world peace" and more of "a platform for the exploitation of disputes and for making ideological propaganda."[96] Anticommunism again animated Afrikaner nationalist thinking. A 1957 report, written against the backdrop of Ghana's independence, claimed that Africans abroad were "being exhorted, by Communists as well as by the Bandung countries under Indian leadership, to resist their 'white rulers,'" not only through "direct propaganda" but also by "provocative speeches in the conference halls of the United Nations where the 'Colonial' authorities (also those of the Union) are described as oppressors."[97] This conflation of communism and Indian criticism served an instrumental end, both flattening anti-apartheid sentiment and freezing the actions of South Africa's critics in a linear, self-referential Cold War paradigm from which the Union government could claim ideological unanimity with Western nations. South Africa's goal, always, was unity with the West.

The tactic generally worked in the postwar years. South Africa stayed on the offensive against liberals and Asian nationalists throughout the 1950s. For instance, when France withdrew from the General Assembly in protest of the U.N.'s discussion of Algeria in 1956, South Africa followed suit, curtailing its presence in New York in a similar effort to pressure its Western allies into condemning criticism of the Union's domestic policies. In a speech on South Africa's foreign policy that year, Louw cast events in positive terms. "In spite of the fact that the opposition has remained strong, I think I can say that we have gained a little ground."[98] Citing conversations with Western policymakers, he argued that while the "struggle against intervention in domestic affairs" had "begun in South

Africa" it was now "a struggle, not only against South Africa, but also against the so-called 'colonial powers' of Africa." Consequently, the Union was receiving a "larger measure of support and also more enthusiastic support" from countries that once ignored political developments in sub-Saharan Africa.[99] In private conversations, the foreign minister candidly explained South Africa's mindset. "I wish to be frank," he said in a meeting with the U.S. ambassador in 1957. "A specific and strong resolution against South Africa voted for by a majority of nations in [the] U.N. does not matter so much as one might expect. What matters more than . . . all other votes put together is [the position] of [the] U.S. in view of its predominant position of leadership in [the] Western world."[100] So long as the Union received the tacit support of the United States and its allies, the country could continue to confront its opponents in the international arena.

American foreign policy (the topic of the next chapter) supported South Africa in these years. U.S. investment and trade in the Union had expanded rapidly in the Truman years. With Cold War tensions escalating in Europe and war spreading through the Korean peninsula, the National Party's unbending anti-communist rhetoric brought it much credit in Washington. U.S-South African relations revolved around South Africa's willingness to produce and sell large quantities of uranium ore exclusively to the United States. So long as nuclear weapons remained an essential aspect of U.S. national security strategy, Pretoria would remain shielded from Western liberals and Indian diplomats.[101] Convinced similarly that communist expansion constituted a major threat to U.S. interests in the world, the Dwight D. Eisenhower administration, especially in its first term, expanded and deepened U.S. relations with South Africa. The growing questions about the immorality of apartheid had little influence on Eisenhower and Secretary of State John Foster Dulles. For most U.S. officials, South Africa was the best source of strategic minerals in the Western world and an ally in the fight against global communism.[102]

The situation began to turn, from the National Party's perspective, only in 1958. Everything pivoted on the United States' stance toward African decolonization. Rather than pushing back against African demands for majority rule, claimed a South African official, U.S. policymakers embraced "gradual independence, neutrality, economic assistance and racial equality" after Ghana's independence in 1957—even though these "very aims [were] vehicles of communist infiltration in Africa." The U.S. civil rights movement, in Louw's mind, was behind this shift, "colouring [America's] external approach" and pushing Washington to acquiesce to Africans to keep pace with Soviet proposals, at the expense of pan-European authority everywhere.[103] The United States, according to National Party officials, shaped the direction of policy in Great Britain, France, and West Germany. When U.S. representatives expressed skepticism about the future of the South West Africa Mandate at the U.N. Trusteeship Council and hardened the West's stance against apartheid in 1958, the Union's ambassador called immediately for a top-level explanation. In private meetings with U.S. officials that year, Louw implored Washington to reverse course. Falling back on common apartheid platitudes, he claimed in October 1958, "Even in Ghana there are signs that Nkrumah . . . is assuming the posture of an African Chief and not a Western Prime Minister." The minister went on, asserting that "a stage will be reached beyond which the United States can not go and there is no guarantee that the African States will not follow the course set by the highest bidder."[104] Only South Africa could truly protect Western civilization in the so-called Dark Continent.

Political currents, however, were moving fast in the opposite direction. In November 1959, a National Party report concluded belatedly that the Eisenhower administration no longer viewed nonalignment as immoral and speculated that the U.S. State Department would probably move toward the doctrine of "'Africa for the Africans' in sub-Saharan Africa" in 1960—a conclusion validated ostensibly by Vice President Richard Nixon's push to establish an autonomous African Bureau within the State Department in the late 1950s.[105] Before the prime minister could respond to this report, Harold Macmillan delivered his famous "winds of change" address in Cape Town in February, blindsiding the National Party by openly questioning the Union's future in the Western bloc. Prime Minister Verwoerd recommended a coordinated response to this emerging Anglo-American entente,[106] but the violence at Sharpeville in March put the Department of External Affairs further on the defensive. By April, the Union's diplomats were defending South Africa not only in private meetings but also at the U.N. Security Council, where African diplomats were already demanding economic sanctions. When American delegates convinced their British counterparts to accept a critical Security Council resolution that month, South Africa's ambassador wrote to Pretoria that the "obvious inference to be drawn" was "that the Union [was] no longer acceptable as a partner in the political field of Africa."[107] As Western protection evaporated rapidly, the Union stood exposed to the postcolonial world and the attacks of the ascendant African Group. "The timing here could not be worse," South Africa's New York ambassador said in mid-April. "I cannot view these trends with anything but deep concern."[108]

The crisis intensified as the African Group's strategy crystallized at the United Nations. "The 'wild men' of Africa are determined to dethrone the white man from his position of power in Africa and put the blacks in power," South Africa's U.N. delegate said in April 1961. Quoting a speech by George Padmore on the nature of the U.N. Charter, the official speculated that the African Group wanted "an 'African Africa'" where the Charter existed simply to support nonwhite political views.[109] An analysis of resolutions on apartheid, conducted the same month, cemented the Union's fears. Whereas India's U.N. resolutions had "embodied generalities concerning human rights and freedoms," the African Group's proposals constituted a "genuine, more dangerous" threat to the country's national security.[110] Yesterday's enemies were "mild" in the face of African protest.[111] Even after India's resolution passed the General Assembly in 1961, South African officials remained pessimistic. "Our stand on Art. 2(7) which was never fully honoured now seems to be finally foredoomed," a report concluded that November. "During the recent vote on the apartheid item only *Portugal* voted against the [Indian] resolution. *Every other country present and voting, voted in favor of the resolution.*"[112] The South African government's future in the international arena was growing dark.

Trends in the economic realm reinforced this conclusion. The foreign capital that had propelled the country's manufacturing growth in the postwar years evaporated rapidly after Sharpeville, as global investors grew restless that South Africa's troubles foreshadowed a coming racial war. In November 1960, banking officials reported that nearly R250,000,000 in private investment capital had left the country that year, halving the Union's gold and foreign exchange reserves in a six-month period.[113] With "the net outflow of capital" having "an appreciably adverse effect on the country's monetary reserves and financial markets," dramatic action was required—the government needed to "exert itself in every possible way to revive the confidence of foreign investors."[114] Reserve Bank officials called on the Department of External Affairs to "bring home" the idea that "the political and economic position" of the Union was "fundamentally different from that in most other parts of Africa," convince the world that "various steps have been taken or are being contemplated to remove causes of Bantu unrest," and provide "local entrepreneurs" with incentives for showing "their confidence openly." Unless "robust" actions were taken soon, the situation would "worsen in the coming years" and possibly destabilize white political hegemony in South Africa.[115]

This diagnosis ironically mirrored the conclusions of the African Group. However, the Nationalist government adopted a different, three-pronged strategy to pursue its goals. Its most prominent moves were defensive in nature. As noted earlier, Verwoerd declared a state of emergency after Sharpeville that curtailed further black political protest and passed legislation that expanded the size and authority of the government's domestic security forces—a move intended explicitly to prevent incidents that attracted "the attention of critics beyond our borders."[116] Second, the prime minister accelerated plans to make South Africa a fully independent Republic, pushing for a referendum in 1960 that ended the Union's political associations with Great Britain and insulated white South Africans from the "whims of Western liberal sentiment."[117] Finally, government officials embraced proactive action in the realm of propaganda and took action to address the recommendations of the Reserve Bank. P. J. Nel, the director of information, diagnosing South Africa's "image" problem in November 1960, explained:

> The public opinion outside our country has reached a stage where it reacts to emotions and no longer to facts. An intelligence effort merely focused on providing the facts cannot succeed because the facts are no longer accepted . . . How far this situation has already progressed is apparent in press reports from the United States: there is no longer any debate or discussion about South Africa. The 'great battle' and the 'day of reckoning' are coming! From a publicity point of view this places our country before a challenge that cannot be successfully faced without real action, assistance from all possible sources and a concentrated programme of action.[118]

Nel's analysis foregrounded the government's genuine frustrations with the intellectual developments of the early 1960s and highlighted the National Party's unique understanding of the global apartheid debate. While the African Group viewed the General Assembly as an instrument to remake international order, Afrikaner elites lamented the forum because it influenced U.S. perceptions and intellectual trends. Rather than focusing on the link between U.N. diplomacy and U.S. policymaking, South African officials centered their attention on an indirect connection—General Assembly resolutions shaped not formal government action but perceptions of that action within the American public sphere, which, in turn, affected the policymaking proclivities of Washington. This diagnosis was crucial. In the minds of South African policymakers, if Pretoria could develop tools to influence the views of U.S. opinion makers, they would subvert and circumvent the threat of Africa's political offensive at the United Nations.

By 1961, most National Party officials agreed that the situation had reached a crisis point. "Everything indicates that the Kennedy regime is going to be strongly influenced by liberal and progressive elements," Ambassador Naude stated after the U.S. election in November.[119] Although Kennedy was not yet prepared to support "formal civil rights legislation," he seemed intent on winning "the support not only of the negro population in this country, but also of the African States in the Cold War struggle"—all of which spelled trouble for the South African government.[120] It was possible for the first time, an official said in April 1961, to "visualize events which could lead to an American intervention [in South Africa] through the United Nations."[121]

The Nationalist government needed its propaganda campaign to be nuanced and targeted to reverse these trends. Although an "information service [could] not be expected to influence the grand strategy of the Western Powers," it could "disprove the assumption" that apartheid's failure was good for the United States.[122] "How can we possibly convince the doubters of the sincerity of the South African Government's intentions?" queried Ambassador Naude in early 1961. The answer, in his mind, was clear: "The Americans have to be convinced—if they are to be influenced substantially—that the implementation of our racial policy respects at least four principles, namely, self-determination for the Bantu peoples, respect of human rights, respect for the dignity of the individual and that the policy enjoys the consent of the Bantu." In his words, "These are the main constituents of the political jargon of the New Frontier."[123] And they held the key to South Africa's political and economic reintegration with the West.

Toward this end, the government's "programme of action" had several distinct components. First, South African diplomats worked to shore up political support within the new Kennedy administration. "Ultra-liberalistic" sentiment was strongest within the U.S. State Department, according to Foreign Minister Louw, where G. Mennen "Soapy" Williams was assistant secretary of state for African affairs.[124] The new assistant secretary was a "thoroughly spoilt . . . child of very wealthy parents," South Africa's ambassador said in 1961, who had sympathy for blacks only because he always "believed in the underdog."[125] To combat and isolate the new assistant secretary, Nationalist officials turned to indirect diplomacy, hiring an American intermediary—former U.S. General Timothy McInerny—to make South Africa's case at the Pentagon, White House, and Congress. McInerny was a lobbyist for Charles Englehard, a prominent American investor with wide-ranging interests in the Union, and he had "close connections" with Lyndon Johnson and several influential members of the American press corps. In defining McInerny's role, the director of intelligence explained that he would work "behind the scenes—firstly, to the outside, where he directs himself as an American at fellow countrymen for the benefit of the country he serves, and secondly, because he can with his contacts in influential circles convey valuable information to the inside, to the government of our country." He would be, "in truth, a high-level 'lobbyist.'"[126]

Conceived as "the first bulwark of counter-attack," this political effort abroad was coupled with initiatives to manage press coverage within South Africa. The government's aim was "planned internal press canvassing." In the director of information's words, "The press should become priority number one. It was the press here that conditioned the adverse popular opinion against South Africa; the press is the major means to be used to remedy the situation."[127] Conceiving this work as the top commitment of the Information Service of South Africa, he recommended the development of close relationships with "important internal correspondents" and "manageable foreign correspondents." Members of the press were to be treated literally as guests of the government. To reinforce the authority of the state, cabinet members and other officials were instructed to release information to the public through press conferences rather than "impersonal" news releases. "No person worth his salt would be able to afford to miss such a conference. The principle should apply: that whoever does not come will not get the news." For the director, these initiatives would not simply dampen the influence of South Africa's critics. They guaranteed better understanding of South Africa's race problems. Demanding in "the strongest terms" that this program be kept secret from "the press, the Parliament and the public," the director confidently asserted that it provided an "answer to press control."[128]

At the same time, the South African government also worked to change fundamentally global perceptions of apartheid, particularly in the United States. With Americans supposedly conditioned to "accept the simplistic solution of an eventual explosion as the only possible outcome" in South Africa, officials turned to private organizations like the Institute for Motivational Research for guidance in reselling their domestic ideology. Utilizing newly developed social science concepts and research methods, the institute and its "team of Ph.D.'s" analyzed the "latent" and "emotional" reasons for anti-apartheid sentiment in the United States. Many Americans viewed the Nationalist government as a colonial power in South Africa. Everyday Americans tended to juxtapose the rigidity of apartheid with the United States' progressive approach toward race. Nonetheless, few understood the economic realities of South African society. "Armed with these data," the director of information declared in 1960, "we can now apply a strengthened information service with a new prospect of success and new techniques to swing public opinion . . . in our favor."[129]

In the months afterward, the South African Information Service's budget increased dramatically. Linked institutionally to the Department of External Affairs, the Service's efforts focused primarily on distributing periodicals, educational pamphlets, and propaganda movies; and coordinating speaking tours by officials disguised as unbiased experts. The Service's propaganda touched on several themes. Most obviously, the Information Agency worked to disconnect the country's domestic race policies from the narrative of anticolonialism. As one official explained, the Republic needed to show that South Africa was "not only multi-racial but also multi-national—ie. one white nation and several black nations." With four million whites of European origin, four million Xhosa, four million Zulu, two million Tswana, and two million Sotho, the "country [had] no single majority group." It was a semantic point with important implications. "Cartographically, Bantu homelands in the Union must be given a distinction similar to that of the Protectorates, and where boundaries are not yet defined they must at any rate be indicated," a government official recommended in 1961.[130] By locating South Africa within the narrative of postcolonial nationalism—divorcing it from themes of pan-Africanism, while institutionalizing the territorial specificity of African ethnic groups in South Africa—National Party propagandists aimed to reframe common perceptions of apartheid. Afrikaner nationalism did not exploit nonwhites so much as it allowed each racial group to proceed down the path of modernization "in a manner congruent with their standards."[131]

South African officials buttressed this argument by announcing the "independence" of one of the African homelands in January 1962.[132] The territory, located in the Transkei region along the Eastern Cape, was pitched as the first step toward a multinational South Africa. In revealing the plan, Prime Minister Verwoerd announced that "despite provocation, criticism, and extremist demands," his government would solve its problems "in such a way that stability and tranquility for all is assured." In his mind, "All nations of the world which seek to protect human dignity and the right to self-determination should give South Africa a fair chance to establish and develop its own Commonwealth of Nations."[133] Behind closed doors, however, Verwoerd emphasized that his move was as much about propaganda as genuine political reform. In a telegram to South Africa's diplomats, the Department of External Affairs said that while the Transkei plan "appear[ed] to point the way towards a federal form of constitutional association . . . the Prime Minister preferred to think in terms of a Commonwealth which will reflect a community of interest without detracting from political status."[134] In other words, the territory would be given the symbolic trappings of independence—an official flag, a capital building and presidential cabinet, and a semiautonomous police force—but would remain economically integrated with the Republic and politically beholden to the Nationalist government. In the months following the Transkei announcement, propagandists closely analyzed the response of the Western press and lobbied journalists and politicians to accept the move as the harbinger of major change in the Republic. Their message was simple—economic development and territorial freedom could be achieved without a commitment to racial equality.[135]

Simultaneously, South African officials worked to cast aspersions on the proposals of the African Group. Their efforts often centered on themes of South African exceptionalism: "Neither in Algeria nor in [Kenya] can the white communities be regarded as constituting a unique, separate and self-contained nation."[136] Using periodicals like *South Africa Digest*, for example, officials stressed that "the forces and influences that have arisen in Algeria, West Africa, the Congo, and East Africa are not coordinated. To believe this would be to misunderstand the confused, shifting and immature character of the African."[137] Similarly, in a speech before a group of Western businessmen, Foreign Minister Louw argued that U.N. declarations from African nations like Ghana were signs of "political immaturity—the sort expected from small boys or a certain modern type of irresponsible teenager." Unrest in places like the Congo, in his mind, would have a "healthy effect" on the Western world by reminding foreigners that South Africa "is the only country with the necessary knowledge to ensure positive trade relations."[138] The government's goal was to convince Western authorities that the rest of Africa was fundamentally different from South Africa—and that Africa was a geographic entity, not a people. "We must show" that "African nationalism and the African personality cannot [be expressed] in South Africa through institutions designed and developed over 300 years to express the Western personality." Black African states were inherently "unstable" and "unpredictable," while South Africa was a bastion of "modern capitalism."[139]

When addressing the unrest in their own borders, government officials continued to harp on the specter of communism. Although the African National Congress had long-standing ties to the South African Communist Party, their relationship was derived primarily from their mutual exclusion from the mainstream political process in South Africa. The African National Congress deepened its patronage ties to the Soviet Union in the 1970s, but few African nationalists—and no one with loyalties to the Pan Africanist Congress—counted themselves as genuine communists in the early 1960s.[140] As criticism of apartheid mounted, however, South African propagandists made the case that black activism and communism were a singular phenomenon. "Nothing would satisfy the Communists except a successful revolution in South Africa, and nothing would satisfy the extremist Africans except the introduction of one-man-one-vote into the constitution," an advertisement claimed in 1962.[141] For many white South Africans these two dangers were interconnected. By positioning themselves between the Western bloc and imaginary communist masses, Pretoria sought to convey the message that it was a defender of Western values in Africa.

Most important, South African propagandists lauded the merits of their industrial society. Nearly every propaganda item from the early 1960s made some reference to the country's high standard of living and complex manufacturing sector. The goal, according to the Information Service, was to "present to the world the true picture of South Africa" by focusing on themes like "industrial and social progress; science and education; cultural development; opportunities for investment; tourist attractions; and the way of life of South Africans at work and play."[142] A pamphlet from 1962 reflected the self-image that propagandists sought to convey, claiming that South Africa "is the only bridge on the African continent between the Old World, for whence thousands of immigrants came and are still coming, and the new technological world of which it is a sturdy representative . . . It is a country of the future—with unlimited possibilities and exciting prospects."[143] Privately, Nationalist officials discussed the intentions behind such phraseology. The goal was "to project an image of national confidence, tolerance and maturity," an official explained in 1961. "In the existing confusion of African affairs this is our trump card." In the coming years, "the emphasis will move from whether a particular nation is multi-racial or uni-racial, heterogeneous or homogeneous to whether it is an efficient and trustworthy partner."[144] By positioning itself appropriately in the near term, Pretoria would be able to reap the benefits of this inevitable shift.

Recognizing that colonial themes of white civilization no longer resonated abroad, the South African government tried to use concepts of multinationalism and modernization to reestablish its place in the Western world. Officials aimed not to engage African nationalists directly in a debate over apartheid but to manipulate underlying Western assumptions about blacks and emphasize the pragmatic importance of social stability and economic vitality. These efforts were not entirely successful, but they revealed important aspects of how the gap between older modes of civilizational thinking and the newer discourse of modernization was bridged in the years after second-wave decolonization. Explicit racial paternalism—the type that defined Nationalist public discourse through the 1950s—receded undeniably from global discourse in the 1960s. However, racialist assumptions did not disappear. South African officials simply recoded and repackaged their arguments in less obvious, more functional ways.

By the time the African Group successfully brought the apartheid question to the Security Council in 1963, this counteroffensive was beginning to yield some positive results. On an economic level, in particular, South Africa had started to recover from the collapse of 1960. In 1961 and 1962, the Nationalist government received a series of loans from the International Monetary Fund, World Bank, and several American corporations to address its economic downturn, and investors from the United States, targeted heavily by South Africa's information campaign, began to reinvest millions as the domestic situation stabilized in the Republic. At the end of 1962, Reserve Bank officials claimed these changes "indicate[d] the beginning of an increase in foreign confidence in the maintenance of order, stability and prosperity in South Africa," and opined that events had turned out "much better than expected."[145]

Events in the political realm were more conflicted. In some respects, it seemed that Pretoria had won support within the Kennedy administration. In a meeting with Ambassador Naude on the eve of the 1963 U.N. Security Council debate, U.S. Secretary of State Dean Rusk offered candid insight on his thinking about the apartheid question. Keeping his comments strictly "off-the-record," Rusk said that the United States would never support U.N. sanctions through chapter VII of the Charter—a major, albeit unknown blow to the African Group—and claimed that the State Department was willing to consider a nonintegrationist solution to South Africa's racial problems. If the Republic shifted fully to a "federal or confederal" political system—along the lines of the Transkei plan—Rusk speculated that white South Africans could eliminate the offensive aspects of apartheid while maintaining exclusive control over "external affairs and defence." Naude—who interpreted this plan as a sign of "fresh thinking and an abandonment of the hackneyed clichés of the New Frontier"—responded with enthusiasm. Writing to Pretoria the following evening, he noted that if South Africa could continue to "present [its] situation in terms of [Rusk's] own terminology [it] might be able to make a great deal of 'progress' in getting the U.S. to understand [its] situation, without moving an inch from [its] declared policies." From South Africa's perspective, the overture was a sign that the Americans were "willing to agree—albeit reluctantly—to explore, if not yet to follow, [the] road of separate development" in South Africa.[146]

In other respects the situation remained negative for the Republic. Rather than publicly insulating South Africa at the Security Council, for instance, the Kennedy administration chose to throw its weight behind the arms embargo in 1963 and issued a surprisingly strong denunciation at the United Nations that linked apartheid directly to civil rights issues in the United States. On its own, the gesture might be excused as political posturing, but it was coupled with a formal Aide-Memoire that explained the United States would support the International Court's upcoming ruling on the legal status of South West Africa. As one Nationalist official explained, although the United States was "strongly opposed to sanctions" under chapter VII there was "no doubt that she [would] consider herself obliged to comply with Security Council action under Article 94."[147] If South Africa lost the case against Ethiopia and Liberia, therefore, sanctions would reemerge as a political possibility. Even more, openly defying the Court's ruling carried serious consequences. "Any openly warlike action on an international plane spells inevitable defeat," a government official stated in 1963. "We could certainly not militarily defend ourselves for long against attacks from within as well as without."[148] The South African government, in its own mind, remained in a highly insecure and vulnerable position at the end of 1963.

When the Group of Experts presented its findings at the United Nations in early 1964, Nationalist leaders tried to adjust to the emerging geopolitical situation. In January, incoming Foreign Minister Dr. Hilgard Muller—who replaced the aging Eric Louw that year—declared, "Under present circumstances long-term and so-called '[grass]-roots' publicity methods are no longer feasible." In his mind, "with the present international trends, even by spending millions of Rands, [South Africa] could not effectively reach the masses whose minds are conditioned daily by the antagonistic press, radio and T.V."[149] The declaration did not reduce the size of South Africa's information machine so much as refocus its efforts on specific, influential actors within the political arena. "The immediate problems facing us are of such an urgent nature that we must find a way of conveying our message directly to the policy and decision-makers in Washington," the new minister explained. "The political and diplomatic aspect has assumed over-whelming proportions."[150]

A "Directive on Policy," issued a few months later, elucidated the minister's plan. "I am convinced that our policy everywhere must not be to explain and excuse small details but to approach the main issues of economic sanctions and punitive intervention in South Africa, particularly on the South West Africa issue."[151] Noting that the "spearhead of the attack" on apartheid was now the International Court, the foreign minister called on his surrogates to lobby "policy influencers and makers" who might shift American attitudes on article 94. His rationale was simple—if the African states failed to force "the West to apply economic sanctions or to establish a UNO presence in South West Africa, their real threat and danger to us will have been completely broken."[152] Nineteen sixty-five promised to deliver not only the Court's verdict on the status of South West Africa, but also the United States' final decision on whether to pass sanctions against the Republic or insulate South Africa from the African Group. A fork in the road was approaching. With a new president in the White House and questions of race rapidly changing in the U.S. arena, no one knew which path Washington would take. Only one thing was certain—the decision would remake the terrain of the apartheid struggle.

3

Africa for the Africans

The United States is keenly aware of the importance which the African peoples attach to racial equality—in Africa and elsewhere in the world. We acknowledge that race discrimination exists in the United States. In pointing to the progress we have made, and to the Government's unequivocal policy of bringing discrimination to an end, we do not expect to win any plaudits nor to gloss over what remains to be solved. We simply say: We are earnestly working away at the problem.
—G. Mennen Williams, *Washington National Cathedral (1961)*

The period surrounding African decolonization marked the highpoint of America's geopolitical predominance in the world. While internal upheavals would soon destroy the cultural consensus of the early Cold War and inflation would erode the economic authority of the Bretton Woods trade system, the United States was in an unparalleled position in the late 1950s and early 1960s. Contemporary politicians frequently claimed otherwise, but the struggle for the "soul of mankind" had become a lopsided and asymmetrical affair, with Washington funneling its wealth toward reconstruction projects in Europe and Asia, building military bases throughout the Pacific Rim and Middle East, and the Soviet Union laboring to meet the basic amenities of its people and maintain its status as a global superpower. "The true measure of hegemony is not power alone," historian Thomas McCormick explains, but "a nation's ability to use that power to realize some approximation of its preferred world order."[1] By such a standard, the United States had become an unquestioned hegemon by the early 1960s. Having internationalized a form of New Deal liberalism through institutions like the United Nations, World Bank, International Monetary Fund, and International Court of Justice after World War II, Washington's influence was cresting in the late 1950s, as West Europeans embraced the Common Market system— an outgrowth of initiatives started under the Marshall Plan—and once great imperial powers succumbed to the authority and leadership of the United States in North Africa, Southeast Asia, and beyond.

The United States' ascendance brought with it paradoxes that shaped global politics in the early 1960s. Although the United States had forcibly conquered much of North America during the nineteenth century, curiously, it denounced empires as obsolete political entities in the early twentieth, at odds not only with free market capitalism but also the very tenets of Western civilization. This stance opened space for new claims on the universality of territorial autonomy and self-determination, even as the U.S. government closed opportunities for self-proclaimed anti-imperialists through self-righteous paternalism and scientific racism.[2] Such contradictions, embedded in the fabric of American society, represented the greatest threat to America's continued hegemony as decolonization spread through Africa and the Caribbean. How could the United States lead a world of free nations it regarded as backward and racially inferior? Washington elites, like their counterparts in Europe, found answers in the discourse of development. Trained in modernization theory and cultural pluralism, U.S. planners stood as champions of social engineering at the height of the Cold War, convinced that the implementation of American ideas could alleviate hunger and social dislocation, reform education standards and agricultural practices, and promote local industrial growth.[3] As U.S. political theorist Walt Rostow explained in 1961, the "whole southern half of the world—Latin America, Africa, the Middle East, and Asia—[was] caught in the adventures of asserting their independence and modernizing their old ways of life," and the United States had a "moral obligation as a wise leader" to guide these pursuits.[4] Self-determination and territorial freedom would thrive, in other words, within a system of political and economic interdependence anchored by the United States.

This chapter explores how Washington's preponderance of power influenced the global apartheid debate. The fight over South Africa's place in the world highlighted how assumptions about the nature of freedom and the meaning of the nation were contested as the international community became more politically diverse and culturally pluralistic. Although the United States did not have a direct stake in the apartheid debate—the U.N. African Group and South African government were always the main protagonists—its status as a global hegemon nonetheless shaped what was politically possible in these years. Global norms, as well as the consequences of breaking those norms, were tethered to the attitudes and assumptions of U.S. elites, who possessed unmatched influence in both independent Africa and the Republic of South Africa. Looking at the fault lines among these individuals and trends within the United States illuminates the country's influence on the political arena outside its borders.

Assistant secretary of state for African Affairs G. Mennen "Soapy" Williams sat at the center of U.S.-African relations in this period. Appointed by the Kennedy administration in 1961, Williams, the former governor of Michigan, attained neither a cabinet position nor a promotion during his five-year tenure in Washington, and many of the goals he set for the African Bureau went unfulfilled in the years after African decolonization. However, his role in the apartheid struggle was paramount. To a degree unmatched by his predecessors or peers, he embraced the legitimacy of African nationalism and worked to meet the expectations of African states by bending U.S. foreign policy away from South Africa. Reflexively progressive and intensely moralistic, Williams viewed modernity as intellectually incompatible with race-based discrimination and felt that America's ascendance mandated the end of racial hierarchy at home and abroad. During his time in Washington, ideas about white supremacy moved from the periphery to the center of U.S. policy thinking, and his constant advocacy, spurred partly by his connections to liberal and civil rights leaders, turned sanctions against South Africa into an imaginable—though not uncontested—policymaking option. Although Williams was not the most powerful politician in the United States, he was the most active and influential American on the chessboard of African affairs.

The assistant secretary's impact manifested itself in two areas. First, he helped formalize the linkage between the U.S. civil rights movement and decolonization in Africa. Like many of his liberal contemporaries in academia, he used African American experiences to frame his understanding of Africa and felt that America's Declaration of Independence obliged the U.S. government to embrace the common pan-African freedom struggle. During the Kennedy years, he promoted civil rights legislation as the United States' best diplomatic tool in Africa and denounced the idea that modernization programs alone would ensure Washington's continued influence in the decolonized world. America's "greatest asset" was "its reputation for generosity, love of freedom and fair dealing," Williams stated often, and its "greatest liability" was its tendency "not to live up to" its "own ideals."[5] When the civil rights movement transformed race relations in the United States in the mid-1960s, Williams conflated the national and the global and argued that reform at home mandated change abroad, most obviously in the form of U.N. sanctions against the white regimes of southern Africa. The argument, panned widely in Kennedy's White House, gained tentative support in the early Johnson years.

Equally important, Williams voiced unyielding support for international law and the United Nations. "The principal object of our foreign policy is *not* one of being the world's leader," he stated in a memo in 1965. "Rather, our purpose is cooperation in a world community—as embodied in the U.N. Charter, our treaties, and legislative acts."[6] Washington was not in the game of bullying nation-states into accepting its will. An influential cohort of liberal policymakers shared this mindset in the immediate postwar years, and for a brief yet important period in the 1960s the United States responded to Third World nationalism not through hard-edged realpolitik but liberal internationalism, reifying U.S. values and expectations through United Nations membership, open trade policies, and international law. A precursor to what political scientists would eventually term "soft power," this formula envisioned America's empire as a system of independent nation-states united in an Americentric capitalist system.[7] Williams believed passionately in this system and felt that U.S. legitimacy ebbed and flowed in relation to the attitudes of new members at the General Assembly. Washington, in his mind, had a moral obligation to establish consonance between its security interests and the expectations of African and Asian nationalists in New York. Finding this balance represented the new frontier of his Cold War.

Williams never affected U.S. policy in places like Vietnam or the Congo, but he shaped how American global power interacted with postcolonial questions. By the mid-1960s, his assertions on civil rights and decolonization had become conventional wisdom in many Washington circles, rationalizing the Johnson administration's strong anti-apartheid stance after its 1964–65 civil rights legislation. Likewise, the assistant secretary's views on international order provided a consistent counterweight to those policymakers apathetic about Third World political demands. His views were not novel, but Williams's place at the center of the policymaking establishment—his ability to introduce these beliefs into high-level discussions and embed them in state-sanctioned thinking—made him influential. U.S. hegemony, cresting in the early 1960s, expressed itself through the tendencies of specific individuals. More than any other figure in Washington, Williams shaped the antagonism that characterized U.S.-South African relations in the mid-1960s.

Windows and Mirrors

Williams was nine months into his tenure as assistant secretary on August 29, 1961. In Northern Rhodesia on his second goodwill trip through Africa, he celebrated the anniversary on an airport tarmac in Lusaka, engaged in small talk with the coterie of local officials who had chaperoned him through the territory during the previous week. "A man came up to us," Lusaka's mayor later explained, "went straight to Mr. Williams, grabbed his lapel with one hand and shouting an offensive remark, hit him straight in the jaw."[8] It was, to say the least, an undignified introduction to politics in southern Africa. Evidently triggered by a speech Williams had given in Salisbury a few days earlier, the punch led to a wave of apologies and regretful editorials the next day, but "behind the official façade . . . caused a great number of smiles and laughter in high official and other circles." According to South Africa's ambassador, "The blow symbolized white . . . public feeling towards the United States and its Africa policy."[9]

It foreshadowed many of the difficulties that would consume the assistant secretary in subsequent years.

In 1961, Williams was the Kennedy administration's point man in Africa. He
was a curious choice by any standard. Heir to an enormous fortune in the personal care industry, the six-time governor was a staunch New Deal liberal,
known widely as the reformer who had remolded Michigan's political establishment in the 1950s by forming an alliance between labor and civil rights activists
in Detroit. Publicly religious and personally righteous, he viewed himself as the
"conscience of the Democratic Party" and assertively championed state power
as the solution to all of society's ills, especially racial inequality, wealth disparity,
and shallow materialism.[10] A one-time candidate for president, Williams had
championed black equality as the "ultimate moral issue" of the 1950s and
openly opposed Lyndon Johnson's 1960 nomination as vice president because
he felt that the Texas senator was too weak on civil rights issues.[11] Disappointed
by Kennedy's decision not to appoint him secretary of Health, Education and
Welfare or secretary of Labor, the governor was slow to embrace his nomination
as assistant secretary of state after the 1960 election. His foreign policy experience was limited to occasional vacations abroad, and he understood—even
better than his many detractors—that he would be an unnatural fit at the
Department of State.[12]

Williams's anxieties were not unwarranted. His predecessor at the African
Bureau, Joseph Satterthwaite, had accepted an ambassadorship to South Africa
eagerly in late 1960, leaving the office understaffed and largely apathetic about
its role in foreign policy, and John Foster Dulles, who dominated the Department of State through most of the Eisenhower administration, was Williams's
political antipode. When it came to the global south, Dulles had infused U.S.
foreign policy with an unbending Cold War reductionism that questioned the
very morality of Third World nationalism.[13] Although Pretoria fretted that the
formation of the State Department's African Bureau would fundamentally alter
U.S. policy, discussions within Washington told a very different story. During
a National Security Council (NSC) meeting on the topic in mid-1958, for
instance, a State Department official lamented openly that the "Spirit of 1776"
was "running wild" through Africa and noted that the "various states and
colonies" wanted "independence now, whether they [were] ready for it or not."
Specifically referencing Ghana's President Nkrumah, the official called such
trends "terrifying."[14]

The mindset permeated other segments of the Eisenhower administration as
well. During another NSC meeting in 1960—called as France relinquished control of its West African empire and Congo and Nigeria gained independence—
Vice President Richard Nixon suggested crudely that "some of the peoples of
Africa have been out of the trees for only about fifty years" and suggested that

"politically sophisticated diplomats" could easily subvert black nationalism and reorient "the African people toward the Free World." President Eisenhower, in similar terms, argued that South Africa was the only country in the entire continent that could actually govern itself. Rejecting the idea that territorial autonomy formed the gateway to economic development, he claimed that African leaders were "putting the cart before the horse" by placing such precedence on political independence.[15] Decolonization, in his mind, was best granted slowly, after territories had achieved a certain standard of social civility and economic progress.

These views—grounded in a particular vocabulary of prewar American race relations—also structured the White House's stance toward South Africa in the late 1950s. When Eisenhower heard that the State Department issued a statement expressing regret about the Sharpeville Massacre in 1960, he called a meeting with Secretary of State Christian Herter. Learning that a bureau chief had issued the statement on his own, the president said that if it were his decision, he would "find another post" for the individual and recommended that the department apologize immediately to the Nationalist government. Concurring with the president's comments, Secretary Herter framed the statement as a "breach of courtesy between two nations."[16] When pressure subsequently built for a U.N. Security Council resolution on the violence in South Africa, Eisenhower held a private meeting with British Prime Minister Harold Macmillan at Camp David to formulate a joint Anglo-American response. "One could not sit in judgment on a difficult social and political problem six thousand miles away," the president said. Noting that the United States had its "own problem" with race and indicating his sympathy with his "friends in Atlanta on some of their difficulties," Eisenhower declared that the Security Council resolution should "express regret about the disturbances" without committing the Western bloc to a serious confrontation with South Africa.[17] Pretoria's economic and political importance in the Cold War was more important than the moral questions that surrounded the apartheid question.

Williams sat on the opposite end of the political and philosophical spectrum. American society was standing on the brink of a revolution in race relations and, in his view, the federal government needed to embrace and celebrate the inevitability of this change. In a letter to an African Studies professor at Pennsylvania State University, penned shortly after he arrived in Washington, the assistant secretary claimed flatly that "America [was] the 'permanent revolution,'" and it needed to upend the "status quo" everywhere in favor of "progress."[18] When commentator Walter Lippmann asked Williams to square his well-known New Deal liberalism with the African situation, the latter sent the columnist a reading list that included William Bascom and Melville Herskovits's *Continuity and Change in African Culture* (1959), Gwendolen Carter's *Politics of Inequality* (1958), Malcolm Hailey's *An African Survey* (1957), and Charles Seligman's

Races of Africa (1957), among others.[19] The books not only showcased Williams's affinity for interdisciplinary anthropology—a relatively new genre with institutional connections to the African Studies program at Northwestern University—they also highlighted how he filtered information about the continent. The common denominator of such scholarship was the cultural structuralism of anthropologist Franz Boas.[20] For many scholars in the 1960s, African culture was an integrated sociological matrix that connected the behavior and thoughts of "indigenous Africans" to that of "the New World Negro."[21] The linkage tacitly connected contemporary civil rights activism, interpreted explicitly by some academics as the byproduct of the interaction between "traditional black values" and "Euroamerican civilization," to the fight against colonialism in Africa, which theoretically emanated from comparable processes.[22] The struggles of Africans and African Americans were two sides of a single coin. If the governor supported the civil rights movement at home, it followed that he had to embrace African decolonization abroad.

Indeed, this sentiment animated Williams's frequent speeches on Africa in 1961. In his first address as a member of the Kennedy administration, he called on Americans to support African independence by educating themselves about the continent, embracing African students and ambassadors, and "most obviously" accelerating the progress toward black equality at home.[23] During his first trip to Africa in February, he sharply rejected the rationale of the Eisenhower years, declaring that the "verdict of history in Africa" was "unmistakable and irreversible." Wrapping his words in the language of postcolonial freedom, Williams cast "human dignity and freedom" as "indivisible," and announced that the "old colonial era" and the "old power relationships" were unequivocally "dead." The Kennedy administration, in his words, would use its "influence in the service of constructive change," and buttress the United Nations as a "forum of the exercise of freedom, a testing ground for the responsible use of power, and an instrument of economic and social progress." He continued:

> We believe that no man is completely free so long as any man anywhere lacks freedom. We know that our place in the human brotherhood is not secure so long as any man anywhere fails to be fully accepted in human dignity. We will work fully to realize that goal at home while promoting it abroad.[24]

Simultaneously, Williams worked to place himself at the political interface between the African American freedom movement and the African nationalist community. By the early 1960s, black internationalists had established a long record of protest against discrimination in South Africa.[25] The *Appeal for Action Against Apartheid*, initiated by George Houser's American Committee on Africa

(ACOA) and sponsored by Martin Luther King Jr. and Albert Luthuli in the early 1960s, cast racial discrimination as a global phenomenon and urged the U.S. government to support U.N. sanctions against Pretoria. "It is tragic that our foreign policy on Africa is so ambivalent," King lamented in 1962. "We decry in some mild manner the apartheid policy of the Union of South Africa but economically we continue 'business-as-usual' in spite of the stringent racist policies being enforced and intensified."[26] When King, James Farmer, A. Philip Randolph, Roy Wilkins, and Whitney Young formed the American Negro Leadership Conference on Africa (ANLC) later that year—announcing explicitly that the "civil rights problem" at home could "not be separated from that abroad"—the assistant secretary adopted an assertively responsive stance.[27] The ANLC's demands differed from the African Group's initiatives abroad, focused as much on hiring practices in Washington as U.N. resolutions in New York, but Williams nonetheless opened the Bureau's doors to African American concerns and formed an advisory committee that included many ANLC members. During subsequent discussions, he "drew a careful line between his responsibilities as a part of the Administration" and "his obvious desire to say that we haven't done enough and would like to do more" on American civil rights issues. According to minutes of these meetings, the assistant secretary "defended the Department . . . and yet encouraged the [ANLC] to continue talking."[28] In later phone discussions and personal correspondence, King, Randolph, and others praised Williams's sincerity—a contrast, in their minds, to their dealings with the Justice Department—and praised his efforts to employ black diplomats.[29]

By building bridges between the activist community and the State Department, Williams broadened the channels of elite interaction and facilitated the emergence of alternative policymaking impulses in Washington. "For the first time I found myself in the 'area of gossip,'" *Ebony* magazine publisher John H. Johnson reflected after serving on one of Williams's advisory committees during the Kennedy years. It was possible to be part of "that informal, social-business climate where, at a club, a wedding, a dinner, or a golf outing, business deals and projections are traded by white men . . . who assume, as a matter of course, that there's nobody here but us chickens, and that everybody in the inner circle has a right to know and does."[30] Johnson's access to this world was possible because of Williams and the assistant secretary's embrace of the ANLC—particularly his efforts to solicit the recommendations of civil rights organizers—opened a space for nongovernmental actors to have a more vocal role in the arena of foreign affairs. In a very real sense, Williams was as a gatekeeper between the administration's foreign policymaking apparatus and the civil rights community—an individual who translated the frustrations of black internationalists into policy proposals in Washington, DC.

In this capacity, the assistant secretary adopted a notably antagonistic stance toward South Africa. In his first meeting with the Republic's ambassador, he stated explicitly that the "Declaration of Independence was a universal declaration— good for the whole world."[31] Similarly, Williams's first memo on apartheid rejected Eisenhower-era ambivalence and announced that Americans faced a "choice between good relations with South Africa and the stability and friendship of the rest of Africa as well as doing the right thing."[32] The Afrikaners of South Africa shared traits with American segregationists, according to Williams, and had to be confronted with unyielding moral certitude. He used his 1961 trip to convey his vision to the region, visiting only Southern and Northern Rhodesia (modern day Zimbabwe and Zambia) after his request to travel directly to South Africa was rejected because National Party leaders feared another "wind of change moment."[33] "The drama of change is the text for our times," he explained in Salisbury on August 25. "It cannot be buried by angry men or hidden in the midst of the sea by those who dislike or fear it unrolling. It is inexorably written in the life stream of our times." While the United States had "yet to achieve the full promise of racial equality," the Kennedy administration supported civil rights and African nationalism with equal vigor, embraced the legitimacy of African culture, and viewed self-determination as the basis of world order.[34] The United States would not blindly impose its will on leaders in southern Africa, but it was time for whites everywhere to "come to terms" with the "reality of decolonization."[35]

Williams's encounter at Lusaka's airport four days later highlighted white resentment of such views. It also foreshadowed the difficulties he would face as he tried turning rhetoric into policy in Washington in the early 1960s. Within months of accepting his post, he was immersed in a bitter, unexpected fight within the State Department over the importance of Africa. While the new administration collectively recognized the futility of pushing Africans to "choose up sides" in the Cold War, not all of Williams's peers accepted his view that the United States itself was "the permanent revolution."[36] Fearing that the assistant secretary's rhetorical flourishes might offend members of the North Atlantic Treaty Organization (NATO), specifically Portugal and France, the State Department's Europeanists openly dismissed his proposals on southern Africa and worked with Defense Department officials to refocus attention on the region's abundant mineral sources and anticommunist credentials.[37] South Africa produced close to 65 percent of the Western bloc's gold in the 1960s— the loss of which would undercut the stability of the Bretton Woods economic system—and possessed an important National Aeronautics and Space Administration (NASA) tracking station, as well as nearly $600 million worth of private American investment.[38] Williams's words, high-minded and progressive, echoed awkwardly in the corridors of power in Washington.

In part, his difficulties were ideological. National security percolated through nearly every level of the U.S. government during the Cold War. Animated by a concern for the United States' long-term physical safety and a desire to project U.S. political values and free enterprise economy abroad, Washington elites embraced a vision of the world that linked the so-called core and periphery in an Americentric web of national security relationships.[39] The balance between these imagined regions, however, was never equal. Because Europe was re-sponsible for the two previous global conflagrations and sat atop the primary fault line between the American and Soviet empires—to say nothing of the deep cultural connections shared between elites in the United States and Western Europe—U.S. officials defined national security always in reference to Great Britain, Germany, and France. For most American policymakers, core values like modernization, justice, and liberty existed in the context of pan-European historical narratives and intellectual debates.[40] Dean Acheson, Rob-ert Lovett, George Kennan, and Paul Nitze—individuals who exerted influence in both Republican and Democratic administrations after World War II—methodically reified this mindset in the early Cold War through a hierarchy of objectives that ranked strength at the West's center, specifically Western Europe, West Germany, and Japan, ahead of strength along the African, Asian, and Middle Eastern periphery.[41] President Kennedy gave rhetorical support to African decolonization, but he was no less dedicated to this vision of national security than his predecessors.[42] For the White House, African issues simply ranked below events in Western Europe and Eastern Asia, and Williams's effu-sive moralism was out of step with the administration's carefully crafted image of unemotional pragmatism.

This ideological disjuncture was buttressed by individual personalities within the Kennedy administration. Intellectually, Williams's closest allies in Washing-ton were Undersecretary of State Chester Bowles and U.N. Ambassador Adlai Stevenson. However, with Bowles's influence limited by his sometimes irrev-erent verbosity and Stevenson's effectiveness hampered by his distance from Washington, neither were particularly effective policymaking partners. Figures like National Security Advisor McGeorge Bundy tended to exercise greater in-fluence over the president in the early 1960s.[43] Although Bundy remained largely silent on nonaligned issues—his efforts centered almost exclusively on Europe and Asia during the Kennedy years—he made no secret of his view that non-aligned nations needed to respect Washington's varied commitments on the global stage. Because "interest and sympathy" often pushed the United States in opposite directions, it was "becoming" that U.S. leaders interact "coolly" with the decolonized world, he explained in a 1962 *Foreign Affairs* article.[44] Bundy's principal aide, Robert Komer, was interested in reorienting the traditional bal-ance between the core and periphery, but was kept occupied by events in India,

Indonesia, and Egypt until mid-1965, when he turned attention toward Africa in the months before the International Court of Justice's decision on South West Africa.[45] Walt Rostow, another Bundy aide, demonstrated interest in Third World issues as well, but focused primarily on economic theory, famously positing that the administration could push new nations toward "economic take-off" through broad-based aid programs that fostered Americentric development and stability.[46] Other prominent policymakers in Kennedy's Washington, such as Secretary of State Dean Rusk and Undersecretary of Economic Affairs George Ball, remained openly antagonistic toward postcolonial nationalism. Colonialism and apartheid were abhorrent, Ball acknowledged, but "abhorrence [was] a state of mind, not a principle of political action." In South Africa, the wisest course of action, in his mind, was to embrace white South Africa's entrepreneurial class and let local elites dictate the terms of nonracial democracy.[47]

The assistant secretary tried to adapt to this milieu. In a 1962 paper to Rusk, he argued that a "strong U.S. European policy" was actually entwined with a "strong U.S. African policy." Listing Washington's various interests in Africa, he explained that the "fact of the matter" was that "a Western European presence in Africa depend[ed] in no small degree upon a significant American presence [there]." Because the United States had "no colonial history in Africa," it could "perform an important function both for independent African countries and their former metropoles by providing an expanded association within which they [could] comfortably continue to do business with each other without being suspect[ed] of neocolonialism." The only prerequisite, in Williams's mind, was that the United States stayed "true to its traditions of self-determination."[48] However, after America's botched invasion of Cuba and Kennedy's difficult Vienna meeting with Soviet Premier Nikita Khrushchev, the president replaced Bowles with Ball as undersecretary of state—part of a deliberate internal shift away from liberal-minded policymakers in 1962 that left the assistant secretary and his African Bureau firmly on the defensive. Speaking off the record, one government official responded to the news with the declaration, "One down and Williams to go!" while another suggested openly that the "trouble with Bowles and Williams was that when they saw a handful of black baboons beating tom-toms they saw George Washington."[49] In an America where southern segregationists still dominated Congress and civil rights legislation appeared to be an impossibility, Williams's worldview had little traction in Washington.

Indeed, racialist precepts continued to undergird thinking in many sections of the State Department. A 1962 policy paper entitled "The White Redoubt," for instance, directly challenged the assistant secretary's triumphal portrait of African decolonization. Connecting the situation in South Africa directly to the revolution in Algeria, officials noted that blacks now faced whites "across a sea of developing hate." The language used was telling, South Africa "is, in effect, a last white stronghold against black invasion from the north and racialist-inspired upheavals from within."⁵⁰ Following the Eisenhower administration's script, the document's authors subtly cast Africans as barbarians at the gates of whiteness and treated the tensions in southern Africa as an outgrowth of black extremism rather than as a byproduct of South Africa's system of racial discrimination. The department's 1962 "Guidelines of Policy and Operations" for Africa adopted a similarly ambivalent stance toward recent events. The "basic strategy" of the United States was to use social and economic development to offset the "destructive tendencies and influences" in Africa. "In an area as volatile as Africa, we make no sharp distinction between 'enemies' and 'friends,' for today's opponent may be tomorrow's friend—or vice versa."⁵¹ Backward and unpredictable, African leaders had to be molded in America's self-image yet approached with caution and skepticism.

For most Kennedy officials, newly independent black nations were important not on their own terms but in relation to the United States' grand strategy at the United Nations. A 1962 NSC paper, discussed widely within the White House and State Department, claimed that "the way to 'move ahead' through [the] predictable storms" of decolonization was to "focus as much attention as [possible] on developing and strengthening the U.N."⁵² The rationale was simple—the organization offered an invaluable "'third man' in international policies" and served as an "antidote to small-nation emotionalism and irresponsibility" by forcing states to filter their demands through "legislative acts at the General Assembly" and "executive functions" of the Security Council. "'Strengthening the U.N.,'" therefore, meant not only "defending it from attacks of the Soviets," but also "using it to remove contentious issues"—most obviously the "hardcore" colonial questions of southern Africa—"from the agenda of world politics." Referring subtly to the African Group's recent U.N. resolutions, American officials declared that the "power of the General Assembly" rested on the willingness of "smaller states" to see that their "self-interest" lay in "demonstrating a greater sense of responsibility" in New York. It was "only in the General Assembly that the small countries [were] equal." If the United States could provide a "politically acceptable framework within which advanced and less-developed countries transfer[ed] skills and resources without implying inequality and domination," it would be possible to "complete the process of decolonization and build a new set of relationships with the former colonies."⁵³ A veritable treatise on American hegemonic thought—articulated in prose reminiscent of Antonio Gramsci's theories of power—the document captured mainstream sentiment in the Kennedy administration during the early 1960s.

It also underscored the nature of American power in the second half of the twentieth century. In a world of nation-states and free market capitalism, the United States' authority flowed not only from its military installations and

economic investments in Western Europe and the Pacific Rim—objects quanti-
fiable as hard power—but also from Washington's ability to guide the agenda of
the United Nations, as well as the International Monetary Fund, World Bank,
and International Court of Justice. The Kennedy and Johnson administrations
"took the United Nations seriously," Rusk wrote in his memoirs, "probably more
so than any administration in the [subsequent] four decades."[54] The organization
legitimized Americentric definitions of development and justice, and, in theory,
so long as other countries accepted its institutional authority and prestige, Washington would continue to shape the rules of the postwar world. The sudden
enlargement and diversification of this system in the early 1960s constituted
both the fulfillment of the United States' discursive commitment to territorial
autonomy and self-determination and a structural test to Washington's status as
the postwar world's principal hegemon. How could the United States lead a
world of free nations it regarded as backward, unpredictable, and inferior? By
bracketing the actions of nationalist leaders coming to power in Africa and elsewhere, the General Assembly was a defensive counterpart to U.S. economic aid
and development programs. The Soviet Union scored propaganda points in
New York in these years—a problem that annoyed Washington throughout the
Cold War—but so long as African elites continued to accept the integrity of the
United Nations, the United States' place at the center of world politics would
remain functionally intact. The overlap between geopolitical order and America's fundamental values, in a word, would persist into the postcolonial era.[55]

It was on this point that Williams departed dramatically from others in the
Kennedy administration. While Secretary Rusk was content attributing the rhetoric of newly independent states to Soviet propaganda and influence, Williams
posited openly and often that the continuation of U.S. legitimacy in New York
depended on Washington's willingness to address the problems that mattered
most to African nationalists.[56] This did not mean that the United States was
obliged to accept the African Group's arguments about the nature of article
2(7), but Washington, in Williams's mind, could not avoid confronting the
apartheid question. Discrimination in South Africa was "the 'gut' issue for all
African countries." It shaped African understandings of "self-interest" at the
international level—far more than the theories of modernization developed by
Rostow and other Washington intellectuals—and challenged the philosophical
basis of African nationalism by decoupling economic development from majoritarian democracy and pan-Africanism. African nationalism's authority at home
and abroad rested on a particular narrative of postcolonial freedom, and so long
as apartheid existed, the African Group's efforts in the international arena would
continue to focus on destroying the intellectual foundations of racism. The African resolutions of 1961 and 1962 flowed not from emotion or immaturity but a
deliberate, sustained effort to mold global norms in Africa's perceived image.

According to Williams, African states would "move even more radically in the U.N. against South Africa" if the United States failed to genuinely address these core concerns.[57] The "problem of South Africa," stated simply, was "an all-Africa problem" that transcended "geographical limits," and as long as Washington possessed "the power to be really effective" against the Republic, African states would continue to use the United Nations to push the United States to form "a credible program of action" that "promise[d] to produce some change in the apartheid situation." There would be "unrest in the rest of Africa until this situation [was] cleared up."[58]

For the better part of two years, Williams's pronouncements fell on deaf ears. Whether dealing with the travails of visiting African diplomats or black rights in the United States, the president and his core advisors simply did not see race questions in moral terms. It was only as young civil rights activists began provoking domestic crises throughout the Deep South—first during the 1961 Freedom Rides and later in the Birmingham crisis of 1963—that top administration officials slowly modified this stance. Kennedy's turn toward civil rights legislation in late 1963 flowed as much from anxieties about the international consequences of U.S. racial upheavals as from genuine concern about the treatment of blacks in America.[59] Images of burning buses and rabid police dogs represented "a severe blow to U.S. prestige," a United States Information Agency (USIA) report explained in mid-1963, and adversely affected America's "position of leadership in the free world." The "masses of 'colored' peoples" in Africa and Asia were "hypersensitive on the question of racial discrimination" and wary of the United States' "condescending attitude . . . towards the 'non-whites.'"[60] Kennedy's landmark nationwide television address on race relations, delivered at the height of the Birmingham movement, revealed the administration's solution to this dilemma. Noting that the United States had "committed [itself] to a worldwide struggle to promote and protect the rights of all who wish to be free," the president admitted that the country now faced "a moral issue" as "old as the scriptures" and "as clear as the American Constitution." The time had come for Americans to square unequivocally their racial traditions with the imperatives of the postcolonial world. "We preach freedom around the world, and we mean it, and we cherish our freedom here at home, but are we to say to the world, and more importantly, to each other that this is a land of the free except for the Negroes; that we have no second-class citizens except Negroes; that we have no class or caste system, no ghettos, no master race except with respect to Negroes?"[61]

The administration's sudden rhetorical change emboldened Williams. In an unsolicited private letter to Kennedy on June 14, he argued that the president's "excellent statement on civil rights [had] arrested but . . . not solved the crisis." The "American Negro knows you have already done as much as or more than any other President," he noted. "But the times, and justice, demands still more. Only determined and decisive action will get us on the road to that. Past and new records will quickly pale if not augmented by broad and further gains. There will be no surcease, no 'cooling off' period until the momentum to the ultimate goal is clear and unequivocal."[62] Cognizant that the administration was planning to step up USIA efforts to spin global news coverage of America's civil rights revolution, Williams suggested that the time for such cynicism had passed.[63] He wrote:

> Today large segments of the Negro population are losing confidence in interracial approaches to the problems of gaining full civil rights. The dialogue between Negro leaders and white liberals clearly runs a danger of being broken. Efforts to solve the present racial problem on the basis of uni-racial rather than interracial leadership [are] not in the best interest of this nation. It is vitally important that we take decisive action now before division sets in. Action is necessary to demonstrate that the moral force of your office is behind the present drive to solve the integration problem.[64]

For Williams, the U.S. government had to do more than co-opt Third World nationalism or black activism within the system of liberal internationalism. The country's responsiveness formed the basis of its social and cultural hegemony. In the face of decolonization abroad and civil rights at home, white liberals had a moral obligation to reinvent themselves to stay at the vanguard of world events. The distinctions between the African Group's initiatives at the United Nations and African American efforts in Birmingham were secondary to the U.S. government's ability to respond positively to the demands of the nonwhite world.

Invigorated by the civil rights breakthrough at home, Williams traveled to Africa in June and July 1963. On returning, he continued to push President Kennedy and Secretary Rusk to recognize the validity of his views. The "preoccupation with the fight for African independence is even more deep-seated and feverish than I had thought before the trip," he wrote in July. "Without exaggeration it can be said that this situation is rapidly reaching crisis proportions." His explanation flowed predictably from his worldview. The situation had grown "precarious (1) because of the need to realize the promise of the President's Civil Rights program, and (2) because of the necessity to demonstrate by concrete action our policies of support for self-determination and self-government." Declaring provocatively that the administration's "efforts heretofore with respect to self-determination and apartheid have been absolutely inadequate," the assistant secretary suggested that Africans had "at best" concluded that Kennedy attached "little importance or urgency to the problem of colonialism," and "at worst" deduced that the United States was "aiding and abetting the South

Africans and Portuguese in the maintenance of the status quo."[65] The president, in Williams's mind, was obliged to follow his civil rights address with comparable measures on the international stage.

For the assistant secretary, the best method of action was an arms embargo against the Republic. Adlai Stevenson had suggested this idea in January to appease the African Group at the United Nations, but the proposal had failed to gain traction in the White House. Williams now recast the embargo in bolder terms. "Both right and self-interest dictate our adoption of an arms embargo posture and the sooner we take it the more effective our position will be," he explained in a letter to Rusk. Referring to the resolutions of the inaugural Organization of African Unity meeting in Addis Ababa in 1963, Williams opined that "all African countries regard[ed] apartheid not only as obnoxious to human dignity but a threat to African freedom," and they judged "all countries . . . friendly or unfriendly on the basis of their positive acts of opposition to apartheid." The governor's rationale for action was twofold. On a moral level, the problem "need[ed] little elaboration." The proof of apartheid's inequity could be seen at the United Nations. Votes at the General Assembly, in particular, provided "ample evidence" that apartheid was loathsome "not only to all colored peoples who are the majority of the world's population but to all civilized people as well." If "another Sharpeville massacre occurred, [the United States] would stand condemned in the eyes of most of the world."

Hoping to secure support from hawks like Ball and Rusk, Williams framed this moral assertion as a national security issue. Inaction would cost Washington U.N. support when it came to China's membership status, and it might encourage African states to take concrete retaliatory actions against the United States. Without an arms embargo against South Africa, Williams explained, the Kennedy administration would likely lose military installations in Libya and Ethiopia, scientific facilities in Nigeria and Zanzibar, and communication facilities in Nigeria and Liberia. The way forward was logical and inescapable. Apartheid was the "archetype of racism in the world," and the "time of good intentions [was] over." Only "concrete action [would] do."[66]

Williams's proposal sparked debate within the top echelon of the administration. "I would draw a sharp distinction between our deep concern with respect to racial discrimination in the United States and the way in which we crusade on that very issue outside the United States," Secretary Rusk wrote in July. "The United States is our responsibility; our failures are our failures . . . But no one has elected us to undertake such responsibilities in other countries. The President has reminded us that we are not interested in a Pax Americana. It seems to me, a fortiori, that we are not the self-elected gendarmes for the political and social problems of other states."[67] Others agreed. The president's special assistant Arthur Schlesinger summarized the situation to Attorney General Robert

Kennedy, expressing his skepticism about Williams's plan. While "the African states [had] history on their side and probably justice too," the United States needed to "evade" any firm decisions on apartheid, lest more space open for the African Group's initiatives in the international arena.[68] The fact that Rusk, Schlesinger, and others refrained from characterizing African demands as irrational was important and likely a reflection of the growing influence of the domestic civil rights movement on the administration, but their comments nonetheless revealed the mindset among Kennedy's top advisors. U.S. hegemony was to be maintained on American, not African terms.

Ironically, this conclusion did not ultimately derail acceptance of the arms embargo. As officials discussed the pros and cons of Williams's proposal, the rationale for action slowly changed. A memo from the National Security Council staff cast the idea in strictly policy terms. It explained, "In the past several years . . . we have sailed an improvised, often erratic course between the antagonists, with a series of minor concessions to the Africans as the pressures mounted, while avoiding an irreparable break with the . . . South Africans. While this has been the most sensible—indeed the only sensible—course open to us, we are beginning to run out of sailing room." It was possible to "gain some space for maneuver, and continue to defer the dilemma, if [the United States] raised [its] present tactic to a deliberate, systematic policy."[69] The arms embargo, in other words, could serve as a symbolic appeasement tool, demonstrating American engagement with postcolonial questions without mandating a meaningful change in U.S.-South African relations.

President Kennedy's own response to the proposal exposed his affinity for such an approach. Silent throughout the first round of debate on South Africa, he formally accepted the arms embargo in mid-July but passed along a revealing rejoinder to Secretary Rusk. "Our discussion with the South Africans should be in the context of our conviction that the course we are adopting represents the minimum changes necessary if we are to be able to assist in preventing much less satisfactory results," he wrote. Referring to the crux of the African Group's political strategy at the General Assembly, he stated flatly that the United States must "oppose chapter VII measures."[70] Because apartheid was not a threat to American peace and security, the United States would never accept action under such auspices. Kennedy's aim in accepting the arms embargo was not to reinvent American power in postcolonial ways but to adjust public optics to give the perception of change. He wanted, in short, to co-opt the African Group through political showmanship. As it became clearer in autumn 1963 that this approach would not succeed, he predictably fell back into a more confrontational mindset. In an October meeting with British officials, called to discuss the African Group's renewed push for economic sanctions at the United Nations, Kennedy drew an unequivocal line in the sand, declaring that the United States had "gone along on the arms embargo" but "would not go beyond that and would not support sanctions." The question, in his mind, was now "how best to stop them."[71]

This turn of events left Mennen Williams in a paradoxical position. The arms embargo ostensibly represented a major policymaking breakthrough, but the White House's rationale departed markedly from the assistant secretary's worldview. The administration had achieved something major but for the wrong reasons. For Williams, and many subsequent chroniclers of the Kennedy administration, the government's internal orientation negated the utility and full significance of the arms embargo against South Africa—an interpretation with only partial merit.[72] The United States had ample reason to maintain close economic and security relations with the Republic in the early 1960s, but it nonetheless distanced itself from a resolute, dependable Cold War ally in 1963. Absent the assistant secretary, this shift simply would not have happened. Although Williams did not achieve his victory on the terms he wanted, his proposal adjusted U.S. policy toward South Africa and shifted the context within which Africans and Afrikaners articulated their competing claims.

Even more, the assistant secretary did so in a manner that carried his views on the civil rights movement and African decolonization. At the United Nations, when the arms embargo was presented to the international community in late 1963, it was cast deliberately as an outgrowth of Kennedy's recent stand on black rights at home. In Adlai Stevenson's words, America's disavowal of domestic racism made support for the "bitter toxic of apartheid" impossible.[73] Regardless of the president's private views, this public stand had consequences, expanding the space for anti-apartheid activism that embraced the language of American civil rights. Ironically, this linkage—not the overt cynicism of top officials—survived the president's assassination in November. As Lyndon Johnson began using Kennedy's public rhetoric to marshal support for comprehensive civil rights legislation at home—the top priority of the new administration—many U.S. officials began misremembering their own anxiety about Williams's arms-embargo proposal. Only months into 1964, some aides, most notably Komer, were openly encouraging the new president to "continue and expand" his predecessor's anti-apartheid efforts to demonstrate the newfound continuity between America's racial policies at home and its stand against discrimination abroad.[74] Once at the periphery of policy thinking, Williams's views were being echoed within Johnson's White House.

Articles and Action

On paper, the assistant secretary's background made him a natural ally of Lyndon Johnson. Like the new president, Williams had entered national politics as a foot soldier of the New Deal, and the two men shared a common faith that the federal government could achieve equality of opportunity for disadvantaged Americans.[75] However, Williams's controversial actions at the 1960 Democratic convention in Los Angeles, when he publicly rejected Johnson's vice presidential nomination on civil rights grounds, lingered as a shadow over their relationship. During their first telephone conversation after Kennedy's death, Johnson did not hesitate to bring up this past awkwardness, declaring preemptively: "We've pulled down the curtain on Los Angeles that night. We're a team." Announcing that Williams would be as "welcome and effective in the White House as [he] had been with Kennedy," the new president implored his assistant secretary to provide feedback on the administration's civil rights efforts, claiming that his success in Michigan gave him "more experience than any of us" and a unique perspective on what "will be good in Mississippi."[76] The overture seemed genuine. When Averell Harriman, a former New York governor and long-time antagonist of Williams, crowed a few months later that his appointment as the administration's ambassador-at-large signified the president's desire to see "a seventh floor man" not a "sixth floor person" dictating African policy, Johnson demanded that Harriman "walk the carpet or apologize or resign."[77] While acknowledging that he was "no intimate of Williams," the president denounced Harriman's swipe as "cruel and unfair"[78] and noted that Williams "work[ed] hard" and had his "complete confidence."[79]

However, Harriman's appointment was not insignificant. From Williams's vantage point—and that of the majority of the Washington press corps—the bureaucratic move eroded the African Bureau's ability to influence policy toward the major issues of the day. According to Williams's biographer, Harriman's "reputation as a master of bureaucratic politics" and his "insatiable lust for power" led to a distinct shift in U.S. foreign policy toward hotspots like the Congo.[80] For instance, Harriman's support for pro-Belgian Moise Tshombe's appointment to prime minister in mid-1964 ran firmly against the views of Williams's African Bureau. Having worked to contain Tshombe's influence throughout the early 1960s—casting the idea of an independent Katanga state as a violation of African unity and independence—the assistant secretary found himself reversing course under Johnson, collaborating openly with the dictator to quell tumult in the Congo.[81] Concerned with his own survival in the new administration, Williams accepted Johnson's controversial plan to use Belgian soldiers in a 1964 hostage crisis, turned a blind eye toward the use of white mercenaries, and acquiesced quietly to U.S. aid plans when General Mobutu seized power in a coup the following year.[82] These policies fit uneasily with the assistant secretary's advocacy of Africa for the Africans and his push to remove the continent from the Cold War game.[83] Against the backdrop of America's growing military presence in Southeast Asia, Harriman's ascension inaugurated a seemingly more conservative stance toward Africa's most controversial problems.[84]

However, it would be a mistake to evaluate Johnson's policy toward South Africa through the lens of the Congo or Vietnam. Unwilling to ever declare America's war in Southeast Asia, the new president had few qualms announcing his war against racism when he entered office in 1964.[85] Despite Williams's perceptions, Johnson believed passionately in civil rights reform. Domestic legislation had the power, in his mind, to place the United States at the apex of the changes sweeping through the world—or, in Williams's lexicon, to help America assume its role as the world's "permanent revolution." The spearhead of this offensive—Johnson's ambitious Great Society programs of 1964–66—promised explicitly to "end poverty and racial injustice" in a single generation and "lead America toward a new age" where "the demands of morality" and "the needs of the spirit" would "be realized in the life of the Nation."[86] Civil rights and economic justice, cast as distractions during much of the Kennedy administration, now formed the twin imperatives of Johnson's Cold War. By ending discrimination and economic hardship, reform would allow Washington to outflank both the communist left and the white-supremacist right and resume its place as the unquestioned hegemon of the international system.[87] "[America's] enemies may occasionally seize the day of change," Johnson declared famously at Howard University in 1965. "But it is the banner of our revolution that they take." The United States stood not just for "equality as a right and a theory" but also for "equality as a fact."[88] Like Williams, the new president wanted to rejuvenate American power by remaking the United States into a model for the non-European world.[89]

Johnson's rhetoric bolstered the assistant secretary in a particular way. The administration's efforts in the Congo and Vietnam—shaped in part by a desire to forestall explosive conflicts that sapped energy from this ambitious reform effort—functioned on a separate plane from the fight against discrimination and poverty, and the highly combustible apartheid debate existed in a political context distinct from many of the other African questions facing Washington policymakers.[90] Williams's policymaking influence bifurcated along these lines during the mid-1960s. Excluded from high-level debates on national security, he emerged nonetheless as the administration's lodestar in the realm of global civil rights—the "conscience" of Johnson's foreign policy team—and a counterweight to those who dismissed the importance of racial justice, decolonization, and diplomacy at the United Nations.

This distinction came into focus as the administration turned more attention to the apartheid question in 1964–65. Not surprisingly, Johnson did not adjust Kennedy's position toward article 2(7); the provision was a bulwark against state-to-state territorial aggression, in his mind, and the African Group's assertion that South Africa's internal discrimination constituted a transnational threat to peace and security was too great a rupture of U.N. precedent at too important a moment in the United States' own racial reconciliation efforts. However, this decision did not mean that Johnson's White House divested itself of the apartheid controversy, nor did it signify an end to the sanctions discussion within the State Department.[91] During Anglo-American talks in January 1964—the first since Kennedy's death and Harold Macmillan's health-related retirement in October—Williams provided a detailed overview of current American thinking on South Africa. Apartheid "got under the skin of Africans" more than any other problem facing Africa, the assistant secretary said, and Washington wanted to begin steps to "get the South African Government into a dialogue with the non-Europeans" and reintroduce the "rule of law in South Africa." British officials pushed back, noting that South Africa's intransigence and Western investment made change unlikely, but Williams moved the discussion quickly toward international law. The issue now was not the limits and scope of chapter VII. It was whether the West would maintain a commitment to the International Court of Justice in the postcolonial era. The Court was currently immersed in a case on the legality of South Africa's Mandate in South West Africa and, according to British minutes of the conversation, Williams's position was unambiguous:

> If, as a result of the International Court's decision on South West Africa, South Africa was in obvious breach of its obligations [to the United Nations], that would be a very serious situation . . . So far our policies had continued some degree of ambivalence, but the harder side of American policy was now being stressed and would be more and more. If our two Governments could really convince the South Africans that we meant business and that defiance of the International Court of Justice created a completely new situation for us, then it might be possible to bring the South Africans to their senses.[92]

Williams's emphasis on South Africa's obligations under international law subtly reframed the apartheid debate. In the same discussion, Harlan Cleveland, assistant secretary of state for International Organization Affairs, offered a rejoinder that related the situation to the Kennedy administration's 1962 NSC paper on the United Nations. "It was increasingly clear that the United Nations situation was crystallizing on colonial [and or] racial issues," he stated. Past attempts to soften postcolonial demands through process and procedure had boomeranged as Africans began to "realize that the repeated passage of mere symbolic resolutions brought them diminishing returns." This cognizance—focused by the fight over chapter VII in 1962–63—was leading to new trends at the General Assembly. "It was no longer a matter of the Africans versus . . . the South Africans with ourselves as the middlemen but the Africans versus the Atlantic community," with the African Group working to "erode" U.S. policy through consistent political pressure—an approach validated by the newfound "inter-action between African pressure and internal [civil rights] politics." The United Nations, as a result, was growing less susceptible to American leadership. According to Cleveland, the actions of those who "believed in change more than in peace" were forcing U.S. policymakers to draw a "sharp distinction" between the "symbolic" resolutions at the General Assembly and the "real" events at the Security Council and International Court—forums less influenced by the "bloc politics" of Africa.[93] Against this backdrop, the ICJ case took on greater significance. If the Court nullified South Africa's Mandate in South West Africa, the African Group's case would move suddenly from the realm of "symbols" into the "real" arena of law, and the Security Council would be asked to take action under article 94(2)—which detailed its enforcement obligations following ICJ rulings.[94] Western inaction, in this scenario, was almost unthinkable. It would shatter the fragile veneer surrounding the newly expanded nation-state system and undermine the foundation of American legitimacy as a postimperial world power.

President Johnson's personal commitment to this formula was tested in 1964, just as he marshaled support for his landmark civil rights legislation at home. Verwoerd's government established a commission to study the situation in South West Africa in 1962, and it seized the resulting "Odendaal Report" in January 1964 to justify the implementation of separate development in the Mandated territory. Timed to influence events at the International Court of Justice, the document's release was a major event in South Africa. The report not only described how economic progress could be squared with racial separation, but it also outlined dozens of projects that would effectively integrate the territory as a fifth province of the Republic. When the African Group predictably protested the move, denouncing it as a violation of the World Court's jurisdiction, U.S. officials suddenly found themselves caught in a diplomatic standoff. According to an NSC briefing paper that March—drafted with significant feedback from Williams—Verwoerd's "contemplated actions" promised to "bring about a critical situation in the Security Council involving strong and legally valid demands" to punish Pretoria for ignoring the contested nature of the Mandate.[95]

The NSC paper formed the basis of National Security Action Memorandum (NSAM) No. 295 and marked Johnson's first direct engagement with the apartheid question. The document not only encouraged top policymakers to use diplomatic action to force the National Party to halt actions in South West Africa, but it also outlined a series of concrete moves to prepare Washington for the aftermath of the ICJ decision, including the relocation of NASA's tracking station to Madagascar, the reaffirmation of the Kennedy administration arms embargo, the withdrawal of government loans and guarantees for investment in the Republic, and the formation of a "program of contact and covert aid" to assist noncommunist African refugee leaders.[96] Nine months earlier, many of these moves had been unimaginable. Now they formed the basis of U.S. policy toward Pretoria.

The action memorandum was a victory for Williams. His ideas had gained unprecedented currency within the White House and upper echelons of the State Department. The Republic succumbed eventually to U.S. pressure and halted the implementation of the Odendaal plan in April 1964, but confrontations over military cooperation continued between Pretoria and Washington. When Ambassador Naude met with Rusk in late April their exchange differed sharply from their previous meetings. "Clouds [are] gathering and [I] frankly [can] not see a patch of blue sky ahead," Rusk declared as the men began their conversation. The primary problem, according to the secretary of state, was South West Africa and the International Court of Justice. When Naude tried bringing up their earlier discussions on the possibility of a "federated" South Africa—claiming that Pretoria was pursuing this suggestion and recent misunderstandings were born simply from the "natural inclination of Americans to fail to grasp or understand anything that was not in the American style or terminology"—Rusk interrupted the ambassador and asked when Africans would gain their civil rights. Williams, present at the meeting, pushed Naude further, demanding that the National Party prove its claims of legitimacy by holding open elections in South West Africa.[97] Relaying these developments to Pretoria, the ambassador speculated that the United States was increasingly using Johnson's approach toward African Americans to frame its stance on apartheid. Naude was ignorant of the exact content of NSAM 295, but he conveyed to his superiors that Rusk and Harriman, as well as Williams and the African Bureau, were now discouraging export trade to South Africa and pushing for the relocation of NASA's tracking facilities. Against the backdrop of Washington's newfound interest in the ICJ case, these developments indicated a "distinct change in U.S. policy" that pointed toward a new "willingness to directly confront" the Nationalist government.[98]

Naude's conclusions were grounded neither in personal paranoia nor unsubstantiated rumor. By July, administration officials had denied a loan guarantee to Chase Manhattan Bank to fund a mining project in South Africa, launched a comprehensive study of sanctions and other enforcement measures, and sent diplomatic demarches that informed Pretoria of the seriousness of the upcoming ICJ decision.[99] In the autumn, when Lockheed attempted to secure government support to sell sixteen aircraft to South Africa, a transaction worth $64 million, Johnson tacitly extended the scope of the Kennedy arms embargo by denying government support—overriding opposition from the Treasury, Commerce, and Defense departments. The original 1963 Security Council resolution had anticipated "strategic exceptions" to the embargo, and the aircraft in question were designed explicitly to strengthen the Republic's submarine capabilities along the South African coastline, but White House officials nonetheless took a firm line, determined to avoid blowback in the General Assembly and criticism from liberals and African Americans in the upcoming U.S. election.[100] William Brubeck, a member of the National Security Council staff, summarized the administration's mindset well, noting that involvement in a "long term aircraft contract would run exactly counter" to NSAM 295 and the president's stated desire to prepare the United States for the exigencies of the ICJ decision.[101]

In January 1965, the Johnson administration formalized its offensive by updating the National Policy Paper on South Africa. The mammoth document—deemed "authoritative" and "comprehensive" by the White House—outlined a detailed plan of formal and informal confrontation, crafted deliberately to push the Republic to comply with the ICJ decision, compel Verwoerd to develop "realistic contingency plans" for South West Africa, and force white South Africans into dialogue with non-Europeans. "An alternative to the status quo policy is needed," the paper declared. In recent months, the United States had found itself in "an awkward position at home and abroad" as it tried to "maintain friendly relations with two hostile factions" and cast itself as a champion of the "principle of racial equality." The ICJ verdict promised to expose the unsustainable nature of this policy. Williams's intellectual influence was self-evident, as the authors tied the rationale for action repeatedly to the civil rights movement and liberal internationalism. "Both the trend in the U.N. and the immediate thrust of U.S. domestic policy [were] running strongly counter to South Africa's practices of racial segregation and domination," and while the Nationalist government possessed a "strong and secure" hold on power, U.S. policymakers nonetheless needed to compel Pretoria to adjust its apartheid policies to prevent a confrontation that would "threaten the authority of the U.N. and the International Court."[102] South Africa's place in the Cold War and its investment-friendly economy were important. But U.S. hegemony flowed from the faith other nations placed in the United Nations, and the apartheid controversy was deflecting attention away from America's long-term strategy of "fostering a cooperative community of free nations across the North-South dividing lines of race and wealth."[103] The sooner Pretoria reformed its racial practices, the sooner the Johnson administration could refocus attention on the global benefits of Great Society liberalism.

This conclusion was coupled with novel assessments of South Africa's policies. Unlike previous national policy papers, the document weighed in on the implications of apartheid and denounced the Nationalist government's defense of apartheid in the global arena. Referring to the Republic's recent propaganda efforts in New York, Washington, and London, the document's authors explained:

In its main effort to placate world opinion and to curtail, artificially, the ratio of Blacks to Whites, the South African Government has recently introduced the concept of the 'Bantustan.' This idea embodies the eventual creation of a series of scattered Black African tribal states in a confederal or 'Commonwealth' system, but with South Africa retaining central direction for several decades to come . . . The plan lacks administrative infrastructure, essential development capital, and clear-cut promises of eventual autonomy or independence. It fails to resolve the problem of the urban African. Thus far, in the Transkei, the South African Government has shown little evidence of good faith in giving the territory adequate economic backing or progressive movement toward actual autonomy.[104]

A year and a half earlier, Rusk had openly entertained the commonwealth idea in discussions with Naude and denounced Williams's call for a pax Americana based on racial equality. Now, his Department of State seemed intent on dismantling the intellectual edifice of race stratification theory. Bolstered by these trends, Williams tried pushing President Johnson to dramatically overhaul American aid programs in Africa in 1965. The style and page length of his plan was criticized sharply by White House officials when it reached the Oval Office that autumn, but Johnson's top officials embraced many of the assistant secretary's ideas. The situation in Africa, in Rusk's words, provided "a unique opportunity to project American ideas and use American resources by means which attract attention to and are consistent with our democratic principles, our commitment to an interracial society, and our concern with human welfare." Williams's proposal, in Rusk's mind, offered an offensive counterpart to U.S. efforts in South Africa that provided Africans with an Americentric "evolutionary, peaceful" alternative to "Wars of Liberation." Rusk did not hesitate to connect this assertion to domestic events. "Just as the American contribution to the postwar rehabilitation of Western Europe drew on many of the politico-economic ideas of the New Deal and Fair Deal, and the policies of the New Frontier were reflected in the Alliance for Progress in Latin America, so would a progressive, responsible concept of our relations with Africa be a particularly appropriate foreign policy counterpart of the Great Society."[105]

The context surrounding Rusk had clearly changed. The southern-based civil rights movement was cresting in 1965, as African American activists dramatized the brutality of Jim Crow in Mississippi, Alabama, and beyond. It had become clear, in the secretary's words, that "how we handled civil rights in the United States" could not be separated from "our relations with the rest of the world."[106] By moving to address America's racial problems through comprehensive civil rights and voting legislation, the president had tacitly legitimized the civil rights movement's definition of discrimination and morality in the United States. "At times, history and fate meet at a single time in a single place to shape a turning point in man's unending search for freedom," Johnson explained in a joint address to Congress following violence in Selma, Alabama, in 1965.[107] The United States had reached such a moment, in his mind, and needed to reinvigorate its moral standing through racial reform and Great Society liberalism. For the better part of four years, Williams had been making a comparable argument, pushing officials around him to accept the inherent symmetry between civil rights at home and apartheid abroad. Now, in the context of Johnson's expansive reform initiatives, his efforts seemed to be leading to concrete action against South Africa. It was not impossible, in the assistant secretary's view, to imagine a scenario where Washington would confront the Nationalist government with economic sanctions.

In November 1965, events tested the depth of these policymaking trends. Since late 1963, when Great Britain began liquidating the Central African Federation, the problem of Southern Rhodesia had hovered in the background of the global apartheid debate. Northern Rhodesia and Nyasaland gained independence in uneventful power transfers in 1964—forming the nation-states of Zambia and Malawi, respectively—but white Southern Rhodesians rejected the idea of open elections, demanded independence on white-settler terms, and eventually elected nationalist Ian Smith in April 1964. London, led now by Harold Wilson's Labour Party, responded by making full sovereignty contingent on five principles, including "progress toward" majority rule, the elimination of "retrogressive" amendments to the constitution, direct African participation in the political process, major steps to end racial discrimination, and concrete evidence that all Rhodesians favored independence. As Smith pushed back against Great Britain's prerequisites in 1964, negotiations ground to a halt and tensions became more acute. By 1965, the situation seemed destined for conflict.[108]

U.S. policymakers treated the impasses as an internal British issue throughout 1963–64 and remained largely uninvolved until Smith announced that Southern Rhodesia was an independent nation on November 11, 1965. This unilateral declaration of independence (UDI) forced the United States into action. At first, it seemed President Johnson would treat the Rhodesian crisis much like the Congo crisis. He immediately appointed George Ball as the administration's point man and initiated a series of symbolic moves that included halting military supplies to the region, publicly denouncing travel to the country, placing travel restrictions on Rhodesians in the United States, and suspending loans and credits to the Smith government.[109] Having worked against many of Williams's initiatives during the Kennedy years, Ball again strove to limit the African Bureau's policymaking influence and deliberately curbed efforts that placed Washington "out in front" of Great Britain. Rather than embracing Wilson's "quick kill" strategy—which proposed using oil sanctions and economic isolation to bring Smith back to the bargaining table—the undersecretary of state offered what he termed a "feasible" alternative, which included a two-year sugar embargo and new regulations on exports to the colony.[110] Wilson, convinced that British pressure would only succeed with American support, countered with a reformulated version of the "quick kill" plan, based on a compromise that would involve U.S.-U.K. embargoes of Rhodesian tobacco and sugar, as well as a sustained effort to end foreign investments in the colony and supply Zambia— now isolated on its south, east, and west borders—with appropriate economic support.[111] This tit-for-tat continued through late 1965. By the time Johnson and Wilson finally met in person in mid-December, officials in London had grown convinced that Ball's team would never accept a plan involving sanctions and State Department officials were talking openly about Wilson's "mismanagement" of the crisis.[112]

The December meeting between the president and prime minister, however, marked a turning point in the initial UDI debate. The two men quickly agreed that the United States would support an oil embargo and organize an airlift to assist Zambia's economy. Although some U.S. aides still lamented that these measures would not work,[113] Johnson overrode skepticism, citing African and African American complaints about the weakness of his Rhodesian policy.[114] By January, the airlift was in place and the Commerce Department was unfurling new trade regulations against Smith's government. In historian Thomas Noer's words, the president's involvement allowed Williams to reemerge "as the major spokesman for U.S. policy" in southern Africa.[115] He did not hesitate to take advantage of the opening. In a speech that January, Williams declared that the United States would never allow "220,000 whites to maintain a 'Governor Wallace type' of racial supremacy over millions of black Africans." If the West failed to act, the "Southern Rhodesian situation could well lead to the downfall of responsible, friendly African Governments" and "their replacement by radical elements." In his mind, sanctions would force Smith to accept the necessity of free and open elections by early summer.[116] In April, this rhetoric was put to the test when Portugal attempted to break the newly established Western oil embargo by allowing a Greek tanker to transport oil to Rhodesia through Mozambique. U.S. officials pushed their British counterparts to orchestrate a response at the United Nations. Working together, British and American representatives guided the passage of a unanimous Security Council resolution on April 9 that granted the Atlantic powers the authority to stop the tanker. Casting Portugal's move as a clear "threat to the peace," the resolution authorized the Council to review the situation and determine enforcement measures under chapter VII.[117]

The resolution's language did not go unnoticed by the African Group. Rather than coalesce around Western leadership and recognize the tanker as the "threat,"

African diplomats contended immediately that Rhodesian independence constituted the true danger to international peace and security. According to the African Group, the precedent existed for universal mandatory sanctions under chapter VII.[118] In the days that followed, the press fueled an environment of uncertainty, reporting that disagreements were proliferating through the Johnson administration and between the Atlantic powers. Behind closed doors, Ball and others indeed lamented the unexpected reintroduction of chapter VII into discussions at the United Nations and blamed the African and International Organization bureaus for their clumsy diplomacy; meanwhile, a host of State Department officials countered that the undersecretary's waffling undermined the consistency, clarity, and effectiveness of the Anglo-American political offensive.[119] By the end of April, it was clear that U.S. policy toward white redoubt in Africa was reaching a crossroads. Washington could either escalate the stand against Southern Rhodesia and prepare for direct conflict with South Africa, or move away from the brink by refocusing attention on the economic and strategic dividends that came from partnering with Salisbury and Pretoria. The middle path between these alternatives was growing increasingly unnavigable.

Mennen Williams had resolute views on this question, but he refrained from lobbying the president that spring. On March 11, in a joint press conference with Johnson, he announced that he was running to become Michigan's junior senator. Forty-eight hours later he was on the campaign trail in Detroit, discussing the state of race relations and labor rights in urban America, and by March 23 his last remaining responsibilities as assistant secretary were passed to Joseph Palmer, an apolitical career diplomat with more than a decade of experience in the State Department.[120] For Williams, the time had come to rebuild the alliance between blacks and unions that had propelled his political career in the 1950s. Eager to reenter the national arena someday as a viable presidential contender, he wanted badly to prove that New Deal liberalism could still solve the problems facing contemporary America. The debate about South Africa and apartheid's contested place in the world now rested on the shoulders of other politicians.

PART TWO

WHITE REDOUBT

WHITE REPORT

4

Halls of Justice

Freedom is like birth. Till we are fully free, we are slaves.
—Mahatma Gandhi

All things are subject to interpretation. Whichever interpretation pre-
vails at a given time is a function of power and not truth.
—Friedrich Nietzsche

Harold Taswell was not a happy man in the summer of 1965. As South Africa's
new ambassador to the United States, he held one of the most important and
prestigious positions in the Republic's Ministry of Foreign Affairs. However,
things were not going well. In August, he presented a less than subtle report to
his superiors in Pretoria: "Could Paul Kruger have avoided war with England
and yet retained the integrity of the Republic? Will we be able to avoid an armed
clash with the United States—or an armed clash with the United Nations
strongly backed by the United States—and still retain our integrity? There is a
parallel between the period preceding the Anglo-Boer War and conditions pre-
vailing today. The situation is equally dangerous."

He went on to outline the nature of the threats facing South Africa. "Powerful
forces" in Washington were out to "goad and provoke [South Africa] into taking
some action which would give America a face saving excuse for applying sanctions
against us, for breaking off diplomatic relations and finally for armed intervention."
Framing President Lyndon Johnson as a "calculating yet quick tempered, impet-
uous man," Taswell further lamented that the American was so committed to
racial integration that he was "push[ing] aside all those who stand in his way . . .
[even] his own Whites." In the ambassador's words, "Our policy and his are diametrically opposed." And the path forward was becoming treacherous: "The
tougher nut we are to crack, the less likely are we to be attacked but we must not
underestimate the American danger and the tremendous military power of this
country. As Oscar Wilde remarked it is easy to choose one's friends but one must
be very careful in choosing one's enemies."[1]

Clearly, all was not quiet on the Republic's Western front. Taswell's anxiety was palpable and tied to a simple, unavoidable fact—the global struggle against apartheid was coming rapidly to its climax. Inspired by the political openings of decolonization, African nationalists had rallied against South Africa in the wake of the Sharpeville Massacre, creating a coherent political bloc at the United Nations that was dedicated to destroying white racism on the African continent. Their efforts went beyond driving a wedge between South Africa and its traditional Western allies; they transformed the dynamics of the Cold War. As one journalist explained in late 1965, the apartheid question was "symbolic of bigger issues," namely whether "the demands of Bandung" would influence the nature of global power in the decolonized world.[2] Taswell's apprehensive telegram reflected the fears and suspicions of many white South Africans as they surveyed these developments in the mid-1960s. The citadel of white redoubt—constructed so methodically by South African leaders in the years after World War II—was now in the midst of a full-scale diplomatic siege. Former allies like the United States could no longer be counted on for moral, economic, or political support.

This chapter examines the International Court of Justice case of 1966 against South Africa, a turning point in this story. South African officials genuinely feared that a negative ruling would lead to sanctions or some type of armed conflict before 1967; African leaders expected fully that a positive ruling would reorient the terms of global legitimacy in their favor and validate their demands vis-à-vis South Africa. The actual verdict delivered by the Court in late July 1966 surprised both sides and sent shockwaves through the international system, redefining the movement against white power in southern Africa. Arguably the most important decision in the Court's history, the trial offers a unique window on how actors in the First and Third Worlds conceptualized—and contested—the notion of political order in the decade after decolonization.[3]

The ICJ case against South Africa was political. The primary aim of the African Group in the early 1960s was to implement sanctions against the National Party and overturn white rule in South Africa. By the mid-1960s, it was growing obvious that the Security Council—specifically the United States and Great Britain—would not accept General Assembly resolutions as evidence that apartheid was a breach of "international peace and security." If the African Group could secure a positive ruling at the International Court, it would break the deadlock over these issues and force the great powers into action through article 94 of the U.N. Charter. Pretoria, meanwhile, hoped that a South African victory at the Court would fragment the international anti-apartheid struggle and eliminate the possibility of sanctions by the United Nations. In both scenarios, the case formed the pivot of a uniquely political game.

At the same time, the ICJ case was about legitimacy. Both sides were drawn to the Court because it represented a source of unbiased authority in the international system. Positioned as the linchpin of the United States' multilateral postwar political order, the International Court of Justice included judges from six continents, and it systemized and reified values for the entire global community.[4] For the African Group, the goal was to defeat South Africa on uniquely postcolonial terms. By formally delegitimizing the apartheid idea, African nationalists thought that they would translate their understanding of universal equality into international law and reaffirm the moral power of the African liberation struggle. The stakes were equally high for the National Party. A victory would not simply insulate the government from sanctions and armed intervention; it would effectively buttress South Africa's assertion that sovereignty trumped nonracial equality in the decolonized world. If anti-apartheid activism could be framed as a mere sideshow in the larger drama between liberal capitalism and communism, South Africa would be free to reposition itself as the West's principal ally on the African continent.

When viewed within these frameworks, the ICJ case emerges as a watershed moment. The Court's verdict was delivered during a period of remarkable turmoil in the international system. Third World nationalists who had rallied to the United Nations in the years after decolonization were beginning to lose their faith in the organization by the mid-1960s. The outcome of the ICJ case reflected and reinforced these trends. It became a powerful symbol, dramatizing the limitations of change in the decolonized world and foreshadowing future directions in the struggle against apartheid in southern Africa.

Apartheid's Achilles Heel

Kenneth Kaunda was emerging as one of Africa's most respected leaders in 1964. As the prime minister of Zambia, the most recently liberated nation in Africa, he was invited to the semiannual Conference of Non-Aligned Countries in Cairo that autumn to speak on behalf of his people. His speech to the conference centered on one basic theme—now was not the time for "new looks" on Third World issues.[5] Opening his address with a few words on the continued moral clarity of nonalignment, he shifted quickly into an extended diatribe on white power in southern Africa. Noting that the "forces of reaction" still loomed large over Africa, Kaunda pointed specifically to the Republic of South Africa, arguing that apartheid would "reap the whirlwind of disaster" if it continued to violate "reason and the fundamental principles of civilisation and human rights." His solution was deceptively straightforward—a renewed commitment to the "diplomacy of peace." White redoubt could only be defeated through international action. "We all know that the United Nations Organization is the only key to international and national security," he explained. "It is through the strength of the General Assembly that the non-aligned nations will be secure until all the powerful nations are politically, economically and socially just."[6]

The speech was an important moment in Kaunda's embryonic political career. It helped elevate his profile among Third World politicians and positioned him to eventually succeed Gamal Abdel Nasser as the secretary general of the Non-Aligned Movement.[7] It also revealed many of the core assumptions of African nationalist thought in the mid-1960s. For leaders of newly independent African countries, apartheid was an affront to the very concept of African political liberation. South Africa's racial policies served as an imaginative foil for pan-Africanism in the years after decolonization, providing an array of politicians—in Africa and the wider Third World—with a common "other" at the international level. Kaunda's comments showcased how many nationalist politicians conceptualized action against the monolith of white redoubt. For Kaunda, the numerical superiority of African and Asian countries at the General Assembly was significant, and the best strategy was not guerilla warfare or aid from communist powers but diplomacy at the United Nations. Decolonized nations did not just have a seat at the table of nations; they had the right to control the conversation about North-South issues. They had the right to use the United Nations to confront white racism in Africa.

Kaunda's speech provides a useful vantage point on the international anti-apartheid movement in the first decade after decolonization. This was a struggle defined not by Western liberals, church leaders, or civil rights groups in the United States but by African nationalists from the Third World. These nationalists adhered to a metanarrative that blended modernization with nonracialism and equated national liberation with socioeconomic progress and territorial autonomy. By the mid-1960s, the African fight against apartheid had reached a paradoxical crossroads. On the one hand, nationalist diplomats had successfully pushed the United States to pass an arms embargo against the Nationalist government and connected the apartheid question to the broader constellation of colonial issues in Southern Rhodesia, Angola, and Mozambique. However, the major prizes—economic sanctions and military intervention—were still out of reach. While the African Group could pass General Assembly resolutions against South Africa with ease and frequency, they found it nearly impossible to move the Security Council beyond a position of symbolic criticism of apartheid.

Members of the African Group understood these difficulties well. In the years after decolonization, many hoped the General Assembly would push the Security Council past this tipping point through article 14 of the U.N. Charter, which gave the Assembly the ability to "recommend measures for the peaceful adjustment of any situation . . . it deems likely to impair the general welfare or friendly relations between nations." African Group leaders initially believed that if they demonstrated that South Africa was a danger to "the maintenance of international peace and security," the Security Council would be obliged to take action under the provisions of chapter VII.[8] By the end of 1965, it was becoming clear that this would not happen. The United States and Great Britain—with their sizeable economic investments in the Republic and positions of influence on the Security Council—were simply unwilling to accept U.N. General Assembly resolutions or Special Committee reports as proof that South Africa was a direct threat to international peace.

Faced with this impasse, African leaders at the United Nations fell back on the second plank of their anti-apartheid strategy. If progress in the political realm had reached its natural limits, the alternative was action through the system of international law. This approach was not entirely unfounded. U.S. planners, determined to prevent a third world war and disillusioned with European-style imperialism, had created an international system based not on power politics and intimidation but on legal structure and multilateralism.[9] This framework opened a range of pathways for Third World activists in the years surrounding decolonization and, so long as the so-called great powers were committed to this liberal international order, a victory against South Africa at the International Court would have serious repercussions. Article 94 of the U.N. Charter explicitly bound the Security Council to uphold Court judgments. In the minds of African Group leaders, a legal victory against apartheid at the Court would put the United States and Great Britain in a political checkmate, forcing both countries to choose between concrete action against South Africa and a veto in support of the National Party.

The Republic's controversial Mandate over South West Africa offered an ideal basis for litigation. The League of Nations had entrusted South Africa with a class "C" Mandate over Germany's colony following World War I. In theory, this Mandate was to become a United Nations Trust Territory after World War II, but South African leaders made an aggressive power play in the late 1940s, arguing that because the United Nations was *not* the natural successor to the League of Nations, the territory no longer belonged to the international community. In their minds, there had been no transfer of power between the League and the United Nations. As such, South West Africa was now sovereign to South Africa. The United Nations responded to this challenge methodically in the early 1950s, soliciting the views of the International Court of Justice in a series of advisory opinions that denounced the National Party's actions as insolent and unlawful. However, the Court's advisory rulings were nonbinding, and South Africa's intransigence went largely uncontested through the first decade of the Cold War.[10] All the African Group had to do was prove in a contentious hearing that South Africa's Mandate was illegitimate. The legal basis for action against apartheid would immediately be established at the United Nations.

A victory on this front would be a major accomplishment. Since crushing the final remnants of domestic unrest in 1964, the National Party had effectively put to rest the notion that it would succumb to internal pressures from the African National Congress and Pan Africanist Congress. South Africa, in the words of one journalist, was not going to be the next Algeria.[11] Most observers abroad were dejected by this turn of events. "South Africa's monolithic police state with all its ramifications of spies and informers makes it impossible for organized violence or boycotts to be planned," one activist lamented at an international conference on apartheid in 1965.[12] The South West Africa Mandate was the chink in the seemingly impenetrable armor of white redoubt. In the minds of many African leaders, the region represented "the Achilles heel of apartheid."[13] While Pretoria could use notions of sovereignty to shield its internal policies from international criticism, its position in the Mandate territory was tenuous at best. As one African nationalist explained, South West Africa was not only a "major issue in world politics" but also a "flashpoint in the international struggle against apartheid—involving not only African nations but the great powers as well."[14] Victory would be more than symbolic. It would create the legal rationale for a rollback process that stopped only at Table Mountain in Cape Town.

In late 1960, the African Group announced that it would bring litigation against the Republic. Although most African countries provided resources to pay for trial expenses, Ethiopia and Liberia coordinated the effort because they had been members of the League of Nations when the Mandate was originally conferred on South Africa. The first hurdle of the case was a large one. The African Group needed to confirm that it had a legal basis to challenge the Republic's policies in South West Africa. To develop their strategy, the Applicants hired a New York-based lawyer with extensive experience in the U.S. State Department—Ernest A. Gross. A former U.S. ambassador to the United Nations, Gross had written extensively on the role of the United Nations in promoting international peace and justice.[15] According to Enuga Reddy, a U.N. official who worked closely with African leaders in the 1960s, Gross was "chosen as the counsel in the hope that he would influence the U.S. Government."[16] His connections in Washington would elevate the profile of the ICJ proceedings in the Foggy Bottom and his intellectual background would ensure that the Africa Group's positions were presented in pro-American language. African nationalists wanted not only to win the case; they hoped to push the United States into their worldwide coalition against apartheid.

Gross approached the job from an equally distinct vantage point. The fifty-four-year-old liberal lawyer viewed the trial as a chance to rectify the growing tension between the politics of postcolonialism at the General Assembly and the politics of the Cold War at the Security Council. In the vernacular of modern legal theory, he was an advocate of "transitional justice." As scholar Elizabeth

Borgwardt explains, this paradigm embraced "an alternative way of thinking about the relation of law to political transformation," treating justice as "distinctive in times of transition—partial, contingent, and shaped by social understandings of prior injustice rather than by abstract, idealized conceptions of the rule of law."[17] For Gross, decolonization was the major transformation of the twentieth century. "New nations explode into being, not like stars in space, but as neighbors on a crowded planet," he wrote in 1962. "New opportunities bring need for corresponding changes in process and structure." If the history of man was a story of "endless struggle toward durable peace and a just order," South Africa was important for one reason—new nations emerging onto the world stage viewed apartheid as an impediment to further human progress. As such, it needed to be confronted.[18]

Gross explained his thinking about South Africa during an informal lunch with members of the African Bureau before he accepted the African Group's job offer in 1960. According to notes of the meeting:

> Gross said the importance of SWA has often been overlooked because of the broader problem of apartheid in the Union. In his view the problem of South West [Africa] arose because of apartheid and was inextricably tied up with it . . . using South West Africa to bring additional pressure against the Union, [the Mandate] might be a handle to get at the apartheid question itself. He said this gave added emphasis to the question of timing and tactics since at some point the question of South West Africa and apartheid would . . . merge into one effort.[19]

This attitude shaped Gross's approach during the initial phase of the case. As counsel to the African bloc, he articulated a two-pronged legal assault that cast the situation in wide terms. The first step was proving that the South West Africa Mandate still existed. Drawing heavily upon the Court's own advisory opinions, Gross's initial Memorial asserted that the General Assembly had replaced the League Council as the primary oversight organization of the Mandate System.[20] Despite South Africa's assertions to the contrary, Pretoria had tacitly accepted the authority of the United Nations by requesting feedback on whether South West Africa could be annexed in 1945. It was only after this request was denied that Nationalist leaders fell back on the thesis of discontinuity. According to Gross, these points meant the Mandate was still an "autonomous territory" with "international character."[21] As such, the South African government was obliged to provide regular reports and petitions to the United Nations and submit to the general will of the world community.[22] This argument was the linchpin of Gross's case. If the Court rejected the claim that South West Africa was within the basic jurisdiction of the United Nations, the Applicants' case would collapse before it even began.

The second part of the African Group's legal assault focused on the terms of the Mandate. Gross went through the original document with methodical care, emphasizing how the National Party had debased its territorial responsibilities and violated the human rights of indigenous peoples. Despite the fact that article 4 of the Mandate explicitly prohibited the creation of army or navy bases in the territory, the Republic had done exactly the opposite. "Armoured corps are not normally used for police protection or internal security," Gross noted with a hint of sarcasm in 1961.[23] South Africa was deliberately turning the territory into a buffer zone for white power, stifling local independence movements while ignoring the development needs of the people.[24]

Human rights questions were featured prominently in the Memorial. Hearkening back to article 2 of the Mandate—which instructed South Africa to "promote to the utmost the material and moral well-being and social progress of the inhabitants of the territory"—Gross's legal team provided nearly one hundred pages of self-proclaimed factual evidence on the "well-being, social progress, and development of people in the territory."[25] Their analysis constituted a veritable *tour d'horizon* of Western development theory in the early 1960s and focused on how South Africa had retarded the economic growth, representative government, citizenship rights, freedom of movement, personal security, rights of residence, and educational opportunities of people living in South West Africa. The result was a damning portrait of neglect.[26]

The logic undergirding Gross's legal brief was fairly self-evident. If the mandate system was built on a "sacred trust" between the Mandatory and indigenous people, South Africa's policies of apartheid breached this agreement. As such, the Mandate needed to be revoked. The New York lawyer was modeling Africa's case on the most prominent human rights trial of the twentieth century, the Nuremberg Trials. Like the litigation against Nazi Party leaders in the 1940s, his argument centered on the idea that inhumane acts committed against civilian populations were indictable as "crimes against humanity." Gross also understood that the South West Africa case had the potential to function as a contest over the meaning of human rights and justice in the postcolonial era. It was essential, therefore, that his attacks link the Republic's failures in the realm of development with its support of inequality and racial separation.[27] Progress was simply incompatible with apartheid in the postcolonial era. In his words:

> The Mandatory has not only failed to promote 'to the utmost' the material and moral well-being, the social progress and the development of the people of South West Africa, but it has failed to promote such well-being and social progress in any significant degree whatsoever. To the contrary, the Mandatory has thwarted the well-being, the social progress and the development of the people of South West Africa

throughout varied aspects of their lives ... The grim past and present reality in the condition of the 'Natives' is unrelieved by promise of future amelioration. The Mandatory offers no horizon of hope to the 'Native' population.[28]

Ipso facto, nonindigenous rule was an inhuman act. It followed, therefore, that political independence—defined literally as control of a fixed territorial space— formed the gateway to economic and social development. A victory on these terms would provide the legal basis for concrete action against the Republic of South Africa. Theoretically, it would also institutionalize the connection between apartheid and moral iniquity and reframe global norms around postcolonial objectives.

These stakes were not lost on the Nationalist government. Afrikaner elites combated the global anti-apartheid movement through a multifaceted program of propaganda, political resistance, and grassroots lobbying during the early 1960s. Their goal was not to engage African nationalists directly in a debate about human rights but to work outside the parameters of the United Nations to subtly reframe the nature of the conversation on apartheid. Pretoria's initial response to the Applicants' charges at the International Court fit into this initiative. The government put its faith in Dawie P. de Villiers, a prominent member of the South African Bar with ties to Prime Minister Hendrik Verwoerd. Not surprisingly, his philosophical attitudes on international law contrasted starkly with Gross's transitional justice. An ardent political and social conservative, the Afrikaner supported a static vision of global order based on national sovereignty and historical tradition.

In forming South Africa's response to the Memorial, de Villiers tried to do an end-run around human rights questions by focusing exclusively on the status of the South West Africa Mandate. His argument unfolded in four parts. Wrapped around a sophisticated interpretation of Western contractual law, the first point claimed that the Mandate could not be viewed as a binding legal agreement because the resolution that created it was termed a "declaration" rather than "treaty or convention."[29] When South Africa refused to recognize the jurisdiction of the United Nations in 1946, it followed that the Mandate ceased to exist.[30] The second and third points attacked the *locus standi* of Ethiopia and Liberia. Pushing the boundaries of circular logic, South Africa asserted that because no country still belonged to the League of Nations, it was technically impossible to challenge South Africa's control over South West Africa. Drawing again on the specific language of the Charter, Nationalist lawyers rationalized this claim by pointing out that article 7—which outlined proper recourse in the case of a dispute over South West Africa—did not say that "former" League members could challenge the Mandate. The third point made this argument in a slightly different way, speculating that the Applicants could not technically have a dispute with South Africa because Mandatory powers were answerable only to the League as an entity. Individual states had no standing.[31] Finally, Nationalist lawyers sought to delay the litigation, claiming that "direct diplomatic intercourse" between the Applicants and South Africa had yet to take place. Previous discussions at the United Nations were meaningless because they had been conducted in a "charged political environment." Until the Republic was given "a real and genuine opportunity to negotiate it can *not* be said that the dispute is one which cannot be settled by negotiation."[32]

South Africa's efforts were almost successful. In a narrow 8–7 decision just before Christmas 1962, the Court accepted the first part of Gross's argument. The Mandate existed despite the dissolution of the League, and Ethiopia and Liberia had the right to challenge South Africa's policies in South West Africa. As one legal scholar explained at the time, the decision symbolically indicated that the "sacred trust" would not be "allowed to go by default and just disappear into thin air."[33] The Nationalist government was accountable for its actions in South West Africa. In an opinion that foreshadowed the next stage of the legal battle, Phillip Jessup, one of the Court's most influential judges, explained that the law was a "living phenomenon which translates the collective exigencies and necessities of each historical moment." Noting that the "social occurrences" of each era were the most important sources of global order, he explained, "Law is not just a mental abstraction, nor the result of repeated application of written jurisprudence, but, rather, a norm of conduct which is rooted in social intercourse."[34] The implications were obvious—momentum was on the side of Gross's "transitional justice."

From Nuremberg to *Brown*

For the Nationalist government, the Court's decision constituted just one part of the much larger—and universally unfavorable—political landscape. Attacks against South Africa came from several directions in the early 1960s. On the one hand, the country's position in the Western bloc was under fire. The Republic was effectively removed from the British Commonwealth in 1961, and it was subjected to an arms embargo by the U.N. Security Council in mid-1963. On the other hand, South Africa's position in southern Africa was growing unstable. The Republic's relationship with Rhodesia was fraught as Ian Smith prepared the country for its unilateral declaration of independence in 1965.[35] Pretoria wanted desperately to avoid the creation of an African nationalist government along its northern border but viewed Smith as a dangerous provocateur who would provoke a U.S.-led sanctions regime in southern Africa.

By the mid-1960s, South Africa stood at a difficult juncture. In the words of Prime Minister Verwoerd, the "crux of the problem" was whether being in the "good books of world opinion" mattered as much as "ensur[ing] the survival of the white race in this country."[36] The answer was obvious to most high-ranking South African officials, even if the consequences were not. Despite a constant stream of propaganda on South Africa's economic and political invulnerability, many officials understood that the country's long-term prospects were intimately entwined with the world. As former Foreign Minister Eric Louw admitted, while South Africa could weather criticism from the U.N. General Assembly, the "attitude of those countries *outside* the Bandung-Communist combination," namely the United States and Great Britain, posed a "serious threat" to South Africa's continued prosperity.[37] According to a top-secret policy review, the "good-will, aid and investment" of the West was simply "more important to South Africa than vice versa."[38] With the United States embroiled in its own civil rights revolution and the apartheid debate sitting at the nexus of postcolonial politics at the United Nations, this uneven relationship meant trouble for the Republic.[39]

In this environment, the second phase of the ICJ case took on tremendous significance. Viewed widely as an unbiased institution of international law, the Court provided a forum where values were contested and normalized for the global community. If the logic undergirding Gross's second argument was accepted by the Court, it was entirely possible that attitudes toward South Africa's situation would harden into outright hostility. As de Villiers explained to his superiors, the ICJ case was one of the "greatest threats facing the Republic."[40] A victory would carry substantial dividends. If the Nationalist government could show that apartheid in South West Africa was not a violation of human rights— if it could decouple concepts of justice from the African liberation narrative— the government would gain leverage to reverse trends toward confrontation with the West. In the minds of South African officials, the ICJ case was the tipping point in the larger contest over the Republic's future in the Western bloc.

South Africa's legal strategy during the second phase of the trial was elaborate. Not surprisingly, de Villiers opened his case by rearguing his original claims on the nature of the Mandate and U.N. succession. He sharpened the thesis of discontinuity, arguing that the Mandate was accountable not to a nebulous "international community" but to a concrete institution, the defunct League of Nations. Consequently, it was not possible for a wholly different institution to have supervisory powers without the Republic's consent. The Applicants' evidence that South Africa had given this consent tacitly in 1946 was countered with a series of previously undisclosed "new facts" that delved deep into the minutiae of the historical record, drawing on a constellation of minor points to muddy the clarity of Gross's original argument.[41] Recognizing that the Court had already ruled on this issue in 1962, de Villiers tried reframing the Court's decision as a narrow verdict on jurisdiction rather than an expansive judgment on the discontinuity thesis. This was not entirely true, but with the Court divided 8–7 a South African breakthrough was not impossible. If one judge accepted the validity of the Republic's "new facts," the original basis of the case would have to be reconsidered. And without evidence of consent, Gross could be pushed into a corner where he would have to argue that the "international community" had boundless supervisory powers over nation-states in the world-system.

The central thrust of South Africa's case was its rebuttal of the African Group's characterization of apartheid in South West Africa. For de Villiers, everything pivoted on showing that segregation could not be conflated with oppression. In a brief that totaled over 1,400 pages, his legal team challenged both the factual and conceptual accuracy of Gross's initial Memorial, explaining that apartheid did not retard social progress but offered each racial group the tools for "separate development." Far from functioning as an agent of race hatred, this program allowed South West Africa's "major ethnic groups to achieve an increasing measure of self-government and to develop toward self-determination in a political and territorial entity of its own."[42] The Republic's rationalization of its approach was twofold. In defensive terms, South African lawyers claimed it was unfair for the white community to sacrifice its "institutions, its culture, [and] its heritage" in the face of a "numerically preponderant and aggressively nationalistic Bantu population."[43] Drawing on popular binaries between civility and barbarism, they suggested that southern Africa's demographic and historic particularities made multiracial unity—the conceptual linchpin of Milner's original vision of the Union—a dangerous myth.

At the same time, de Villiers and his associates cast separate development as a positive alternative to the "cultural imperialism" of "European universalism." Rejecting the civilizational language of early twentieth-century racial thought, South Africa instead used social science to show that ethnic groups were "different" in objective ways and deserved the chance to develop in line with their own standards. Quoting Prime Minister Verwoerd, de Villiers asserted that South Africa's policy of race separation was not a by-product of white supremacy, but a practical way to allow groups to live "next to one another as good neighbors and not as people who are continually quarrelling over [power]."[44] The issue was not racism but conservative Christianity. Apartheid was South Africa's practical response to the biblical lessons of Babel.[45]

On the strength of this framework, de Villiers proceeded to reject each accusation of the Applicants' Memorial. In the economic realm, he asserted that whites were more powerful than indigenous people in South West Africa because Natives were uninterested in private property and modern capitalism. Drawing on ethnographical evidence and expert testimonies, South African lawyers suggested that most Africans chose to remain independent of the "money economy" because they preferred subsistence farming and local trade networks. Those individuals who bucked these trends generally gravitated to regional mining industries, where they avoided trade unions because of their illiteracy and the linguistic diversity of African workers. Framing government policies in munificent terms, de Villiers suggested that Nationalist officials only represented Natives on labor boards so that their welfare was protected from "unscrupulous troublemakers."[46]

The same principles applied to the political realm. Although Africans were not allowed to participate in white political institutions, they were given complete control over their local, tribal, and territorial affairs. The Applicants' suggestion that these Native Reserves—or Bantustans—were unfunded and overcrowded was placed next to South Africa's widely publicized "Odendaal Report," which promised to spend over £75 million on a five-year social modernization program in the territory. It would probably take "one-hundred years or more" to get indigenous people ready for full self-determination, but the Nationalist government was willing to commit the necessary resources.[47]

Finally, in the area of education, South African lawyers framed apartheid as an agent of development. In their minds, direct comparisons between white and nonwhite education levels were deceptive because African "tribes" were so widely opposed to universal European instruction standards. Education was a source of identity and power for local groups. Nationalist officials coupled this point with evidence that, despite these barriers, the government was able to increase school attendance among African children by 46 percent between 1950 and 1961, a number that compared favorably with Ethiopia's 5 percent and Liberia's 23 percent.[48] Returning to article 2 of the Mandate—which instructed the Mandatory to "promote to the utmost the material and moral well-being and social progress of the inhabitants of the territory"—South Africa concluded that Gross's entire case was baseless. Despite assertions to the contrary, apartheid was implemented in good faith in South West Africa, proving that racial separation was not incompatible with the project of development.[49]

To hammer this point home, South Africa made a bold move as oral arguments commenced on March 30, 1965. Standing before the Court for the first time since 1962, de Villiers invited the judges to conduct an on-site inspection of South West Africa. The only condition was that they also visit Ethiopia, Liberia, and a former Mandate territory like Tanzania. With this comparative understanding of the "African reality," the Court would be better equipped to "form a general impression of comparable conditions and standards of the material and moral well-being and social progress of the inhabitants."[50] The request was a shrewd tactical maneuver. De Villiers understood that Gross was modeling his case on the Nuremberg Trials and hoped the invitation would highlight the flaw that undergirded the historical analogy. The Allied case against Nazi Germany's leadership worked because American lawyers could show that German policies resulted in the wholesale violation of human rights during World War II. If the Nationalist government could prove through concrete, comparative evidence that its policies were not resulting in the ends alleged by the Applicants, the African Group—or at least the judges at the International Court—would be forced to reassess the basic charge against apartheid. South Africa's racial policies certainly stood in juxtaposition to trends toward nonracial integration in the First and Third Worlds. But that did not necessarily mean apartheid was "genocide masquerading under the guise of a civilized dispensation of justice."[51]

The gamble paid off. Gross's legal team was surprised by the South African move. Refusing to accept the proposal, the Applicants claimed that such a trip would sap the Court's resources and unnecessarily extend the trial. It was "unnecessary, expensive, dilatory, cumbersome and unwarranted."[52] However, as some observers pointed out at the time, Gross's declarations masked the fact that de Villiers had placed the African Group in a genuine catch-22.[53] Without tangible evidence of oppression in South West Africa, the case against apartheid lacked substance and depth. But to obtain concrete evidence of oppression, the Applicants would have to open their own internal policies to scrutiny and examination. In essence, de Villiers was asking his opponents to move their charges from the realm of rhetoric into the world of reality. If the Court went through with the trip and supported South Africa's argument, the rationale of the African Group's international political program—in particular the argument that political liberation formed the gateway to economic development—would be discredited. In de Villiers' own words, the dilemma was "unenviable."[54]

Gross responded by moving the case to purely theoretical grounds. Although he intended to challenge systematically each point of South Africa's Counter-Memorial, he announced in early April that the Republic's entire brief had been "immaterial."[55] The issue was no longer oppression in South West Africa, but the fact that the National Party's policies violated the "international human rights norm of non-discrimination or non-separation."[56] According to Gross, this norm was created by the U.N. Charter and the Universal Declaration of Human Rights and solidified in the early 1960s with the General Assembly's Declaration on the Elimination of All Forms of Racial Discrimination.[57] Although these documents—the last of which was passed because of African Group's own efforts in 1962–63—did not explicitly trump South Africa's national sovereignty, they gave "specific and objective" meaning to international agreements like the Mandate and bound international organizations such as the United Nations to certain forms of behavior.[58] The implications were self-evident when applied to the South West Africa case. Article 2 could not be upheld without a parallel commitment to nondiscrimination and nonseparation. As one legal expert explained at the time, "The sole issue was the existence of an international legal norm which absolutely and categorically prohibited apartheid. Neither South Africa's motives in instituting apartheid in South West Africa, nor the effects of that policy on the territory's inhabitants were now at issue."[59] In Gross's mind, the ball was back in South Africa's court.

However, this line of reasoning dramatically changed the rules of the game. Gross was now modeling the African Group's case not on the Nuremberg Trials, but on the United States' landmark *Brown v. Board of Education* case. Because "separation [was] inherently unequal," it followed that apartheid automatically suppressed human rights in South West Africa, irrespective of the evidence presented by the Nationalist government.[60] Linking this situation directly to U.S. law, Gross argued, "The Respondent's policy of racial segregation in . . . the Territory is even more affirmative, explicit and far-reaching than the racial bar struck down by the *Brown* decision."[61] If the United States government was willing to support the norm of nondiscrimination, it followed that the Court would have to deliver a comparable judgment against racial separation in South West Africa.

Gross was getting to the same end—the incongruity of apartheid and development—through different means. During the initial phase of the trial, the Applicants' case had pivoted on the idea that apartheid was illegitimate because it impeded the development of local South West Africans in tangible and observable ways. This argument did not fundamentally change during the second phase of the trial, but the emphasis shifted from local dynamics to international structure. In very natural ways, the raison d'être of the African Group's position came to the forefront. The case was as much about legitimizing African nationalism as it was about the intrinsic morality of events in South West Africa; apartheid was significant not only because it oppressed black South Africans but because it held symbolic importance at the international level. Through its theoretical sophistication and political intransigence, apartheid challenged the very idea that history was moving in a linear fashion toward a political order based on territorial liberation, racial equality, and economic development. Faith in this narrative was the source of Africa's political power in the years surrounding decolonization. By reframing the charge against Pretoria around the global norm of nondiscrimination, the Applicants sought not only to invalidate the logic and rationale of South Africa's policies but also to reify the authority and prestige of the African Group's larger political agenda.

This shift was a huge leap for the Court. Beyond the basic quandary of whether one sovereign's domestic law had universal, transnational value was an even weightier question: Was there a single moral system for the world? Gross felt that if he could convince the Court that such a system existed, he would obtain a favorable ruling on apartheid in South West Africa. Even more, a positive judgment on these terms would institutionalize a new balance between traditional "European" notions of global order—based on restrictive national sovereignty—and an emerging "postcolonial" vision of power based on universal racial equality. The implications of the argument were extraordinary. But, as de Villiers had envisioned, the Applicants' case now rested on tenuous, uncharted ground. Did the "international community" truly have boundless supervisory powers over nation-states in the world-system?

Historical Inevitabilities

This contest did not unfold in a vacuum. Put plainly, litigation at the International Court mattered because Washington was listening. Having created the basic scaffolding of the postwar international system, the United States gave life to notions of transnational law and enforced the Court's authority at the U.N. Security Council. Most U.S. leaders may not have been emotionally vested in the issues discussed at The Hague, but American attitudes nonetheless shaped the parameters of what was politically possible in the outside world.[62]

U.S. policy toward apartheid was conflicted in the 1960s. The State Department tended to treat the National Party as a political and propaganda liability. With the creation of the African Bureau in the late 1950s, liberals such as Mennen Williams obtained an institutional platform to push the United States toward confrontation with the Republic. U.S. policymakers did not see the same linkages as African leaders like Kaunda, but they generally accepted a progressive vision of history and social justice.[63] Apartheid was significant, in their minds, because it distracted the global south from the benefits of Great Society liberalism and pushed the region into an unnecessarily combative anti-Western stance.[64] Robert Komer, the president's deputy special assistant for National Security Affairs, framed these fears in November 1965, saying that if the United States failed to back the anti-apartheid movement then it would be viewed as opposing the "historically inevitable" rise of African majority rule.[65] Few members of the State Department equated support for African nationalism with an armed intervention against South Africa, but many felt that sanctions against Pretoria would eventually become unavoidable.[66]

By contrast, the Pentagon, Joint Chiefs of Staff, and Central Intelligence Agency tended to frame the Nationalist government as the United States' main ally in Africa. Placing precedence on concrete U.S. interests in the region—namely a NASA tracking station and over $600 million worth of private investment—they castigated the "radicalism" that percolated through the State Department. Maxwell Taylor, the chairman of the Joint Chiefs of Staff, put it best: "As long as communist penetration and racial discord in Africa remain an active threat to Free World interests, stability in South Africa is desirable and the United States should do everything that its political and moral position permits to contribute to this."[67] Self-rule in the Third World might have been historically inevitable, but that did not negate Washington's national security interests or lessen the dangers of the Cold War.

President Johnson sided generally with the State Department in the mid-1960s. "I feel that the prime determinant of U.S. influence in Africa will be the stance the U.S. takes on those political issues of primary concern to the Africans themselves," he explained in a private memo to Secretary of State Dean Rusk in November 1965. "U.S. concern for African problems must be demonstrated by actions, and in terms, which will have an immediate appeal to the people of Africa."[68] The result was a foreign policy that tilted toward confrontation with South Africa. Although a workable solution was admittedly "difficult to identify," the U.S. national policy review on the Republic nonetheless opened with the declaration that the "status quo" needed to be overturned in the region. The authors presented a conceptual map that mirrored the African Group's own understanding of the situation. While the rest of the world was "moving fast in one direction," the Nationalist government was "moving fast in the opposite direction." With America's own racial situation "in an acute stage of resolution," an equivocal approach toward apartheid was no longer acceptable.[69]

However, opposition to South Africa did not automatically mean support for African diplomats at the United Nations. The president's decision to confront South Africa was driven not by his deep-seated concern with African affairs but by his overriding desire to address black and white extremism at home and abroad. His goal, stated plainly, was to invigorate faith in America's stewardship of world affairs. Like any power structure, the liberal international order constructed by U.S. leaders in the late 1940s functioned because member-states around the world tacitly invested in its authority. Apartheid challenged this balance in two interlocking ways. Most obviously, it distracted attention from the United States' own goals and obfuscated the moral primacy of U.S.-centered internationalism at the United Nations. On a deeper level, however, South Africa's refusal to adjust its policies in the face of General Assembly criticism—and the Security Council's reluctance to punish the apartheid government for its obstinacy—eroded faith that the United Nations could still be an agent of justice in the decolonized world. Taken together, these trends spelled trouble for the United States. In the minds of many liberals, the intellectual infrastructure of American hegemony was buckling under the weight of postcolonial politics. A new status quo in South Africa would not only counteract these trends, but it would also help the United States reconsolidate its political authority in the international realm.

The case at the International Court focused these abstract concerns in concrete ways. As a State Department paper explained, the trial was "the first major confrontation between the world community and South Africa" and a major challenge to the "authority of the U.N."[70] The Johnson administration's overriding goal was to avoid the African Group's "all-or-nothing" checkmate and prevent an angry explosion at the U.N. General Assembly.[71] Receiving most of their information about the day-to-day proceedings at The Hague directly from Gross—who nurtured his connections in Washington throughout the trial—State Department officials assumed that the ICJ judgment would go against South Africa on all counts and worked to preempt the consequences by mollifying the National Party's policies in South West Africa. Their efforts amounted to an aggressive tactical initiative. Not only was the arms embargo of 1963 continued, but the administration also began discussing the removal of NASA and DOD facilities from South Africa and asked lending agencies to suspend economic activity with the Republic.[72] Mennen Williams and his African Bureau furthermore gained the green light to coordinate a series of meetings with prominent businessmen to discourage investment in the Republic.[73] Even the Pentagon got involved, canceling the U.S.S. *Independence*'s layover to Cape Town in May 1965.[74] These efforts were coupled with a series of planning papers that explored the feasibility and desirability of economic sanctions and/or military action in southern Africa.[75] By the end of the year, the United States—working in conjunction with Great Britain—was in the midst of a full-scale diplomatic battle with the Republic over the implementation of apartheid in South West Africa.[76] This culminated with a pair of Aide-Mémoires in 1965 and 1966 suggesting, with calculated subtlety, that the West would support economic sanctions if the National Party failed to comply with the ICJ decision.[77]

This turn of events surprised Pretoria. Writing from Washington in 1965, Ambassador Taswell speculated that the American public was being "softened up" for an attack on the Republic. South Africa's "most dangerous enemies" were those out "to win the Negro vote in the United States and win the goodwill of the black man in Africa and the Afro-Asian group as a whole." For many members of the Johnson administration, the "white man in Africa" was merely an "expendable obstacle."[78] Others pushed against such "over-simplified" sentiments. "The majority of the United States policy-making elements [were] not yet aware enough of the South African situation to have fixed views for or against," lectured Donald Sole, the deputy secretary of Foreign Affairs. "In simple terms, we are not 'Communists' nor are we 'Fascist' enough (vide Franco) to be classified as 'enemy.'" There was still time to improve U.S.-South Africa relations.[79] M. I. Botha, South Africa's U.N. representative in the mid-1960s, agreed with this sentiment but still felt the United States was guilty of ideological hubris. The Americans, in his mind, were incapable of distinguishing "between the racial situation in the United States and that in South Africa. To them nationhood is somehow only nationhood in the image of the United States which is an all-embracing nation—as Whitman called it, 'a nation of nations.'"[80]

This intellectual egotism—or perhaps this propensity for seeing South Africa in Milner's terms—did not bode well for the Republic. Nationalist officials were angered primarily by Washington's unwillingness to acknowledge that the trial itself was tipping definitively in South Africa's favor. De Villiers spent much of 1965 burying the Court under documentary evidence and highlighting the implications and contradictions of Gross's norm of "nondiscrimination" and "non-separation." Turning the concept on the Republic's enemies, he argued first that the internal policies of India, Liberia, Ethiopia, and dozens of other states in Africa, Asia, Europe, and North America fully supported ethnic, economic, religious, and racial stratification. Although the ideal of "nondiscrimination" was rhetorically ubiquitous at the U.N. General Assembly, the concept still did not exist concretely anywhere in the world.[81] Furthermore, if the Court accepted the logic of the Applicants' accusation, it would open the door for infinite, unrestrained, and politically charged litigation at the International Court of Justice. Would "untouchables" in India be able to attack their government for its legacy of discrimination? Were African Americans entitled to prosecute the United States for housing and employment segregation in the urban North? De Villiers did not provide answers to these questions, but his message was clear—categories of discrimination and equality were not static, self-evident, or one dimensional. They were fluid and subjective terms used by actors with particular political agendas.

The second part of de Villier's counterattack tried to highlight the "true" origins of Gross's legal strategy. Drawing selectively on expert knowledge from Europe, South Africa, and the United States, the South African legal team presented a litany of witnesses to lament the "indiscriminant use of racial discrimination, segregation, separation, apartheid, [and] Nazism" at the General Assembly and bemoan apartheid's false association with racial superiority, doctrines of expansionism, and racial hatred. Politics rather than "law and history" were driving these linkages.[82] Once de Villiers established this point, he turned his attention again to South Africa's own policies. Adeptly wrapping his government's social program in the language of social science, he contrasted the African Group's "fairytale" history of global unity and pan-racialism with the Republic's "judicious" story of global diversity and separate development.[83]

For de Villiers and his associates, the case climaxed in mid-October with the testimony of Dr. Stefan Possony, a sociologist from the Hoover Institution at Stanford University. In an exchange South African propagandists' highlighted often after the judgment, the professor suggested that even if Gross's norm existed, it could only be applied to interstate relations and not to the domestic policies of individual nations.[84] Dr. Possony concluded by rejecting the philosophical underpinnings of the Applicants' case:

> Mankind with all its diversities has never accepted a single writ. To impose a single formula would be ideological imperialism. Given the ideals of humanity—the hopes of advance as well as the promises of

human rights—but given also a manifold reality, the best principle, it seems to me, is to tailor methods or responses to specific challenges . . . As Hegel taught, reality is always reasonable in its own way. Reality can be changed, and of course it should be improved. But continuity and respect for the historical tradition remain as the unavoidable framework of human betterment.[85]

When South African politicians tried making this point directly to U.S. policymakers in the months before the Court's verdict, they were met with indifference and hostility. In a meeting with Assistant Secretary of State Williams, Ambassador Taswell was told that the "sincerity" of apartheid did not matter. The Republic was "sitting on a time-bomb and heading for a racial collision."[86] Similar sentiments were expressed by Secretary of State Dean Rusk in late 1965 in a discussion with South Africa's minister of Foreign Affairs, Dr. Hilgard Muller. According to the American diplomat, everything turned on the fact that apartheid was alienating member-states at the United Nations. "There may be differences between nations," he explained, "but the abandonment of the elementary structure [of the United Nations] would put civilization back about 500 years—there would simply be no other channel of communication on the approach to differences." In referencing the ICJ decision, Rusk dismissed Muller's contention that South Africa would win the case and referred suggestively to a conversation he had had with a Russian official several years earlier. "The law is like the tongue of a wagon," the secretary of state claimed. "It goes in the direction in which it is pointed."[87]

This mindset was internalized in Washington by mid-1966. During Anglo-American talks that year, U.S. officials explained that "if South Africa refused to comply with the judgment [Washington] would have to apply an ascending scale of pressures. Sanctions came at the top of the scale." While Rusk had not officially "committed himself to the use of sanctions . . . he had agreed that the U.S. Government should consider their use for the purpose of enforcing the rule of law. If this were allowed to be flouted, the whole structure of the United Nations might be endangered."[88] In a National Security Council meeting on the eve of the Court's decision, Undersecretary of State George Ball—already well-known for his opposition to sanctions under chapter VII—opened the conversation by speculating that the judges would rule against South Africa on all counts. Although an armed U.N. intervention was still unfathomable, the United States could not give "the black Africans the idea we are laying down, nor can we permit a breakdown of the International Court and the international legal system." Debate erupted almost immediately on the utility of sanctions under article 94, with CIA Director Richard Helms and Treasury Secretary Henry Fowler suggesting that South Africa was "one of the least vulnerable countries in the world" to such action. President Johnson, however, was less definitive. He called for the establishment of a task force to plot a course to "relieve some of the pressure" of the Court's decision. In typically colloquial terms, the president explained that "even a blind hog [could] find an acorn."[89]

Few observers were distracted by such euphemisms. British officials, watching the situation from Europe, summarized, "It is almost inconceivable that the Americans would be prepared to cast their first veto in favour of the White man in southern Africa, let alone veto an attempt to uphold the rule of law which had been flouted by the White minority."[90] Johnson did not reveal his thoughts on this topic explicitly, but his willingness to place Arthur Goldberg—a well-known liberal who supported action against South Africa and now served as U.S. ambassador at the United Nations—at the helm of the ICJ task force suggests the veracity of British sentiment. Having just passed legislation that ended Jim Crow in the American South, the president appeared poised to implement symmetrical action against apartheid in South Africa. Sanctions under article 2(7) of the U.N. Charter remained a political impossibility. But if the African Group successfully obtained a rationale for sanctions under article 94, thereby making the African position legitimate under international law, then the United States would be obliged—in some ways even forced—to support action against the Nationalist government. Inaction would not just be tantamount to turning away from the political order invented by the United States after World War II; it would directly undercut the Americentric moral majority forged tentatively by Johnson's foreign policy team in 1964–65. The ICJ ruling, as Gross had envisioned in the early 1960s, would place Washington in the equivalent of a political checkmate.

There was only one catch—the Court's final judgment. After seven months of deliberations and five years of litigation, the ruling finally came on July 18, 1966. As the world watched in anticipation, the International Court of Justice unveiled a startling 8–7 decision.[91] According to the Court's new majority, the Applicants no longer had sufficient "legal right or interest" in the South West Africa Mandate to obtain a judgment on the merits of their case. "Humanitarian considerations can constitute the inspirational basis for rules of law," the Court explained, but unless given "jurisdictional expression" and "clothed in legal form," it was impossible for them to "generate legal rights and obligations."[92] The Applicants' arguments, in this regard, were "based on considerations of an extra-legal character, the product of after-knowledge" more suited for the political realm than the legal system.[93] It was not the job of the Court to "fill in the gaps" of international law.[94] This decision not only reversed the logic, content, and implications of the Court's 1962 ruling; it shattered the idea that the Court would act as an agent of transitional justice.

The ruling stunned the African Group. In the days that followed countries throughout Africa reacted with visceral anger. Ghana's U.N. ambassador summarized the mindset in late July, saying that the Court was so "out of tune with the tempo of [the] modern world" that no country from the global south would ever again acknowledge its "jurisdiction" or "authority."[95] The decision meant, according to Guinea's U.N. delegate, "that there is no grounds for belief or hope that this issue [apartheid] can be settled by reasonable means."[96] In testimony before the U.S. Congress in August, Gross suggested that the decision had "introduced a new element of uncertainty into international adjudication at a time when predictable and systematic legal order needs to be established." So long as the judges were "pro-Western and [bound] to international law which is essentially European," Third World countries would resist and question the power of the Court.[97] In commentary that foreshadowed the events of the early 1970s, the New York Times said, "The decision on South-West Africa may appear to [African states] to confirm the growing suspicion that if Black Africa is to get help against South Africa . . . it must look to the Communist bloc."[98] Diplomacy at the United Nations, on the surface, had run its course.

African Americans and American liberals—key constituents within President Johnson's domestic coalition—also expressed disappointment over the decision. Floyd McKissick, national director of the Congress of Racial Equality (CORE), denounced it immediately as "vague" and "confused," and Roy Wilkins, the NAACP's executive director, called the outcome a direct blow to the Court's "prestige among the disadvantaged peoples of the world." Having accepted Gross's claim that the case was the global equivalent of the Brown decision, activists and liberals alike rallied around The Nation's assertion that the decision was "white, Eurocentric, and quite 'colonialist' in spirit"—an affront to history itself.[99] A constellation of left-leaning U.S. congressmen— Charles Diggs, Robert Nix, Benjamin Rosenthal, and John Culver, among many others—had gone so far as to orchestrate formal hearings on U.S.-South Africa relations earlier in 1966 to pressure Johnson to curtail U.S. relations with Pretoria.[100] And five weeks before the ICJ ruling, Senator Robert Kennedy, a liberal icon, had traveled to South Africa to deliver a series of speeches about the region's importance on the world stage.[101] Convinced privately that the war in Southeast Asia was sapping America's authority in the decolonized world, he attempted to cast the fight against racism as the true raison d'être of the Democratic Party. His words had invoked the rhetorical clarity of Mennen Williams, with whom the Senator corresponded regularly in 1965–66.[102] Although governments and peoples invariably "march[ed] to the beat of different drummers," all nations were morally obliged to move "toward increasing freedom; toward justice for all; toward a society strong and flexible enough to meet the demands of all of its people, whatever their race, and the demands of a world of immense and dizzying change that face us all," Kennedy told students at the University of Cape Town in June.[103] The ICJ decision, against this backdrop, was a lost opportunity to reorient U.S. attention and resources away from the conflict in Vietnam toward the "true" frontline of international politics in the postcolonial age—the Republic of South Africa.

Officials in the Johnson administration agreed that the decision was a turning point. The CIA's report on the decision—passed along to the president by members of his National Security Council in August—was entitled appropriately "South Africa on the Crest of the Wave." It declared candidly that Verwoerd's government had turned a corner in its fight against African nationalists at the United Nations. "The court's decision not to rule on the substance of the case [has] deprived South Africa's opponents of any hope that they would soon have more leverage in their efforts to persuade the West to impose sanctions." If the African states continued to push the apartheid issue in the international arena the "most likely result" would be "South Africa's withdrawal or expulsion from the U.N., its continued defiance of any [General Assembly] resolutions, and the exposure of the U.N.'s weakness."[104] South Africa, plainly stated, had won the first phase of the apartheid debate. It remained to be seen whether this conclusion would meaningfully alter the State Department's position on the Republic or, more important, affect the stance of President Johnson himself, but the CIA's conclusion held significant implications. For much of the mid-1960s, the Johnson administration had worked from the assumption that a peaceful outcome in South Africa would be contingent on a new status quo—one that involved universal political representation and nonracial democracy in the Republic. The International Court decision served to fracture the African Group's strategy on apartheid and undermine American assumptions about the possibilities of change in South Africa.

South African officials, for their part, looked at the judgment with a sense of measured ebullience. In a formal statement to the international community after the ICJ ruling, Prime Minister Verwoerd declared sanctimoniously that the Republic would "not crow over [its] opponents," even though "impartial observers" had determined their claims of oppression to be "unfounded." The "door of friendship" would be left open, but he warned that "intervention in each other's affairs" would benefit no one and lectured that "world peace" would come only through economic development, not "jealousy, interference and conflict."[105] A secret briefing paper further elaborated on these points in early August. "It has always been clear that the main purpose of the promoters of the South West Africa case was to obtain a Judgment in contentious proceedings, which if not complied with, could lead to an invocation of Article 94 of the Charter," the authors explained. "Our adversaries have consequently not succeeded in obtaining a basis for invoking Article 94 of the Charter. This is probably the most significant effect of the Judgment." Although the political game between the African Group and South Africa would continue at the General Assembly, the possibility of legal recourse was "definitively shut-down." The situation had returned to pre-1960 conditions.[106]

The Status Quo

It is abundantly clear, from experience, that the United Nations Organisation has become an instrument of manipulation of the imperialist powers, particularly the United States of America. To ignore this fact is to ignore reality.
—*Pan Africanist Congress, Memorandum (1969)*

Fervor is the weapon of choice of the impotent.
—Frantz Fanon, *Black Skin, White Mask (1952)*

No matter where one looked in mid-1966, the world was changing. In the realm of science, the United States' *Surveyor 1* spacecraft was on the moon and the Soviet Union's *Luna 10* was orbiting above. The Beatles were culturally "bigger than Jesus," and the Beach Boys had just released *Pet Sounds*. France was leaving the North Atlantic Treaty Organization, and England was on its way to its first World Cup championship. New political elites were coming to power throughout the Third World. By March, Indira Gandhi was prime minister of India, Suharto was acting-president of Indonesia, and Kwame Nkrumah—the man once heralded as the "undisputed voice of Africa"—was exiled in Guinea. These dramatic transformations unfolded against the backdrop of a major turning point in the Cold War. Between February and April 1966, sixty thousand U.S. soldiers poured into South Vietnam, pushing the total U.S. troops to over a quarter-million. The Vietnam War, having long symbolized the global struggle between colonial power and Third World nationalism, was now an American war.

These changes reshaped global politics in the late 1960s. However, in July 1966, most observers assumed the future would be much like the recent past. When the International Court of Justice unveiled its controversial ruling on South West Africa that month, African nationalists responded with surprise and indignation, born from the widespread conviction that international trends had coalesced already around progressive, postcolonial ends. South Africa was the new Nazi Germany, according to African Group delegates, and "any hesitation to support decisive action" against it would be "judged by history as appeasement and abetment of racism and fascism."[1] Many U.S. policymakers also viewed events that month through the prism of older narratives. In a policy review released just four days after the ICJ decision, officials in the U.S. State Department proudly framed American programs in "less developed countries" as evidence that the United States was moving beyond the short-term, self-interested policies of former colonial powers. Drawing on tenets of Great Society liberalism, the authors confidently declared, "We can, if we wish, be increasingly single-minded in the pursuit of long-range economic development in the world."[2]

This was an exciting and contentious time. Concepts of justice, freedom, and order—long defined in ways that reified pan-European ideas—were being reassessed to accommodate the moral imperatives of decolonization. The actors who participated in this global discussion often conceptualized their conversation differently and framed its stakes in contradictory ways, but they shared one common assumption about the world they inhabited—it was moving forward. For African nationalists, American policymakers, and countless other groups, the lines around what seemed possible were broad. This latent sense of optimism gave debates like the one surrounding the apartheid question a sense of vitality and dynamism. For the protagonists, it was not unimaginable that South Africa's "outmoded" system of racial discrimination—sitting defiantly in the path of the progressive history itself—could be defeated in their lifetime.

By the end of the decade, however, stories of postcolonial justice were giving way to widespread disillusionment and cynicism. As these transformations accelerated, pessimism began to take hold in many intellectual circles, and the linear vision of world events which garnered such influence in the years after decolonization fell rapidly by the wayside. The Americanization of the Vietnam War eroded the power of the U.S. economy and undermined faith in Washington's development mission abroad; it also convinced many members of the global community that the United States could no longer be viewed as a neutral arbiter in the struggle against colonialism. Nkrumah's fall in Ghana, likewise, foreshadowed upheavals that swept through Africa in the late 1960s. When coupled with urban riots in the United States, these changes brought new, difficult answers to old questions about black equality and civil rights. Only ten days after the ICJ decision on South West Africa, South Africa's ambassador in the United States surveyed contemporary trends and presciently speculated that, for South Africa's enemies, the situation would "get worse before it [got] better." And "when it [was] all over there [would] be changes in the lives of everyone, Negro and White alike. What, no one can foretell." But it would be a very different world.[3]

This chapter examines one small part of the story of the late 1960s. Focusing on the period between 1966 and 1968, it looks at how the African Group at the

United Nations reformulated its international political strategy in the wake of
the ICJ decision. For six years, African diplomats had used their institutional
authority in the General Assembly to build a case for U.N. sanctions against
South Africa, passing an assortment of resolutions and establishing a durable
alliance with Asian nations at the United Nations. In the wake of the ICJ's ruling,
the African Group took unprecedented action by demanding the unilateral revocation of South Africa's Mandate over South West Africa. The action shocked
some members of the international community. In subsequent months, as the
limits of the Group's influence grew increasingly self-evident, efforts at the
United Nations began to shift from the sanctions fight to propaganda activities,
with broadly inclusive concepts of human rights supplanting African nationalist
discourse at the thematic forefront of the international apartheid debate. This
shift not only eroded the authority of African nationalism; it reoriented the geopolitical terrain of the struggle against South Africa in the late 1960s.

The United States seemed to sit on the sidelines of these transformations.
To most observers in the Third World, American policy toward South Africa
changed very little in the late 1960s, defined still by criticism of apartheid,
support of the arms embargo, and opposition to economic sanctions under
chapter VII of the U.N. Charter. Under the surface, however, subtle changes
were taking place in Washington, DC. As the war in Vietnam escalated and
the U.S. gold standard buckled under the weight of "growth liberalism,"[4] bureaucratic momentum in the Johnson administration swung sharply from the
State Department's African and International Organization bureaus toward
the Department of Defense, the Central Intelligence Agency, and the Department of Treasury. The result was the abandonment of the confrontational
mindset that shaped U.S. foreign policy during the mid-1960s. By the end of
1968, Washington had accepted the status quo in South Africa and was beginning to discuss ways to curtail the influence of anti-apartheid advocates at the
international level. The foundation for rapprochement between the United
States and South Africa was established by the time Richard Nixon entered
the White House in early 1969.

When viewed together, these parallel stories reveal an important intersection
in global history. For African nationalists, the debate over South Africa was
always bigger than the internal policies of the Nationalist government. It was the
barometer of African political power, offering a concrete way to measure the international community's engagement with Third World nationalism. The United
States, although not entangled directly in this fight, shaped the arena of political
possibility during the early and mid-1960s. Criticism of South Africa's policies
certainly did not dissipate with the U.S. policy shift of 1968, but the mindset of
the U.S. government came to limit the space for particular forms of anti-apartheid
criticism. The unique linkages that buttressed and empowered the international

anti-apartheid movement in the years after Sharpeville—based on the fragile marriage of territorial autonomy and economic development with pan-racial unity and postcolonial justice—ballooned and then deflated in the final years of the Johnson administration. A much stronger National Party and a very different anti-apartheid movement emerged from this collapse.

Cutting the Knot

As early as August 1965, a year before it was handed down, African diplomats were publicly casting the ICJ ruling as a turning point in the anti-apartheid struggle, claiming that if the Security Council failed to assume its responsibilities in South West Africa, the "movements of liberation would . . . draw their own conclusions" about the U.N.'s future role in global affairs.[5] Behind closed doors, the discussion was no less candid. In a memorandum to the U.N. secretary-general that July, Enuga Reddy, secretary of the Apartheid Committee, admitted that while the "Special Committee and the African group [would] continue to press for economic sanctions" in autumn 1965, committee members were aware that the United States and United Kingdom would not take action that preempted "the International Court decision on South West Africa in 1966."[6] When the Court made its decision in July 1966, African nationalists suffered an undeniably acute strategic blow.

The ruling came at an inopportune time for the African bloc. Its relationship with the liberation movements of southern Africa, always awkward, was growing increasingly strained in the months before the decision. The first signs of trouble had appeared at the inaugural meeting of the Organization of African Unity in 1963, when the liberation movements of southern Africa collectively submitted a memorandum that asked African heads of state to reject "discrimination or differentiation . . . among us African peoples" and to allow nonstate movements to attain legal rights within African countries and "associate member" status at the semi-annual African Summit meetings. Wrapping their request in the language of pan-Africanism, the movements asserted that because "all Africans" were "freedom fighters," it followed that the stateless peoples of southern Africa deserved "a status commensurate to our position as brothers and comrades . . . who have already won their independence."[7] Citizenship, in other words, should be grounded not in national identity but continental race unity.

The argument highlighted the unreconciled paradox of African nationalist discourse. What was the proper balance between pan-racialism and postcolonial freedom? In the case of the liberation movements, did racial heritage entitle exiled black Africans to equal rights in West, East, and North Africa, or was territorial autonomy—bureaucratic control, literally, of a spatially concrete "nation"—the

only possible pathway to freedom? On the surface, the fight against apartheid softened the edges of such queries in the early 1960s by giving African politicians a
shared project and a defined "other" on the global stage, but beneath the façade
sat an intractable disjuncture that underscored the difference between postcolonial imaginings and governance in postindependence Africa. The African Group,
whose legitimacy flowed from its narrative of postcolonial justice and its claim to
speak for one unified Africa, had a vested interest in downplaying such ideological
contradictions. African nationalist elites needed the tacit support of the liberation
movements as much as nonstate organizations required material assistance from
African governments.

This unresolved paradox led to tensions in the mid-1960s. The OAU's initial
solution had been the African Liberation Committee (ALC). Formed in 1963,
the committee, which consisted of nine OAU member nations, was tasked with
"harmonizing" the relationship between African nation-states and the liberation
movements of southern Africa. It would ensure that African freedom fighters
were "received properly" in African countries, given "training in all sectors," and
provided with necessary "material aid."[8] From the perspective of the liberation
organizations, the arrangement was less than ideal. Within two years the ALC
had cemented the power of African nation-states over exile movements and fragmented older, looser networks of transcontinental cooperation by outsourcing
aid distribution to regional powers like Tanzania and Zambia, which shared borders with Mozambique and Southern Rhodesia.[9] Once free to draw patronage
directly from nationalist leaders through informal clearinghouses like the Bureau
of African Affairs in Accra and the African Association in Cairo, stateless African
organizations now faced fewer options and more regulations.[10] Because nationalist diplomats were at the helm of anti-apartheid strategy, New York City came
to function as the frontline of the fight against the Republic, with events in
southern Africa inexorably recast as debate points, important not on their own
terms but in reference to the overarching idea that only U.N. sanctions could
prevent a racial war in Africa.[11]

The backlash against this system had come into focus by early 1966. At the
African summit meeting in Accra the previous year, the PAC led thirteen other
liberation movements in an open challenge to the ALC's leadership, claiming in
a press conference that the committee no longer "represented Africa's collective
interests."[12] Only seven nonstate organizations—primarily those benefiting
from the ALC's resource distribution methods—did not join in the event. By
November, six of those seven were frustrated enough to participate in a round-
table conference in Algiers, sponsored by the trade-union journal *Revolution et
Travail*, to discuss the future of the ALC. The journal's editors, who also invited
the National Liberation Front of South Vietnam to participate, opened discussions with a damning statement that the "present international conjuncture" was

"characterized by a world-wide imperialist assault" and the "retreat of the revolutionary movement."[13] In discussing recent events, one participant explained that
exiled Africans had "wanted to be part of [the ALC] and not simply observers—
we wanted to take part in the discussions." Another openly attacked the efforts of
the African Group at the United Nations, claiming that "meaningless resolutions" and "sterile accords" harmed "not only the revolutionary movements of
Africa but the true unity of this continent."[14] The conference concluded with the
prescient recommendation that African liberation movements see their fight not
in terms of African nationalism but as part of a shared Third World struggle
against pan-European imperialism.[15] As such, it was time for the movements to
develop material and ideological relationships beyond Africa.

The South West Africa case was a chance for African Group leaders to counter
these trends. It was an opportunity, perhaps the last, to demonstrate that nationalist elites could meaningfully remold the international system in their own
image and force the great powers to take action against the South African government. In the months before the decision, African diplomats made a series of
overtures to the liberation movements, inviting the Pan Africanist Congress and
several South West African organizations to New York City to present their views
at the Special Committee of Twenty-Four and adopted fresh resolutions at the
General Assembly that reaffirmed the legitimacy of the black freedom struggle
for self-determination. The ICJ decision, against this backdrop, was a shock and
a major setback, both eliminating the possibility of U.N. action under article 94
and undermining these tentative overtures to the liberation movements. When
the U.N. General Assembly reconvened in the autumn, the African Group was in
an undeniable bind. Its efforts against South Africa, on the surface at least, had
run their natural course.

In September, the bloc responded with the only move left in its political arse-
nal. The time had come, announced Ghana's delegate in a subcommittee meeting,
to "move beyond talk" and "legal nonsense" and "accept the need for concrete
action." Because the International Court had failed to accept its "moral responsibilities to the oppressed peoples of southern Africa," it fell on the General Assembly itself "to exercise the right of reversion" and "assume responsibility for
the direct administration of the territory" of South West Africa.[16] The proposal's
logic flowed from Ernest Gross's case at the International Court of Justice. The
Republic had forfeited its right to administer the mandated territory ipso facto
because it supported the philosophy of apartheid, an ideology doctrinally opposed to the universal norm of nondiscrimination. Although the Court had
refused to rule on this argument's validity, Africa's U.N. delegates presented their
case directly to their peers at the General Assembly and challenged them to openly
reject its veracity. "Is there a single person who honestly expects that South
Africa—the South Africa of Mr. Verwoerd and Mr. Vorster—will be persuaded to

fulfill its obligations and discharge its responsibilities?" queried the Guinean representative in late September.[17] Apartheid itself—irrespective of the Republic's assertions and evidence—nullified the ability to perform either task. Bolstering this thesis with a General Assembly resolution that officially termed South Africa's policies a "crime against humanity," the African Group outlined a formal plan on September 19. The United Nations would seize control of South West Africa, hold elections within six months on the basis of universal adult suffrage, and oversee the formation of a wholly independent new nation. If the Republic refused to cooperate, the international community had but one logical recourse—action through chapter VII of the U.N. Charter.[18]

Framed by Ghana's representative as the "last chance for peace" in South Africa, the move exposed the mindset among African nationalists in the mid-1960s. The African Group's position derived from a basic assumption: if the United Nations was a truly representative and responsive body, then the organization had a legal and moral obligation to address the demands of its largest constituency. If the international community, particularly the Security Council, failed to acknowledge the demands of this constituency, it followed that African assumptions about decolonization were fundamentally flawed. The end of empire—or the creation of nation-states with voting power at the United Nations—was not the harbinger of genuine independence. The proposal to unilaterally revoke the South West Africa Mandate and use the United Nations to create a new government focused this abstract claim on a concrete issue and forced a Manichean choice upon the rest of the global community. Countries could either support postcolonial justice by terminating the Mandate or acquiesce to neocolonial domination by accepting South Africa's system of apartheid. There was no middle ground. As Guinea's delegate said on September 27, the time had arrived for "the Great Powers"—specifically the "all powerful" United States—to decide "here and now" whether they placed "the principles they profess ahead of their profits."[19]

The ultimatum came to the American policymaking establishment at an awkward time. Assuming falsely that the ICJ case would invalidate the legality of the South West Africa Mandate, State Department officials had spent much of 1965–66 exploring the feasibility of economic sanctions and military action in southern Africa, pushing their Defense Department counterparts, and even private companies, to curtail connections in the Republic, and lobbying the Nationalist government directly to modulate the apartheid system. Members of the Johnson administration understood that the apartheid debate would reach a turning point in the summer of 1966, and their goal was to avoid a showdown that would undermine the prestige of the United Nations. The organization, for U.S. policymakers, was not an agent of postcolonial revolution but a forum for cooperation, collective security, and American-centered consensus. "The SWA issue will be a cruel test of the U.N.," a National Intelligence Estimate summarized in June 1966.

"Should [the organization] prove unable to take substantive action in the case, [it] will receive a damaging blow." Disillusioned by failure, the African Group and its supporters might turn away from Washington's vision of liberal international order. "On the other hand, a decision to take action, e.g., mandatory sanctions against South Africa, could also seriously damage the U.N. if they were not fully imposed or were otherwise not effective." If the United States failed to garner enough support for action at the Security Council—and neither Great Britain nor France seemed willing to take concrete measures after the ICJ decision—then sanctions would cease to function as a meaningful political deterrent in the global arena.[20] The impasse, in the minds of American policymakers, constituted a genuine conundrum.

These geopolitical calculations were complicated by domestic events in the United States. America's racial issues had burst onto the world stage in the form of the civil rights movement in the mid-1950s and early 1960s, culminating after much effort in the landmark civil rights legislation of 1964 and 1965. U.S. officials, particularly those working in the Johnson White House, had come to see the situation in South Africa through the lens of the United States' day-to-day race questions at home. It was in response to domestic issues, for instance, that the president had delivered a high-profile address to African ambassadors just two months before the ICJ decision, explicitly relating the administration's recent civil rights legislation to events at the United Nations.[21] "We will not support policies abroad which are based on the rule of minorities or the discredited notion that men are unequal before the law," the president stated on May 26. "We will not live by a double standard, professing abroad what we do not practice at home or venerating at home what we ignore abroad."[22] Johnson's words, while divorced from the minutiae of the Mandate debate and intended mostly for short-term political consumption—specifically the desire to "make it difficult for Bobby [Kennedy] to get far ahead of [the administration]" on "the question of political liberty for Negro Americans"—nonetheless influenced U.S. tactical options as the African Group articulated its up-or-down proposal on South West Africa that autumn.[23] American policymakers needed to navigate the thicket surrounding the Mandate question at the United Nations in a way that protected Johnson's newly established high ground on questions of race in the United States.[24] By any standard it was a difficult task.

The State Department, particularly the International Organization and African bureaus, headed by Arthur Goldberg and the newly appointed Joseph Palmer, respectively, understood these stakes well. There was little naïveté about the African Group's aims, which centered on the quest to "overthrow the apartheid system in South Africa itself."[25] A State Department report on September 21, issued just days before the African Group submitted its resolution to the General Assembly, explained, "Since the Court judgment of July 18 virtually ruled out the possibility of obtaining a judgment which would provide the basis for action against South Africa under Article 94(2), the Africans must revert to their original objective of mounting their attack on the South African regime under Chapter VII of the Charter." However, because the Security Council had rejected already the argument that apartheid itself constituted a "clear threat to the peace," the African Group's only path forward was "to establish that South African defiance of international law constituted a threat to the peace," which was contingent on the presupposition that "international law" flowed from the African Group's own resolutions at the General Assembly. The State Department would have preferred to send these questions back to the International Court, but it recognized that "the Africans, in their present mood of frustration, [were] likely to reject such deliberate procedure." It was inevitable that the next step would "be debated, not in a legal forum, but in the highly charged political arenas of the Assembly and Security Council."[26]

American officials did their best to parry the African Group's diplomatic offensive. While State Department lawyers admitted that the International Court's earlier advisory decisions had indeed given the U.N. legal authority in South West Africa, they urged Assembly members to appreciate the "financial and organizational limitations of the United Nations," as well as the "authority of the Security Council vis-à-vis the General Assembly."[27] Working in conjunction with Canada, Italy, Ireland, and Japan, Americans developed a counterproposal in October that replaced the words "terminate" and "revoke" with a broader statement that South Africa had "forfeit[ed] its rights under the Mandate" and recommended the formation of a smaller, Western-centric ad hoc commission—not an administrative body under General Assembly control—to "find ways to achieve the purpose of the Mandate" and "recommend means" to help South West Africans "exercise their right of self-determination."[28] The goal, once again, was not to solve the crisis but to keep the United Nations an arena of consensus. By establishing subtle openings for discussion and compromise, the State Department hoped both to push South Africa into negotiations in New York and subvert the African Group's efforts to use the General Assembly in a historically unprecedented way. "This is an action proposal," Goldberg said in a speech on October 12. "It is designed to provide the community of nations promptly with a considered blueprint for united and peaceful action for the benefit of the people of South West Africa." On this "transcendently important issue," the United Nations needed a plan that was "intrinsically sound" and "widely supported," one that would solve the Mandate question without eroding "the authority and prestige of this world body."[29]

These efforts yielded modest, yet important, results. Most obvious, Latin American countries coalesced behind the most important part of the U.S. proposal in late October. On October 26, Mexico and twenty-one other nations submitted a formal amendment to the African resolution that replaced the plan for direct General Assembly administration with an ad hoc committee to "recommend practical means by which the territory should be administered." In presenting these measures, Mexico's representative underscored the importance of consensus and collaboration, explaining that "only through unanimity" could "the United Nations deal with the final stages of this question."[30] But the Latin American amendment, in exchange for African support, did not soften the language of the Mandate's termination. On October 27, U.S. representatives tried attaching a subamendment that replaced the statement that South West Africa was now "the direct responsibility of the United Nations" with the legalistically flexible, "the United Nations has a direct responsibility to preserve the international status of the territory . . . under conditions which will enable South West Africa to exercise its right to self-determination and independence."[31] Nonetheless the Assembly rejected the move, placing State Department officials in an unwelcome bind—they could either abstain from a resolution they had successfully moderated or accept a proposal they half supported.

The State Department chose the latter option, setting the stage for a pair of confrontations in early 1967. The first clash centered on Anglo-American relations. With the British Labour Party's election in 1964 and Southern Rhodesia's controversial unilateral declaration of independence in 1965, the United States and Great Britain had embraced a common policy toward southern Africa in the mid-1960s, culminating in their joint diplomatic entente against Ian Smith and Hendrik Verwoerd in 1965–66. The reasons underlying this effort, however, were dissimilar. Sir Martin Le Quesne, deputy under-secretary of the British Foreign Office, observed in mid-1966 that the Anglo-American partnership had been driven from the mid-1950s through the early 1960s by a shared commitment to decolonization and a mutual fear of communist expansion in Africa. "I think we have now come to the end of this period," he stated in a memorandum that June, after Prime Minister Harold Wilson received a letter from President Johnson suggesting that the president's May speech to African Ambassadors form the cornerstone of Western policy in Africa. "The fact remains that on the question of South Africa the American *optique* is quite different from our own." Le Quesne went on:

> Our attitude is, in a nutshell, that, despite South African unwillingness to lend us the backing which would make our policy against Rhodesia effective, and despite their unwillingness to satisfy the U.N. either over South West Africa or over their racial policies, we simply cannot afford for economic reasons to be drawn or pushed into an economic war with South Africa . . . But in purely economic terms the Americans could afford infinitely more easily than we could to engage in economic sanctions

against South Africa. Indeed I suppose that perhaps their major interest in South Africa is not economic at all.[32]

This underlying disjuncture came into focus during the South West Africa debate.[33] As the United States worked to foster compromise at the General Assembly, concerned primarily with maintaining the organizational integrity of the United Nations, Great Britain openly challenged the "doubtful legality" of the African Group's proposal. During the final plenary meeting on October 27, Lord Hugh Caradon, the United Kingdom representative who had served as a private citizen on the apartheid expert committee only two years earlier, noted that there was no way his country could endorse the Afro-Asian bloc's current plan. The General Assembly was not designed for unilateral, majoritarian political action. Under the Charter, he emphasized, its power was limited to passing a "formal declaration" that ended "the South African Government's rights under the Mandate" and forming a new "advisory commission to study all aspects to the action."[34] Great Britain coupled this public declaration with a private rejoinder to the United States acknowledging explicitly that Whitehall would be "forced into a veto in the Council" if the African plan survived the ad hoc committee. From a semantic perspective, it was essential, according to the Foreign Office, to frame the upcoming conversation around "how people of the territory are to be enabled to exercise their right to self-determination— rather than how South West Africa can be administered by the United Nations." If "tailored to this end," South African administration of the territory could be presented as "not automatically incompatible" with the revocation of the Mandate.[35]

The overture foreshadowed a second confrontation, which unfolded within the ad hoc committee in early 1967. Although the African Group's influence was curtailed by the composition of the committee—members included Canada, Chile, Ethiopia, Italy, Japan, Mexico, Nigeria, Pakistan, Senegal, the United Arab Republic, and the United States—African diplomats acted quickly, submitting a proposal in March that mirrored their October draft resolution. The General Assembly would take "direct temporary control" of the territory through a United Nations Council for South West Africa, which would oversee the withdrawal of South African personnel and establish a constituent assembly to draft a constitution, before holding elections and granting the territory its independence no later than June 1968. In outlining these proposals, Ethiopia's delegate acknowledged that the African bloc was forming a new precedent. "The two previous examples of a United Nations administration"—Libya and West Papua—"had been carried out at the behest of, and by agreement with, the principal parties concerned." In the case of South West Africa, however, "the existing administration in the territory was based on the unacceptable principles of apartheid" and the United

Nations would need to "start from scratch."[36] Attempting to forestall Western criticism, Nigeria's delegate demanded that the ad hoc committee focus solely on this task. There was no need to "chase additional information and consider other issues like economic and social conditions in the territory, or legal questions surrounding the status" of South West Africa. A "crash training program" could be provided to form "the core of the country's future leadership," but nothing was possible until the United Nations pushed South Africa out of the territory.[37]

The position flowed directly from the logic of African nationalism. African elites had emerged from an intellectual milieu where European colonialism, framed often in monolithic terms, was understood as the source of all social discontent in Africa—responsible for the fragmentation of the continent's natural value systems and the retardation of its economic progress. This assumption was tacitly affirmed by the United Nations itself, where membership and prestige hinged on bureaucratic control of fixed territorial space and economic development existed as a universal principle delivered by agents of government. The effort to institutionalize and legitimize Africa's own understanding of the nation—to make apartheid literally inconsonant with membership in the world community—had been the cornerstone of African discourse since before 1960. However, with liberation movements turning away from nationalist leadership and African heads of state confronting unexpected forms of domestic upheaval in the mid-1960s, the internal contradictions of this ideology were growing more apparent.[38] The South West Africa question provided clarity at an ambiguous moment. If the African Group could prove its case and push the United Nations into action on African terms, it could potentially bolster its prestige on the world stage, shore up support at home, and bring the liberation organizations back into the nationalist fold.

It was an ambitious and somewhat desperate task. Because Latin American and Western countries were unwilling to acquiesce to African demands, debate at the ad hoc committee quickly took the form it had in the autumn of 1966. This time, however, the African delegates refused to revise their position. "There can be no negotiation since there is nothing to negotiate," Ethiopia's delegate announced in mid-April. The Western proposals—which envisioned a special U.N. representative who would make a "comprehensive survey" of the situation to determine the conditions necessary for independence[39]—"were vague and permissive," based on the view that South Africa held de facto power in the territory.[40] Latin American proposals too were insufficient. Supportive of the council idea but eager to promote dialogue with South African authorities, their plan "fail[ed]" to articulate the "terms of negotiation" or outline proper coercive measures if the Republic "proved obstructive."[41] Africa's proposals alone were realistic, according to Guinea's representative, because they "confront[ed] the possibility of South

Africa's refusal to co-operate." They accepted that because "[n]o-one was [now] lawfully responsible for the administration of South West Africa," the United Nations was "duty-bound to fill the vacuum."[42]

None of the three sides budged in April, leading the ad hoc committee to submit three separate proposals to the General Assembly at the end of the month. The breaking point in this diplomatic morass came when the United Nations called a Special Session—only the fifth in its twenty-year history—to deal with South West Africa. The Soviet Union, which had lent support to nearly every other African resolution on southern Africa in the 1960s, opened the meeting with a speech that pointedly questioned the wisdom of the African proposal. "In every other former colonial territory it has been demonstrated that problems such as the establishment of a government apparatus can be solved [only] under conditions of independence without outside interference," the Russian delegate stated on April 24. Why then would the Africans embrace a U.N. council that the "Western Powers would surely" use to "delay" the territory's freedom? It was better, according to the Soviet delegate, to grant South West Africa its independence and turn the whole issue over to the OAU.[43] The move—rejected vehemently by the African Group—underscored the U.S.S.R.'s "great power dilemma," a British official in New York City explained on May 10. "On the one hand they seek to pose as strong supporters of Black Africa against Pretoria. On the other hand they do not want active intervention in South West Africa since United Nations intervention to them still means American intervention."[44] Confronted with the opportunity to establish a new precedent, the Soviet Union decided instead to send a clear message to the Africans that the Eastern bloc's threshold of support had been reached.

The unanticipated move robbed the African Group of its diplomatic cover at the Security Council and highlighted the Cold War's continued importance in the decolonized world. Although African elites claimed that the fight against apartheid was bigger than the superpower contest, their contentions existed within a particular geopolitical context. Their tenuous gains in the early and mid-1960s unfolded in space opened by the West's desire to establish equilibrium between its Cold War security interests and the Third World's moral rhetoric. As Harold Macmillan had explained in the early months of 1960, Western policymakers accepted Africa's "national consciousness" as an irrevocable aspect of global politics and wanted badly for African leaders to build partnerships with the West in the postcolonial era. However, neither Washington nor London ever recognized apartheid as an existential threat to the international community. Even the most ardent supporters of sanctions against South Africa always saw the Republic's importance through the prism of Western hegemony. Within this geopolitical environment, Moscow's tactical shift eliminated the final rationale for Western action against South Africa. The Security Council was now unanimous in its rejection of the Council of South West Africa plan. The African Group's position in New York now rested on a controversial, fragile assertion: the General Assembly had a right to dictate the terms of Security Council action.

The United States took a hard line as discussions climaxed in late April. As the Africans entered last minute negotiations for a compromise resolution with the Latin Americans, Goldberg outlined the U.S. position at the General Assembly.[45] "The world is already suffering from too many confrontations," he said on April 26. "We have no case to imitate the conqueror Alexander, who when challenged to solve the puzzle of the Gordian knot took a sword and cut it through. In this day and age the U.N. should not be in a hurry to use the sword; rather we must apply ourselves to the task of untying the knot."[46] When Africans and Latin Americans emerged with a proposal to use the Council of South West Africa to discuss withdrawal options with South Africa—omitting whole paragraphs that explicitly called on the Security Council to punish the Republic under chapter VII—the United States nonetheless labeled the measures "unreasonable" and "extreme" and led a wave of thirty abstentions against the resolution.[47] By the time the Council of South West Africa formed officially in mid-June, it was a shadow of its imagined self, devoid of superpower support and hampered by meager finances. In August, council members wrote a letter of protest to the Nationalist government; that winter, it recommended renaming the territory "Namibia." By 1968, it had effectively ceased to function.

Beyond the Turning Point

Kitwe, Zambia, was an unusual place to convene a major gathering on apartheid. Established as a railway depot and mining town by imperialist Cecil Rhodes during the 1930s, the city embodied many of the ambiguities of the region's colonial past. The individuals who converged there in mid-1967 shared these ambiguities. Scion of one of Uganda's well-connected families, Apollo Kironde could easily have been a bureaucrat in the imperial system—he had read law in Europe and passed the bar in Great Britain—but he served instead as his country's first ambassador to the United Nations and the assistant to the secretary-general. On U Thant's behalf, Kironde delivered the event's opening speech on July 25, 1967. "It is my honour and privilege to welcome all of you who have responded to the invitation to attend the international Seminar on *apartheid*, racial discrimination and colonialism," he said to the partially full assembly hall. Apologizing for the last minute change in venue—the proceedings had been slated to take place in Dar-es-Salaam until late June, when Tanzania's president unexpectedly rescinded his country's invitation to play host—Kironde noted that the participants' flexibility was a "sure indication of the importance [of] the subject before us."[48]

The meeting had been pitched to the General Assembly as an international brainstorming session that would bring together an array of diplomats, nongovernmental organizations (NGOs), and political experts. The delegates in attendance, however, hailed almost exclusively from Africa and Asia.[49] In the months before the seminar, discussions among the organizers had centered primarily on United Nations' future role in the anti-apartheid struggle. "I have a feeling that we agree that U.N. activity should enter a new phase," said an official in a private letter to one of the liberation movements that May. The time had come to reassess the "whole question of legitimacy and legality."[50] For the past six years, the African Group had tethered its understanding of both concepts to action through the United States' liberal international system. Militarily weak and economically undeveloped, African states had used their influence at the General Assembly—politically through their committee posts and resolutions, and intellectually through postcolonial discourse—to push Asian nations and the United States toward the anti-apartheid cause. Gains could be registered, but dissension was acute in 1967. As delegates gathered in Kitwe, the Nationalist government sat "stronger than ever" in Pretoria, and African leaders—frustrated by their own setbacks in the global arena—were beginning to express private "contempt" for the liberation movements of southern Africa.[51]

Kironde's speech effectively framed the transitional nature of the moment. "Where there is no vision, the people perish," he told his audience that morning. The fight against South Africa had commenced with "the unanimous adoption by the General Assembly of the Declaration of the Granting of Independence to Colonial Countries and Peoples" in 1961—a resolution that linked independence to racial equality and equated freedom with territorial autonomy, giving Africans the institutional leverage to push the Security Council toward the arms embargo of 1963. These measures had sent a "clear signal" to the international community that the United Nations was dedicated to eradicating all "vestiges of racialism and discrimination in the municipal law of Member States." In 1965, this mission was extended, Kironde continued, when "for the first time" the "processions of Chapter VII of the Charter were invoked against the illegal minority regime of Southern Rhodesia." The "imposition of economic sanctions against a regime which had violated the commonly accepted principles of nations was a major step with far-reaching consequences in international relations." However, as exemplified in the South West Africa debate in April, the anti-apartheid movement had subsequently stalled. Harkening back to former British Prime Minister Harold Macmillan's famous Cape Town address of 1960, Kironde concluded:

> The winds of change have swept right across the continent of Africa from west to east and from north to central Africa but they seem to have come up against a stony wall running somewhere across the southern

part of the African continent. Not only have the winds produced no change beneficial to the non-white people living in this part of Africa but the attitude of the white minority groups that have settled in these areas seems to have hardened and the attainment of self-determination of the non-white inhabitants of these regions indefinitely deferred.[52]

For nearly two weeks, seminar participants debated how to change this dynamic. Discussion sessions in Kitwe explored the relationship between the West's foreign policy and its financial interests in southern Africa, apartheid's affect on international peace and security, and the feasibility of new tactical measures against the Republic and its allies. U.N.-appointed experts—including the chairman of the Apartheid Committee, the president of the Mozambique Liberation Front (FRELIMO), and a well-known anti-apartheid writer—presented papers, and government officials engaged in lengthy discussions with the liberation groups. "This Seminar has been convened not as an academic exercise, but to analyse the weakness of international action so far and formulate recommendations for more effective action in consultation with the spokesmen and leaders of the oppressed people of southern Africa and her friends," the chairman of the seminar declared on August 4. "We did not come here to exchange formalities and to agree on meaningless platitudes. We came here to discuss more effective *action*."[53]

The seminar's final proposals, however, flowed mostly from the African Group's well-trod initiatives. Participants called, for instance, for the creation of a U.N. office to document examples of South Africa's crimes against humanity and for more funds for refugee assistance. They asked for additional donations to the U.N. Trust Fund and protested the treatment of prisoners in South Africa. Most important, the delegates returned to chapter VII of the Charter, lamenting innumerable times that Africa's peace and security rested on the implementation of sanctions against the Republic.[54] The seminar broke new ground most obviously on the rhetorical level. Its final communiqué explicitly linked Africa's recent domestic upheavals to the policies of discrimination in southern Africa for the first time. The "forces of apartheid"—with the Nationalist government "playing the primary role"—were no longer content simply to oppress black South Africans; they were now engaged "in a deliberate and calculated attempt" to undermine "the rightful and lawful Governments of independent Africa." The recent coups in Ghana and elsewhere were the result of Pretoria's "psychological warfare, espionage activities, and sabotage." The West's refusal to stop apartheid—its unwillingness to support the African Group's proposal to form the new nation of Namibia—had resulted in neocolonialism in Africa.[55]

This mindset formed the cornerstone of the vision that emerged from the Kitwe Seminar. Although many African delegates had drifted toward anti-American views in the mid-1960s—particularly after the U.N. intervention in Congo and the U.S. takeover of the Vietnam War—the Group generally appreciated that the United States, because of its unique influence over Great Britain and France and distinctly anticolonial national narrative, was the pivot in the diplomatic fight against South Africa and the key to passing sanctions at the Security Council. The discussions and presentations at Kitwe denounced this view and painted a negative, conspiratorial portrait of Washington's intentions in the world. An "unholy alliance" had formed from the "Cape to Katanga," claimed one research paper, supported by a "giant economic complex" that originated in the United States. Economic sanctions were still "the most appropriate peaceful measures under the United Nations Charter," but it was "unrealistic to ignore the fact that the main trading partners of southern Africa" were simply "unwilling to implement these measures."[56] The United Nations had become the "graveyard of African subjects and matters," an African representative explained. "Small nations have no voice: they can speak but they will be ignored. We have no hope." The seminar's "one useful purpose" was to "put a page in the record of history" so "that when other generations come, they will see that people at this particular point were disappointed in what was being done in southern Africa."[57]

With this deepening pessimism came new assertions about the relationship between African nation-states and the liberation movements. Because exile communities faced both suppression from "South African racists" and "certain international conspiracy," violence stood as "the only means of salvation."[58] On the surface, this conclusion built logically on the African Group's admonitions that conflict would become inevitable if Western states failed to join the anti-apartheid cause. However, it was coupled with a subtle yet significant rejoinder. "Whatever we do at the international level—whether as governments or in anti-apartheid movements and other popular organizations—we need to recognize in all humility that our role is but secondary," suggested the chairman of the Apartheid Committee in one of the seminar's most widely discussed papers. "We do not aspire to liberate—which would be tantamount to substituting ourselves for the South Africa people—but to assist the liberation, as that is our duty if we are loyal to our convictions."[59] Violence, in other words, was not a pan-African project. It fell squarely on the shoulders of black South Africans.

The semantic shift highlighted the widening fissure between the ideals of African nationalism and the realities of the liberation struggle. African delegates had confidently cast themselves as the senior statesmen of the anti-apartheid movement in the wake of second-wave decolonization, responsible for patronage and leadership in the fight against South Africa. Now, with the various prongs of the Group's strategic initiative defeated on the international stage, African leaders pushed away from their own promises of change. Pan-racial identity was important, but only indigenous South Africans could truly topple the Nationalist government. For many African representatives, steeped increasingly in regionally specific, national narratives that conflated conditions in southern Africa with earlier circumstances in the rest of the continent, the liberation organizations deserved blame for the setbacks of recent years. The world was "cruel and cold," Zambia's foreign minister declared at the seminar. "Therefore the freedom fighters, wherever they are and whatever they are doing, must get down to earth. Making good speeches in Lusaka, Cairo, Dar es Salaam or anywhere else [was] not the answer to the fight."[60] The liberation movements—classified now as distinct from the broader community of African peoples—held principal responsibility for their freedom.

Collectively, these sentiments added a powerful subtext to the seminar's final recommendations. Chapter VII was important, no less than it had been in 1961, but the African Group was not responsible for adjusting Western policy. Having approached the United Nations as a political battleground through the early and mid-1960s—a forum to pursue concrete strategic objectives—delegates at Kitwe now outlined a more restrictive vision of the organization. Indeed, the seminar's only original "action" proposal focused on information and nonstate activism, rooted in the emerging view that the United Nations was best utilized to "counteract the massive and misleading propaganda campaign" of South Africa and encourage "non-governmental organizations to play a more effective role in opposition to racism and colonialism."[61] Neither premise was wholly novel in 1967, but Kitwe effectively formalized the primacy of such tactics over the fight for sanctions and elevated what had been means in the anti-apartheid contest to an end in its own right.[62] The United Nations was a "knowledge source" and "organizing center," one expert paper explained.[63] Its activities would not liberate South African blacks, but they could help legitimize the activities of freedom fighters south of the Zambezi River. The U.N.'s principal importance, in short, came from its ability to wrap nongovernmental activism in the cloth of moral authority.

Many observers grasped the significance of this strategic change. As the U.N. Secretariat centralized anti-apartheid information activities in 1967—a move mandated by the Kitwe Seminar and orchestrated by the newly formed Special Unit on Apartheid—permanent members of the Security Council lamented the newly porous boundary between politics and knowledge at the United Nations. Examining the Special Unit's initial publication in 1967, British officials commented that while the document was simply "an up-dating of similar studies" previously "circulated by the Special Committee on Apartheid," the "new format" underscored the unit's "clear intention to promote publicity through the U.N. sales network." It was unclear whether readers would garner new knowledge on the "evils of apartheid," the official continued, but the document gave "maximum publicity to Western investment in South Africa." This newfound emphasis gave the British government pause. "We could of course protest that apartheid is a human rights question and that foreign trade does not determine the political systems within a country, but we would find the United Nations impervious to this argument."[64] Americans articulated a similar diagnosis. For all intents and purposes, the African Group had been halted in the political realm. However, the result was not the end of anti-apartheid activism but a series of unintended consequences. The creation of the Special Unit was leading to "efforts at persuasion" that were "less [politically] specific" but more ubiquitous, with the apartheid question, in the process, being transformed from a "regional [African] problem" into a flashpoint in a larger, integrated story of neocolonial power in the world. The use of U.N. funds to promote the linkage between Western economic interests and white racism in southern Africa, problematic on its own terms, was setting an "unnerving precedent" with "wide implications" for Washington's continued leadership in New York.[65]

Anxiety over this development was not limited to representatives of Western governments. In early August 1967, only a week after the publication of the Kitwe Seminar's conclusions, G. L. Obhrai, an Indian official at the U.N. Office of Public Information (OPI), bristled at the implications of Africa's new proposals. "The question seems to me to boil down to this: is the Office of Public Information henceforth to be permitted, indeed required, to function, not merely as a purveyor of objective and factual information about the aims and activities of the United Nations, but also as a public-relations agency actively engaged in the actual promotion of those activities and the attainment of those aims?" He continued, "Are we to remain an Office of Information or become an agency for political action?" Quoting former U.N. Secretary-General Dag Hammarskjold, Obhrai forcefully answered his own question:

> The United Nations should not indulge in propaganda—*for itself or any of the positions taken within the Organization.* Thus, public information activities are information activities in the true sense of the word, not a selling operation in any kind of disguise. One sometimes hears it said that there is nothing wrong in making propaganda for something that is good. This argument seems to me to be a very dangerous one, as everyone resorting to propaganda certainly feels that he is serving a good purpose, whatever his aims may be.[66]

Enuga Reddy—the former secretary of the Apartheid Committee and now head of the Special Unit on Apartheid—had participated in the Kitwe discussions in July and August, and he did his best to deflect such criticism. To Western officials, he argued that the unit's emphasis on economic investment was simply a reflection of discussions among U.N. member-states. The unit was merely a "dumping ground for resolutions on any aspect of Apartheid."[67] To fellow U.N.

bureaucrats, he took a stronger line, pushing back against the idea that Kitwe's recommendations broke exceptional ground. Although "the O.P.I." was being asked to "intensify information on the work of the U.N. organs on apartheid," it was not "undertak[ing] any research or initiat[ing] any 'propaganda,'" he explained in a memorandum in September. "The effectiveness of the information would depend mainly on the work of the Committee."[68] The distinction was perhaps clearer to those within the U.N. building than to outside observers—even Reddy admitted later that his efforts were probably "improper for a civil servant who was supposed to be 'neutral'"—but his rationalizations nonetheless garnered the support of the secretary-general. Anti-apartheid publications proliferated at the United Nations after 1967.[69] The Special Unit on Apartheid, despite its relatively meager budget and small staff, slowly supplanted the African Group at the nexus of U.N. anti-apartheid activities. By linking official committee reports at the General Assembly with papers by the United Nations Educational, Scientific and Cultural Organization (UNESCO), the International Labor Organization, and other expert organizations, the unit helped institutionalize a uniquely activist portrait of the problems in southern Africa.

The unit's understanding of anti-apartheid activism, however, differed markedly from African nationalist discourse at the General Assembly. In private correspondence, Reddy openly articulated the aims and views of his unit. Because "the African group ceased to be a dynamic force" in 1966, it was essential to diversify the struggle and reach out to new groups interested in the future of South Africa. "To keep the issue alive," he explained, "all organizations" needed "to engage in great activity at their *own* level and according to their *own* policies." Some efforts "may be purely humanitarian. Others may be pacifist or limited to specific aspects, etc. Action at any level is useful. It is only by involvement that people will learn and take the next step."[70] The unit strove, with this in mind, to shift the language of anti-apartheid criticism from African nationalism to universal human rights. By foregrounding publications on topics like education, law, and prison conditions in South Africa—downplaying abstract debates on the relationship of race and the nation—the unit appealed intentionally to "larger groups in the world" with interests in "humanitarian and human rights" questions. This effort, far from "diverting the issue," offered a way "out of the impasse" at the General Assembly.[71] The United Nations would provide information on South Africa, encoding apartheid as a global crisis with broad moral implications, and nonstate activists and organizations would take autonomous action in their own local environments.

This strategy, advanced principally and purposely in the discursive realm both reflected and reified the global shift away from territorial forms of political consciousness in the late 1960s. For six years, the African Group, sitting at the forefront of the apartheid struggle, had rooted its identity in a particular vision of the postcolonial nation—an entity juxtaposed imaginatively to empire, capable of delivering economic development and racial justice to people within the space known as Africa—and treated apartheid as both a threat to African nationalism and the unifying "other" of pan-Africanism. U.N. intervention in South Africa was necessitated by the supposed universality of this postcolonial state, as well as Africa's control of the agenda of the United Nations.[72]

What emerged from the milieu of 1967 was a less discrete and more pervasive anti-apartheid movement. The seeds of this shift were woven into discussions dating from 1946—nongovernmental actors had long appealed to the United Nations for moral support and political leverage and the anti-apartheid movement in North America and Europe was expanding incrementally throughout the 1960s.[73] These efforts bloomed in the months surrounding the Kitwe Seminar, as the African diplomats surrendered their claims of leadership in the anti-apartheid fight and U.N. bureaucrats adopted a more explicitly activist stance on the global stage.[74] Nineteen sixty-eight, declared the Year of Human Rights by the United Nations, saw the Republic's policies framed as morally unjust not simply for pan-African or postcolonial reasons, but because apartheid disregarded liberties inherent to all humans, such as life, security, freedom of assembly, freedom of movement, and equality under law.[75] These linkages, reified by the U.N. Office of Public Information as it published "millions of pamphlets in over sixty languages" that year, became the centerpiece of anti-apartheid discourse at the United Nations for years to come.[76] The norm of nondiscrimination, formulated at the International Court of Justice in the mid-1960s, reemerged in strictly positivist terms, framed as an individual birthright rather than a philosophical national imperative. Apartheid was illegitimate not simply because it defied the inevitability of decolonization, but because it embodied a worldview that was out of step with the shared values of all peoples in the world community. As a delegate at the 1968 Human Rights conference in Tehran explained, "Neither borders nor military power" would "delay indefinitely" the South African people's "achievement of rights fundamental to all men."[77]

This subtle semantic shift—an outgrowth of the African Group's setbacks—overlapped with equally important changes in Washington. Ironically, just as African diplomats were publicly renouncing the United Nation's capacity to deliver postcolonial justice, American policymakers were quietly asking new questions about the organization's future as the "forum" and "safety valve" of the global arena.[78] The Johnson administration's leadership efforts were buckling everywhere in 1967. That March, Martin Luther King Jr.—a supporter of the president's effort to revive and reform liberalism—gave a widely publicized speech against the Vietnam War, tacitly linking the plight of nonwhite people in the United States to the treatment of Vietnamese citizens on the other side of the world. The next month, thousands of activists converged on the U.N. building in

New York, previewing the march in October that would bring over one hundred thousand protesters to Washington. Placed alongside racial violence in cities around the United States that summer, these developments formed a dark cloud on Johnson's domestic political horizon. The outlook was no better in the global arena. In May, Egypt's Gamal Abdel Nasser challenged U.S. efforts in the Middle East by expelling the United Nations Emergency Force, stationed in the region after the 1956 war, from the Sinai Peninsula, setting the stage for Israel's preemptive attack and the divisive Six-Day War. President Johnson may have viewed himself as a moderate man of the political center but the world around him was rapidly clustering toward either end of his imagined political spectrum.

As global politics grew more tumultuous, bureaucrats in Washington began reconsidering American policy toward apartheid. In late 1966, William Duggan of the Policy Planning Council outlined a case for "Constructive Reinvolvement" in South Africa. Subtly lamenting Mennen Williams's heightened influence on U.S.-South Africa relations between 1963 and 1966, the paper—circulated to a small coterie of top officials in the White House, State Department, and Defense Department—argued that U.S. policy had bifurcated in recent years, with a cohort of liberal officials pushing disengagement on the basis of the "marriage" between U.S. civil rights goals and black South African aims, and others developing policy based on concrete economic, strategic, and political factors. Recent events made it clear that Washington needed to reconcile the tension between these approaches. "It is the prime thesis of this paper that an international program of full or partial sanctions against South Africa would *not succeed*," Duggan stated. By pretending otherwise in recent years, the United States had simply eroded its own power and falsely heightened the expectations of African states hoping to influence the administration's behavior. After outlining possible courses of action, Duggan proposed a plan that involved a three-year "moratorium" on South African issues and direct diplomacy in South Africa on the basis of no sanctions. By drawing the Republic as close as possible to the West— through exchange programs, cultural and information activities, economic relations, VIP visits, and technology sharing—the White House could "evolve" the apartheid system in ways that reflected American values.[79]

The Defense Department agreed fully and began pushing against the State Department's affinity for U.N. diplomacy in early 1967. In January, Assistant Secretary of Defense John McNaughton asked Secretary Robert McNamara to open a dialogue directly with Dean Rusk to counter the "strong forces favoring a more extreme position" against South Africa. "Up to now, the U.S. seems to have been working on the promise that we must make every effort to satisfy African aspirations on Southern Africa issues," McNaughton claimed. "The wiser course of action—particularly when looking to longer-term relationships—would seem to lay in dealing more frankly with key African leaders," not the African

Group as a whole. The United Nations was more a distraction to U.S. interests than a reflection of American values in the world—and it was time for a more "realistic" stance abroad.[80]

The first step involved a hard look at American interests in South Africa. Economic sanctions would cost the United States between $250–300 million, and the United Kingdom about $840 million, which effectively precluded any chance of British participation. Furthermore, McNaughton explained, South Africa controlled over 70 percent of the West's annual gold output, giving the country powerful leverage in an economic war. Then there were military issues. To blockade South West Africa, the United States would need to commit four carrier task forces, consisting of four carriers, twenty-four destroyers, and three submarines. "In [the] face of present U.S. military involvement in Vietnam, it would be impossible to participate in a military operation of this magnitude without a substantial increase in our present military posture, including a call-up of reserves."[81] The State Department African Bureau's embrace of sanctions in 1965–66 had been nothing more than liberal adventurism based on a naïve, increasingly outmoded, sense of moral certitude.

McNaughton's argument dovetailed with sentiment in many sectors of the State Department in 1967. A department paper entitled "African Problems," prepared for a National Security Council meeting in July, offered an equally pessimistic, almost cynical assessment of the United States' waning influence over the apartheid debate. "Facing the problem of opposing tendencies—to associate with South Africa or to disengage from it entirely—the pressure has been strong [in recent years] to take actions which swing between the two extremes," the paper explained. A fully consistent policy was "probably impossible at this time, since the policies at each end of the spectrum" had "strong attraction and considerable support."[82] The United States lacked the ability to appease its critics and protect its interests. Newly appointed Undersecretary of State Nicholas Katzenbach framed the problem more succinctly during the NSC meeting itself, bluntly concluding that "no solution" existed to the current impasse at the General Assembly.[83]

By September, when the NSC convened again to discuss the upcoming U.N. session, Arthur Goldberg—perhaps the administration's strongest remaining advocate for action against South Africa—was on the defensive. Acknowledging that his views no longer "prevail[ed] in the Administration," he lamented that American "dealings with South Africa [were] over-extensive and [did] not advance our national security." The United States gained few military advantages from the Republic, in his mind, and American investments in Africa were "many, many times larger than U.S. holdings in South Africa." However, Katzenbach and others flatly rejected such views, and insisted that Congress would never support sanctions or military action in southern Africa.[84] The planning paper for the meeting captured the emerging consensus within the administration, explaining that African delegations had gone beyond the United States' threshold of support in pursuit of "movement" and "change in the status quo" in South Africa. Although Washington's "failure since the 21st GA to meet African expectations ... [would] make [it] a target for more widespread attacks than in the past," policymakers needed to "continue with positions that discourage illusions, among others, that the U.S. might be willing to move further than we know to be the case."[85] Two and one-half years earlier, the State Department's official policy paper on South Africa had used similar words quite differently, declaring that the time had arrived for an "alternative to the status quo policy" toward Pretoria.[86] Now, with 53 percent of Americans disapproving of the president's approach toward foreign policy and Third World nations openly framing U.S. policy in neocolonial terms, the administration adopted a more restrictive stance toward affairs in the region.

This shift reflected the institutionalization of new conclusions about both the liberation movements and the African nation-states. Whereas State Department officials had considered political violence in South Africa inevitable during the early and mid-1960s, the intelligence community sharply rejected such claims in 1967. "The often widespread negative feelings of the blacks of southern Africa toward the white regimes have not automatically translated into positive allegiance to the liberation cause, much less to a particular liberation group," a National Intelligence Estimate stated in November. "Especially to the blacks in the bush, the liberation movements are often unknown, distant, or even alien, as in cases where they are identified with hostile tribes."[87] This diagnosis mirrored the intelligence community's conclusions on the upheavals within independent African states. Unrest in Accra and elsewhere was not the consequence of communist subversion or capitalist intrigue. "The most immediate threat to African governments [was] internal and indigenous," a CIA memorandum explained in October. "It usually stem[med] from disaffected native elements often motivated by narrow tribal, personal, or professional considerations."[88] Taken to their logical conclusion, such analyses offered a strong disincentive for further confrontation with South Africa over apartheid. The alternative to white rule—once embraced by segments of the U.S. government as a solution to Washington's credibility problem among African nationalists—was now anathema.

By December, Katzenbach and Undersecretary of State for Political Affairs Eugene Rostow were even reassessing the wisdom of the 1963 arms embargo. For Rostow, it was time "to move towards a more realistic" approach, more "in line with the present British" stance on weapon sales in southern Africa,[89] which had been rolled back substantially earlier that year.[90] Although both officials understood that the African Bureau and International Organization Bureau felt policy changes would have disastrous political repercussions in Africa and at home and send the "wrong signal" to the South Africans, their discussion largely dismissed the viewpoints of Palmer and Goldberg. Disparate expectations and standards, Rostow explained, had undermined the utility of the embargo and eroded the U.S. government's support among American manufacturers and European governments. The "net result" of the current approach was that both the U.S. and U.K. balance of payments suffered, and the United States created unnecessary and unproductive friction with its European allies. In Rostow's words, it was time to "examine the problem rationally." While new embargo guidelines—which would make it easier to sell aircraft with American parts to South Africa—would provoke a backlash in some quarters, it was a "sensible" move "balanced by advantages."[91]

President Johnson and his closest advisors expressed few opinions about this bureaucratic wrangling, primarily because the Vietnam War and its effect on Great Society liberalism at home and abroad consumed their attention in the final years of his administration. By 1968, in fact, the president's only direct engagement with South African issues came in the form of gold policy negotiations. The fighting in Southeast Asia combined with social spending that year undercut the stability of the Bretton Woods economic system and threatened the scaffolding of the administration's programs at home and abroad. The crisis reached its apex in March, when global investors made a series of runs on the dollar that dramatically depleted the global gold pool.[92] Suddenly South Africa's mineral riches— which had propelled the United States' interest in the region during the early Cold War[93]—mattered far more than apartheid. U.S. government officials began pushing Pretoria to support a two-tiered gold system that established an official gold market for central banks and major lenders, which would keep the value of gold at $35 per ounce, and an unfixed private sector for industries and speculators.[94] In a calibrated effort to drive up the price of gold, however, South Africa refused to participate in the American plan. The Republic's balance of payments situation meant it could not suspend gold sales indefinitely, but the country possessed enough of a balance of payment surplus to maintain the embargo through the end of 1968, guaranteeing continued economic instability during the American election year.[95] For the first time in the postwar era, South Africa had the upper hand over the United States.

The State Department's formal "National Policy Paper on South Africa," updated in November 1968, reflected these changed political conditions. Explaining that Washington's "relationship with Africa" was "under pressure" because Johnson supported both "the aspirations of the African states" and U.S. "material and strategic interests in the white-controlled states," officials called for an approach that would be "damage-limiting for the range of U.S. interests in Southern Africa."[96] Although State Department planners framed this proclamation in terms of continuity, underscoring America's ongoing commitment to the "middle way" between black and white extremists in Africa, the paper differed notably from previous policy declarations. No longer would the U.S. government strive explicitly to adjust South Africa's domestic policies; the aim was to reduce threats to American interests as Washington navigated between "two unsatisfactory alternatives."[97]

The distinction was made clear during a Senior Interdepartmental Group meeting in early December. Reiterating McNaughton's earlier criticisms of the State Department, Deputy Secretary of Defense Paul Nitze asserted that firmer distinctions needed to be drawn between America's "tangible 'action' interests"—involving "very precise and well defined" economic and strategic concerns—and its "'declaratory' policy on human rights," which encapsulated the "postur[ing] in the United Nations." Eugene Rostow agreed tacitly, lamenting that the United States could do a better job differentiating political symbolism from national security: "We should clearly oppose the black liberation movements" and build up "influence in South Africa affirmatively and constructively." The U.S. government could manage the inevitable backlash by minimizing its exposure to the African bloc and expanding direct aid to influential African countries like Zambia and Tanzania. Defending their analysis and recommendations, the State Department officials who had drafted the paper noted that on substantive matters "there was no disagreement" between the Department of Defense and Department of State. Both sides agreed that it "was not plausible that . . . South Africa would be persuaded to change its domestic policies in response to external representations." Even more, in the current "out of control" environment at the General Assembly, they concurred it was not inconceivable that the State Department would "apply [its] veto on one or two United Nations resolutions."[98] While the Treasury Department asserted the new policy paper was still "overly subtle,"[99] and the Joint Chiefs of Staff objected to many of its details,[100] the meeting nonetheless revealed a degree of consensus unimaginable two years earlier. The United States could not change the status quo in South Africa. All it could do was limit the damage to U.S. interests.

6

Looking Outward

The United States is strongly aware of the fact that the white race in the world is in the same position as it is in South Africa, namely, in the minority. The twentieth century simply has to come to terms with this. A way must be found of eliminating race in international affairs.
—Dean Rusk, *private discussion with Hilgard Muller (1967)*

Today there are thirty independent countries in Black Africa. Fifteen of these countries have populations less than the State of Maryland, and each has a vote in the U.N. Assembly equal to that of the United States. There were twelve coups in Black Africa in [1966–67]. Not one of the thirty countries has a representative government by our standards and the prospects that any will have such a government in a generation or even a half-century are remote.
—Richard Nixon, *public lecture at Bohemian Club (1967)*

South African Ambassador Harold Taswell spent July 1967 at Rehoboth Beach, Delaware, an island of white privilege, sequestered in a moment of unprecedented tumult in the United States. Race riots had recently flared in Tampa, Florida, and Buffalo, New York, sparked in both cases by clashes between African American youth and white police officers, only to be followed by explosions in Newark, New Jersey, and Detroit, Michigan, later that month. The violence in Detroit, referred to in many quarters as a full-scale black rebellion, gripped the United States for a week, forced President Johnson to deploy the National Guard, and left 43 people dead, 467 injured, over 7,200 arrested, and more than 2,000 buildings burned down.[1] The ambassador relished the moment. "While basking in the sun today and meditating on what all the experts have to say on the . . . latest spate of American riots, my thoughts turned to Sharpeville," he wrote to the South African Embassy on July 31. "Could you have someone check back on our records and see whether [the U.S. government] said anything about our problems back then?" he queried. "I'd like to have it on record for a few little informal digs when I meet certain gentlemen. Sorry old Soapy has left the State Dept."[2]

The winds of change were shifting direction. Throughout the 1960s, apartheid was one of the most visible and complex problems in the global arena—an issue that sharpened the political lines between the so-called First and Third Worlds, and highlighted how government elites contested the meaning of and relationship between territorial autonomy, economic development, and racial equality. While the proclivities of G. Mennen Williams and others in the Johnson administration had placed the South African government firmly on the defensive in the mid-1960s, the backlash against Great Society liberalism, as well as the United States' escalating involvement in Southeast Asia, and developments at the International Court of Justice and General Assembly were altering the political landscape. Taswell's confidence—palpable as he relayed his thoughts from the beaches of Delaware in 1967—would have been unimaginable two years earlier, when National Party leaders confronted the possibility of U.N. sanctions and international intervention in South West Africa. As the clarity of postcolonial narratives were clouding everywhere, the ambassador's past fears seemed an ephemeral chimera.

This chapter looks at how the Nationalist government capitalized on the changing context of the late 1960s. The ascension of Prime Minister John Vorster in 1966 inaugurated a series of novel initiatives and assumptions within the apartheid state. As African nationalism faltered on the international stage, Vorster's government began building relationships with neighboring African nation-states—part of a broad, ambitious effort to establish South Africa's legitimacy north of the Zambezi River and expand the wedge between the African liberation movements and their traditional patrons in the continent. Cast shrewdly in apolitical terms, this one-sided detente was directed as much at Washington as at Africa, and framed as a peaceful, orderly alternative to the divisive and intractable imbroglio surrounding the apartheid question. These efforts did not halt criticism of the Republic's domestic policies, but they did earn the new prime minister measurable dividends in the late 1960s; some members of the African Group accepted a rhetorical ceasefire with Pretoria, and the newly elected Richard Nixon administration openly denounced the political demands of "micro-states" at the General Assembly. At first glance, it appeared that these changes heralded a new era of Afrikaner security in the global arena.

However, dynamics elsewhere painted a more complex story. At nearly the same moment Ambassador Taswell found himself reflecting on the state of U.S.-South African relations, ANC members were devising ways to transform the nature and structure of the anti-apartheid movement. "Tribute must be paid to the tireless work of those at the United Nations," ANC Acting-President Oliver Tambo said in late 1967. But "the long struggle for freedom in our country has entered a vital new phase" that required an "armed invasion" of South Africa. On August 13, the ANC partnered with the Zimbabwe African Peoples Union

(ZAPU) to send two units of Soviet-trained guerillas into Southern Rhodesia with the explicit aim of sparking a "second Algeria" in South Africa.[3] The guerillas were apprehended within a few months, but the campaign signaled the beginning of major transformations in southern Africa. "The people were at their lowest ebb" in the months before the invasion, explained Joe Slovo, a devout communist and prominent ANC member. "When [the invasion] happened, it was as if we had salvation. At least we knew something positive was happening . . . We were getting out of the lull."[4]

This chapter also explores the paradoxical revitalization of the African National Congress. Having toiled at the periphery of the apartheid debate through much of the 1960s—isolated ideologically from the African nationalist political movement and treated by most sub-Saharan governments as a supplicant of the Pan Africanist Congress—ANC leaders began to capitalize on the African Group's failures in the late 1960s. As U.N. officials started framing anti-apartheid propaganda in explicitly human rights terms after the 1967 Kitwe Seminar, the ANC moved to reclaim its status as the "legitimate" voice of nonwhite South Africans. In part, these developments flowed from Oliver Tambo's instincts for self-preservation. Faced with mounting discontent among exiled black South Africans in Zambia and Tanzania, his Executive Council bolstered its authority among the liberation activists. The organization's distinct background gave form to these efforts, providing the African National Congress with a coherent alternative to African nationalism that seamlessly married multiracial solidarity and human rights with labor unity and Leninist anti-imperialism. The ANC's initiatives—calibrated to take advantage of the exigencies of the late 1960s—formed a counterpoint to the National Party's diplomacy, helping the organization expand its material relations with the Soviet Union, even as it built new ideological connections in South and Southeast Asia, Eastern and Western Europe, North Africa and the Middle East, and the United States.

When viewed from a distance, the dual efforts of the Nationalist government and the African National Congress outlined the contours of a new apartheid debate. The formula that had animated the anti-apartheid struggle for nearly ten years, contingent on the assumption that change would come through the postwar international system, lay in tatters, along with the legitimacy of many postcolonial nationalists and faith in the nation-state as an instrument of development and freedom. The changes that accompanied the late 1960s in Africa, one small part of the upheavals sweeping through North America, Europe, Asia, and elsewhere, reinforced the emerging conclusion—prominent especially among young activists and transnational intellectuals—that "true" independence came not from decolonization but from the networks and identities that transcended, contested, and subverted the nation-state.[5] This conviction not only bifurcated the apartheid debate along government and nongovernmental lines—allowing the National Party to achieve a modicum of security even as the African National Congress gained authority as the voice of nonwhite South Africa—it underscored the increasingly complex intersection of politics and people in the late twentieth century and the way globalization was transforming the Cold War.

Toward Security

The haze over Table Mountain hung low on September 6, 1966. Monday had been a public holiday in South Africa and most white Capetonians settled slowly into their normal work routines that Tuesday morning. At the House of Assembly, government officials prepared diligently for the afternoon session, where Prime Minister Hendrick Verwoerd was scheduled to speak on his historic meeting three days earlier with Lesotho's Chief Leabua Jonathan. It had been the first meeting on South African soil between the premier of South Africa and the leader of a black state, and it was coupled with a path-breaking joint communiqué on the importance of cooperation without interference in internal affairs, crafted deliberately to attack the African Group's efforts in the international realm. At 2:14 p.m., with bells ringing to summon members of Parliament to their seats, Verwoerd took his place in the Assembly chamber and began reviewing the main points of his speech. Few government officials noticed the unassuming, slightly disheveled parliament messenger who entered the hall briskly from the lobby entrance. Within seconds, however, the man—later deemed schizophrenic by South African doctors—was standing over the prime minister. As members of government looked on in horror, the man unsheathed a knife and plunged it deep into Verwoerd's neck and chest four times. Members of Verwoerd's cabinet wrestled the man to the ground, while five doctors—four of them members of Parliament—rushed to the aid of the prime minister. But it was too late. Dr. Hendrick Verwoerd, the principal intellectual architect of apartheid and the political giant of the National Party, died on the floor of the House of Assembly two days before his sixty-fifth birthday.[6]

Verwoerd was struck down at the height of his political power. At home and abroad, his accomplishments were unprecedented in South African history. Despite accusations of being a totalitarian dictator, Verwoerd had led the Nationalists to an electoral rout in March 1966, gaining twenty seats in the House of Assembly and winning over 58 percent of the vote. It was the National Party's fifth-straight general election victory, and it showcased Verwoerd's burgeoning popularity among English-speakers in Natal, where whites had historically resisted the Afrikaner ethos of the National Party.[7] In his first radio broadcast after the election, the prime minister offered an explanation for his success. Pointing an accusatory finger at the United States and Great Britain, he asked whether it was "too much to expect the Great Powers to realise that chaos in southern Africa . . . would constitute a mortal danger to their own power and survival?"[8] Observers everywhere understood the subtext. The Dutch *Nieuwe Roterdamse Courant* noted that the speech highlighted the growing sense of betrayal among South Africans who once "counted on Britain and the United States for support of the White cause,"[9] while the *Financial Times* opined that the "two white races in South Africa [were] learning to overcome their past differences as they consolidate[d] their common position in dealing with the Coloured races."[10] By mobilizing latent fears among white South Africans, Verwoerd had effectively built a permanent political majority that enshrined the power of the apartheid state.

This political order sat atop the prime minister's vision of apartheid. Verwoerd was the champion of "grand apartheid." Drawing a distinction between racial segregation and racial partition, he repackaged South Africa's domestic policies in the 1960s using the language of modernist social engineering and state-led economic development. In practical terms, these efforts meant the creation of artificial, all-black "nations" within a white-dominated South Africa. These black nations, termed Bantustans by Verwoerd and his surrogates, were given all the trappings of independence—capital cities, parliaments, universities, flags, police, and social services—even as they remained economically reliant on Pretoria. In Verwoerd's mind, apartheid was South Africa's answer to the challenge of decolonization. If territorial autonomy truly formed the gateway to political, economic, and racial freedom, then the Bantustan social order theoretically complemented visions of postcolonial freedom elsewhere in Africa by providing native Africans with space to develop on their own terms. This vision was riddled with problems—specifically its inability to rationalize the forced removal of 60 percent of the black population living and working in so-called white urban centers and non-Bantustan rural areas, or the existence of cosmopolitan non-whites who directly challenged apartheid's essentialist racial categories—but it reshaped South African politics in the 1960s.[11]

The prime minister's accomplishments were equally apparent in the international arena. In the minds of many white South Africans, the 1966 ICJ case was a test. Framing the ruling in its broadest terms, Verwoerd acknowledged over the radio in July that, "the legal proceedings formed only part of a wider political campaign against South Africa" waged by "African States at the United Nations." Because the goal was always to use the United Nations to isolate South Africa, the verdict held wide significance. It marked not only the "failure of this particular form of attack" but was also a rebuttal of the logic undergirding African attacks on apartheid. Verwoerd explained:

Although the judgment of the court apparently rest[ed] on a fairly narrow basis, it [was] clear from the proceedings that the applicants suffered defeat... For instance, they started the case with the same type of allegations of oppression and discrimination against the non-Whites in South West Africa as [were] regularly submitted to the United Nations. After South Africa's exposition on the true facts in the pleadings before the court, the applicants were, however, compelled to abandon these allegations, accept our facts, and confine themselves to a legal contention to the effect that all forms of official differentiation, however beneficial, are unlawful.[12]

White South Africans embraced Verwoerd's explanation of events. Johannesburg's the *Star* claimed that "from every angle, the judgment is a major victory for South Africa." Although the verdict did not declare South Africa blameless, the "court shrewdly and probably finally notified the African States that it will not... pull their political chestnuts out of the fire." Through a legal technicality, "it informed them that it [was] a court of law, not a political forum."[13] Cape Town's *Die Burger* similarly editorialized that an "ugly weapon" on an "important front" had been removed from the African Group,[14] and the *Cape Argus* suggested presciently that the decision had placed South Africa's opponents in a difficult position. "They could go ahead to the United Nations with all kinds of pressure on South Africa," but their efforts would lack "some of its authority and much of its prestige because of the failure of the legal attempt."[15]

As South Africans recovered slowly from the shock of Verwoerd's murder, one thing was clear—the prime minister had left the National Party more powerful than he found it. Its control over nonwhites at home was nearly complete, and its message had deep support among white South Africans. In the days after the assassination, Nationalist elites rallied behind an equally imposing, right-wing politician to lead the country—Balthazar Johannes [John] Vorster. Appointed minister of justice in 1961, the fifty-one-year-old Vorster had a reputation for two things: efficiency and brutality. His mantra was simple. "In normal circumstances you can play the game according to the rules," he explained to his biographer. "But these are not normal times" and "to play according to the rules would be like fighting an implacable and vicious enemy with one hand tied behind your back."[16] In the early 1960s, Vorster used his position as minister of justice to pass legislation that expanded the power of his Security Police and authorized covert attacks on nonwhite political networks. In 1962, editors at *Rand Daily Mail* suggested that his behavior confirmed "in the mind of the outside world the belief that we have a fascist-style government in South Africa."[17] But Vorster, who had spent World War II in prison because of his ties to the Nazi Party, saw the situation differently. His critics were "communistic liberals," and their words simply revealed their tacit support for the "revolution that [aimed] to destroy the South African way of life."[18]

At first glance, Vorster's efforts seem best understood in terms of continuity with Verwoerd's policies. Building on his efforts as minister of justice, Vorster passed the Prohibition of Political Interference Act (1968), which outlawed all mixed-race political collaboration, and the Black States Constitutional Act (1971), which accelerated the development of Verwoerd's Bantustan program. He also built up the Republic's conventional and nonconventional military power, transforming the Ministry of Defense into a major player in Pretoria.[19] In 1969, Vorster revamped the intelligence service by forming the Bureau of State Security (BOSS), a unit which became a crucial instrument of Pretoria's "counter-terrorism" efforts in the 1970s, infiltrating refugee and guerilla camps in neighboring black states and targeting exiled black political parties in Europe. The rivalries between BOSS and the traditional defense establishment mushroomed in later years, spawning legendary power struggles in Pretoria and Cape Town, but for Vorster these agencies were novel extensions in government authority.[20] Confidence, in his mind, flowed from strength—and the new prime minister was determined to continue his predecessor's iron-fisted initiatives.

However, Vorster was more than a one-dimensional authoritarian. South Africa's apartheid policies remained unaltered under his tenure, but the atmosphere within the National Party changed in notable ways. One cabinet member later explained, "Verwoerd wanted to make all the decisions. [He] was a very strong character [who] dominated the cabinet completely." Vorster, in contrast, "would listen to his ministers, question them, make suggestions . . . [but] never give orders."[21] Over time, this subtle shift created a new mindset among South African policymakers. "While Verwoerd was largely a dictator, Vorster brought us back to true cabinet rule and true cabinet responsibility," another government official said.[22] Even Lesotho's Chief Jonathan noted the difference. After working with both men, he commented in 1967 that Verwoerd's approach toward race relations had been "a bit difficult, indeed very difficult" because he was a philosopher, and "philosophers always want you to accept their philosophy." Vorster, however, was "a bit more realistic and practical," partly because he was "a lawyer, and they [were] more amenable."[23]

The new prime minister's pragmatism produced major changes in the realm of external affairs. Whereas Verwoerd personally resented criticism of his domestic policies and worked assiduously to delegitimize his opponents, Vorster seemed uninterested in debates on the inherent morality of separate development. Addressing a National Party political rally in mid-February 1967, he announced that South Africa needed to put aside its differences with African nationalists and fulfill its true destiny in the world. Because of its linguistic and cultural diversity, he suggested that the Republic was the "best laboratory in the world" to explore how groups could learn to "coexist in peace and harmony." Although apartheid was not a perfect social system, neither were the alternatives provided by the African states and the United States. What mattered, in Vorster's mind, was not the intellectual supremacy of apartheid's inner logic, but its ability to ensure peace based on mutual respect and economic development. According the prime minister, if white South Africans demonstrated their commitment to these dual principles, they would eventually regain the acceptance of the international community.[24]

South African newspapers immediately grasped the significance of Vorster's words. For the *Star*, it was "clear that Mr John Vorster's Government set itself the laudable objective of abandoning the cry of the earlier Nationalist regimes . . . for the world to stop so that they could get off."[25] *Die Burger*, which had strongly supported Verwoerd's foreign policy, also admitted that the new prime minister's approach was "in direct conflict with the 'laager mentality' so frequently ascribed to the Afrikaner in general and the Nationalist in particular. Here we have an appeal and a challenge to move out into the world, to look outwards, to become involved, to seek our national salvation in participation instead of in separation."[26] In the months that followed, South African journalists termed Vorster's approach the "outward policy." Although Verwoerd had entertained the establishment of relations with African states, Vorster shifted this discussion to the terrain of functional politics. "Not only do we live in a changing world, but we live in a world that has already changed," he explained to supporters in 1967. In the current environment of disillusionment and detente, the National Party had an opportunity to champion a "conservative and realistic path" that demonstrated the compatibility of South Africa's interests and Africa's material future. If the world would "accept South Africa as part of Africa and just as it is," then Vorster was more than willing to provide "practical aid to enable [African states] to help themselves."[27]

The prime minister's outward policy centered on building economic relations with black Africa. The initial step involved bolstering the Nationalist government's ties to the former High Commission Territories of Botswana, Lesotho, and Swaziland. Whereas Verwoerd had treated these states with disdain, as they moved toward independence in 1966, publicly telling them that "their political interests [would] be dominated by their economic interests," Vorster adopted a more collaborative stance in public and private.[28] He put in motion, for example, customs arrangements that better compensated each country for trade with South Africa, nearly tripling their annual budgets in two years.[29] Simultaneously, the prime minister reached out to the leaders of Malawi, offering funds to build a sugar mill, and a R19 million loan to pay for a new capitol building in Lilongwe and a railway line along Lake Malawi.[30] Hastings Banda, Malawi's first president, rewarded South Africa immediately, breaking publicly with other African leaders in 1967 and denouncing the African Group's confrontation with Pretoria over South West Africa. "Idealism is all right, but we must make a mixture of idealism and realism," Banda explained in a speech. "I hold strongly that African leaders are doing themselves no good—and are doing Africa no good—by living in the air instead of on the ground."[31]

These initial breakthroughs established a foundation for success elsewhere. The following year, Pretoria successfully formed economic relations with Madagascar, culminating in a R2.3 million loan to tar roads, repair regional airports, and fund a resort in Nosy Be, and by 1970, the island Mauritius had altered its laws to allow South African exports to pass quietly through Port Louis en route to states in East, Central, and West Africa, allowing the country to trade discreetly with Gambia, Gabon, Cote D'Ivoire, Central African Republic, Nigeria, Kenya, and Ghana, among others.[32] "Our government's approach is one of cordial readiness to help," Foreign Minister Hilgard Muller claimed in 1967. Economic dividends would not be "granted condescendingly nor would South Africa ever try to dictate how other states should manage their affairs, for this would be in conflict with South Africa's cardinal principle of non-interference."[33] The Republic, according to Vorster, was committed simply to helping Africans "achieve their own salvation without losing their self-respect."[34]

This economic offensive paralleled diplomatic efforts in Southern Rhodesia. Having propped up Salisbury through clandestine economic and military aid in the period surrounding Ian Smith's unilateral declaration of independence, South Africa expanded its presence in the country as it implemented the outward policy elsewhere in Africa, countering U.N. economic sanctions directly by sending oil across its border and expanding regional trade.[35] In private, Vorster found Smith an unpredictable ideologue and viewed Southern Rhodesia as a weak ally.[36] But these reservations had little influence on the prime minister's political initiatives. South Africa "enjoy[ed] the best of all worlds" with Salisbury in the late 1960s, according to historians James Barber and John Barratt. The country "prov[ed] sanctions ineffective (and profit[ed] from it)" while expanding its influence as a "middleman" on the diplomatic front.[37] Guerilla activity was at minimal levels in Southern Rhodesia, and Vorster's government entered the 1970s with confidence that it was beginning to gain control of regional developments.

The centerpiece of Pretoria's diplomatic efforts was Zambia. President Kenneth Kaunda's respected status within the Nonaligned Movement made him an appealing target for cooperation. In 1967, Vorster reached out to Lusaka with an offer of technological and scientific cooperation and protection against Southern Rhodesia and Portugal. When Kaunda responded negatively, asserting that apartheid undermined the basis of good-faith agreements, Vorster pointed to South Africa's connections in Malawi, Botswana, and Lesotho and reiterated his offer, explaining that Zambia held "the key to the extension of co-operation to all countries in Southern Africa."[38] This game of cat-and-mouse continued until mid-1968, when Kaunda finally met with South African officials in Lusaka and opened tentative economic relations with Pretoria. In a subsequent letter to Vorster, Kaunda opened a window, suggesting that majority rule—the only way out of the impasse in Southern Rhodesia—was "not applicable to the situation in South Africa." Admitting personal ignorance of apartheid theory, Kaunda noted coyly that the "final objectives" of separate development "would be of interest to the critics of South African policy." He intimated that the Smith regime in Southern Rhodesia—not the apartheid policies of South Africa—was the "key or the obstacle in the path towards better understanding" between Africa and the Republic.[39] If Pretoria would help isolate its neighbor to the north, in other words, Zambia, implicitly, would accept the permanence of the National Party in South Africa.

Vorster grasped at the opening, proposing an open referendum to determine a new government in Rhodesia, but he demanded that further negotiations occur face-to-face in either Lusaka or Pretoria.[40] Kaunda, cognizant of the implications of such a meeting, balked and instead moved to marshal support among East and Central African nation-states for a public declaration of African views on South Africa. The resulting "Lusaka Manifesto," published following a two-day meeting of heads of state in April 1969, called for the isolation of the Republic and reiterated the African Group's long-standing commitment to racial equality but simultaneously renounced "African imperialism"—defined as any territorial claim based on pan-racial identity—and declared that African leaders would "prefer to negotiate rather than destroy, to talk rather than kill." The document, like the conclusions emanating from the Kitwe Seminar in 1967, deliberately downplayed the ideological importance of African nationalism and expanded the distance between independent African nation-states and the liberation organizations. The most widely quoted section of the manifesto read:

> If peaceful progress to emancipation were possible, or if changed circumstances were to make it possible in the future, we would urge our brothers in the resistance movements to use peaceful methods of struggle even at the cost of some compromise on the time of change.[41]

South African officials recognized the significance of such words. Discussing the document in the House of Assembly in May, Muller speculated, "Realism [was] beginning to appear in Africa," as well as "modesty . . . in regard to [African] achievements," and a new willingness to accept the place of whites in South Africa.[42] After suffering political defeat at the International Court and at the General Assembly, African nationalists no longer possessed the tools or the

ambition to fundamentally alter the Republic's domestic policies. In private discussions, the minister admitted that the manifesto was a "fascinating" template
for relations, with "encouraging" and "very cleverly phrased" sections that effectively isolated the liberation movements. Kaunda, in Muller's mind, was aiming
to walk the line between the "extremist" and "very moderate elements" in the
rapidly changing African political arena. This willingness, alone, signaled a political victory for the South African government.[43]

Elsewhere in Africa, Vorster's detente provided even greater dividends. Ivory
Coast's President Félix Houphouët-Boigny, for instance, openly dismissed those
who resisted dialogue with Pretoria. His rationale veered toward cynicism.
"Although it is true that discrimination exists in South Africa," there was "also
discrimination in countries such as the United States, where the Red Indians
were killed by the whites," and no African country saw fit to refuse aid from
Washington. Observing that more people were "being killed in southern Sudan
than in South Africa," Houphouët-Boigny argued further that "refugees in Dar es
Salaam [were] not competent" to relay authoritative information about conditions in the Republic—an explicit reference to the exiled liberation movements
living in Tanzania.[44] In private discussions with African leaders, the president
was no less blunt and unequivocal. "[We] have nothing to be ashamed of,"
Houphouët-Boigny's aide stated during a meeting with representatives of
Malawi, Madagascar, Gabon, Central African Republic, Ghana, and Lesotho in
May 1971. "[Our] method of communication and persuasion [is] just as re-
spectable as any other method hitherto employed in the campaign against apartheid and [we] should, therefore, sally forth and explain [our] point of view, as
others did theirs, and counter the accusations leveled at [us] instead of simply
absorbing them."[45] The Ivory Coast, in short, aimed to dissolve the U.N. African
Group.

Such sentiment played perfectly into Vorster's hand. Houphouët-Boigny's
"courage and forceful personality" was leading a "break-away faction among the
Africans" and opening doors for South Africa in the global arena, a South African official declared in May 1971.[46] The effects seemed instantaneous. Only a
month after Ivory Coast's announcement, United Nations Secretary-General U
Thant himself flirted with dialogue, indicating through intermediaries that he
would support South Africa's outward policy if evidence emerged that "normal
inter-state relations" could alleviate the tensions surrounding the apartheid
debate.[47] The Republic was "within sight of being 'over the hump' in its struggle
to turn back the tide of international criticism and pressure [from] Black Africa,"
one news commentator wrote that year.[48] The "common thread" of anti-apartheid
activism that had "provided the independent African states with . . . ideological
cement" in the early 1960s was being eroded by Pretoria's detente initiatives,
another reporter claimed in May. It was not unimaginable that South Africa

would reemerge as a legitimate member of the Western bloc in the coming years.[49]

Vorster agreed but with an important rejoinder. "The forces unleashed by the granting of independence" were giving way to nonideological, practical approaches in Africa, he acknowledged in an interview in 1971. However, it would be up to the United States to ensure the maintenance of this "newly non-polemic" geopolitical environment.[50] Washington's position of geopolitical authority, in the prime minister's mind, set the boundaries of international affairs and made American policymakers the referees in the fight between Pretoria and African nationalists. The debate over South Africa's policies would continue, therefore, until the United States threw its weight definitively behind the Nationalist government. Only then would Vorster accept victory.

Toward Order

When Vorster entered office in mid-September 1966, U.S.-South African relations were undeniably at a low. Influenced by civil rights reform and international law, as well as the anti-apartheid proclivities of certain policymakers in the State Department, the Johnson administration had purposefully distanced itself from the Republic between 1964 and 1966, suggesting openly in 1965 that it would accept sanctions under article 94 if South Africa defied the authority of the International Court of Justice. Dynamics within Washington had begun to turn in 1967, as momentum within the capital shifted away from the State Department toward the Defense and Treasury departments. However, National Party officials left little to fate in the final years of the Johnson presidency. The outward policy, in many ways, was calibrated to appeal as much to Washington elites as to moderate Africans.

Having established an ambitious "programme of action" in the early 1960s—focused principally on propaganda and private suasion—the Republic turned toward direct diplomacy in the late 1960s. Pretoria, in the minds of South African diplomats, possessed a strong political hand. Confident that "'heads [were] roll[ing]' as a result of the total misinterpretation of the outcome of the South West Africa case,"[51] Ambassador Taswell and others pushed Undersecretary of State George Ball and newly appointed Assistant Secretary of State Joseph Palmer to accept the ICJ decision as a major South African victory. If your "client was suspended over the sea from a precipice by a chain which you had formed and one of the links broke it wouldn't help him very much to say that the rest of the links were fine," Taswell stated flatly in a meeting in late 1966. It was impossible, therefore, according to the ambassador, for the United States to continue to entertain the possibility of sanctions now that the final pillar of the African

Group's anti-apartheid campaign had been defeated.[52] Foreign Minister Muller articulated similar claims in meetings with Secretary of State Dean Rusk in 1967, noting that the "'seventh floor' of the State Department"—where Rusk and other top officials worked—needed to appreciate that South Africa's neighbors were growing "more conservative and less hostile" because of Vorster's regional initiatives. Claiming that America's "colour problem" too often undermined "rational" U.S. policymaking toward South Africa, he speculated that "the atti- tude of the U.S.A. would change to one of appreciation" as the "true aims and results" of apartheid grew more obvious.[53]

This hard-nosed diplomacy was coupled with indirect pressures. For instance, Michael Banghart—an American businessman who communicated regularly with South Africa's Ministry of Foreign Affairs—berated Assistant Secretary Palmer in late 1966 for "reversing" the U.S. government's long-standing tradition of giving assistance to businessmen in South Africa. Positioning himself as an unbiased observer with material interests abroad, Banghart lectured, "Sooner or later the U.S. would have to say 'NO' to the Afri-Asians [sic], and this was a good time to start." These efforts aimed not only to push Palmer away from the policy positions of his predecessor, G. Mennen Williams, but also to isolate other African Bureau liberals who "falsely conflated" America's civil rights movement with the situation in southern Africa.[54] A host of American investors—all with substantial interests in South Africa and extensive personal relations with the Nationalist government—took comparable arguments to members of the U.S. Treasury Department in 1967–68, successfully pushing Johnson officials to loosen restrictions on South African imports and provide backing for U.S. capital in southern Africa. Trade with South Africa consequently skyrocketed in the final year of the Johnson presidency, ostensibly limiting any incentive for sanc- tions and buttressing Pretoria's economic security.[55]

National Party operatives also outflanked State Department liberals at Con- gress, working assiduously in the late 1960s to open relations with influential figures like Senator Michael Mansfield. In late 1966, Taswell candidly informed the Democratic majority leader that the United States was "the only country that could cause any real threat" to South Africa and warned that "forces within the State Department were intent on working in that direction." Pointing an accusa- tory finger at former Assistant Secretary Williams, the ambassador provided a laundry list of complaints, as well as suggestions on how relations between South Africa and the United States could be improved.[56] When a committee in the House of Representatives began hearings on apartheid in 1966, the Republic wrestled over how best to influence the trajectory of the discussion. "South Africa obviously cannot become *directly* involved in the hearings," Ambassador Taswell explained. But it could "*indirectly* arrange for influential people who are well-disposed towards South Africa to appear, to be briefed, etc." Lining up an array of professors and other intellectuals who "lacked direct investments in South Africa," government intermediaries quietly positioned experts to dampen criticism of apartheid and to keep attention in Washington focused on the benefits of Vorster's outward policy in Africa.[57]

At the same time, the Republic expanded its traditional propaganda initiatives. In August 1968, Vorster appointed Connie Mulder as minister of information and provided the Information Service more independence to pursue a robust information campaign in the United States. Under the leadership of Eschel Rhoodie, Mulder's confidant and department secretary, South Africa expanded its programs dramatically, increasing its budget by over R7 million between 1968 and 1973. "My department will not remain on the defensive," Mulder announced in the early 1970s. "We have now gone over to the offensive."[58] One of the centerpieces of this effort was the "South West Africa Survey," distributed widely to Western leaders and businessmen in the late 1960s. The document attempted to refocus elite foreign opinion on the 1966 ICJ decision, providing vivid images from the territory to show the high standard of living among native Africans. "South Africa makes no claim to perfection," the survey explained. It wanted only to provide a "fair picture" so that non-South Africans "may appreciate the unremitting and by no means unsuccessful efforts which have been made in difficult circumstances to do the best possible for all the Territory's peoples, in leading them to self-determination and stable self-realization." Such efforts, flowing from the directives of the early 1960s, carefully appropriated postcolonial discourse and wrapped apartheid in the language of modernization theory.[59]

Nationalist officials attempted to muddy the linkage between race problems in the United States and South Africa as well, sending frequent pamphlets to newspaper editors, opinion writers, and policymakers in the United States during the late 1960s. Calibrated carefully to appeal to American audiences, these materials followed highly specific themes—developed with the assistance of U.S. advertising firms—and worked to demonstrate that apartheid provided security and mutual respect, as well as "justice and prosperity for all South Africans."[60] As the U.S. civil rights movement moved northward in 1966, shifting national attention to problems of urban poverty and economic injustice, and race riots engulfed American cities in 1967 and 1968, National Party operatives amplified these efforts, juxtaposing American unrest with South African stability and wrapping their views in the discourse of the emerging American conservative movement. According to Harold Taswell, "Some of the white man's grievances against the black man (the sort of things which were said in private among friends) now come out into the open." If the Republic could position itself as the "champion of law and order" in Africa, it would benefit from the growing "White backlash" in the United States.[61] In December 1968, as Johnson prepared to hand over the reins of government to Richard Nixon, Ambassador Taswell wondered whether the winds of change might finally be blowing at South Africa's back. In his words:

> While it is unfortunate that our side of the story cannot be heard at all at certain forums over here, we can draw solace from the fact that we are not the only ones who have problems. Americans themselves are also "white pigs" and often have a much rougher passage than we do. Student militancy, unrest and unreasonableness have reached major proportions in the United States. Discipline has not been enforced, liberalism and the cult of irresponsibility have broken down law and order at many educational institutions.[62]

As Taswell understood, these were the themes of Richard Nixon's 1968 presidential campaign. Not surprisingly, Nationalist officials waited with bated breath as Republicans took over the White House in 1969. At first, a major policy change appeared unlikely. Henry Kissinger, the new president's widely hailed national security advisor, seemed to be "very strongly anti-South African," the Republic's deputy secretary of foreign affairs speculated in December 1968. Citing an American informant, the secretary suggested that the former Harvard professor would likely "approach the situation in South Africa as if it were a recrudescence of Nazism."[63] In the early months of 1969, however, these anxieties dissipated, as signs began to proliferate that Vorster's outward approach had supporters in Washington. In February 1969, Texas Senator John Tower informed Taswell that Nixon and Kissinger hoped to remove racial considerations from U.S. policymaking and to repair relations with Pretoria,[64] and, in March, during the ambassador's first meeting with new Secretary of State William Rogers, America's top diplomat openly blamed anti-apartheid sentiment on "irrational" radicals. Laughing that his own nomination to Foggy Bottom would likely have been rejected if people had realized his role in expanding Twentieth Century Fox's South African outlets in the mid-1960s, Rogers tacitly praised the Nationalist government's ability to prevent a Nigeria-style "tribal war" among black Africans. "I feel more optimistic than I ever did after a discussion with Mr. Rusk," Taswell wrote in late March. Although the United States would likely continue to "slither around and juggle with words" at the United Nations, "an element of goodwill" was being "introduced at the top."[65]

By mid-1969, a major policy change toward southern Africa seemed imminent. According to the National Party's sources in the administration, Nixon's team was moving toward a position of "studied indifference" in the region. This "low-key" approach would eliminate "any semblances of a confrontation" without providing an open endorsement of Vorster's domestic and foreign policies, allowing President Nixon to "move slow[ly] and undramatical[ly]" toward better relations with South Africa while preventing a backlash from congressional Democrats or nonstate activists.[66] Vorster took the cue and ordered Taswell and others to lower their profiles as much as possible so that Nixon's approach could come to fruition. With Senator Edward Kennedy's presidential hopes unexpectedly destroyed by the 1969 Chappaquiddick incident,[67] the Republic suddenly had an unprecedented opportunity to "profit in the long-term from an eight year association with the Nixon Administration."[68] It was incumbent upon South Africa to do its part to strengthen the thirty-seventh president's political hand.

American foreign policy, indeed, changed rapidly during the early Nixon years. Under the auspices of National Security Action Memorandum 39, Henry Kissinger had ordered a comprehensive review of U.S. policy in southern Africa in 1969. The African Bureau, led by Assistant Secretary David Newsom, a career diplomat with experience as the U.S. ambassador to Libya, tried to keep this debate tethered to the State Department's 1968 "damage limiting" National Policy Paper. However, Kissinger's Interdepartmental Group (IG), influenced by the Defense Department's Richard Kennedy and the NSC's Roger Morris, pushed for a cleaner departure from the Johnson administration and argued for the relaxation of anti-South African measures at the United Nations and elsewhere. Even former Secretary of State Dean Acheson weighed in, providing a proposal for the full normalization of relations with Pretoria.[69] When Kissinger finally presented the IG's formal options to Nixon in January 1970, he threw his weight behind relaxation. In his mind, the United States needed to lower its profile at the United Nations, roll back the embargo on dual-use civilian/military items, expand military contacts in South Africa, and keep interactions with African nation-states on strictly bilateral terms.[70] On South West Africa, now renamed Namibia by the General Assembly, Kissinger acknowledged that official disassociation from President Johnson's legal positions would cost the administration "more than it would be worth" but argued still that there was "no reason to make the Territory an issue in our bilateral relations with South Africa." The impasse of the late Johnson years exemplified a situation where the United States could observe "black African sensitivities in public" and end "disdainful lecturing" in "private diplomatic dealings."[71] According to former Kissinger aide Anthony Lake, the national security advisor hoped to promote "peaceful change" within southern Africa in a way that rewarded business constituents who had suffered because of the previous administration's confrontational initiatives during the mid-1960s.[72] It was time, in Kissinger's mind, for policymaking based on tangible material interests rather than the ethereal dictums of liberal internationalism.

Readily accepted by Nixon, these proposals altered the dynamics surrounding the global apartheid debate. In March 1970, the administration orchestrated the

United States' first veto at the Security Council—openly condemning an African-sponsored resolution on Southern Rhodesia in an effort to demonstrate Washington's disdain for further discussions of sanctions or intervention. Cognizant that Great Britain already planned to reject the African proposal, Nixon's team led the veto push for largely symbolic reasons. It was up to African states, not the United States, according to Kissinger, to reconcile their passion toward discrimination with the reality of their weakness in the international system.[73] Richard Kennedy, who moved from the Defense Department to the NSC in 1970, cast the situation in rhetorical terms:

> Africans are fighting uphill; won't they run out of steam as they make demands that are more and more impossible of realization? Resignation must set in. Isn't the Lusaka Manifesto evidence of something of this sort? Now that the U.S. has shown that it has the guts to use the veto, the whole U.N. context of African issues may have been altered considerably; the debate . . . cool[ed] down very quickly in the U.N. after the U.S. veto. How can the Africans get carried away again on a bandwagon that clearly isn't going anywhere?[74]

This stance—centered on eliminating African expectations at the United Nations—built on and accelerated policymaking trends from the final years of the Johnson administration. The aim was not to respond to African nationalism but to reassert American power. In 1971, when the International Court of Justice issued a nonbinding advisory ruling that supported the legality of the General Assembly's 1967 decision to terminate the South West Africa Mandate, Nixon officials scoffed at the decision. In a background paper to the president, Kissinger chided the State Department's past naïveté toward the supposedly "defunct" International Court of Justice—a statement that clashed starkly with the consensus that had reigned in the Johnson administration—and claimed that any U.S. response to the ruling would simply "irritate the South Africans, irritate the black Africans, contribute nothing to a practical solution to the problem, and force us to cast another Security Council veto."[75] Liberal institutions like the Court, in other words, would have no influence over Washington's geopolitical considerations on Kissinger's watch. In a discussion with Minister Muller in late 1970, Secretary of State Rogers went even further, rejecting not only the content of Ernest Gross's 1966 pleadings—specifically the suggestion that American laws and values held meaning beyond U.S. borders—but also the scaffolding of the Johnson administration's liberal international vision, connecting international law itself to a lost era when dominant international principles had shared common European reference points. Now, in the decolonized world, "everybody stated principles to support their own conclusions," leaving "enough principles flying around to support any conclusion."[76] It was incumbent on American leaders, in his words, to deal "realistically" with challenges of this newly relativistic world.

This mindset dovetailed with the White House's domestic political strategy. A brilliant political tactician, Nixon rose to power in 1968 on an amorphous, opportunistic electoral platform that appealed not to the historical inevitability of nonracial justice but to the "silent majority" of Americans disheartened by anti-Vietnam War protests and dissatisfied with the results of Great Society liberalism. His victory, in effect, signaled the symbolic end of the political coalition that had supported the Democratic Party since 1932. The Republican Party that emerged from 1968 was not politically beholden to African Americans and white liberals, and unconcerned with either the institutional authority of the United Nations or the imperatives of decolonization. There was no place for someone like G. Mennen Williams in Nixon's Washington. The new president's reelection hopes for 1972 ebbed and flowed in relation to his "southern strategy," designed explicitly to capitalize on the backlash among white conservatives in the Deep South and urban North. Such shifts practically ensured liberal internationalism's death as an operational ideology. Nixon, his advisors, and his constituents were more concerned with building a sustainable domestic political coalition—one that reflected and refined the fragmentation of contemporary America and guaranteed the Republican Party's continued preeminence in Washington—than dealing with the tumult of second-wave decolonization. The apartheid question was simply a noisy, unsolvable distraction.[77]

This transformation led predictably to a rollback of the Johnson administration's earlier initiatives in southern Africa. For instance, Nixon's State Department revisited the utility of economic sanctions against Southern Rhodesia, eventually making it easier for American businesses to access certain minerals and protect their long-term investments in the region. These efforts, which unfolded in 1970–71, culminated in the signing of the so-called Byrd Amendment in late 1971, a resolution sponsored by senators from the Deep South and supported by the administration, which explicitly authorized the importation of seventy-two "strategic and critical materials" from Southern Rhodesia, including chrome, ferrochrome, and nickel.[78] In public, Nixon framed these moves in positive terms. His yearly addresses to Congress paid heed to America's "historical commitment to racial equality and self-determination," while emphasizing the necessity of closer association with the Nationalist government. Because "the 1960s have shown all of us—Africa and her friends alike—that the racial problems in the southern region of the Continent cannot be solved quickly," it followed that contact and moral suasion, not force and violence, were the logical pathways toward "constructive change" in the Republic.[79] Privately, the president acknowledged that change in Africa ranked near the very bottom of his geopolitical concerns. Decolonization and North-South issues simply distracted attention from the East-West Cold War and American relations with the Soviet Union, China, and Europe. If Washington had a dependable surrogate in Pretoria, there was no reason to allow moral questions to muddy the waters of political and economic certainty.[80]

The president's "grand design" abroad, to the extent it existed beyond tactical improvisation, centered on adapting U.S. power to the reality of America's decline in the early 1970s. The United States was not only embroiled in a military quagmire in Vietnam; it also faced the economic challenge of sustaining the Bretton Woods system in the face of domestic inflation. These dual problems loomed at the forefront of Nixon's political mind. His administration hoped to retain U.S. influence in a manner that recognized the practical limits of American power. At the macro-level, this approach led to detente in Moscow and Beijing—part of a sustained effort to bolster Washington's geopolitical status through high-level direct and indirect diplomacy—and the formation of a network of "special relationships" with smaller nations willing to safeguard U.S. interests in the Middle East, Latin America, Asia, and Africa.[81] The Republic of South Africa appeared to be the ideal American surrogate. Its record of anti-communism combined seamlessly with its economic strength and political durability. The administration's new approach toward Pretoria, therefore, formed simply one part of the larger "Nixon Doctrine"—evident in Saigon, Tel Aviv, Tehran, Amman, Riyadh, and elsewhere—which provided military and economic aid to regional proxies that acted as guarantors of American-defined stability in different corners of the world.[82]

What animated the thirty-seventh president's grand strategy? Fear of democratic chaos and global disorder form part of the story.[83] However, in public and private, Nixon cited not just an amorphous global revolution of young people but the failure of certain institutions, such as the United Nations, the North Atlantic Treaty Organization, and the United States Information Agency, to deal with specific problems, ranging from the proliferation of small nations and nuclear technology to the collapse of U.S. prestige in the global south. Nixon's policies, in other words, flowed from the perceived shortcomings of Lyndon Johnson's approach to the transformations of the 1960s—specifically, the former president's belief that liberal institutions like the United Nations and International Court of Justice could be viable instruments of American intellectual and political power in the postcolonial world. Nixon frequently explained this worldview in local terms. The globe would be one "great city" by the end of the twentieth century, he claimed in a lecture before entering the White House, connected through transportation and communication technologies yet divided sharply along entrenched economic and ideological fault lines.[84] Neither postwar institutions nor liberal platitudes would properly empower American elites to lead in this environment—only a respect for authority and the return of great men could ensure stability and progress for the United States and the world.[85]

At the heart of the president's words lay the deeper dilemma of global governance in the decolonized world. Base agreements, covert interventions, and bilateral trade arrangements helped the United States project its influence and slow the growth of Soviet power, but America's grand strategy went beyond the markers of hard power. For much of the mid-1960s, liberal internationalism—institutionalized by the United Nations, International Court of Justice, World Bank, and International Monetary Fund—had shaped the form of American hegemony, propelling the processes that led to decolonization while formalizing U.S. assumptions about the world that followed.[86] For Nixon, soft power's inherent weakness—dramatized by Washington's inability to control the behavior of new member-states within the liberal world order—destabilized the entire edifice of this model. It was time, in his mind, to reorient Washington's patronage networks and economic relationships and reinvigorate the idiom of American power. The Nixon Doctrine, in effect, constituted a reimagination of how the United States wielded the tools of global governance.

Henry Kissinger, cited widely as the architect of Nixon's foreign policy, discussed this dilemma openly. The origins of the "structural problem" facing the administration was not university activism but decolonization in the Third World, he explained in a series of essays published in 1969. "For the two decades after 1945, [America's] international activities [had been] based on the assumption that technology plus managerial skills gave [Washington] the ability to reshape the international system and to bring about domestic transformations in 'emerging countries.'" The normalization of American views was supposed to have cemented Washington's influence in the world. However, "political multipolarity"—Kissinger's codeword for campaigns like the one waged by the African Group in the 1960s—had made it "impossible to impose an American design" abroad, necessitating the creation of an alternative system that acknowledged the failures of liberal institutions.[87] The American empire, like previous great powers, was plagued with long arms but weak fingers.[88] The national security advisor aimed not to upend the logic of the Cold War but to strengthen these fingers—to reorient the way the United States operated in the cacophonous postcolonial world.

These developments strengthened the position of the Nationalist government in the early 1970s. American direct investments soared from $600 million to $1.5 billion in the 1970s, and both the CIA and the Defense Department expanded their relations with Vorster's enlarged security state.[89] By the time Nixon resigned from office in August 1974, the foundations of a fundamentally new relationship—one that would be tested and deepened in Angola in the 1970s and 1980s—were established.[90] In the minds of its critics, South Africa was emerging as the right arm of an American imperial war machine. From Vor-ster's perspective, however, South Africa was emerging from the long storm of the postcolonial decade. With the African Group's sanctions campaign all but finished at the United Nations and with U.S. support growing in the realm of state-to-state relations, the Republic's possibilities seemed boundless. On the surface and in the minds of South Africa's leaders, the Nationalist government was emerging victorious in the global apartheid debate.

Toward Legitimacy

The reality, however, was more complex. Anti-apartheid criticism was growing less politically specific but more ubiquitous in the late 1960s, as the African Group faltered on the international stage and as the Unit on Apartheid began to recast criticism of segregation in the inclusive language of human rights. The end of the sanctions threat boomeranged in the Nationalist government's favor in the short term, but pathways beyond the purview of national power were prolif-erating rapidly, providing new outlets for nonstate organizations and alternative forms of legitimacy within the international system. This messy and knotted process, termed "postcolonial globalization" by historian A. G. Hopkins, con-fronted the liberation organizations—the Pan Africanist Congress, African National Congress, South West African People's Organization (SWAPO), Zimbabwe African Peoples Union, and Zimbabwe African National Union (ZANU), among many others—with an assortment of possibilities and pitfalls in the late 1960s.[91] The ANC's eventual reemergence as the authoritative voice of nonwhite South Africa resulted as much from decisions made in this period as from the organization's historical connections to the Republic before 1960.

The ANC's rise was entwined with the decline of the African Group. The tense relationship between African nation-states and liberation movements de-teriorated rapidly in the years after the 1967 Kitwe Seminar, so that by 1969, when the U.N. Apartheid Committee traveled to Lusaka to consult with the ANC, SWAPO, and ZANU, meetings consisted mostly of a series of accusa-tions and counteraccusations.[92] Members of the committee, hailing from North, East, and West Africa, lamented the ignorance of stateless Africans toward the nuances of New York politics and the economic needs of indepen-dent Africa, while liberation activists complained vehemently of the ineffec-tiveness of the African Group's campaign at the General Assembly. "In the final analysis," announced Abdulrahim Abby Farah, chairman of the U.N. com-mittee, "it was the people of South Africa who must bear the brunt of the struggle." And "unless there were continued acts of violence, no matter how just the cause, nobody would pay any attention. Sharpeville hit the headlines because many were killed and maimed. Today, unless there were more Sharpevilles, there would be indifference."[93]

This message differed sharply from the African Group's promises during the early 1960s. In the immediate wake of second-wave decolonization, African nationalists had rallied to the anti-apartheid cause, promising to use U.N. economic sanctions to create the conditions for change in South Africa, while using the apartheid issue to sharpen, extend, and institutionalize a particular definition of the nation in the postcolonial world. For a time, the liberation movements had invested in this model of activism. "Once, our people had believed that only the United Nations could save them," SWAPO members explained to the committee in 1969. "But now"—in the aftermath of the failed attempt to liberate the Mandated territory of South West Africa and, more recently, the controversial Lusaka Manifesto—"the people of Namibia ... hate[d] the United Nations because of the non-implementation of its resolutions."[94] The impasse was partly generational. Liberation activists of the late 1960s were critical of the failings of the Africa's postcolonial leaders, especially their inability to chart a course toward greater unity, more equality, and less European influence.[95] But SWAPO's frustration—common among freedom fighters—was also linked to the growing gap between the promise of decolonization and the reality of Africa's weakness in the decolonized world. Unlike nationalists of the late 1950s, liberation fighters tended to define freedom in juxtaposition to the trappings of the American-defined liberal world order. True independence, in their minds, was contingent not on control of a territorial space and membership in the United Nations—factors that had anchored earlier iterations of African nationalism—but on the defeat of U.S. imperialism and the emergence of a fundamentally new international system.

The Pan Africanist Congress did not adapt well to these intellectual currents. Having modeled itself narrowly in the image of Kwame Nkrumah, the organization began to struggle when the Ghanaian president's fortunes soured after 1963 and—despite a brief embrace of Maoism in the mid-1960s—proved slow to respond to the exigencies of the period after the ICJ decision. Ineffectual leadership exacerbated this decline. Moving regularly between Ghana, Tanzania, and Zambia after his expulsion from Basutoland (Lesotho) in 1963, Potlako Leballo, the PAC's de facto leader-in-exile, seemed reflexively insecure, and prone to flamboyant outbursts directed toward not only the ANC and Nationalist government but also toward subordinates who questioned his authority or made decisions without his approval.[96] As problems mounted in the 1960s, PAC members grew convinced that their leader was squandering funds to pay for a lavish lifestyle in Accra and Dar-es-Salaam.[97] Eventually, in 1968, they attempted to expel Leballo from the organization. Although Leballo managed to survive the Organization of African Unity's decision to suspend funds to his organization that year, by becoming a police informant in Dar-es-Salaam,[98] the Pan Africanist Congress entered the 1970s a shadow of its former self.

The ANC's fortunes followed an inverse path. At the highpoint of African nationalism in the early 1960s, the organization had struggled mightily to find African patrons, accelerating plans for an armed struggle in 1961, in part, to demonstrate its international legitimacy as a liberation movement.[99] When the Nationalist government arrested the top echelon of the ANC's military wing, Umkhonto we Sizwe, in a suburb outside Johannesburg in 1963—eventually putting Nelson Mandela, Walter Sisulu, and Govan Mbeki on public trial in 1964—Deputy President-General Oliver Tambo found himself the ANC's de facto leader.[100] He, too, faced challenges from subordinates in these years. Tennyson Makiwane and Robert Resha, dynamic African activists in their own right, frequently disregarded Tambo's instructions, particularly on the allocation of ANC funds, and the South African Communist Party's Vella Pillay—the organization's initial conduit to the Eastern bloc—used his access to the Soviet government often as political leverage in these years.[101] Privately, Tambo complained bitterly of this situation. "Each representative office of the ANC" was functioning as "a kingdom unto itself," in his mind, and "each leader [seemed] bound by nothing except his own ideas and decisions."[102]

The deputy president-general survived this turmoil, however, and the African National Congress eventually came to define the postnationalist anti-apartheid movement. For many observers, the reason was tied to Tambo's unique combination of humility, openness, and integrity. "He [was] able to talk to anybody, able to communicate—he was a really extraordinary man, you see, [because he was] democratic," ANC leader Joe Matthews explained.[103] Comparable portraits abound among ANC scholars. Luli Callinicos, Tambo's official biographer, characterized the deputy president-general as "a man of consistent and substantial character,"[104] and historian Sifiso Mxolisi Ndlovu suggested that Tambo "always avoided the alienating behavior associated with intellectual and political posturing."[105] Without these unique personality traits, the African National Congress would have collapsed as an exile political movement in the 1960s.

Tambo, indeed, possessed undeniable political acumen. Rather than confronting his internal opponents directly at the organization's political nadir in 1964–66, the deputy president-general shrewdly organized a consultative conference in Morogoro in May 1965 to discuss broadly the ANC's future with its National Executive Committee (NEC). The resulting measures gave Tambo the official title of Acting President, which, in turn, bolstered his ability to critique his opponents in a series of meetings with mission heads in 1966.[106] Tambo softened these attacks by requesting an official review of his own performance, but his criticism was unmistakable—ANC members were abusing funds, disregarding instructions, moving between countries with inadequate correspondence, and engaging in unacceptable interpersonal behavior.[107] Without significant internal reform, the organization would succumb to factionalism.

These moves, however, did not single-handedly revive the African National Congress. Money was the lifeblood of every liberation movement during the Cold War, and ANC members undeniably benefited from non-African forms of economic aid. Unlike the PAC, the ANC possessed ties to the Soviet Union and East Germany. After the collapse of Umkhonto we Sizwe in 1963, Tambo traveled to Moscow, requesting both direct aid and access to military-training facilities. The trip—which resulted in an immediate $300,000 funding package—gave the deputy president-general not only the connections to circumvent the SACP's authority within the Congress Alliance but also the clout to centralize many operations under his control in Dar-es-Salaam.[108] Mission heads had to listen to Tambo's complaints in 1966, in other words, because he controlled access to the organization's most important funding source. Although the acting president was not a communist, he deftly expanded his relationship with the Soviet Union in the mid-1960s. Following a second visit to Moscow in 1965, he secured another $560,000 and systemized a route to the Soviet Union—dubbed the "Freedom Trail" by contemporary ANC members—that helped the organization endure its marginalization in Africa and rebuild Umkhonto we Sizwe externally.[109] The ANC's ability to create a "visible, well-trained army" was of "absolutely vital political importance," a member of Tambo's inner circle explained in 1969. "The [OAU's] Liberation Committee and other groups hostile to us would have been able to wipe us out if they did not have this stubborn fact in front of them."[110]

In the short term, the ANC's reliance on Moscow led to problems. The failed 1967 invasion of Southern Rhodesia, for instance, highlighted the weakness of this Soviet-trained military force, and the subsequent backlash against Tambo and the NEC, spearheaded by Umkhonto we Sizwe members politicized in Russia, underscored the continued fractiousness of ANC politics in the late 1960s.[111] However, in the long term, the organization's embrace of Marxism—institutionalized at the 1969 Morogoro consultative conference—provided the conceptual tools for the African National Congress to reposition itself at the vanguard of the global anti-apartheid movement.[112] "One of the cardinal errors in any assessment of the political struggle in southern Africa at the present phase is to think and calculate *territorially*, to examine territorial situations and draw territorial conclusions," a top-ranking ANC member explained just before the Morogoro meeting.[113] With nation-states throughout the continent "falling under the spell of White South Africa" and succumbing to Pretoria's "subtle outward policy," it was an opportune time to articulate an alternative to African nationalism. The framework itself had grown bankrupt, along with previously sacrosanct assumptions about the relationship between territorial power and economic development. Political independence through the United Nations was not the gateway to postcolonial freedom. Only the destruction of the global capitalist system would guarantee the end of apartheid.[114]

This conclusion proliferated within the African National Congress in the years after the Morogoro conference. Umkhonto we Sizwe guerillas living in Tanzania and Zambia were enrolled in education programs—aimed to "militer-ise [sic] the mind"[115]—that focused explicitly on topics like proletarian interna-tionalism, Marxism-Leninism, dialectical materialism, and world imperialism.[116] The coming ANC-led revolution, one instructor explained, would lead to a "fundamental transformation and effective transfer of power from one class to another, from the colonizers to the colonized, from the exploiters to the exploited." These arguments, drawn freely from the work of Frantz Fanon, Albert Memmi, and other contemporary theorists, denounced members of the "African petite bourgeois"—African nationalist elites—as "slaves to Western imperialism" and rejected the utility of working within the current, Western-dominated international system. The African National Congress was not a "civil rights movement content with superficial changes and cosmetic reform." It was a "total revolutionary movement" that would transform "not only the military and economic, the political and social, but also the ideological and educational" bases of society in South Africa.[117]

Such declarations marked an intellectual departure in the apartheid story. The era of "build[ing] support through the African image" was over, according to a discussion paper prepared for the NEC in 1969. The African National Congress needed to project a more inclusive approach toward anti-apartheid activism—geared as much toward Indians, Coloreds, and whites as native Africans—that framed apartheid in economic terms and placed the organiza-tion at the head of the "diffuse solidarity campaigns" spreading through Europe, North America, Asia, and Africa.[118] The first step was focusing atten-tion on the "main enemy" of the South African people—American imperi-alism. Washington had "embarked upon a global strategy" of "counter-attack" in the Third World, ANC leaders claimed, deliberately creating "hot beds of war" with the help of political proxies such as South Africa and Israel. The United States had "systematically engineered" coups in Latin America to over-throw its critics and used aid, loans, and unequal trade to sow division among independent peoples in much of the rest of the world.[119] Anti-Americanism served as the lodestar of Third World politics in the 1970s in the same manner that anti-Westernism had served as the linchpin of earlier pan-Asian and pan-African visions of global order.[120] It provided, in the words of one ANC planner, a "rallying point," a common denominator of oppression that facili-tated and expanded non-African engagement in causes like the anti-apartheid movement.[121]

The African National Congress understood it lacked the financial resources, military weapons, and political clout to fight the American monolith at the state level. But direct confrontation was never its intention. The ANC's goal centered always on using anti-Americanism to build alliances with other disaffected non-state organizations—establishing legitimacy in the spaces between the contemporary nation-state system. NEC members targeted a long list of "progressive and peaceful" organizations—defined as such because they opposed the United States—which included the World Federation of Trade Unions, the Women's International Democratic Federation, the World Federation of Democratic Youth, the International Union of Students, the World Peace Council, the Afro-Asian Solidarity Organization, the Institute of Jurists, the Afro-Asian-Latin American Solidarity Organization, the Afro-Asian Writers Organization, the All-African Trade Union Federation, and the Pan-African Youth Movement, among many others.[122] "We are a part . . . of the forces of the world that seek justice," an ANC publication explained in the early 1970s. "We fight for freedom and independence, for peace, for a nonracial, ultimately non-national world society; a society without class."[123] By placing the African National Congress in the middle of such an eclectic network and defining its political goals in such broad terms, Tambo and his compatriots hoped to expand their authority by making apartheid the focal point of anti-American criticism, while simultaneously arousing the passions of people *within* nation-states, undermining Washington's ability to justify its support for South Africa.

In defining this plan, the African National Congress hearkened explicitly to the experiences of Algeria and Vietnam. "The centre of the Algerian Revolution was never inside the country in eight years of struggle," an ANC strategy paper claimed in 1969. "It was in the international realm.[124] The Vietnamese Liberation Front, too, benefited from the "solidarity actions" of "the peace and progressive forces of the world." The central lesson needed little elaboration—the "growing identification of common purposes, common interests and common enemies" meant that a calibrated information campaign was now essential to the success of the liberation struggle.[125] In Africa, the Middle East, and Asia—specifically urban nodes such as Lusaka, Dar-es-Salaam, Cairo, Algiers, Beirut, Hanoi, and New Delhi—the ANC spearheaded this effort with the journal *Sechaba*. Propagandists developed articles that connected global affairs to "Marxist ideology, South African legislation, the lives of refugees, [and] women in the struggle" and showcased "poetry, fiction, essays of a committed nature, [and] reviews of books on Southern Africa." As a member of Tambo's NEC explained, it was not for *Sechaba* "to try to report events as they occur." The journal was the "mouthpiece of our ideology," published to "set right the record of things" and build support among "anti-imperialists around the globe."[126] By joining the "mass of mankind" fighting the same enemy, the ANC would obtain "moral and material support for [its] own struggle."[127]

Strident anti-Americanism did not preclude activism within the United States. The "ruling circles" in Washington were set on "aiding and abetting" the Nationalist government, but "growing numbers of people and organizations vigorously oppose[d] the pro-Apartheid lobbies" in North America—part of an "unprecedented upsurge of youth and student action all over the world largely sparked off by the war in Vietnam." ANC propagandists tried to tap into the energy of this emerging network, first, by appealing to Americans who responded to apartheid for "humanitarian reasons." These groups typically did not support armed revolution in South Africa, but they did view apartheid as a violation of universal human rights. If the African National Congress could position itself as a champion of such values, it would invariably elicit "moral and material aid." Second, ANC propagandists appealed directly to African American organizations. The similarities between the "demand for freedom and equality in the U.S. and in South Africa" made "co-ordination and co-operation not only possible but essential." ANC agents reached out both to emerging black power movements in urban centers—receptive already to themes of American imperialism—and older, less militant organizations with connections to black churches and local political establishments. The goal was not so much to "gain material aid" but to link apartheid to American racism and to ensure the ANC's place at the vanguard of grassroots discussions in the United States.[128]

Similarly, the African National Congress expanded its connections in Western Europe. Cognizant that notions of Third World revolution were "only effective with political parties who by their very nature" understood the ANC "ethos," the organization dampened its rhetoric and adopted slogans that catered to trade unions, writers, and left-leaning university activists. The aim was to "fragment" the ANC message "to suit the fragmented character of the organizations in Europe" and present the organization's political objectives in ways that appealed to "the attitudes of each section" of European society. Stated plainly:

> In the trade unions it [would be] necessary to prepare a document showing how our whole struggle is in the concrete a struggle of the workers. Peasants [in South Africa] were not only fighting for their *national* rights but also against *anti-worker* fascist laws. It [was] best therefore to [focus] not only [on] the laws affecting the black workers but also the persecution and execution of [all] the workers who fought against these laws.[129]

By framing apartheid in the language of Marxist class struggle, the African National Congress strove to make the apartheid crisis bigger than Africa. And if the problem was larger than the continent—larger than the ideology of African nationalism—then the solution required not only national independence but also unity with other oppressed peoples around the world.

This goal, in part, was defined in reference to the rhetoric of the emerging New Left movement. Inspired by the writings of Herbert Marcuse, C. Wright Mills, and others, the movement had begun in Frankfurt, Germany, and spread through Paris, London, and other European cities, before crossing the Atlantic and making a deep impact on the U.S. civil rights and antiwar movements in the late 1960s and early 1970s. In meetings with figures like Breyten Breytenbach, a well-known anti-apartheid poet living in Paris, and Jean-Paul Sartre, the influential writer, literary critic, and philosopher, Tambo and other ANC leaders emphasized their nonracial ideological convictions and developed joint projects that heightened the ANC's political profile among white leftists. Even more, ANC leaders involved themselves in countless conferences in Paris, Stockholm, and London during the late 1960s and early 1970s.[130] So long as "the white man identif[ied] completely with blacks," skin color was "irrelevant," Tambo explained in a letter in 1969.[131]

When viewed from a distance, the irony of the ANC's ambitious propaganda offensive was inescapable. Necessitated by the "failure" of U.N. agents to secure "tangible results in the form of sanctions against South Africa," the organization's campaign closely mirrored the tactics adopted by the Nationalist government in Washington, New York, and London in the early 1960s.[132] For Tambo, this was not a coincidence. Pretoria's ability to survive the tumultuous 1960s was closely tied, in his mind, to its success in the information realm—to the relationships that government representatives had established with businessmen, politicians, and policymakers outside traditional international institutions.[133] It followed logically, therefore, that the ANC needed to adopt a comparable approach, based on fighting South Africa not at the United Nations but through the pathways that existed around, between, and within the nation-state system.

What did this move mean for the wider anti-apartheid movement? According to ANC leaders, decolonization had been the harbinger of false change. It was these transnational networks—tying hundreds of nongovernmental organizations together across enormous swaths of physical space—that formed the basis of a truly "new world order," free of American imperialism and animated politically by the creative tension between global thinking and local action. If the African National Congress could place the apartheid question at the heart of this emerging worldwide network, it would not only survive and thrive in this globalized world—it would eventually topple the citadel of whiteness from within. "Victory is inevitable," an ANC publication claimed in 1969, not because the African National Congress possessed conventional military and economic strength, but because it possessed people power, or the ability to shape how individuals outside the corridors of government discussed and debated the apartheid issue.[134] If the organization embraced these information tactics and took the long view in its fight against Pretoria, victory would emerge organically from the imperatives of globalization. When the organization's message eventually reached South Africa itself, the ANC would be positioned to define the terms of the postapartheid world.

It is tempting to conclude with a scorecard on how the National Party, U.S. government, and the African National Congress navigated the multifarious transformations of the late 1960s and early 1970s. However, notions of winners and losers would mask the contradictions of this tumultuous historical moment. The South African government turned back the threat of U.N. sanctions and successfully cemented its security relationship with the United States, but criticism of apartheid spread in creative new directions in the late 1960s, and the country, in public, remained a pariah on the global stage. The Nixon administration, likewise, seemed to alter the optics of U.S. power in the world, initiating detente with China and the Soviet Union and establishing proxies in the Middle East, Africa, and Asia. However, the structural problem that propelled these changes— "multipolarity"—proliferated nonetheless in these years, and the White House's hubris eventually accelerated its undoing in the mid-1970s. The ANC suffered innumerable setbacks, as it fought to regain its bearings after the fall of the African Group, but managed to build alliances in Africa, Europe, and North America and to reinvigorate criticism of the Republic through the discourse of Marxist internationalism.

The postcolonial apartheid debate ended, in other words, on an immensely complex note. Stated plainly, people around the world were coming together through new pathways in the late 1960s and early 1970s, rallying around particular political causes in diffuse yet powerful ways, with government elites embracing more concrete, at times cynical, strategies to protect and project their authority on the global stage. As these changes unfolded, the contours of a fundamentally new apartheid debate started to come into focus. Bifurcated sharply along state and nonstate lines, this arrangement allowed the South African government to achieve a modicum of security even as the African National Congress gained influence as the legitimate voice of nonwhite South Africa. These developments underscored the increasingly muddled intersection of politics and people in the late twentieth century and demonstrated, often in vivid terms, the tension between American ideals and interests, and how actors on every end of the spectrum competed to wrap their viewpoints in the cloth of legitimacy. Perhaps better than any other contemporary issue, the apartheid question highlighted the paradoxes of the postcolonial world—and illustrated how concepts of nationalism, development, justice, and self-determination took on new meanings as Cold War superpowers supplanted European empires in the cockpit of global affairs. South Africa was the quintessential border of this world—a physical and imaginative place that focused political differences and epistemological contra-dictions, and revealed points of commonality and divergence between politicians, policymakers, and activists in the First and Third Worlds.

Did the 1960s mark the triumph of the modern nation-state system or the rebirth of empire in neocolonial garb? The answer rests on the vantage point. For the African National Congress and countless other nongovernmental organizations, neocolonialism offered a powerful and persuasive conceptual map to explain events in the late 1960s. For members of the Nixon and Vorster governments, the nation-state remained the central entity of the international system. Studying the evolution of the apartheid debate does not elucidate a singular answer to such a difficult question—it opens a window on the processes, decisions, and frustrations that led to an international system where states functioned within layered networks of autonomy and where formal and informal power took on increasingly unexpected forms. The 1960s witnessed the un-making of a liberal political order and the birth of our postmodern world-system—a world capable of bringing actors together in unprecedented ways yet fragmenting the very notion of fixed meaning. For a brief period in this decade, the United Nations and the vision of internationalism embodied therein seemed to function as an inclusive intellectual and political umbrella of this world.

That moment, however, ended. Today, we exist in the ambiguous aftermath.

Conclusion

Toward a New Order

We have ceased to think in terms of colour.
—Nelson Mandela, *interview with British press* (1990)

The antislavery movement, the anticolonial movement, and the anti-apartheid movement have been subjected to relentless irony, for their humanistic claims can be set off against the exclusions and hierarchies they reinscribed and the whiggishness that narrating their history seems to imply. But such movements were not simply entrapped in a framework of European beliefs; they profoundly changed what Europeans thought they believed.
—Frederick Cooper, *Postcolonial Studies and Beyond* (2005)

The international press corps barely noticed Nelson Mandela's arrest in August 1962. The same could not be said of his release from prison in early 1990. The seventy-one-year-old Mandela was greeted by thousands of supporters and a throng of national and foreign reporters when he walked through the gates of Paarl's Victor Verster prison on February 11. As he triumphantly thrust his fist in the air, relishing his freedom after twenty-eight long years in jail, Mandela found himself beset immediately by "a long, dark, furry" object. "I recoiled slightly," he recalled, "wondering if it were some newfangled weapon developed while I was in prison." Standing at her husband's side, Mandela's wife informed him that it was a microphone.[1]

The ANC leader did not take long to familiarize himself with the device. Almost immediately, Mandela embarked on a public speaking tour, traveling throughout his country, as well as Africa, Europe, and North America in an effort to accelerate the movement toward majority rule in South Africa. The world that confronted him in those momentous years was dramatically different than the one he left in 1962. The Berlin Wall—erected one year before the Nationalist government apprehended him outside Natal—lay now in rubble, and the Cold War between Washington and Moscow was lumbering inexorably through its final chapter. The economic order that once defined the postwar world had been replaced by a system of floating currencies and free capital movements, and the number of nongovernmental organizations on the global stage had grown ten-fold.[2] "What struck me most forcefully," Mandela reflected after he surveyed his new surroundings, "was how small the planet had become during my decades in prison."[3] Globalization had literally remade the world in his absence.

The early 1990s were a joyous and eventful time for the African National Congress. The program that Oliver Tambo and his compatriots began to implement during the late 1960s bore its fruit in these years, paving the way not only for Mandela's release from prison but also for the fall of the National Party and the rise of the "New" South Africa in 1994. Mandela brought his organization's message to a masterful crescendo. In Havana, the ANC's new leader railed against the "vicious imperialist-orchestrated campaign to destroy the impressive gains made in the Cuban revolution"; in Washington, he celebrated the Declaration of Independence's universality and praised Thomas Jefferson, Abraham Lincoln, and Martin Luther King Jr.[4] "We have a vision of South Africa as a united, democratic, non-sexist and non-racial country," he explained to Swedish lawmakers in March 1990. "We see ourselves as not aligned to any military blocs. At the same time, we shall be firmly aligned with regard to the fundamental and universal issues of human rights for all people, the right and possibility of every individual to full and unfettered development, the right of every country to determine its future, protection of the environment and peace in a world that should be free of regional conflicts and the threat of a nuclear war."[5] Mandela's message—crafted with care and precision by a team of ANC speechwriters—was all things to all audiences.

The African National Congress did not end apartheid. But the organization capitalized brilliantly on the communication and social revolutions that accelerated during the final quarter of the twentieth century. Driven by relatively small numbers of well-educated young people with connections in New York, London, Geneva, and Paris—and a knack for getting their perspectives expressed at outlets such as the *New York Times*, the BBC, and *Le Monde*—these revolutions did not reward abstract arguments about nationhood and international law but activism that embraced tropes of power/resistance and shamed oppressors by explicating their cruelty to the world. Within this milieu, the ANC's victories were as subtle as they were pervasive. Although the organization directed neither the strategy nor the tactics of the multifarious individuals who championed its cause after the 1960s, its leaders gained tremendous dividends from their opaque ideological message. "Ideology mattered, but on its own it wouldn't have won the race," British Labour Party politician Hugh Bayly extolled during an interview about his collaboration with South African exiles in the 1970s. "No, it was simply clear to us that the ANC could lay claim to broader support."[6] Real or imagined, such sentiment gave the African National Congress staying power and shaped the nature of the political system that emerged in apartheid's wake. The

commitment to racial reconciliation demonstrated by ANC leaders during subsequent negotiations to end apartheid, and the extent to which this commitment
continued after the National Party relinquished power, resulted directly from the
international solidarity that marked the anti-apartheid cause.[7] Even if apartheid's
collapse grew from a heterogeneous set of domestic and international factors,
this sense of solidarity and interconnection—which permeated Mandela's
nimble, crosscutting speeches during the early 1990s—influenced the contours
(and contradictions) of South African life after 1994.

What was the global solidarity campaign to end apartheid? Linked initially to
the effort to rethink nationhood, statehood, and world order during the mid-
twentieth century—a process entwined with decolonization and centered at the
United Nations—the anti-apartheid movement changed notably as international
affairs became more democratic, plural, and transnational after the 1960s. Like the
campaigns for nuclear disarmament and abortion rights, the grassroots solidarity
movement gained sustenance from an educated middle-class in the pan-European
world. Interest in South Africa's problems stemmed partly from the new type of
consciousness that accompanied the growth of television and photojournalism
and partly from a new style of Western politics that eschewed older, class-based
concerns and embraced causes that affected people emotionally and psychologi-
cally. To affluent and aroused young people, apartheid was a blank screen and
shaming white South Africans into reform was as much about accountability in
pluralist democracy—forcing traditional elites to listen to the moral concerns of
diverse voters—as ending the particular mechanics of the National Party's racial
policies. At its core, the anti-apartheid solidarity campaign was about challenging
the authority of those who stood aloof in the face of globalized "people power"—
and reifying a particular discourse of freedom and justice.

This process took different forms in different countries, but it followed a con-
spicuous chronological arc. In the United Kingdom, the seeds of mass protest
were planted in mid-1959 with the formation of a Boycott Movement—renamed
the Anti-Apartheid Movement (AAM) in March 1960—but civic outrage came
in sporadic bursts during the next two decades, shaped by a small coterie of hardcore activists who mobilized high-profile events, such as the 1969–1970 "Stop of
Seventy Tour" against South Africa's rugby and cricket teams. At the grassroots
level, widespread support for their cause arose only in the late 1970s. The numbers
hint at an interesting story: the AAM's London staff grew from one administrator
to a staff of twenty-three during the 1980s; its initial 2,500 supporters—drawn
from a cross-section of trade unions, student groups, political parties, and the
Council of Churches—expanded threefold in the same period, and the organization's newsletter went from a circulation of 7,000 to approximately 20,000. By the
time Mandela arrived in London in 1990, Britain's Anti-Apartheid Movement
had the support of approximately 200 Labour parties, 708 trade union branches,

and 91 student unions and the ability to summon hundreds of thousands of people to rock concerts and demonstrations.[8] This growth was less from the inevitable consequence of preceding activism and more a reflection of the distinct transformations that accelerated through Britain after the 1960s.

In Sweden, grassroots mobilization expanded in a comparable way. Again, the seeds of solidarity were planted in the early 1960s by activists angered by the Sharpeville Massacre, as well as popular journalists such as Per Wastberg and Herbert Tingsten who published books and articles that castigated South Africa's political order as oppressive and racist. But the breakthrough came during the 1970s. The rise of Prime Minister Olaf Palme—educated in the United States during the 1940s and influenced strongly by the American labor movement—transformed Stockholm into one of the world's preeminent backers of Third World liberation. An advocate of nonalignment and Cold War neutrality, Palme established direct political relations with the African National Congress in 1973, supplying Tambo with aid comparable to that of the Soviet Union—around $200 million between 1977 and 1991—which both alleviated the organization's financial hardships and gave credibility to ANC claims of Cold War neutrality. In the years that followed, Swedish anti-apartheid groups proliferated in many directions, providing support to South African expatriates, free education and health care at ANC training camps, and holding mass street demonstrations in Stockholm. By the time Palme was assassinated in 1986—the first such killing in modern Scandinavian history—Sweden had become such a vocal opponent of South Africa that many observers suspected Pretoria had authorized the murder.[9]

A similar pattern marked the American anti-apartheid movement. Despite a few sporadic protests during the 1960s—including the formation of George Houser's American Committee on Africa in 1953 and Students for a Democratic Society's (SDS) picketing of Chase Manhattan in 1966—grassroots sentiment was confined almost exclusively to lobbying until the late 1970s. With the formation of TransAfrica in 1978, African Americans and other groups amplified the scope and scale of their efforts to influence U.S. foreign policy. Within Congress, the newly formed Black Caucus, established in 1971 to advance the gains of the civil rights movement, implemented a multipronged legislative strategy to force the White House to impose economic sanctions on South Africa; on the streets of Washington, the Free South Africa Movement launched a civil disobedience initiative that used famous personalities to draw attention to sit-ins outside South Africa's embassy; and elsewhere in the United States, college students and union leaders collaborated to push for the divestment of South African interests from shareholdings and pension funds at universities and city governments. Although this movement was less centrally coordinated than its European counterparts, its various threads came together dramatically during the mid-1980s when Congress overrode President Ronald Reagan's veto of the

Anti-Apartheid Act—a twentieth-century precedent in the foreign policy realm—and a constellation of banks and corporations abruptly left South Africa, triggering an economic crisis that accelerated Pretoria's turn toward genuine democracy. "We had an impact," one African American activist later reflected. "Reagan was accountable to me!"[10]

The statement captures the essence, as well as the irony, of the anti-apartheid solidarity campaign. The movement's protagonists were not so much oppressed by South Africa's policies as aware of South African oppression, and—just as ANC leaders had grasped during the late 1960s—their particular passions were as diverse as their economic, ethnic, and national backgrounds. It is useful to consider AAM's 1960 Boycott Movement and SDS's 1966 Chase Manhattan protests as harbingers of the activism that culminated with Mandela's release from prison. However, the road that linked the postapartheid and postcolonial moments was neither straight nor straightforward. The former reflected and reified a transnational conversation about plurality and morality; the latter was really a debate about the implications of second-wave decolonization. *Gordian Knot* narrated the prehistory of Mandela's triumph: a critical and misunderstood juncture in South Africa's journey to the present, and a transformative yet underappreciated period that saw the black Atlantic enter the community of nation-states. The echoes of the 1960s could be heard outside Victor Verster prison and in the living rooms of millions of television viewers in 1990, but these conceptual connections were muffled at best—and imbued with dozens of distinct meanings. South Africa's "long walk to freedom" was not the inevitable result of good's fight against evil. It was a political contest that ebbed and flowed in various directions as different doors opened and closed on international and domestic stages.

Reading the history of the apartheid debate forward—uncovering stakes as they existed in the 1960s rather than reflexively viewing South Africa's past on the terms of the early 1990s—reveals fresh insights about our world today, especially the nation-state's journey through the mid-twentieth century. For African nationalists, Pretoria's racial policies tested the conceptual ballast of decolonization itself, specifically the marriage of economic development and territorial autonomy with racial equality and human rights. For Afrikaner nationalists, independent Africa was an equally existential threat to theories of European sovereignty, separate development, and racial stratification. The supporters of these competing nationalisms adhered to dissimilar political strategies and utilized disparate tactics to navigate the international system in the 1960s, but they shared a common desire to legitimize their positions on the stage of global affairs. African diplomats used their numerical advantage at the U.N. General Assembly to isolate South Africa, while Afrikaner policymakers turned to private powerbrokers to translate colonial thinking into the language of modernization—and their campaigns formed the outlines of a very different conversation than the ones that surrounded Mandela in 1990. At stake was not only the future of nonwhite people living in South Africa, but the nature (and location) of the international community and the meaning of nationhood in the post-imperial age.

By virtue of America's extraordinary influence in the postwar world, policymakers in Washington, and to a lesser extent London, acted as reluctant referees in this contest. During the first decade of the Cold War, the United States typically viewed South Africa as a reliable member of the anticommunist coalition. Pretoria supported America's strategic goals in the world, gave a home to a NASA facility, and provided Western corporations with millions of dollars in revenue annually. However, decolonization—specifically the transformation of the U.N. General Assembly and the growth of black activism in the United States— altered the policymaking calculus surrounding apartheid in the 1960s. As the tentative breakthroughs of the Kennedy years gave way to the reform impulse of the Johnson administration, U.S. leaders adopted an increasingly antagonistic stance toward South Africa, and by 1966, it seemed to many observers that sanctions against Pretoria rested only on the outcome of the South West Africa case at the International Court of Justice. Having confronted racial discrimination in the Deep South, American liberals appeared ready to confront inequality and segregation within the Republic.

The ICJ decision both fragmented these trends and captured the contradictions of the postcolonial apartheid debate. Stripped of pretense, the initiatives of African nationalists rested on an affirmative answer to an undeniably controversial question: Did politicians at the U.N. General Assembly have the right to direct the actions of the Security Council? As African diplomats amplified their push to liberate South West Africa after the ICJ decision—formally renaming the territory Namibia, granting it unilateral independence in 1967, and establishing a council to govern the territory from abroad—the implications of this query came into focus for Washington policymakers. With domestic race riots and antiwar protests on the rise, the Johnson administration predictably scaled back its approach toward racial justice in the global arena. By the time Nixon entered the White House in 1969, the United States was already committed to limiting the effects of decolonization and establishing more constructive relations with Pretoria.

Out of this milieu emerged an empowered National Party and a deflated African Group. For a period after the 1955 Bandung meeting, it looked as though new nation-states would be able to use their numerical dominance of the U.N. General Assembly to wield real influence on the international stage and reorient the world agenda—imagined in singular terms—toward global north-south concerns of white racism and economic manipulation. However, decolonization never signified the "leveling" of the geopolitical playing field. Washington viewed diplomacy at the United Nations always as a means toward establishing

Americentric consensus in the world. African nationalists achieved a number of victories in these years, altering assumptions about racial discrimination and postcolonial territoriality in the process, but the setbacks of the late 1960s were inevitable, born of deeper disagreements about the nature and meaning of decolonization itself. As frustrations mounted in the mid-1960s, global politics started to bifurcate sharply along state and nonstate lines, leaving South Africa politically secure yet devoid of legitimacy and positioned opposite an amorphous legion of transnational activists who found solace in broad discourses of human rights, Third Worldism, and Marxist internationalism. The era of European imperialism ended in the 1960s. But postcolonial freedom—imagined so vividly in the years surrounding Africa's independence—was nothing more than a chimera by 1970. For diplomats and activists in the First and Third Worlds, events had not coalesced around nonracial equality, territorial autonomy, and economic progress but political cynicism, moral relativism, and economic individualism.

This book narrates the history of the apartheid debate during these contentious years to shed light on a moment of political and epistemological upheaval. Apartheid's apparent intractability made the fight for the Republic's future a combustible *entrepôt* of political and intellectual exchange. The contest over South Africa's future exposed the uneven nature and the inherent contradictions of American hegemony after World War II, as well as the multifarious ways that diplomats, policymakers, and activists traversed the context of their times. The story of the postcolonial apartheid debate hints both at the political trends that underlie the postmodern intellectual revolution and the frustrations that powered the boom of new forms of nongovernmental activism after 1970. Narratives that reflexively pit white oppressors against black liberators fail to adequately capture the complexity of this period. But process-oriented histories—calibrated to explain the dynamic interplay of politics and ideas—have the ability to genuinely remap the past of the present and give today's cosmopolitans a more sophisticated framework to reimagine tomorrow. This book, hopefully, is a small step in that direction.

NOTES

Introduction

1. Richard Wright, *Black Power* (New York, 2008), 535–38.
2. Ibid., 543, 547. For work on the Bandung conference, see George McTurnan Kahin, *The Asian-African Conference* (Ithaca, 1956); G. H. Jansen, *Afro-Asia and Non-Alignment* (London, 1966); Carlos Romulo, *The Meaning of Bandung* (Chapel Hill, 1956). For more recent scholarly analysis, see Vijay Prashad, *The Darker Nations* (New York, 2008); Christopher J. Lee, ed., *Making a World after Empire* (Athens, 2010); See Seng Tan and Amitav Acharya, eds., *Bandung Revisited* (Singapore, 2008); Cary Fraser, "An American Dilemma: Race and Realpolitik in the American Response to the Bandung Conference, 1955," in *Window on Freedom*, ed. Brenda Gayle Plummer (Chapel Hill, 2003); Matthew Jones, "A 'Segregated' Asia? Race, the Bandung Conference, and Pan-Asianist Fears in American Thought and Policy, 1954–1955," *Diplomatic History* 29:5 (November 2005): 841–68; Jason C. Parker, "Cold War II: The Eisenhower Administration, the Bandung Conference, and the Reperiodization of the Postwar Era," *Diplomatic History* 30:5 (November 2006): 12–25.
3. For useful texts on American power in the Cold War, see Melvyn P. Leffler, *Preponderance of Power* (Stanford, 1992); Melvyn P. Leffler, *For the Soul of Mankind* (New York, 2007); John Lewis Gaddis, *Strategies of Containment* (New York, 2005); Michael J. Hogan, *The Marshall Plan* (New York, 1987); Wm. Roger Louis, *Imperialism at Bay* (New York, 1978); Mark Atwood Lawrence, *Assuming the Burden* (Berkeley, 2005); Charles S. Maier, *Among Empires* (Cambridge, MA, 2006); Marc Trachtenberg, *A Constructed Peace* (Princeton, 1999); and Odd Arne Westad, *The Global Cold War* (New York, 2005).
4. For scholarship on the Eastern bloc in the Cold War, see Vladislav M. Zubok, *A Failed Empire* (Chapel Hill, 2007); Vladislav M. Zubok, *Inside the Kremlin's Cold War* (Cambridge, MA, 1996); Chen Jian, *Mao's China and the Cold War* (Chapel Hill, 2001); Jonathan Haslam, *Russia's Cold War* (New Haven, 2011); Lorenz M. Luthi, *The Sino-Soviet Split* (Princeton, 2008); Odd Arne Westad, ed., *Brothers in Arms* (Stanford, 1998); Jeremy Scott Friedman, *Reviving Revolution* (PhD diss., 2011).
5. For work on the Korean War, see Bruce Cumings, *The Origins of the Korean War*, vol. 1–2 (Princeton, 1981, 1990); Rosemary Foot, *Substitute for Victory* (Ithaca, NY, 1990); Chen Jian, *China's Road to the Korean War* (New York, 1994); William Stueck, *The Korean War* (Princeton, 1995); as well as James Matray, "The Korean War," in *A Companion to American Foreign Relations*, ed. Robert D. Schulzinger (Oxford, 2003).
6. For a primer on scholarship about postcolonial thought, see Robert J. C. Young, *Postcolonialism* (London, 2001); and Leela Gandhi, ed., *Postcolonial Theory* (New York, 1998). For a useful summary of the field of postcolonial studies, see Ania Loomba et al. eds., *Postcolonial Studies and Beyond* (Durham, 2006). For excellent snapshots of the colonizer/colonized

binary over time, see Frantz Fanon, *The Wretched of the Earth* (New York, 1963); Frantz
Fanon, *Black Skin, White Masks* (New York, 1967); Albert Memmi, *The Colonizer and the
Colonized* (Boston, 1965); Edward Said, *Orientalism* (New York, 1978); Ngugi Wa Thiongo,
Decolonising the Mind (London, 1986). For influential recent works on subaltern dimensions
of postcolonial thought, see Homi Bhabha, *The Location of Culture* (New York, 1994);
Dipesh Chakrabarty, *Rethinking Working-Class History* (Princeton, 1989); Partha Chatterjee,
Nationalist Thought and the Colonial World (Tokyo, 1986); Partha Chatterjee, *The Nation and
Its Fragments* (Princeton, 1993); Frederick Cooper, *Colonialism in Question* (Berkeley, 2005);
Frederick Cooper et al. eds., *Confronting Historical Paradigms* (Madison, 1993); Frederick
Cooper and Ann Laura Stoler, eds., *Tensions of Empire* (Berkeley, 1997); Paul Gilroy, *The
Black Atlantic* (Cambridge, MA, 1993); Ranajit Guha, "Dominance Without Hegemony and
Its Historiography," in *Subaltern Studies 6* (Delhi, 1989); Achille Mbembe, *On the Postcolony*
(Berkeley, 2001); David Scott, *Conscripts of Modernity* (Durham, 2004); James Scott, *Domi-
nation and the Arts of Resistance* (New Haven, 1990); Todd Shepard, *The Invention of Decolo-
nization* (Ithaca, NY, 2006); Ann Laura Stoler, *Carnal Knowledge and Imperial Power*
(Berkeley, 2002); Ann Laura Stoler, *Haunted by Empire* (Durham, 2006).

7. For a useful essay, see Emily S. Rosenberg, "Considering Borders," in *Explaining the History
of Foreign Relations*, ed. Michael J. Hogan and Thomas G. Paterson (Cambridge, UK, 2005).

8. For useful literature reviews, see Frederick Cooper, "Conflict and Connection: Rethinking
Colonial African History," *American Historical Review* 99:5 (December 1994): 1516–45;
Frederick Cooper, "Africa's Pasts and Africa's Historians," *Canadian Journal of African
Studies/Revue Canadienne des Éstudes Africaines* 34:2 (2000): 298–336; Christopher J. Lee,
"Between a Moment and an Era: The Origins and Afterlives of Bandung," in his *Making A
World After Empire* (Athens, 2010). For useful scholarship on postcolonial Africa, see Fred-
erick Cooper, *Africa since 1940* (New York, 2002); James Ferguson, *Global Shadows* (Dur-
ham, 2006). For relevant international relations scholarship, see Bertrand Badie, *The
Imported State* (Stanford, 2000); Robert H. Jackson, *Quasi-states* (Cambridge, UK, 1990).

9. For a useful essay, see Michael Geyer and Charles Bright, "World History in a Global Age,"
American Historical Review, 100 (October 1995): 1034–60. For classic treatments of apart-
heid debate, see Janice Love, *The U.S. Anti-Apartheid Movement* (New York, 1985); Robert
Kinloch Massie, *Loosing the Bonds* (New York, 1997); Bernard Makhosezwe Magubane,
The Ties That Bind (Trenton, 1987); William Minter, *King Soloman's Mines Revisited* (New
York, 1986); George Shepherd Jr., *Anti-Apartheid* (Westport, 1977); Les de Villiers, *In
Sight of Surrender* (Westport, 1985); as well as George M. Fredrickson, *White Supremacy*
(New York, 1981); George M. Fredrickson, *Black Liberation* (New York, 1995); and John
W. Cell, *The Highest Stage of White Supremacy* (New York, 1982). For more recent treat-
ments, see Francis Njubi Nesbitt, *Race for Sanctions* (Bloomington, 2004); Donald R. Cul-
verson, *Contesting Apartheid* (Boulder, 1999); and Eric J. Morgan, "Into the Struggle:
Confronting Apartheid in the United States and South Africa, 1964–1990" (PhD diss.
2009). Other relevant works that examine South Africa's place in the world include Carol
Anderson, *Eyes Off the Prize* (New York, 2003); Lewis V. Baldwin, *Toward the Beloved Com-
munity* (Cleveland, 1995); Thomas Borstelmann, *Cold War and the Color Line* (Cambridge,
MA, 2002); Thomas Borstelmann, *Apartheid's Reluctant Uncle* (Oxford, 1993); Mary
L. Dudziak, *Cold War Civil Rights* (Princeton, 2002); Penny von Eschen, *Race against
Empire* (Ithaca, 1997); Kevin K. Gaines, *American Africans in Ghana* (Chapel Hill, 2006);
Larry Grubbs, *Secular Missionaries* (Amherst, 2011); Calvin Holder, "Racism Towards
Black African Diplomats During the Kennedy Administration," *Journal of Black Studies*
14:1 (1983): 31–48; Marilyn Lake and Henry Reynolds, *Drawing the Global Colour Line*
(Cambridge, UK, 2008); Brenda Gayle Plummer, *Rising Wind*; James H. Meriwether,
Proudly We Can Be Africans (Chapel Hill, 2002); Thomas J. Noer, *Cold War and Black Lib-
eration* (Columbia, 1985); Nikhil Pal Singh, *Black is a Country* (Cambridge, MA, 2005);
Alvin B. Tilley, Jr., *Between Homeland and Motherland* (Ithaca, 2011); Ronald Walters, *Pan
Africanism in the African Diaspora* (Detroit, 1997).

10. For some excellent work on the intellectual, political, and social dimensions of decoloniza-
tion, see Cemil Aydin, *The Politics of Anti-Westernism in Asia* (New York, 2007); Frederick
Cooper, *Decolonization and African Society* (Cambridge, UK, 1996); Matthew Connelly, *A
Diplomatic Revolution* (New York, 2003); Pransenjit Duara, ed., *Decolonization* (New York,
2004); Wm. Roger Louis, *Ends of British Imperialism* (New York, 2007); Erez Manela, *The
Wilsonian Moment* (New York, 2007); Jason C. Parker, *Brother's Keeper* (New York, 2008);
Martin Shipway, *Decolonization and Its Impact* (Oxford, 2008); James D. Le Sueur, ed., *The
Decolonization Reader* (New York, 2003); Robert Tignor, *Capitalism and Nationalism at the
End of Empire* (Princeton, 1998).

11. Pioneered initially by the Wisconsin school in the 1960s and 1970s, arguments about
American imperialism gained wider legitimacy among foreign relations historians when
postrevisionist scholars embraced it during the 1980s and 1990s. For two prominent exam-
ples, see John Lewis Gaddis, *We Now Know* (New York, 1997); and Geir Lundestad,
"Empire by Invitation? The United States and Western Europe, 1945–1952," *Journal of
Peace Research* 23:3 (September 1986): 263–277. In recent years, the question of imperial
continuity has taken on new meaning. For just a few prominent examples, see Chakrabarty,
Provincializing Europe (Princeton, 2000); Maier, *Among Empires*; Mark Mazower, *No
Enchanted Palace* (Princeton, 2009); and Westad, *The Global Cold War*. For examples of
scholarship about globalization, see Matthew Connelly, *Fatal Misconception* (Cambridge,
MA, 2008); Nick Cullather, *The Hungry World* (Cambridge, MA, 2010); Niall Ferguson et
al., eds., *The Shock of the Global* (Cambridge, MA, 2010); Jessica Gienow-Hecht, "Cultural
Transfer," in *Explaining the History of American Foreign Relations*, ed. Michael J. Hogan and
Thomas G. Paterson (Cambridge, UK, 2004); Akira Iriye, *Global Community* (Berkeley,
2002); Erez Manela, "Writing Disease Control into Cold War History," *Diplomatic History*
34:2 (April 2010): 299–323. For useful context on the field of world history, see Ross
Dunn, ed., *The New World History* (New York, 1990); and Patrick Manning, *Navigating
World History* (New York, 2003); as well as Thomas Bender, ed., *Rethinking American History in a Global Age* (Berkeley, 2002).

12. For a useful conceptual analysis, see Tony Smith, "New Bottles for New Wine: A Pericentric Framework for the Study of the Cold War," *Diplomatic History* 24:4 (December 2002):
567–91.

13. For an influential call to remove the Cold War, see Matthew Connelly, "Taking Off the Cold
War Lens: Visions of North-South Conflict during the Algerian War for Independence,"
American Historical Review 105:3 (June 2000): 739–69.

14. For useful works, see Elizabeth Borgwardt, *A New Deal for the World* (Cambridge, MA,
2005); David Bosco, *Five to Rule Them All* (New York, 2009); David Ekbladh, *The Great
American Mission* (Princeton, 2009); Robert Hilderbrand, *Dumbarton Oaks* (Chapel Hill,
1990); John Ikenberry, *After Victory* (Princeton, 2001); Michael Latham, *The Right Kind of
Revolution* (Ithaca, 2011); Amy Staples, *The Birth of Development* (Kent, OH, 2006).

Chapter 1

1. James Clarke, ed., *Like It Was* (Johannesburg, 1987), 171.
2. "Macmillan Set to Begin Africa Tour," *Guardian*, January 10, 1960, BTS 22/2/20/9, vol. 1,
National Archives of South Africa (hereafter NASA).
3. Telegram of C.R.O., February 2, 1960, PREM 11/3072, National Archives of United Kingdom (hereafter NA).
4. Full speech quoted in Nicholas Mansergh, ed., *Documents and Speeches on Commonwealth
Affairs, 1952–1962* (London, 1963), 347–51; for a description of the presentation see
"Macmillan Spoke to Unseen Ears," *Cape Times*, February 4, 1960, BTS 22/2/20/9, vol. 1,
NASA.
5. "Macmillan Spoke to Unseen Ears," *Cape Times*, February 4, 1960, BTS 22/2/20/9, vol. 1,
NASA.

6. "Macmillan's 'Very Object' Defeated," *Cape Times*, February 4, 1960, BTS 22/2/20/9, vol. 1, NASA.

7. No title, *Die Burger*, February 8, 1960, BTS 22/2/20/9, vol. 1, NASA.

8. "The Union Must Brace Up," *Cape Times*, February 11, 1960, BTS 22/2/20/9, vol. 1, NASA.

9. Rodney Davenport and Christopher Saunders, *South Africa* (New York, 2000); Leonard Thompson, *A History of South Africa* (New Haven, 2000), 110–53; William Worger, *South Africa's City of Diamonds* (New Haven, 1987).

10. F. A. van Jaarsveld, *The Awakening of Afrikaner Nationalism, 1868–1881* (Cape Town, 1961); T. Dunbar Moodie, *The Rise of Afrikanerdom* (Berkeley, 1975); Leonard Thompson, *The Political Mythology of Apartheid* (New Haven, 1985); Hermann Giliomee, *The Afrikaners* (Charlottesville, 2003).

11. Thomas Pakenham, *The Boer War* (New York, 1979); Peter Warwick, ed., *The South African War* (London, 1980).

12. P. Eric Louw, *The Rise, Fall, and Legacy of Apartheid* (London, 2004), 6. P. Eric Louw should not be confused with South Africa's minister of foreign affairs Eric Hendrik Louw, who served Pretoria until his retirement in 1963.

13. Alfred Milner, *The Nation and the Empire* (London, 1913); Cecil Headlam, ed., *The Milner Papers* (London, 1931, 1933); Walter Nimocks, *Milner's Young Men* (Durham, 1968); Jonathan Crush et al., *South Africa's Labour Empire* (New York, 1991).

14. Headlam, *The Milner Papers*, 308.

15. See William Beinart, Peter Delius, and Stanley Trapido, eds., *Putting a Plough to the Ground* (Johannesburg, 1986); John W. Cell, *The Highest Stage of White Supremacy* (New York, 1982); George Frederickson, *White Supremacy* (New York, 1981); Merle Lipton, *Capitalism and Apartheid* (Totowa, 1985); Francis Wilson, *Labour in the South African Gold Mines* (New York, 1972).

16. See Giliomee, *The Afrikaners*; Moodie, *The Rise of Afrikanerdom*; Thompson, *The Political Mythology of Apartheid*.

17. See William Beinart, *Twentieth Century South Africa* (Oxford, 2001), 62–87; Thompson, *A History of South Africa*, 154–86; Davenport and Saunders, *South Africa*, 293–324; Heribert Adam and Hermann Giliomee, *Ethnic Power Mobilized* (London, 1979).

18. For broad literature on Afrikaner nationalism, see Dan O'Meara, *Volkskapitalisme* (Johannesburg, 1983); Adam and Giliomee, *Ethnic Power Mobilized*; Giliomee, *The Afrikaners*; van Jaarsveld, *The Awakening of Afrikaner Nationalism, 1868–1881*; van Jaarsveld, *The Afrikaner's Interpretation of South African History* (Cape Town, 1964); Moodie, *The Rise of Afrikanerdom*; J. H. P. Serfontein, *Brotherhood of Power* (London, 1979); Thompson, *The Political Mythology of Apartheid*. See also Hendrik Verwoerd, "Die bestryding van armoede en die herorganisasie van welvaartswerk," in *Verslag van die Volkskongres oor die armblankevraagstuk*, ed. P. Du Toit (Cape Town, 1935).

19. Nico Diederichs, *Nasionalisme as lewensbeskouing en sy verhouding tot internasionalisme* (Bloemfontein, 1936).

20. Geoffrey Cronje, *In Tuiste vir die Nageslag: Die blywende Oplossing van Suid-Afrika se Rasse-Vraagstukke* (Johannesburg, 1945).

21. For discussion of terms, see Giliomee, *The Afrikaners*, 475–541; Deborah Posel, *The Making of Apartheid, 1848–1961* (Oxford, 1992); Adam, *Modernizing Racial Domination*.

22. Giliomee, *The Afrikaners*, 533–61.

23. Louw, *The Rise, Fall and Legacy of Apartheid*, 31.

24. See Giliomee, *The Afrikaners*, 475–80; Louw, *The Rise, Fall and Legacy of Apartheid*, 30–36; O'Meara, *Volkskapitalisme*, 48–59.

25. Quoted in Giliomee, *The Afrikaners*, 374.

26. See Louw, *The Rise, Fall and Legacy of Apartheid*, 30–36; Willem de Klerk, *The Puritans of Africa* (Harmondsworth, 1976), 114; J. Lochner, *Taal en Hegemony: Die ontwikkeling van Afrikaans as uitsaaitaal, 1923–1948* (Johannesburg, 2002).

27. See Thompson, *A History of South Africa*, 154–86.
28. The urbanization rate among black Africans was 32 percent in 1960. Although this was much lower than the 84 percent rate among whites, it meant that approximately one million more blacks than whites were moving to cities; James Tarver, ed., *Urbanization in Africa: A Handbook* (London, 1994), 315–38; Bernard Magubane, *The Political Economy of Race and Class in South Africa* (New York, 1979), 102–9, 119–62; *South African Prospects and Progress* (Pretoria, 1963), 13–20. Also see Mahmood Mamdani, *Citizens and Subjects* (Princeton, 1996).
29. For discussion of new liberal internationalism see Elizabeth Borgwardt, *A New Deal for the World* (Cambridge, MA, 2005). For effects in South Africa, see Beinart, *Twentieth Century South Africa*, 114–40; Moodie, "The Moral Economy of the Black Miners' Strike of 1946," *Journal of South African Studies*, [hereafter *JSAS*] 13 (1986): 1–35; Tom Lodge, *Black Politics in South Africa since 1945* (London, 1983).
30. For an overview of early the National Party, see Louw, *The Rise, Fall and Legacy of Apartheid*, 57–58, Gilmomee, *Afrikaners*, 489–501.
31. Quoted in Giliomee, *Afrikaners*, 477.
32. Ibid., 478.
33. The literature on early apartheid policy is rich. See Adam, *Modernizing Racial Domination*; Douglas Hindson, *Pass Controls and the Urban African Proletariat* (Johannesburg, 1987); Posel, *The Making of Apartheid*; Ian Goldin, *Making Race* (Harlow, 1987); Marks and Trapido, *The Politics of Race*; John Western, *Outcast Cape Town* (London, 1981); Alan Mabin, "Comprehensive Segregation: The Origins of the Group Areas Act and its Planning Apparatuses," *JSAS* 18:2 (1992): 405–429; Bonner et al., *Apartheid's Genesis, 1935–1962* (Johannesburg, 1993).
34. For a broad overview, see Beinart, *Twentieth Century South Africa*, 143–69.
35. "Race Policy Explained," *Fortnightly Digest of South African Affairs*, 3:19, 5.
36. Hendrik Verwoerd, *Separate Development* (Pretoria, 1958).
37. Mamdani, *Citizens and Subjects*, 3–34.
38. Quoted in Alexander Hepple, *Verwoerd* (Baltimore, 1967), 120.
39. See Bonner et al., *Apartheid's Genesis, 1935–1962*; Jonathan Hyslop, "State Education Policy and the Social Reproduction of the Urban African Working Class," *JSAS* 14:3 (1988): 446–476; Peter Kallaway, ed., *Apartheid and Education* (Johannesburg, 1984).
40. Posel, *The Making of Apartheid, 1948–1961*, 226.
41. For broad analyses of grand apartheid, see Bonner et al., *Apartheid's Genesis, 1935–1962*; Posel, *The Making of Apartheid, 1948–1961*; Goldin, *Making Race*; Marks and Trapido, *The Politics of Race*; Nancy Clark and William Worger, *The Rise and Fall of Apartheid* (New York, 2004), 59–61. Also useful is Union of South Africa, *Summary Report of the Commission for the Socio-Economic Development of the Bantu Areas within the Union of South Africa*, UG 61, otherwise known as the Tomlinson Commission.
42. Bonner et al., *Apartheid's Genesis*; Posel, *The Making of Apartheid*, 246–71.
43. For best overview, see Andr Odendaal, *Vukani Bantu!* (Cape Town, 1984).
44. Quoted in Peter Walshe, *The Rise of African Nationalism in South Africa* (London, 1970), 38.
45. Quoted in Odendaal, *Vukani Bantu!* 273–74.
46. For discussion of SANNC, see Beinart, *Twentieth Century South Africa*, 88–95.
47. Walshe, *The Rise of African Nationalism in South Africa*, 30–35.
48. See Manela, *The Wilsonian Moment* (New York, 2007).
49. Quoted in Carter and Worter, *The Rise and Fall of Apartheid*, 24.
50. For overview of patterns, see Beinart et al., *Plough to the Ground*; Beinart, *Hidden Struggles in Rural South Africa* (London, 1990); Lipton, *Capitalism and Apartheid*; Colin Bundy, *The Rise and Fall of Peasant Communities* (London, 1979); Shula Marks, *Reluctant Rebellion* (London, 1970); Donald Crummey, ed., *Banditry, Rebellion and Social Protest in Africa* (Johannesburg, 1986); Nicholas Cope, *To Bind the Nation* (Pietermaritzburg, 1993).

51. For overview of patterns, see Crush et al., *South Africa's Labour Empire*; Moodie and Vivienne Ndatshe, *Going for Gold* (Berkeley, 1994); Belinda Bozzoli, ed., *Town and Countryside* (Johannesburg, 1983); Belinda Bozzoli, ed., *Class Community and Conflict* (Johannesburg, 1987); Denis MacShane et al., *Power! Black Workers, Their Unions, and the Struggle for Freedom in South Africa* (Nottingham, 1984); Bonner et al., *Holding Their Ground*; Bonner, "The Allure of Violence: Men, Race and Masculinity on the South African Goldmines, 1900–1950," *JSAS* 24:4 (1998): 669–694.

52. Beinart, 88–95.

53. See Helen Bradford, *A Taste of Freedom* (Johannesburg, 1988).

54. See Bengt Sundkler, *Bantu Prophets in South Africa* (London, 1948); Robert Edgar, *Because They Chose the Plan of God* (Johannesburg, 1988); Robert Edgar and Hilary Sapire, *African Apocalypse* (Johannesburg, 1999); Charles van Onselen, *Social and Economic History of the Witwatersrand* (Johannesburg, 1990); Charles van Onselen, "The Cows of Nongoloza: Youth, Crime and Amalaita Gangs in Durban, 1900–1936," *JSAS* 16:1 (1990): 79–111.

55. Leroy Vail, ed., *The Creation of Tribalism* (London, 1990); Bonner et al., ed., *Holding Their Ground*; Beinart, *The Political Economy of Pondoland* (Cambridge, 1982); Kenneth Grundy, *Soldiers without Politics* (Berkeley, 1983); Shula Marks, *The Ambiguities of Dependence in Southern Africa* (Johannesburg, 1986).

56. "ANC Youth League Manifesto" (1944), www.anc.org.za/, accessed August 28, 2008. For the best overview of Youth League activities, see Gail Gerhart, *Black Power in South Africa* (Berkeley, 1978), 1–84.

57. "ANC Youth League Basic Policy Documents" (1948), www.anc.org.za/, accessed August 28, 2008.

58. Gerhart, *Black Power in South Africa*, 45–123.

59. Ibid., 45–84.

60. Robin Kelley, "But a Local Phase of a Global Problem," *Journal of American History* 86: 3 (1999): 1045–1077; see also Toyin Falola, *Nationalism and African Intellectuals* (Rochester, 2001); Tajudeen Abdul-Raheem, *Pan Africanism* (New York, 1996); Kinfe Abraham, *Politics of Black Nationalism* (Trenton, 1991); A. B. Assensoh, *African Political Leadership* (Malabar, 1998); Thomas Hodgkin, *Nationalism in Colonial Africa* (New York, 1957); J. Ayodele Langley, *Pan-Africanism in West Africa* (Oxford, 1973); Ndabaningi Sithole, *African Nationalism* (London, 1959); Immanuel Wallerstein, *Africa and the Modern World* (Trenton, 1986); Immanuel Wallerstein, *Africa: The Politics of Independence* (New York, 1961); Henry S. Wilson, *Origins of West African Nationalism* (London, 1969).

61. See writings of Nnamdi Azikiwe, *My Odyssey* (London, 1970); Nnamdi Azikiwe, *Renascent Africa* (London, 1968); Jomo Kenyatta, *Facing Mount Kenya* (New York, 1965); Ali A. Mazrui, *Towards a Pax Africana* (London, 1967); Kwame Nkrumah, *Africa Must Unite* (London, 1963); Kwame Nkrumah, *Towards Colonial Freedom* (London, 1962); Kwame Nkrumah, *Ghana* (London, 1957); George Padmore, *Pan Africanism or Communism?* (London, 1956).

62. See writings of Nnamdi Azikiwe, *My Odyssey* (London, 1970); Nnamdi Azikiwe, *Renascent Africa* (London, 1968); Jomo Kenyatta, *Facing Mount Kenya* (New York, 1965); Ali A. Mazrui, *Towards a Pax Africana* (London, 1967); Kwame Nkrumah, *Africa Must Unite* (London, 1963); Kwame Nkrumah, *Towards Colonial Freedom* (London, 1962); Kwame Nkrumah, *Ghana* (London, 1957); George Padmore, *Pan Africanism or Communism?* (London, 1956).

63. Cooper, *Decolonization and African Society*; Cooper, "The Dialectics of Decolonization: Nationalism and Labor Movements in Postwar French Africa," in his *Tensions of Empire*, 406–35; Cooper, "Postcolonial Studies and the Study of History," in his *Postcolonial Studies and Beyond* (Durham, 2006). For variations on this theme, see subaltern theory such as Chatterjee, *Nationalist Thought and the Colonial World*; and Chakrabarty, *Provincializing Europe*.

64. For analysis of early notions of territoriality, see Eric Weitz, "From Vienna to the Paris System," *American Historical Review* 113:5 (2008): 1313–43.

65. See James T. Campbell, *Songs of Zion* (New York, 1995); Gilroy, *The Black Atlantic*. See also Gilroy, "Nationalism, History and Ethnic Absolutism," *History Workshop*, 30 (Autumn 1990): 114–20; Gilroy, "One Nation Under Groove: The Cultural Politics of 'Race' and Racism in Britain," in *Anatomy of Racism*, ed. David Goldberg (Minneapolis, 1990). Other interesting works in this vein are Kwame Appiah, *In My Father's House: Africa in the Philosophy of Culture* (New York, 1992); Bhabha, *The Location of Culture*. Useful recent reformulations of pan-Africanism are Thomas Holt, *The Problem of Race in the Twenty-first Century* (Cambridge, MA, 2000); and Nikhal Pal Singh, *Black is a Country* (Cambridge, MA, 2004).

66. See Abdul-Raheem, *Pan Africanism*; Willie E. Abraham, *The Mind of Africa* (Chicago, 1962); Molefi Kete Asante, *The Afrocentric Idea* (Philadelphia, 1987); Richard Bjornson, *The African Quest for Freedom and Identity* (Bloomington, 1991); John DeGraft-Johnson, *African Glory* (London, 1954); Emmanuel Chukwudi Eze, ed., *African Philosophy* (Oxford, 1998); Imanuel Geiss, *The Pan-African Movement* (London, 1974); Robert W. July and Petern Benson, eds., *African Culture and Intellectual Leaders and the Development of the New African Nations* (New York, 1982); Colin Legum, *Pan-Africanism* (New York, 1962).

67. The literature on this topic is sprawling. A few representative works include Allen Isaacman, "Peasants and Rural Social Protest in Africa," *African Studies Review* 33:2 (Sept. 1990): 1–120; Luise White, "Separating the Men from the Boys: Colonial Constructions of Gender in Central Kenya," *International Journal of African Historical Studies* 23:1, 1–26.

68. Alex Quaison-Sackey, *African Unbound* (New York, 1963), 37.

69. The best work on this topic is Cooper, *Decolonization and African Society;* John D. Hargreaves, *Decolonization in Africa* (London, 1988); Tignor, *Capitalism and Nationalism at the End of Empire;* and Bill Freund, *The Making of Contemporary Africa* (Boulder, 1998).

70. An emerging literature deals with the dialogue over development in Africa. Some examples include Monica van Beusekom, *Negotiating Development* (Portsmouth, 2002); Carolyn Brown, "Struggles over the Labor Process: Enugu Government Colliery, Nigeria during World War II," *Comparative Studies of South Asia, Africa and the Middle East* 15:2 (1995): 47–63; Timothy Oberst, "Transport Workers, Strikes and the 'Imperial Response': Africa and the Post World War II Conjuncture," *African Studies Review* 31:1 (1998): 117–34.

71. Anton Lembede, "Why General Smuts' Proposals Will Be Rejected," *African Advocate*, July 1947.

72. Ibid.

73. Lembede, "Policy of the Congress Youth League," *Inkundla ya Bantu*, May 1946.

74. Ibid.

75. Lembede, "African Nationalism and the New African Masses," *Ilanga lase Natal*, June 21, 1947.

76. These points are broadly discussed in Cooper, *Decolonization and African Society*. For older interpretations, see A. Adu Boahen, *General History of Africa* (Berkeley, 1985); James Smoot Coleman, *Nigeria* (Berkeley, 1958); and Thomas Hodgkin, *Nationalism in Colonial Africa* (New York, 1957); as well as the autobiographies of Kwame Nkrumah, Nnamdi Azikiwe, Jomo Kenyatta. For reflections on new historiographical trends, see Cooper et al., *Confronting Historical Paradigms;* Frederick Cooper and Randall Packard, eds. *International Development and the Social Sciences* (Berkeley, 1997).

77. Cooper, *Decolonization and African Society*.

78. Ibid.

79. For two views, see David Birmingham, *Kwame Nkrumah* (Athens, 1990); and Richard Rathbone, *Nkrumah and the Chiefs* (Athens, 2000).

80. Three useful works on this struggle include, Lodge, *Black Politics in South Africa Since 1945;* Gerhart, *Black Power in South Africa;* and Jackie Grobler, *A Decisive Clash?* (Pretoria, 1988).

81. Lembede, "Policy of the Congress Youth League," *Inkundla ya Bantu*, May 1946.

82. Gerhart, *Black Power in South Africa*, 85–123.

83. *ANC Freedom Charter* (1955), www.anc.org.za/, accessed August 28, 2008.

84. Quoted in Mary Benson, *South Africa* (New York, 1966), 209.
85. Good overviews of this period are found in Lodge, *Black Politics in South Africa Since 1945*; and Gerhart, *Black Power in South Africa*.
86. Robert Sobukwe, "The State of the Nation," August 2, 1959, Robert Sobukwe Collection, Liberation Archives, University of Fort Hare (hereafter UFH), www.liberation.org.za, accessed September 12, 2008.
87. P. K. Leballo, "This is Our Land," *Africanist*, December 1955, 11.
88. "African Unity," *Africanist*, March 1958, 18.
89. Quoted in Grobler, *A Decisive Clash?* 120.
90. Sobukwe, "The State of the Nation," August 2, 1959, Robert Sobukwe Collection, UFH, www.liberation.org.za, accessed September 12, 2008.
91. See Gerhart, *Black Power in South Africa*, 204–11. According to her interviews with prominent PAC members, Padmore's *Pan-Africanism or Communism?* was "compulsory reading among South African nationalists" in the late 1950s. Even more, the PAC's flag showed a green field with a black map of African and a gold star in the northwest, beaming in light southward from Ghana.
92. See Nelson Mandela, *Long Walk to Freedom* (New York, 1995), 227; Luli Callinicos, *Oliver Tambo* (Cape Town, 2004), 157–249; *The Road to Democracy in South Africa* (Cape Town, 2004), 257–318; Gerhart, *Black Power in South Africa*, 167–256.
93. Sobukwe, "Time for Action," July 11, 1959, Robert Sobukwe Collection, UFH, www.liberation.org.za, accessed September 12, 2008.
94. For the best account, see Gerhart, *Black Power in South Africa*, 173–236.
95. Quoted in Edward Roux, *Time Longer Than Rope* (Madison, 1966), 150–51.
96. Gerhart, *Black Power in South Africa*, 236.
97. Ibid.
98. For a full retelling of the Sharpeville drama, as well as a thorough overview of historiography, see Tom Lodge, *Sharpeville* (New York, 2011). For contemporary government version of events see *A Précis of the Reports of the Commissions Appointed to Enquire into the Events Occurring on March 21, 1960 at Sharpeville and Langa* (Johannesburg, 1961); for a contemporary reporter's version see Bernard Sachs, *The Road From Sharpeville* (New York, 1961).
99. "S.A. the West's Most Faithful Ally in Africa," *South Africa Digest* 7:7, 3–9.

Chapter 2

1. Oliver Tambo to E.S. Reddy, May 6, 1964, Oliver Tambo: Correspondence, E. S. Reddy Papers, Yale University Manuscripts and Archives (hereafter YUMA).
2. "Areas of Co-operation and Common Interest Between the United States and South Africa (Secret)," no date, BTS 1/33/3, vol. 1, Archives of the South African Ministry of Foreign Affairs (hereafter ASAMFA), emphasis in original.
3. Gerhart, *Black Power in South Africa*, 205.
4. Sobukwe, "Opening Address," April 4, 1959, in *From Protest of Challenge*, vol. 3, ed. Thomas Karis and Gwendolen Carter (Stanford, 1977), 513.
5. "Manifesto of the Africanist Movement," in ibid., 521–22. In discussing African nationalism privately, Padmore and Nkrumah often framed this vision of a singular African nation-state in geopolitical terms. "Brother, you ask me how the fishes live in the sea?" Padmore asked Nkrumah in the mid 1950s. "I answer, as the great powers live—they eat up the little ones." A singular African nation-state would both enhance Africa's power abroad and buttress Nkrumah's personal authority among African politicians. Personal correspondence, May 10, 1954, box 154–41, Kwame Nkrumah Papers, Moorland-Spingarn Research Center at Howard University (MSRC).
6. Gerhart, *Black Power in South Africa*, 208.
7. Personal Correspondence, August 5, 1955, box 154–41, Kwame Nkrumah Papers, MSRC; as well as *From Protest of Challenge*, ed. Karis and Carter, 523. Padmore was especially

influential in casting African nationalism in juxtaposition to both communism and liberal capitalism. He hoped to "spread confusion in the imperialist camp" and "pose the problem: either Pan African freedom if the West wants to retain African friendship or Communism caused by disappointment and frustration." In his mind, this rhetorical strategy put "John Bull and the West . . . in a hell of a dilemma." Personal correspondence, August 5, 1955 and January 19, 1956, box 154–41, Kwame Nkrumah Papers, MSRC.

8. Sobukwe, "One Central Government in Africa," March 1960, *From Protest of Challenge*, ed. Karis and Carter, 562. Nineteen sixty-three was the target date set at the conference for complete decolonization in Africa.

9. Ibid., 563.

10. "Notes for the Delegates to the All-Africa People's Conference to Be Held in Accra," Ghana, December 1958, MF-13332, *African National Congress Collection, 1928–1962* (microform).

11. Joe Matthews, "Africanism under the Microscope," July 1959, in *From Protest of Challenge*, ed. Karis and Carter, 537.

12. Z. K. Matthews, "Non-White Political Organizations," *Africa Today*, November–December 1957; quoted in Gerhart, *Black Power in South Africa*, 205.

13. Mandela, *Long Walk to Freedom*, 238.

14. "Statement by the Emergency Committee of the African National Congress," April 1, 1960, quoted in *From Protest of Challenge*, ed. Karis and Carter, 574.

15. For many historians of South Africa, the banning of the liberation movements and the arrest of the ANC's leadership were important turning points because they ended aboveground protests against apartheid. The Sharpeville Massacre precipitated both events. The domestic side of the story, recounted by numerous South African historians, remains in the background of this narrative. However, it is worth noting that in the months following Verwoerd's decision to illegalize domestic protest in the Union, the PAC and ANC struggled to come to terms with the new restrictions placed on their activities. In May 1961, Mandela organized the All-In African Conference to unify the African protest movement and open negotiations with the National Party. However, Verwoerd (and many PAC members) ignored the meeting. In the subsequent months, the PAC and ANC shifted their efforts toward strategic violence. In June 1961, Mandela, Walter Sisulu, and others announced the formation of Umkhonto we Sizwe—designed to function as the armed wing of the ANC—and established a headquarters on the small farm of Rivonia outside Johannesburg. The PAC, similarly, formed a guerilla organization named Poqo, focusing its initiatives mostly on the Cape region. For useful overviews, see Lodge, *Black Politics in South Africa since 1945*; Grobler, *A Decisive Clash?*; and more recently *The Road to Democracy*.

16. Callinicos, *Oliver Tambo*, 263. It's worth noting that in 1960, neither the new leaders of Africa nor the PAC were advocating for violent action in South Africa. This approach would emerge as a viable option only in subsequent years and it would be supported fully by the ANC.

17. Aziz Pahad, interview by Luli Callinicos, August 11, 1993, quoted in Callinicos, *Oliver Tambo*, 263.

18. Quoted in ibid., 264.

19. Ibid., 264. Scott Thomas offers a useful overview of the ANC's Ghanaian experiences in *The Diplomacy of Liberation* (London, 1996), 28–37.

20. *African Digest*, September 1960; Sifiso Mxolisi Ndlovu disagrees with the conventional view that African leaders like Nkrumah pushed for the formation of the United Front but lacks evidence to support this claim.

21. "Statement on Behalf of the South Africa United Front," 1960, www.anc.org.za/, accessed December 18, 2008.

22. "UNO and Colonialism," *Congress Voice*, November 1960.

23. "Report of the 46th Annual National Conference," December 13–14, 1958, MF-13332, *African National Congress Collection, 1928–1962* (microform).

24. "UNO and Colonialism," *Congress Voice*, November 1960.
25. Signs of trouble between the Congress Alliance and PAC emerged at the 1961 All-In African Conference in South Africa, when the PAC delegation used the presence of communists as an excuse to withdraw from the conference. As both groups turned to violence in subsequent months, their differences widened, with Poqo—the PAC's armed unit—using violence and terrorism to fight the Nationalist government, and Umkhonto we Sizwe—the ANC's military wing—using symbolic sabotage against the apartheid state. See Brown Bavusile Maaba, "The PAC's War against the State, 1960–1963"; Sello Mathabatha, "The PAC and POQO in Pretoria, 1958–1964"; Sifiso Mxolisi Ndlovu, "The ANC in Exile, 1960–1970," all in *The Road to Democracy*.
26. Quoted in George Houser, *No One Can Stop the Rain* (London, 1989), 269.
27. "Boycott and Economic Sanctions," ANC London Papers, MCHO2-1, box 1, UFH.
28. *Yearbook of the United Nations* (New York, 1961), 108–15.
29. "Statement by the South African United Front," no date, see: www.anc.org.za/, accessed December 18, 2008.
30. The organizational structure of the UF was interesting. The PAC's Vusi Make and the ANC's Mzwai Piliso staffed the Cairo office; the PAC's Peter Molotsi and the ANC's Tennyson Makiwane managed the Accra office; and the PAC's Nana Mahomo, SWANU's Fanuel Kozanguizi, and the ANC's Yusuf Dadoo led the London office. For an overview see Callinicos, *Oliver Tambo*, 265–74, and Thomas, *The Diplomacy of Liberation*, 49–70.
31. "Resolutions Passed by the Second Conference of Independent African States," June 14–26, 1960, *Second Conference of Independent African States* (Addis Ababa, 1960), 105.
32. Ibid., 101–2.
33. "Address by His Imperial Majesty Haile Selassie," June 14, 1960, *Second Conference of Independent African States*, 26.
34. For an overview of London activists, see Christabel Gurney, "'A Great Cause': The Origins of the Anti-Apartheid Movement, June 1959–1960," *JSAS* 26:1 (March 2000): 213–244.
35. Ibid., 240–44.
36. Denis Herbstein, *White Lies* (Cape Town, 2004); Callinicos, *Oliver Tambo*, 268.
37. Callinicos, *Oliver Tambo*, 269.
38. Quoted in Tor Sellström, *Sweden and National Liberation* (Nordiska Afrikainstitet, 1999), 102–3.
39. Callinicos, *Oliver Tambo*, 269. Callinicos relates a story from Wästberg, who claims Tambo "was constantly visiting" Canon Collins's church in the early 1960s. "He just knocked on the door without phoning, and he went into the kitchen if we were having breakfast or afternoon tea. He sat at the fireplace in winter and discussed things; he was extremely relaxed with John Collins. I mean, they really loved each other."
40. Ndlovu, "The ANC in Exile, 1960–1970," in *The Road to Democracy*, 432.
41. Cited in Allison Drew, ed., *South Africa's Radical Tradition*, vol. 2 (Cape Town, 1997), 359–62.
42. "Nelson Mandela's Diary," Pan African Freedom Movement of East and Central Africa, Department of Justice, WLD 578/64, vol. 1, NASA. For Mandela's later recollections of this trip, see Mandela, *Long Walk to Freedom*, 286–302.
43. Ndlovu, "The ANC in Exile, 1960–1970," in *The Road to Democracy*, 432–35.
44. Mandela, *Long Walk to Freedom*, 287. See also Lodge, *Black Politics in South Africa since 1945*, 231–60.
45. Mandela, *Long Walk to Freedom*, 286–307.
46. Ibid.
47. Brown Bavusile Maaba, "The PAC's War Against the State, 1960–1963," in *The Road to Democracy*, 285–88; Hili Zwili Bantu, November 5, 1962, *Voice of Africa*, BTS 14/11, vol. 7, ASAMFA.
48. Focused on domestic events—and often relying upon subsequent interviews and oral histories—most historical accounts of the PAC and ANC tend to overlook the context

surrounding the shift toward violence in the early 1960s. The domestic side of the story remains important, but the decision to form MK and Poqo cannot be fully understood without acknowledging the contemporary influence of African nationalism. The shift toward strategic violence was as much an outgrowth of each movement's search for patrons as a byproduct of National Party oppression. For overviews of the turn to violence, see Lodge, *Black Politics in South Africa since 1945*; Grobler, *A Decisive Clash?*; and more recently *The Road to Democracy*.

49. For a documentary overview of Indian protest at the U.N. see U.N., *The United Nations and Apartheid, 1948–1994* (New York, 1994), 221–42.

50. "Excerpts of the Statements in the U.N. Resolution on South Africa," *New York Times*, April 1, 1960, 4.

51. Nkrumah, *Ghana*, 34; quoted in Francis Wilcox, *UN and the Nonaligned Nations* (New York, 1962), 13.

52. "Osagyefo at the United Nations," September 23, 1960, www.nkrumah.net, accessed on January 12, 2006.

53. "Excerpts of the Statements in the U.N. Resolution on South Africa," April 1, 1960, *New York Times*, 4.

54. Quaison-Sackey, *Africa Unbound*, 138.

55. Conference of Independent African States, Secretariat of the Informal Permanent Machinery, Document IAS/613, Annex III.

56. The most comprehensive overview remains Thomas Hovet, Jr., *Africa in the United Nations* (Chicago, 1963).

57. U.N. General Assembly, Resolution 1514 (XV), "Declaration of Independence to Colonial Peoples and Territories," December 1960, www.un.org/en/documents/index.shtml, accessed January 5, 2009.

58. Quaison-Sackey, *Africa Unbound*, 140.

59. U.N. Security Council, Resolution 134, "Question Relating to the Situation in the Union of South Africa," April 1, 1960, www.un.org/en/documents/index.html, accessed January 5, 2009.

60. Cape Town to New York, April 7, 1961, BTS 14/11, vol. 2, ASAMFA.

61. Statement by Alex Quaison-Sackey, April 18, 1961, 15th session, 981st meeting, BTS 14/11, vol. 5, ASAMFA.

62. Statement in the Special Political Committee of the General Assembly, April 4, 1961, BTS 14/11, vol. 5, ASAMFA.

63. Ibid.

64. U.N. General Assembly, Resolution 1663 (XVI), "The Question of Race Conflict Resulting from the Policies of Apartheid of the Government of the Union of South Africa," September 27, 1961, www.un.org/en/documents/index.shtml, accessed January 5, 2009.

65. Kwame Nkrumah, *I Speak of Freedom* (New York, 1961), 226.

66. Mansergh, ed., *Documents and Speeches on Commonwealth Affairs, 1952–1962*, 387.

67. ILO and Secretary-General, July 25, 1961, series 286, box 2, file 4, United Nations Record Office (UNRO); similar actions were taken at the Economic Commission for Africa, the World Health Organization, and the conference on International Trade and Tourism in 1962 and 1963.

68. *Yearbook of the United Nations* (New York, 1961), 108–15.

69. Mr. Wachuku (Nigeria), October 10, 1961, 16th session, 1031st meeting, BTS 14/11, vol. 8, ASAMFA.

70. See Westad, *The Global Cold War*; Robert McMahon, *The Cold War on the Periphery* (New York, 1994).

71. Nkrumah, *I Speak of Freedom*, 231.

72. "United Nations Debate," November 7, 1962, BTS 14/11, vol. 7, ASAMFA.

73. Ibid.

74. *Yearbook of the United Nations* (New York, 1962), 93–99.

75. Quoted in Dudziak, *Cold War Civil Rights*, 172–73.
76. "Agenda Item II: Apartheid and Racial Discrimination," *Organization of African Unity: Basic Documents and Resolutions* (Addis Ababa, 1963), 19–20.
77. Many American historians have missed this point. See Dudziak, *Cold War Civil Rights*, 170–78; Borstelmann, *Cold War and the Cold Line*, 157–64.
78. Statement by Diallo Telli, September 13, 1963, BTS 14/11, vol. 10, ASAMFA.
79. U.N., "Summary of the Report of the Special Committee on the Policies of APARTHEID of the Government of the Republic of South Africa," *Apartheid in South Africa* (New York, 1963), 42.
80. *Yearbook of the United Nations* (New York 1963), 13–24; U.N., *A New Course in South Africa: Report of the United Nations Group of Experts* (New York, 1963), 32–35.
81. Statement by Diallo Telli, Chairman of Special Committee on Apartheid, July 18, 1963, *Speeches at the United Nations*, see www.anc.org.za, accessed January 5, 2009.
82. E. S. Reddy, ed., *Oliver Tambo* (New Delhi, 1991), 6–7.
83. U.N., *United Nations and Apartheid, 1948–1994*, 254–57. For useful overviews of the arms embargo, see Ryan Irwin, "Wind of Change? White Redoubt and the Postcolonial Moment, 1960–1963," *Diplomatic History* 33:5 (November 2009): 897–925; Anna-Mart van Wyk and Jackie Grobler, "The Kennedy Administration and the Institution of an Arms Embargo against South Africa, 1961–1963," *Historia* 46:1 (May 2001): 109–33.
84. Verbatim Record of Political Committee Meeting, October 11, 1963, BTS 14/11, vol. 10, ASAMFA.
85. U.N. General Assembly, Resolution 1904 (XVIII), "Declaration on the Elimination of All Forms of Racial Discrimination," 1963, www.un.org/en/documents/index.shtml, accessed January 5, 2009.
86. Statement of Representative of Guinea, Provisional Summary Record of Special Political Committee, November 1, 1963, BTS 14/11, vol. 11, ASAMFA, emphasis in original.
87. Statement of Representative of Denmark, 380th meeting of the Special Political Committee, BTS 14/11, vol. 10, ASAMFA. For scholarship on North Europe's engagement with apartheid issues, consult Sellström, *Sweden and National Liberation*; Rore Linne Eriksen, *Norway and National Liberation in Southern Africa* (Uppsala, 2000); Iina Soiri and Pekka Peltola, *Finland and National Liberation in Southern Africa* (Uppsala, 1999); Christopher Munthe, *Denmark and National Liberatin in Southern Africa* (Uppsala, 2003).
88. United Nations Document, S/5658, April 20, 1964, BTS 14/11, vol. 11, AFAMSA.
89. David Kay, *The New Nations in the United Nations, 1960–1967* (New York, 1970), 70.
90. United Nations Document, S/5773, June 18, 1964, BTS 14/11 vol. 10, ASAMFA.
91. Die Sekretaris Van Buitelandse Sake, January 5, 1961, BTS 1/33/3/1, vol. 1, NASA, emphasis in original.
92. For full explanation of the department's organization, see Louw's statement to Senate, May 23, 1956, BTS 4/1/6/1, vol. 1, NASA.
93. Eric Louw, Radio Address, December 12, 1957, BTS 14/1/11, vol. 1, ASAMFA.
94. Louw, "Western Policy in Africa," April 1959, BTS 1/33/8/3, vol. 2, ASAMFA.
95. Ibid.
96. Memo to Secretary, April 26, 1956, BTS 4/1/6/1, vol. 1, NASA.
97. "World Situation," March 30, 1957, BTS 4/1/11, vol. 1, NASA.
98. Louw, No Title, March 1957, BTS 4/1/11, vol. 1, NASA.
99. Louw, No Title, April 26, 1956, BTS 4/1/6/1, vol. 1, NASA.
100. Telegram, Embassy in South Africa to the Department of State, November 7, 1958, *Foreign Relations of the United States, 1958–1960*, 14: 732 (hereafter *FRUS*).
101. Borstelmann, *Apartheid's Reluctant Uncle* (New York, 1993), 4.
102. Noer, *The Cold War and Black Liberation*, 44.
103. "United States and Emerging Africa," May 28, 1958, BTS 1/33/8/3, vol. 1, ASAMFA.
104. Talk between Minister and Ambassador Satterthwaite, October 16, 1958, BTS 1/33/8/3, vol. 1, ASAMFA.

105. Washington to Pretoria, November 13, 1959, BTS 1/33/8/3, vol. 2, ASAMFA. See Noer, *Cold War and Black Liberation*, 49–55. For a recent interpretation of creation of the African Affairs Bureau, see George White, Jr., "Big Ballin'!?: Vice President Nixon and the Creation of the Bureau of African Affairs in the U.S. Department of State," *Passport* 41:2 (September 2010): 5–11.
106. Sy Edele die Eerste Minister, March 13, 1960, BTS 22/2/20, vol. 2, NASA.
107. Message to Secretary (Top Secret), April 22, 1960, BTS 1/33/8/3, vol. 3, ASAMFA.
108. "Situation at UNO (Secret)," April 30, 1960, BTS 1/33/8/3, vol. 3, ASAMFA.
109. New York to Pretoria, April 25, 1961, BTS 14/11, vol. 4, ASAMFA.
110. "Analysis of Resolutions on Apartheid," 1958–1961, April 1961, BTS 14/11, vol. 4, ASAMFA.
111. Ibid.
112. "Deterioration in the Attitude of Britain toward South Africa as Witnessed in the Voting and United Nations Debate during the Years 1958–1961," November 1961, BTS 14/11, vol. 4, ASAMFA, emphasis in original.
113. "Report of the Fortieth Ordinary General Meeting," *South African Reserve Bank* (Pretoria, 1960), 14–16.
114. Ibid., 13–15.
115. Ibid., 18–19.
116. Circular telegram, April 5, 1961, BVV 10/3/1, vol. 1, NASA.
117. Circular telegram, November 14, 1960, BTS 14/11, vol. 3, ASAMFA.
118. Program om Openbare Betrekkinge in die V.S.A. te verbeter, November 30, 1960, BTS 1/33/3/1, vol. 1, NASA.
119. Ibid.
120. "African Freedom Day," April 21, 1961, BTS 1/33/8/3, vol. 6, ASAMFA.
121. "Interference in Internal Affairs of States," April 27, 1961, BTS 1/33/8/3, vol. 6, ASAMFA.
122. "Principles Determining Information World in the 'post-Cape Town' Situation," March 3, 1961, BTS 22/2/20, vol. 2, NASA.
123. New York to Pretoria, November 20, 1961, BTS 14/11, subfile, vol. 4, ASAMFA.
124. Besoek van mnr. Williams aan Afrika, December 15, 1960, BTS 1/33/8/3, vol. 5, ASAMFA.
125. Report on Soapy's Senate Testimony, February 10, 1961, BTS 1/33/8/3, vol. 5, ASAMFA.
126. Program om Openbare Betrekkinge in die V.S.A. te verbeter, November 30, 1960, BTS 1/33/3/1, vol. 1, NASA.
127. Ibid.
128. Ibid.
129. Ibid.
130. "Principles Determining Information World in the 'post-Cape Town' Situation," March 3, 1961, BTS 22/2/20, vol. 2, NASA.
131. Persoonlik en Vertroulik, 4 Maart 1960, BTS 22/2/20, vol. 2, ASAMFA. For propaganda examples, see *Progress Through Separate Development* (New York, 1965), 27–32.
132. "Each a Roof of His Own," March 8, 1962, Advertising Campaigns and Reactions, BKL, 318–25, NASA.
133. Press Release, January 24, 1962, BTS 14/11, vol. 4, NASA.
134. Telegram to All Heads of Missions, October 13, 1960, BTS 144/11, vol. 1, NASA.
135. "Publicity Reaction to the Transkei Announcement," BTS 14/11, vol. 5, NASA; Verbod op Gemengde Maatskaplike Verkeer, February 21, 1962, BTS 14/11, vol. 8, NASA.
136. Persoonlik en Vertroulik, 4 Maart 1960, BTS 22/2/20, vol. 2, ASAMFA.
137. "Many Do Not Come to U.N. with Clean Hands," *South Africa Digest* 7:22, 15.
138. "S.A. Unjustly Attacked by Africa Countries," *South Africa Digest*, 10:5, 2.
139. "Principles Determining Information World in the 'post-Cape Town' Situation," March 3, 1961, BTS 22/2/20, vol. 2, NASA.
140. For an explanation of the relationship between the Communist Party and ANC see Lodge, *Black Politics in South Africa since 1945*; Thompson, *A History of South Africa*; Marks and

Trapido, eds., *The Politics of Class & Nationalism in Twentieth Century South Africa*; Magubane, *The Political Economy of Race and Class in South Africa*; Mandela, *Long Walk to Freedom*, 73–75, 91, 115–17.

141. "Praemonitus, Praemonitus," September 21, 1962, Advertising Campaigns and Reactions, BKL, 318–25, NASA.
142. Memorandum to Secretary for Information, December 1, 1962, BKL, 318–25, NASA.
143. *South Africa Prospects and Progress* (New York, 1962), 79.
144. "Principles Determining Information World in the 'post-Cape Town; Situation," March 3, 1961, BTS 22/2/20, vol. 2, NASA.
145. *South African Reserve Bank* (1962), 10–11.
146. "United States/South Africa Relations (Top Secret)," July 24, 1963, BTS 1/33/3, vol. 1, ASAMFA.
147. Samesprekings Met Mnr. Jooste Insake Openbare Skakelwerk, Januarie 5, 1963, BTS 1/33/3/1, vol. 1, ASAMFA.
148. "Areas of Co-operation and Common Interest Between the United States and South Africa (Top Secret)," May 29, 1963, BTS 1/33/3, vol. 1, ASAMFA.
149. "Public Relations Counsel in the U.S.," January 5, 1964, BTS 1/33/3/1, vol. 1, ASAMFA.
150. Ibid.
151. "Directive on Policy," August 21, 1964, BTS 1/33/3/1, vol. 2, ASAMFA.
152. Ibid.

Chapter 3

1. Thomas McCormick, *America's Half-Century* (Baltimore, 1995), 213.
2. For useful texts, see Michael Omi and Howard Winant, *Racial Formation in the United States*, 2nd ed. (New York, 1994); Gary Gerstle, *American Crucible* (Princeton, 2002); Mai M. Ngai, *Impossible Subjects* (Princeton, 2004); Ira Katznelson, *When Affirmative Action Was White* (New York, 2005); Bruce Nelson, *Divided We Stand* (Princeton, 2001); Martha Biondi, *To Stand and Fight* (Cambridge, MA, 2006); Thomas Sugrue, *The Origins of the Urban Crisis* (Princeton, 1996); David Roediger, *The Wages of Whiteness*, revised ed. (New York, 2007); Matthew Frye Jacobson, *Whiteness of a Different Color* (New York, 2000).
3. For thoughtful considerations of nation and development, see Cooper and Packard, eds., *International Development and the Social Sciences*; Cooper, *Colonialism in Question*; as well as David Ekbladh, *The Great American Mission* (Princeton, 2010); and Michael Latham, *Modernization as Ideology* (Chapel Hill, 2000).
4. Quoted in Westad, *The Global Cold War*, 34–35.
5. "Guidelines for Policy and Operations: Africa," March 1962, RG 59, Records of G. Mennen Williams, 1961–1966, Classified Records, Lot 68D8, box 1, United States National Archives and Records Administration (hereafter NARA).
6. Williams to Rostow, April 9, 1965, RG 59, Records of G. Mennen Williams, 1961–1966, Classified Records, Lot 68D8, box 1, NARA.
7. Joseph S. Nye, Jr., *Bound to Lead* (New York, 1990); Joseph S. Nye, Jr., *Soft Power* (New York, 2004).
8. "Williams 'Recoiled but Stood His Ground,'" August 30, 1961, *Rand Daily Mail*, BTS 1/33/8/3, vol. 6, ASAMFA.
9. "Mr. Mennen Williams and the Federation," September 1, 1961, BTS 1/33/8/3, vol. 6, ASAMFA.
10. Noer, *Soapy*, 83–168.
11. Ibid., 203–14.
12. Ibid., 224.
13. See Borstelmann, *Cold War and the Color Line*, 113–14.
14. Memorandum, "Discussion at the 365th Meeting of the National Security Council," May 8, 1958, *Foreign Relations of the United States (FRUS) 1958–1960*, 14: 49.

15. Memorandum, "Discussion of 432nd Meeting of the National Security Council," January 14, 1960, *FRUS 1958–1960*, 14: 75–76.
16. Editorial Note, *FRUS 1958–1960*, 14: 741–42.
17. Memorandum of Conversation, March 30, 1960, *FRUS 1958–1960* 14:745–46; the United States was in a position to influence the resolution because Ambassador Lodge was the chair of the Security Council in April 1960.
18. Williams to William Monat, February 22, 1962, RG 59, Records of G. Mennen Williams, 1961–1966, Chronological File, 1961–1966, box 2, NARA.
19. Williams to Walter Lippmann, December 4, 1961, RG 59, Records of G. Mennen Williams, 1961–1966, Chronological File, 1961–1966, box 1, NARA.
20. For information on the intellectual legacy of Northwestern University, see Jerry Gershen-horn, *Melville J. Herskovits and the Racial Politics of Knowledge* (Lincoln, 2004); as well as Ryan M. Irwin, "Mapping Race: Historicizing the History of the Color-Line," *History Compass* 8:9 (September 2010): 984–99.
21. Introduction in William Bascom and Melville Herskovits, eds., *Continuity and Change in African Cultures* (Chicago, 1959), 5.
22. Ibid., 1–14.
23. Assistant Secretary G. Mennen Williams, "The Challenge of Africa to the American Citizen," January 20, 1961, *Department of State Bulletin* 154: 1130 (Washington DC, 1966), 259–62.
24. Assistant Secretary G. Mennen Williams, "The United States and Africa: Common Goals," February 17, 1961, *Department of State Bulletin* 154: 1133 (Washington DC, 1966), 373–76.
25. For scholarship on this topic, see Carol Anderson, "International Conscience, the Cold War, and Apartheid: The NAACP's Alliance with the Reverend Michael Scott for South West Africa's Liberation, 1946–1952," *Journal of World History* 19:3 (September 2008): 297–326; Baldwin, *Toward the Beloved Community*; Culverson, *Contesting Apartheid*; Love, *The U.S. Anti-Apartheid Movement*; Massie, *Loosing the Bonds*; Magubane, *The Ties that Bind*; Minter, *King Soloman's Mines Revisited*; Nesbitt, *Race for Sanctions*; Shepherd Jr., *Anti-Apartheid*; and Morgan, "Into the Struggle: Confronting Apartheid in the United States and South Africa, 1964–1990," (PhD diss., 2009). For broader scholarship on nongovern-mental activism, Anderson, *Eyes Off the Prize*; Borstelmann, *Cold War and the Color Line*; Dudziak, *Cold War Civil Rights*; von Eschen, *Race against Empire*; Horne, *Black and Red*; Plummer, *Rising Wind*.
26. Cited in Baldwin, *Toward the Beloved Community*, 40.
27. Williams to Fredericks and Abernathy, December 1, 1962; Fox to Williams, December 10, 1962; "Resolutions of the American Negro Leadership Conference on Africa," November 1962, all in RG 59, Records of G. Mennen Williams, 1961–1966, box 16, NARA.
28. "GMW Meeting with Call Committee of American Negro Leadership Conference on Africa," December 17, 1962, RG 59, Records of G. Mennen Williams, 1961–1966, box 16, NARA.
29. Handwritten conversation notes, no date; Randolph to Williams, December 19, 1962, both in RG 59, Records of G. Mennen Williams, 1961–1966, box 16, NARA.
30. Quoted in Plummer, ed., *Window on Freedom*, 5.
31. Meeting with Mennen Williams, April 4, 1961, BTS 1/33/8/3, subfile to vol. 6, ASAMFA.
32. Williams to Fredericks, June 9, 1961, RG 59, Records of G. Mennen Williams, 1961–1966, Chronological File, 1961–1966, box 1, NARA.
33. "Mr. Mennen Williams and the Federation," September 1, 1961, BTS 1/33/8/3, vol. 6, ASAMFA.
34. G. Mennen Williams, "Basic United States Policy," August 25, 1961, BTS 1/33/8/3, vol. 6, ASAMFA.
35. Meeting in Salisbury, August 27, 1961, BTS 1/33/8/3, vol. 6, ASAMFA.
36. Report to the Honorable John F. Kennedy by the Task Force on Africa (confidential), December 13, 1960, Pre-inaugural Papers, box 949, John F. Kennedy Presidential Library (hereafter JFKL).

37. For an overview, see Noer, *Cold War and Black Liberation*, 61–95.
38. Memorandum, Acting Assistant Secretary of Defense (Bundy) to the Deputy Secretary of Defense (Gilpatric), June 7, 1961, *FRUS, 1961–1963,* 21: 595–97; Memorandum, President's Special Assistant for National Security Affairs (Bundy) to President Kennedy, July 13, 1963, National Security Files, box 159, JFKL.
39. Melvyn Leffler, "National Security," in *Explaining the History of American Foreign Relations,* ed. Michael Hogan and Thomas Paterson (New York, 2004), 135. While divided deeply over the question of intent—namely whether American national security interests led to offensive or defensive behavior toward the Soviet Union and the global south—most U.S. diplomatic historians accept national security as the ideological ballast of American foreign policy after World War II. For useful historical monographs, see Leffler, *A Preponderance of Power;* Gaddis, *The United States and the Origins of the Cold War, 1941–1947* (New York, 1972); Gaddis, *We Now Know.* For useful essays, see Jeremi Suri, "The Early Cold War," in *A Companion to American Foreign Relations,* ed. Robert Schulzinger (Oxford, 2006); and Michael Hogan, ed., *America in the World* (Cambridge, 2005).
40. For the recent ideological interpretations of U.S. hegemony, see Ekbladh, *The Great American Mission;* Westad, *The Global Cold War.*
41. Leffler, "National Security," in *Explaining the History of American Foreign Relations,* 134.
42. Some historians point to Kennedy's willingness to meet with new African leaders as evidence of his innate sympathy toward the continent. This conclusion mirrors the views of several prominent African elites—Sékou Touré and Julius Nyerere, among others—who openly praised the president's interpersonal acumen after his assassination in 1963. Many African leaders, indeed, spoke positively of Kennedy, especially in interviews after his death. However, their comments do not provide sufficient evidence to overturn conventional depictions of Kennedy's foreign policy priorities. First, it is essential to distinguish perceptions of the president based often on anecdotes from high-level meetings from comprehensive studies of Kennedy's foreign policy based on primary sources from the period. Second, it is important to recognize that the characteristics often praised by African leaders—namely the president's ability to ask informed questions about Africa—were the direct result of briefing reports written by Mennen Williams. The assistant secretary (1) insisted that Kennedy meet with new African leaders in 1961–62, and (2) provided enormous background papers on each country, which formed the basis of the informed conversations later cited and celebrated by African leaders. For background information, see Noer, *Soapy,* 223–69; and Philip E. Muehlenbeck, *Betting on the Africans* (New York, 2012).
43. Andrew Preston, *The War Council* (Cambridge, MA, 2006).
44. McGeorge Bundy, "Friends and Allies," *Foreign Affairs* 41:1 (October 1962): 22.
45. For excellent overview, see Robert Rakove, "A Genuine Departure: Kennedy, Johnson, and the Nonaligned World" (PhD diss., 2009), 86–90.
46. See Walt Rostow, *The Stages of Economic Growth* (New York, 1960); Walt Rostow and Max Milikan, *A Proposal* (New York, 1957). See also Latham, *Modernization as Ideology.*
47. George Ball, *The Discipline of Power* (Boston, 1968), 245–59; quoted in Rakove, "A Genuine Departure," 115.
48. Williams to Rusk, October 30, 1962, RG 59, Records of G. Mennen Williams, 1961–1966, Chronological File, 1961–1966, box 1, NARA.
49. Cited in Noer, *Soapy,* 247; see also Harris L. Wofford oral history interview, November 29, 1965, JFKL, available online at http://www.jfklibrary.org/Asset-Viewer/Archives/JFKOH-HLW-01.aspx; and Harris Wofford, *Of Kennedy's and Kings* (New York, 1980), 371.
50. "The White Redoubt," June 28, 1962, National Security Files, box 159, JFKL.
51. "Guidelines of Policy and Operations: Africa, March 1962," RG 59, Records of G. Mennen Williams, 1961–1966, Classified Records, Lot 68D8, box 1, NARA.
52. For a discussion of the paper, see George Ball to President Kennedy, August 16, 1962, National Security Files, box 311, JFKL; Memorandum of Conversation, August 21, 1962,

National Security Files, box 311, JFKL; Circular Airgram to Certain Posts, August 30, 1962, RG 59, Central Files 1960–1963, 320/8-3062, NARA; Rusk to President Kennedy, no date, National Security Files, box 311, JFKL.

53. "United States Strategy at the 17th General Assembly," August 16, 1962, RG 59, Records of G. Mennen Williams, 1961–1966, Classified Records, Lot 68D8, box 1, NARA.

54. Dean Rusk, *As I Saw It* (New York, 1990), 409.

55. For different interpretations of American foreign policy and liberal internationalism, see Borgardt, *A New Deal for the World*; Mazower, *No Enchanted Palace*; Stephen Schlesinger, *Act of Creation* (Cambridge, MA, 2003); and Paul Kennedy, *The Parliament of Man* (New York, 2006). For interesting ruminations on the relationship between U.S. policymaking and the "race revolution" of the mid-twentieth century, see Jason Parker, "Cold War II? The Eisenhower Administration, the Bandung Conference, and the Re-periodization of the Postwar Era," *Diplomatic History* 30:5 (November 2006): 867–892.

56. Circular Airgram to Certain Posts, August 30, 1962, RG 59, Central Files 1960–1963, 320/8-3062, NARA.

57. Williams to Elbert Matthews, November 12, 1963, RG 59, Records of G. Mennen Williams, 1961–1966, Chronological File, 1961–1966, box 3, NARA.

58. Williams to Rostow, November 15, 1963, RG 59, Records of G. Mennen Williams, 1961–1966, Chronological File, 1961–1966, box 3, NARA.

59. See Dudziak, *Cold War Civil Rights*, 152–248.

60. USIA report, May 29, 1963, *Civil Rights during the Kennedy Administration, 1961–1963* (Fredrick, MD, 1987), reel 3:121.

61. Kennedy Radio and Television Address, June 11, 1963, President's Office Files—Speeches, box 45, JFKL.

62. Williams to Kennedy, June 15, 1963, RG 59, Records of G. Mennen Williams, 1961–1966, Chronological File, 1961–1966, box 3, NARA.

63. See White to Abernathy, July 19, 1963; "Position Paper Civil Rights in the United States," September 14, 1963; "Meeting on Civil Rights and Africa," July 17, 1963, all in RG 59, Records of G. Mennen Williams, 1961–1966, box 16, NARA.

64. Williams to Kennedy, June 15, 1963, RG 59, Records of G. Mennen Williams, 1961–1966, Chronological File, NARA.

65. "Africa Trip Report," June 22–July 9, 1963, RG 59, Records of G. Mennen Williams, 1961–1966, Chronological File, 1961–1966, box 3, NARA.

66. Williams to Rusk, July 12, 1963, RG 59, Records of G. Mennen Williams, 1961–1966, Chronological File, 1961–1966, box 3, NARA.

67. Rusk to Harriman, July 15, 1963, National Security Files, box 3, JFKL.

68. Memorandum, President's Special Assistant (Schlesinger) to Attorney General Kennedy, July 1, 1963, *FRUS 1961–1963*, 21: 496–97.

69. Brubeck to Bundy, October 29, 1963, National Security Files, box 159, JFKL.

70. Bundy to Rusk, July 17, 1963, National Security Files, box 159, JFKL.

71. Memorandum of Conversation, October 4, 1963, *FRUS 1961 1963*, 21: 471.

72. Richard Mahoney, *JFK: Ordeal in Africa* (New York, 1983); Noer, *Cold War and Black Liberation*; Borstelmann, *The Cold War and the Color Line*.

73. Adlai Stevenson, "Statement at the Security Council," *The United Nations and Apartheid, 1948–1994* (New York, 1994), 254–57.

74. "Briefing Paper Prepared in the Department of State," March 10, 1964, *FRUS, 1964–1968*, 24: 579.

75. For an excellent analysis of Johnson's early years, see Mitchell Lerner, "'To Be Shot at by the Whites and Dodged by the Negroes,'" *Presidential Studies Quarterly* 39:2 (June 2009): 245–274.

76. White House telephone conversation, Lyndon Johnson and Mennen Williams, December 2, 1963, K6312.01, Lyndon Baines Johnson Presidential Library (hereafter LBJL).

77. The comment referred to the location of the African Bureau within the State Department. Rusk and top officials held offices on the seventh floor; Williams's office was one floor below.

78. White House telephone conversation, Lyndon Johnson and Dean Rusk, April 4, 1964, WH6404.05, LBJL.

79. White House telephone conversation, Lyndon Johnson and George Reedy, April 4, 1964, WH6404.05, LBJL.

80. Noer, *Soapy*, 278.

81. Ibid., 280–85.

82. Quoted in ibid., 283.

83. Ibid., 284.

84. For work on Johnson and Vietnam, see Fredrik Logevall, *Choosing War* (Berkeley, 1999), Robert Schulzinger, *Time for War* (New York, 1999); Marilyn Young, *The Vietnam Wars* (New York, 1991).

85. For an excellent overview of Johnson's policies, see Mitchell Lerner, ed., *Looking Back at LBJ* (Lawrence, 2005); as well as Warren Cohen and Nancy Tucker, eds., *Lyndon Johnson Confronts the World* (Cambridge, UK, 1995); H. W. Brands, *Wages of Globalism* (New York, 1997); Diane Kunz, *Diplomacy of the Crucial Decade* (New York, 1994); Robert Dalleck, *Flawed Giant* (New York, 1998); and, of course, the scholarship of Robert Caro.

86. Lyndon Jonson, "The Great Society," May 22, 1964, LBJ Library and Museum, http://www.lbjlib.utexas.edu/johnson/lbjforkids/gsociety_read.shtm, accessed November 12, 2009.

87. Borstelmann, *The Cold War and the Color Line*, 180.

88. Lyndon Johnson, "To Fulfill These Rights," June 4, 1965, History and Politics Out Loud, http://www.hpol.org/lbj/civil-rights, accessed November 12, 2009.

89. Quoted in Borstelmann, *The Cold War and the Color Line*, 178.

90. Most foreign relations historians who have attempted to explain U.S.-Africa relations in this period have focused on the administration's economic aid to the region. For an excellent example, see Terrence Lyons, "Keeping Africa Off the Agenda," in *Lyndon Johnson Confronts the World*, ed. Cohen and Tucker. Such work underscores the fact that Johnson did not actively seek to supplant the economic place Great Britain and France in Africa after decolonization. The region always "ranked" below Europe, Asia, and Latin America in the minds of Cold War policymakers. However, by focusing only on economic aid, an important aspect of U.S.-Africa relations remains unexamined. As demonstrated in chapter 2, African diplomats put precedence not only on bilateral relations with the superpowers but also politics at the U.N. General Assembly. U.S. engagement with African issues mirrored this two-part diplomatic game. Second-wave decolonization, as explained earlier, gave the so-called Third World (i.e., Afro-Asian bloc) the votes to control the General Assembly's agenda, thereby undermining tacitly Washington's soft power on the international stage. The administration's effort to take a stand on race issues in the United States and South Africa—a story often overlooked by U.S. diplomatic historians because it cuts across country files in most U.S. archives—was central to the administration's engagement with Africa. And it was on this level that Williams played his most important role.

91. Thomas Noer is incorrect when he asserts "the feeble push for sanctions" ended with the ascension of the Johnson administration in *Cold War and Black Liberation*, 162. Noer separates his analysis of the arms debate from considerations of the ICJ case, and does not investigate the pathways that would have actually made U.N. sanctions legally possible. Thomas Borstelmann offers a more persuasive ideological portrait of Johnson's motivations—connecting his analysis to the civil rights movement rather than the Vietnam War—but he too neglects the legal questions surrounding the sanctions debate, focusing instead on the broad connections between the civil rights movement and the anti-apartheid struggle.

92. "Anglo-American Talks in Washington," January 27–28, 1964, DO 183/273, NA.

93. Ibid.

94. The Court's importance was further buttressed by the political situation at the United Nations in 1964–65. The organization faced an acute budget shortfall in the years following

second-wave decolonization, and American policymakers found themselves in a bitter fight with France and other states over the precise relationship between voting rights and financial obligations. The United States brought its argument to the International Court of Justice in 1962 in an effort to legitimize the thesis that voting rights were contingent on a state's financial good standing at the organization. As American officials admitted openly, it would have been contradictory to embrace the ICJ's legitimacy (and enforcement powers) on these budget questions, and then deny the ICJ's authority when it came to the South West Africa mandate.

95. "South Africa and South West Africa," March 10, 1964, National Security Files, box 78, LBJL, emphasis added. See also National Security Action Memorandum No. 295, LBJL, www. lbjlib.utexas.edu/johnson/archives.hom/nsamhom.asp, accessed July 20, 2009.

96. Ibid. (both citations).

97. Memorandum of Conversation, April 22, 1964, National Security Files, box 78, LBJL.

98. Moontlike Ontwikkelings in Amerikaanse Beleid teenoor die Republiek, April 21, 1964, BTS 1/33/3, vol. 1, ASAMFA.

99. Status Report on NSAM No. 295 of April 24, 1964—South Africa, July 30, 1964, RG 59, S/S-NSAM Files, Lot 72D316, NARA.

100. For background debate, see Hodges to Rusk, September 16, 1964; Stevenson to Rusk, September 16, 1964; William Brubeck to McGeorge Bundy, September 22, 1964; Brubeck to Bundy, September 23, 1964, all in National Security Files, box 78, LBJL.

101. William H. Brubeck to McGeorge Bundy, September 22, 1964, National Security Files, box 78, LBJL.

102. "National Policy Paper—South Africa," January 18, 1965, RG 59, S/P Files, Lot 72D139, NARA.

103. "Paper Prepared in the Department of State," March 25, 1963, National Security Files, box 3, JFKL.

104. "National Policy Paper—South Africa," January 18, 1965, RG 59, S/P Files, Lot 72D139, NARA.

105. "Strengthened African Program," October 14, 1965, National Security Files, box 76, LBJL.

106. Rusk, *As I Saw It*, 587.

107. Lyndon Johnson, "The American Promise," March 15, 1965, National Security Files, box 77, LBJL.

108. Noer, *Cold War and Black Liberation*, 185–91; see also Roy Welensky, *Welensky's 4000 Days* (London, 1964); Ian Douglas Smith, *The Great Betrayal* (London, 1997); Vulindlela Mtshali, *Rhodesia* (New York, 1967); Martin Loney, *Rhodesia* (Harmondsworth, 1975); Elaine Windrich, *Britain and the Politics of Rhodesian Independence* (New York, 1978); Kenneth Young, *Rhodesia and Independence* (London, 1967); Ralph Zacklin, *The United Nations and Rhodesia* (New York, 1974).

109. "Outline of the Rhodesian Problem," December 1, 1965, National Security Files, box 97, LBJL.

110. Ball to Johnson, November 18, 1965, National Security Files, box 97, LBJL; "Outline of the Rhodesian Problem," December 1, 1965, National Security Files, box 97, LBJL.

111. Noer, *Cold War and Black Liberation*, 197–200; Young, *Rhodesia and Independence*, 158–70.

112. Noer, *Cold War and Black Liberation*, 203–4.

113. Mann to Johnson, December 22, 1965, National Security Files, box 1, LBJL.

114. Read to Bundy, December 17, 1965, National Security Files, box 97, LBJL; see also Harold Wilson, *The Labour Government, 1964–1970* (London, 1971), 186–88.

115. Noer, *Cold War and Black Liberation*, 208.

116. Assistant Secretary Williams, "The Crisis in Southern Rhodesia," January 28, 1966, *Department of State Bulletin* 54: 1391 (Washington DC, 1966), 265–79.

117. Statement by Ambassador Arthur Goldberg, "The Question of Intervention in the Domestic Affairs of States," January 1966, *Department of State Bulletin* 54: 1387 (Washington DC, 1966), 124–33.

118. *Yearbook of the United Nations* (New York, 1965), 291.
119. Noer, *Soapy*, 206–10.
120. Ibid., 297.

Chapter 4

1. "Relations with the United States (Secret)," August 13, 1965, BTS 1/33/3, vol. 1, ASAMFA.
2. "Minority Rule in Africa," July 7, 1965, BTS 1/99/1, vol. 23, ASAMFA.
3. The goal here is not to provide a blow-by-blow account of the trial itself. My aim, rather, is to frame the case in its wider context, drawing out the main points made by both sides, the general shifts in their legal strategies, and the trial's importance in global history. For detailed accounts of the trial by legal scholars consult John Dugard, ed., *The South West Africa/Namibia Dispute* (Berkeley, 1973); and Slonim Soloman, *South West Africa and the United Nations* (Baltimore, 1972).
4. American foreign relations historians are only beginning to explore the concept of legitimacy, but an excellent literature exists among IR theorists. For a useful introduction, see Ian Hurd, *After Anarchy* (Princeton, 2007); and Alexander Wendt, *Social Theory of International Politics* (Cambridge, 1999).
5. Kenneth Kaunda, *Zambia, Independence and Beyond* (London, 1966), 64.
6. *Conference of Heads of State and Governments of Non-Aligned Countries*, Cairo, Egypt, 5–10 October 5, 1964 (Cairo, 1964), 149–54.
7. The Non-Aligned Movement (NAM) was formed in Belgrade in 1961. Although Indian diplomat Krishna Menon coined the phrase "nonaligned" in 1953, the organization was the brainchild of Yugoslav President Josip Tito, Indian Prime Minister Jawaharlal Nehru, Egyptian President Gamal Abdel Nasser, Ghanaian President Kwame Nkrumah, and Indonesian President Sukarno. Throughout the Cold War—and especially during the 1960s and 1970s—NAM sought a third way to the superpower conflict. For an overview of nonaligned politics, see Peter Willetts, *The Non-Aligned Movement* (New York, 1978); and Prashad, *The Darker Nations*, (New York, 2007).
8. *Yearbook of the United Nations* (New York, 1961), 108–15.
9. Borgwardt, *A New Deal for the World*; and Mazower, *No Enchanted Palace*, as well as Ekbladh, *The Great American Mission*. For additional insight on intellectual context of 1940s, see Robert Hilderbrand, *Dumbarton Oaks* (Chapel Hill, 1990); Brian Urquhart, *Ralph Bunche* (New York, 1993); Jay Winter, *Dreams of Peace and Freedom* (New Haven, 2006); Mary Ann Glendon, *A World Made New* (New York, 2003); Paul Kennedy, *The Parliament of Man* (New York, 2006); Samantha Power, *A Problem from Hell* (New York, 2002). For an especially useful biography, see Robert McMahon, *Dean Acheson* (Washington, DC, 2009). For other thoughtful ruminations on these topics, see John Ruggie, *Constructing the World Polity* (London, 1998); John Ikenberry, *After Victory* (Princeton, 2001); John Ikenberry, *Liberal Order and Imperial Ambition* (London, 2006); as well as contributions by Inis Claude, Anne-Marie Slaughter, Andrew Williams, Clark Eichelberger, Ruth Russell, and Brian Simpson.
10. An impressive literature exists on the establishment and evolution of the International Court of Justice. Created in 1945 by the U.N. Charter, the Court was the successor to the Permanent Court of International Justice. It exists to settle legal disputes between member states of the United Nations and to give advisory opinions on legal questions forwarded by authorized international organs, agencies and the General Assembly. It is distinguished from the Permanent Court of International Justice because members of the United Nations are automatically subject to its jurisdiction. The ICJ is composed of fifteen judges elected to nine-year terms by the U.N. General Assembly and the U.N. Security Council. Judges serve nine-year terms and may be reelected for two additional terms. Elections take place every three years, with one-third of judges retiring each time, in order to ensure continuity within the court. Candidates are put forward by the secretary-general, who solicits recommendations from an

assortment of national organizations. No two judges can come from the same country. The goal is to ensure that the Court represents the principal legal systems of the world.

The Court hears two types of cases—advisory cases and contentious cases. Advisory decisions are made upon request from the United Nations. Often complex in nature, these cases require the Court to independently elicit information from states and nongovernment organizations. Although the decisions are nonbinding they are not without legal effect. The reasoning reflects the Court's authoritative view on the subject and often provides guidance (and moral authority) for governments hoping to chart a "legitimate" course of action. Contentious hearings produce binding rulings and are enforced by the Security Council. Only governments can participate. The case begins with the submission of the Applicants' Memorial, which typically outlines the basic charges of the case. The Respondent then has an opportunity to file a Counter-Memorial, which often rebuts the Applicants' allegations.

Cases at the Court often unfold in two phases. First, the Applicants must establish that the ICJ has jurisdiction to rule on the merits of the case. Because of the tenuous relationship between sovereignty and international law, this is often the most contentious phase of the trial. If the Court approves its jurisdiction, the trial then proceeds to merits. During this phase, each side presents its legal rationale, offers expert witnesses, and forwards evidence to support its position. For a brief overview of the Court's organizational history, see Arthur Eyffinger, *The International Court of Justice, 1946–1996* (Boston, 1996); Nagendra Singh, *The Role and Record of the International Court of Justice* (Boston, 1989.

11. "South Africa Stronger Than Ever," August 12, 1964, BTS 1/99/1, vol. 25, ASAMFA.
12. "National Conference on South African Crisis and American Action," March 24, 1965, BTS 1/33/3, vol. 1, ASAMFA.
13. "Namib Today," October 15, 1965, RG 59, Bureau of African Affairs, 1958–1966, box 55, NARA.
14. Ibid.
15. Ernest Gross, *The United Nations* (New York, 1962).
16. Enuga Reddy, personal correspondence, January 2, 2009.
17. Borgwardt, *A New Deal for the World*, 245.
18. Gross, *The United Nations*, 5, 10.
19. Memo of Conversation, June 15, 1960, RG 59, Office of East and South African Affairs, 1951–1965, box 3, NARA.
20. International Court of Justice, Pleadings, Oral Arguments and Documents, *South West Africa Cases: Ethiopia and Liberia v. South Africa*, vol. 1 (The Hague, 1962), 88–95.
21. Ibid., 94.
22. Ibid., 103.
23. Ibid., 182.
24. Ibid., 181–82.
25. Ibid., 110–78.
26. Ibid., 166. For scholarship on development theory in the American context, see Ekbladh, *The Great American Mission*; Latham, *Modernization as Ideology*. For the non-American context, see Cooper and Packard, *International Development and the Social Sciences*.
27. For information on strategy, consult Ernest Gross, "The South West Africa Cases: On the Threshold of Decision," *Columbia Journal of Transnational Law*, 3 (1964): 19–25; "Legal and Political Strategies of the South West Africa Litigation," *Law in Transition Quarterly* 4 (1967): 8–43.
28. ICJ Pleadings, *South West Africa Case*, vol. 1, 161–62.
29. "Legal Analysis of Western Legal System," no date, BTS 1/18/15/3 (1), vol. 11, ASAMFA.
30. ICJ Pleadings, *South West Africa Case*, vol. 1, 298–360; vol. 7, 29–156, 326–28, 376, 382.
31. Ibid., vol. 1, 361–71; vol. 7, 156–99.
32. Ibid., vol. 7, 248, emphasis in original.
33. Slonim, *South West Africa and the United Nations*, 311.

34. "Analysis of ICJ Judgment on Preliminary Objections of South West Africa Case," January 23, 1962, RG 59, Office of East and South African Affairs, box 3, NARA.
35. Sue Onslow, "A Question of Timing: South Africa and Rhodesian UDI 1964–1965," *Cold War History* 5:2 (2005).
36. Quoted in Hepple, *Verwoerd*, 192.
37. Statement by the South African Minister of External Affairs, the Hon. Eric H. Louw, BTS 4/1/13/3, vol. 1, NASA, emphasis in original.
38. "Relations between South Africa and the United States: Summarized Balance-Sheet," no date, BTS 1/33/3, vol. 1, ASAMFA.
39. For an overview of these themes see Borstelmann, *The Cold War and the Color Line*; Dudziak, *Cold War Civil Rights*; Massie, *Loosing the Bonds*; and James Meriwether, *Proudly We Can Be Africans* (Chapel Hill, 2002).
40. Report on ICJ Preliminary Decision, January 13, 1963, BTS 1/99/1, vol. 17, NASA.
41. ICJ Pleadings, *South West Africa Case*, vol. 2, 170–93; vol. 5, 85–99; vol. 8, 582–83.
42. Ibid., vol. 2, 460.
43. Quoted in Slonim, *South West Africa and the United Nations*, 229.
44. ICJ Pleadings, *South West Africa Case*, vol. 2, 472.
45. For useful primers, see Davenport and Saunders, *South Africa*; Thompson, *A History of South Africa*; Louw, *The Rise, Fall, and Legacy of Apartheid*, 1–27, 105–31.
46. ICJ Pleadings, *South West Africa Case*, vol. 2, 410–11, 419–21; vol. 3, 23–31, 38, 92–93, 243–45.
47. Ibid., vol. 3, 105–7, 234–36.
48. Ibid., 341–42, 444–46.
49. Ibid., 195–339, 341–540.
50. Ibid., 278–79.
51. Reddy, *Oliver Tambo*, 6–7.
52. ICJ Pleadings, *South West Africa Case*, vol. 9, 15–16.
53. See Anthony D'Amato, "Legal and Political Strategies of the South West Africa Litigation," *Law in Transition Quarterly*, 4 (1967); Elizabeth Landis, "South West Africa Cases: Remand to the United Nations," *Cornell Law Quarterly*, 52 (1967).
54. *Ethiopia and Liberia v. South Africa: The South West Africa Cases, Occasional Papers No. 5* (Los Angeles, 1968), 17.
55. ICJ Pleadings, *South West Africa Cases*, vol. 9, 21.
56. This concept had been discussed earlier by the Applicants, but it moved to the forefront of their case. The definition of the norm was provided after the submission of the Respondent's Counter-Memorial. In the Applicants' words, "The terms 'non-discrimination' or 'non-separation' are used in their prevalent and customary sense: stated negatively, the terms refer to the absence of governmental policies or action which allot status, rights, duties, privileges or burdens on the basis of membership in a group, class or race rather than on the basis of individual merit, capacity or potential: stated affirmatively, the terms refer to governmental policies and actions the objective of which is to protect equality or opportunity and equal protection of the laws to individual persons as such." Ibid., vol. 6, 493.
57. Ibid., 494–95.
58. *Ethiopia and Liberia v. South Africa: The South West Africa Cases, Occasional Papers No. 31–41*, 35–38.
59. Slonim, *South West Africa and the United Nations*, 246.
60. ICJ Pleadings, *South West Africa Case*, vol. 12, 373–91.
61. Ibid., vol. 4, 373.
62. "Authority of USA to Stop SA Trade," March 26, 1965, FO 371/182125, NA.
63. Report of the Task Force on the Review of African Development Policies and Programs, July 22, 1966, *FRUS, 1964–1968*, 24: 334–49; Paper Prepared in the Department of State, undated, *FRUS, 1964–1968*, 24: 369–75; Discussion on Southern Africa, March 1, 1966, FO 371/188149, NA.

64. Memorandum, Secretary of State Rusk to President Johnson, October 14, 1965, *FRUS, 1964–1968*, 24: 311.
65. Memorandum, President's Deputy Special Assistant for National Security Affairs (Komer) to President Johnson, November 23, 1965, *FRUS, 1964–1968*, 24: 313.
66. Memorandum for the President, May 3, 1964, *FRUS, 1964–1968*, 24: 987–88; AF Priority Issues, April 3, 1963, RG 59, Office of East and South African Affairs, box 3, NARA; Analysis of US/U.K. Approach, April 1965, FO 371/182126, NA; Telegram from Pretoria, June 23, 1966, FO 371/188149; Interview by the Minister of Information, August 5, 1964, BTS 1/33/3, vol. 4, ASAMFA; U.S.-U.K. Policy on Southern Africa, July 8, 1965, BTS 1/33/3, vol. 5a, ASAMFA.
67. Memorandum, Joint Chiefs of Staff to Secretary of Defense McNamara, May 22, 1964, *FRUS, 1964–1968*, 24: 991.
68. Memorandum, President Johnson to Secretary of State Rusk, November 28, 1965, *FRUS, 1964–1968*, 24: 315.
69. "National Policy Paper South Africa (Secret)," January 18, 1965, RG 59, S/P Files: Lot 72 D 139, NARA.
70. Ibid.
71. "Possible US/UK Approaches to South West Africa Problem," January 24, 1963; "Next Steps on South West Africa," February 8, 1963; "South West African Contingency Briefing Paper," March 4, 1963, all in RG 59, Office of East and South African Affairs, box 3, NARA; "The International Court of Justice on South West Africa," June 22, 1966, FO 371/188149, NA.
72. National Security Action Memorandum No. 295, April 24, 1964, *FRUS, 1964–1968*, 24: 985–86; Status Report on NSAM No. 295, July 30, 1964, *FRUS, 1964–1968*, 24: 995–98; Status Report on NSAM No. 295, July 31, 1965, *FRUS, 1964–1968*, 24: 1032–38.
73. Ibid.; "State Department Action to Discourage U.S. Investments in South Africa (secret)," February 15, 1965, BTS 1/33/3, vol. 4a, ASAMFA; "Mr. Mennen Williams Brief United States Businessmen (secret)," July 29, 1965, BTS 1/33/3, vol. 4a, ASAMFA.
74. Telegram, Embassy in South Africa to the Department of State, May 5, 1965, *FRUS, 1964–1968*, 24: 1026–27; Vliegdekskip: Independence, July 26, 1965, BTS 1/33/3, vol. 4a, ASAMFA.
75. Secretary of Defense McNamara to Secretary of State Rusk, May 3, 1965, *FRUS, 1964–1968*, 24: 1025–26; "Intelligence Report Prepared in the Central Intelligence Agency," November 1, 1966, *FRUS, 1964–1968*, 24: 1061.
76. Telegram, Embassy in South Africa to the Department of State, February 12, 1964, *FRUS, 1964–1968*, 24: 969–70; Telegram, Department of State to the Embassy in South Africa, April 13, 1965 *FRUS, 1964–1968*, 24: 1025–26; Memorandum, William H. Brubeck of the National Security Council Staff to the President's Special Assistant for National Security Affairs (Bundy), March 18, 1964, *FRUS, 1964–1968*, 24: 974–75.
77. Telegram, Department of State to the Embassy in South Africa, April 13, 1965, *FRUS, 1964–1968*, 24: 1022–24; "US/U.K. Talks," April 2, 1965, FO 371/182125, NA; "Meeting with State Department," August 10, 1965, FO 371/182125, NA; "Anglo-American Talks on the U.N.," March 4, 1966, FO 371/188149, NA; "The International Court Case on South West Africa," June 22, 1966, FO 371/188149, NA; "Anglo-American Talks on the South-West Problem," July 6, 1966, FO 371/188150, NA.
78. "Relations with the United States (Secret)," August 13, 1965, BTS 1/33/3, vol. 1, ASAMFA.
79. Mr. Taswell's Report 8/6 of August 13, 1965, September 3, 1965, BTS 1/33/3, vol. 5, ASAMFA.
80. "Informal Talks with Members of United States Administration," January 21, 1965, BTS 1/33/3, vol. 4a, ASAMFA.
81. ICJ Pleadings, *South West Africa Case, vol. XI*, 643–708.
82. Ibid., 703.
83. Ibid., vol. 12, 392–451.

84. Ibid., vol. 11, 643–708.

85. Ibid., 708.

86. Interview with Governor Williams (Secret), February 10, 1965, BTS 1/33/3, vol. 4a, ASAMFA.

87. Interview with Secretary of State in NY (Secret), September 30, 1965, BTS 1/33/3, vol. 7a, ASAMFA.

88. "Anglo-American Talks," February 1–3, 1966, DO 216/30, NA.

89. "Summary Notes of the 561st Meeting of the National Security Council," July 14, 1966, *FRUS 1964–1968*, 24:1052–53.

90. "The International Court Case on South West Africa," June 22, 1966, FO 371/188149, NA.

91. The story of why the Court overruled its earlier opinion is fascinating in its own right. Without delving too deeply into the internal dynamics of the Court in the mid-1960s, it is worth noting that one of the judges—Bustamante y Rivero of Peru—was unable to participate in the 1966 decision because of illness. Under normal circumstances, a replacement judge would hear the case on his behalf. However, the president of the Court—Sir Percy Spender—refused to appoint such a figure because the replacement judge had been involved with nonaligned politics and lobbied to serve as the African Group's Ad Hoc judge for the SWA case in 1960. Because this spot was left open, the court was split seven to seven in 1966, and Spender was able to cast a tie-breaking vote. This was extremely controversial at the time. Many members of the African bloc labeled Spender a racist and colonialist. See Interview with Expelled Judge, August 1, 1966, RG 59, Bureau of African Affairs, box 55, NARA.

92. ICJ Judgment, *South West Africa Case*, 34.

93. Ibid., 49–51.

94. Ibid., 48.

95. Interview with Ghana's Ambassador, July 20, 1966, BTS 1/18/15/3 (62), vol. 5, ASAMFA. These sentiments point toward the ICJ's immensely interesting history *after* the South West Africa decision. Incensed by the ruling, members of the so-called Afro-Asian bloc pushed for a series of Court reforms in the late 1960s and early 1970s that actively curtailed the influence of Western judges. In their minds, the African Group had lost the decision because the Court lacked sufficient Third World viewpoints. The resulting changes, mandated by the General Assembly in the immediate wake of the ruling, gave a fixed number of seats to each "regional group." The so-called West received five seats, Asia three, Africa three, Latin America and the Caribbean two, and East Europe two. The aim, explicitly, was to provide Afro-Asian representatives with the numbers to balance the West. Since then, the process of electing judges has been notably politicized. For useful overviews, see Shabtai Rosenne, *The World Court* (Leiden, 2003); James Crawford and Tom Grant, "International Court of Justice," in *The Oxford Handbook to the United Nations*, ed. Thomas Weiss and Sam Daws (New York, 2007); Thomas Franck, *Judging the World Court* (New York, 1986).

96. Quoted in "The World Court Decision," *Hartford Courant*, July 21, 1966.

97. Congress Interview with Gross, August 8, 1966, BTS 1/18/15/3 (62), vol. 6, ASAMFA.

98. "Anti-climax at The Hague," *New York Times*, July 29, 1966.

99. "Decision Due on 'Black Power' in Africa," *Hartford Courant*, July 17, 1966; "South West Africa," *Nation*, December 26, 1966, BTS 1/18/15/3 (62), vol. 1, ASAMFA.

100. For detailed overview of the hearings, see U.S. Congress, House, *Hearings Before the Subcommittee on Africa of the Committee on Foreign Affairs*, parts 1–3, 89th Cong., (1966). For South African analysis of hearings, see BTS 1/33/3/3, vols. 1–5, ASAMFA.

101. Kennedy was invited to South Africa by a student organization called NUSAS. For an interesting overview see Massie, *Losing the Bonds*, 128–45.

102. For correspondence, consult RG 59, Records of G. Mennen Williams, 1961–1966, Chronological File, 1961–1966, box 2, NARA.

103. Robert Kennedy, "Day of Affirmation Address," June 6, 1966, JFKL, www.jfklibrary.org/Historical+Resources/Archives/Reference+Desk/Speeches/RFK/Day+of+Affirmation+Address+News+Release.html.

104. "South Africa on the Crest of the Wave (Top Secret), Directorate of Intelligence," August 30, 1966, National Security Files, box 79, LBJL.

105. Statement by Prime Minister Verwoerd (Press Release), July 18, 1966, BTS 1/18/15/3 (62), vol. 1, ASAMFA.

106. "Implications of ICJ Case," no date, BTS 1/18/15/3 (62), vol. 9, ASAMFA.

Chapter 5

1. Achkar Marof, "Statement on the Occasion of the Publication of the Interim Report of the Special Committee," June 17, 1965, United Nations Collection, UFH.

2. Report on the Task Force on the Review of African Development Policies and Programs, July 22, 1966, *FRUS, 1964–1968*, 24: 311.

3. "The Negro: After the Riots," July 29, 1966, BTS, 1/33/10, vol. 4, ASAMFA.

4. Robert M. Collins, "The Economic Crisis of 1968 and the Waning of the 'American Century,'" *American Historical Review* 101:2 (April 1996): 396–422.

5. Achkar Marof, "Statement at a Press Conference on the Occasion of the Publication of the Annual Report of the Special Committee on Apartheid," August 10, 1965, BTS 14/11, vol. 20, ASAMFA.

6. Enuga Reddy, "Note on the Further Consideration of the Question of Apartheid," July 30, 1965, series 286, box 2, file 5, UNRO.

7. Quoted in Immanuel Wallerstein, *Africa, the Politics of Unity* (New York, 1967), 153–55.

8. *Organization of African Unity: Basic Documents and Resolutions* (Addis Ababa, 1964), 12–13.

9. Zambia gained its independence in1964, and it became a member of the ALC in 1965. See Wallerstein, *Africa:The Politics of Unity*, 152–75.

10. As Wallerstein notes, the ALC was the product of inter-African political calculations—specifically the desire of many heads of state to counterbalance the influence and prestige of Ghana's Kwame Nkrumah and Egypt's Gamal Nasser. Wallerstein, *Africa: The Politics of Unity*, 152–75.

11. Wallerstein, *Africa: The Politics of Unity*, 152–75.

12. "Africa Must Pose and Take Stock," May 25, 1965, *PAC News & Views*, vol. 1, no. 8, box 14, E. S. Reddy Collection, YUMA; Matthew Nkoana, "Kill or Be Killed," November 1966, *The Pan Africanist Congress of South Africa: Material from the Collection of Gail Gerhart*, reel 4, microfilm, MF—6030, 221, PAC, *Collections and Documents*.

13. "La Revolution et Africa," *Revolution et Travail*, Novembre 26, 1965, Yale University Newspaper and Microfilm Reading Room (hereafter YUNMR).

14. Ibid.

15. Ibid.

16. Quoted in *Yearbook of the United Nations* (New York, 1966), 598.

17. Achkar Marof, "No Compromise with Racism: Statement at the Plenary Meeting of the General Assembly, Introducing the Afro-Asian Draft Resolution on South West Africa," September 27, 1966, United Nations Collection, UFH.

18. *Yearbook of the United Nations* (New York, 1966), 598–99.

19. Marof, "No Compromise with Racism," September 27, 1966, United Nations Collection, UFH.

20. "Probable Repercussions of the South-West Africa Issue," June 2, 1966, National Security Files: African General, box 76, LBJL.

21. Memorandum, President's Special Assistant (Moyers) to President Johnson, May 26, 1966, 3/66–5/66, National Security Files: African General, box 76, LBJL.

22. Lyndon Johnson, "The United States and Africa: A Unity of Purpose," May 26, 1966, *Department of State Bulletin* 54:1407 (Washington DC, 1966), 915.

23. Memorandum, President's Special Assistant (Moyers) to President Johnson, May 26, 1966, 3/66–5/66, National Security Files: African General, box 76, LBJL. See Robert Massie, *Loosing the Bonds*, xi–xii, 212–63.

24. Circular Telegram, Department of State to All African Posts Except Pretoria, May 25, 1966, RG 59, Central Files: POL 15-1, NARA.

25. "South West Africa: Action Following the International Court of Justice of 18 July and Likely Developments," September 26, 1966, RG 59, Bureau of African Affairs, 1958–1966, box 55, NARA.

26. Ibid.

27. Clark to Palmer, October 3, 1966, RG 59, Bureau of African Affairs, 1958–1966, box 55, NARA.

28. "South West Africa: Background Paper," October 14, 1966, RG 59, Bureau of African Affairs, 1958–1966, box 55, NARA.

29. Arthur Goldberg, "United States Urges Concrete U.N. Action on South West Africa," October 12, 1966, *Department of State Bulletin* 55, 1427 (Washington DC, 1966), 691.

30. Quoted in *Yearbook of the United Nations* (New York, 1966), 600–601.

31. Ibid., 601.

32. Le Quesne to Killick, FO 371/187695, NA.

33. For an excellent overview to the lead up to the Anglo-American break, see "An Assessment of British Commitments in Africa," October 25, 1966, RG 59, Bureau of African Affairs, 1958–1966, box 2, NARA.

34. Quoted in New York to Pretoria, October 28, 1966, BTS 14/11, vol. 20, ASAMFA.

35. Memorandum on South West Africa, January 20, 1967, FCO 25/588, NA.

36. New York to London, Speech Excerpts, February 10, 1967, FCO 25/588, NA.

37. New York to London, Speech Excerpts, January 24, 1967, FCO 25/588, NA.

38. Cooper, *Africa Since 1945*, 156–90.

39. *Yearbook of the United Nations* (New York, 1967), 691.

40. New York to London, Speech Excerpts, April 24, 1967, FCO 25/525, NA.

41. Ibid.

42. Ibid.

43. "Provisional Verbatim Record of the Fifteen Hundred and Fourteenth Plenary Meeting, Question of South West Africa," May 5, 1967, FCO 25/525, NA.

44. "Soviet Attitude on South West Africa," May 10, 1967, FCO 25/525, NA.

45. A prominent labor lawyer who served as chief legal advisor during the Congress of Industrial Organizations (CIO) merger with the American Federation of Labor (AFL) in 1955, Arthur Goldberg served as secretary of labor and an associate member of the Supreme Court during the Kennedy administration. In 1965, shortly after Adlai Stevenson's death, President Johnson convinced Goldberg to leave the Supreme Court to become ambassador to the United Nations. Goldberg accepted the post principally because he hoped to convince Johnson to end the Vietnam War. Following Williams's departure from the administration, Goldberg was perhaps Washington's most forward-leaning liberal voice. Tellingly, however, his engagement with the apartheid issue was limited to the 1967 debates about South West Africa (Namibia). For a comprehensive overview of Goldberg's career and influence, see David Stebenne, *Arthur J. Goldberg* (New York, 1996).

46. Arthur Goldberg, "Statement of April 26," *Department of State Bulletin* 56, 1459 (Washington DC, 1967), 891. For similar sentiment, see Circular Telegram, Department of State to Certain Posts, April 15, 1967, *FRUS, 1964–1968*, 24: 636.

47. Goldberg, "Statement of May 5," *Department of State Bulletin* 56, 1459 (Washington, DC), 893.

48. Statement by the Secretary-General to the Seminar, July 25, 1967, International Seminar on Apartheid, Racial Discrimination and Colonialism in Southern Africa (hereafter Intl. Seminar on SA), series 0196, box 12, file 6, UNRO, emphasis in original.

49. The Soviet Union and several East European countries were in attendance, along with Scandinavian nations. The United States sent several State Department officials, but they arrived after the opening ceremony and left before the conclusion of the conference. "Organization of the Seminar," Intl. Seminar on SA, series 0196, box 12, file 6, UNRO.

50. E. S. Reddy to Oliver Tambo, May 19, 1967, Oliver Tambo: Correspondence, E. S. Reddy Collection, YUMA.

51. Ibid.

52. Statement by the Secretary-General to the Seminar, July 25, 1967, Intl. Seminar on SA, series 0196, box 12, file 6, UNRO.

53. Concluding Statement by the Chairman of the Seminar on August 4, 1967, Intl. Seminar on SA, series 0196, box 12, file 6, UNRO, emphasis in original.

54. Conclusions and Recommendations of the Seminar, August 4, 1967, Intl. Seminar on SA, series 0196, box 12, file 6, UNRO.

55. Final Declaration of the Seminar, August 4, 1967, Intl. Seminar on SA, series 0196, box 12, file 6, UNRO.

56. Achkar Marof, "The Crisis in Southern Africa with Special Reference to South Africa and Measures to Be Taken by the International Community," August 4, 1967, Intl. Seminar on SA, series 0196, box 12, file 6, UNRO.

57. Concluding Statement by the Minister of Foreign Affairs of the Republic of Zambia, August 4, 1967, Intl. Seminar on SA, series 0196, box 12, file 6, UNRO.

58. Final Declaration of the Seminar, August 4, 1967, Intl. Seminar on SA, series 0196, box 12, file 6, UNRO.

59. Marof, "The Crisis in Southern Africa," August 4, 1967, Intl. Seminar on SA, series 0196, box 12, file 6, UNRO.

60. Concluding Statement by the Minister of Foreign Affairs of the Republic of Zambia, August 4, 1967, Intl. Seminar on SA, series 0196, box 12, file 6, UNRO.

61. Report of the International Seminary on Apartheid, Racial Discrimination and Colonialism in Southern Africa held in Kitwe, Zambia, July 25–August 4, 1967, series 0196, box 12, file 6, UNRO.

62. Nonstate organizations suggested some of these proposals in the early 1960s. Their first formal expression came at a U.N. conference in Brasilia in 1966.

63. Colin Legum, "The Future of Apartheid," August 4, 1967, Intl. Seminar on SA, series 0196, box 12, file 6, UNRO.

64. New York City to London, May 23, 1967, FCO 25/706, NA.

65. Report on the Kitwe Seminar on July 25–August 4, 1967, RG 59, Bureau of African Affairs, POL3-6, NARA.

66. G. L. Obhrai to J. Rolz-Bennett, August 9, 1967, series 0196, box 12, file 6, UNRO, emphasis in original.

67. New York City to London, May 24, 1967, FCO 25/706, NA.

68. Reddy to Narasimhan, September 14, 1967, series 0196, box 12, file 6, UNRO.

69. Personal Correspondence with Reddy, January 10, 2009.

70. Reddy to Tambo, June 3, 1968, Oliver Tambo: Correspondence, E. S. Reddy Collection, YUMA, emphasis added.

71. Ibid.

72. For a reflection on the theme of territoriality, see Charles Maier, "Consigning the Twentieth Century to History: Alternative Narratives for the Modern Era," *American Historical Review* 105:3 (June 2000): 807–31; Maier, *Among Empires*.

73. For excellent overviews of early nongovernmental anti-apartheid activism, see Carol Anderson, "International Conscience, the Cold War, and Apartheid: The NAACP's Alliance with the Reverend Michael Scott for South West Africa's Liberation, 1946–1952," *Journal of World History* 19:3 (September 2008): 297–326; Baldwin, *Toward the Beloved Community*; Culverson, *Contesting Apartheid*; Love, *The U.S. Anti-Apartheid Movement*; Massie, *Loosing the Bonds*; Magubane, *The Ties that Bind*; Minter, *King Soloman's Mines Revisited*; Nesbitt, *Race for Sanctions*; Shepherd Jr., *Anti-Apartheid*; and Morgan, "Into the

Struggle: Confronting Apartheid in the United States and South Africa, 1964–1990," (Phd diss., 2009). For broader scholarship on nongovernmental activism, Anderson, *Eyes Off the Prize*; Borstelmann, *Cold War and the Color Line*; Dudziak, *Cold War Civil Rights*; von Eschen, *Race against Empire*; Plummer, *Rising Wind*.

74. For a description of this shift, see Paul Gordon Lauren, *Human Rights* (Philadelphia, 2003), 233–47.

75. Ibid., 246. For an introduction to scholarship on human rights, see Samantha Power, "*A Problem from Hell*" (New York, 2002); Mary Ann Glendon, *A World Made New* (New York, 2002); Jeri Laber, *The Courage of Strangers* (New York, 2002); as well as Sarah B. Snyder, *Human Rights Activism and the End of the Cold War* (Cambridge, UK, 2011).

76. *Yearbook of the United Nations* (New York, 1968), 536. For instance, when the General Assembly called on the Security Council to expel South Africa from the United Nations in 1974, this request was cast in the language of human rights rather than postcolonial nationalism. Although the Security Council did not take action, the Assembly nonetheless voted to rescind the Republic's credentials. South Africa was unable to participate in General Assembly debates until 1994.

77. Report on the International Human Rights Conference, April 22–May 13, 1968, series 0196, box 12, file 1, UNRO.

78. "21st General Assembly," September 15, 1966, National Security Files, NSC Meetings, box 2, LBJL.

79. William Duggan, "Southern Africa in the Next Decade: A Case for Constructive Reinvolvement," August 23, 1966, National Security Files, box 78, LBJL.

80. Memorandum, Assistant Secretary of Defense for International Security Affairs (McNaughton) to Secretary of Defense McNamara, January 18, 1967, *FRUS, 1964–1968*, 24: 406.

81. Ibid.; for direct exchanges between State and Defense departments, see letter, Deputy Secretary of Defense (Nitze) to the Undersecretary of State (Katzenbach), October 19, 1967, *FRUS, 1964–1968*, 24: 647; letter, Undersecretary of State (Katzenbach) to the Deputy Secretary of Defense (Nitze), November 15, 1967, *FRUS, 1964–1968*, 24: 648.

82. "African Problems," no date, National Security Files, Africa—General, 6/66-1/69, box 77, LBJL.

83. "African Problems," July 13, 1967, National Security Files, NSC Meetings, box 2, LBJL.

84. "22nd General Assembly," September 15, 1966, National Security Files, NSC Meeting Minutes, box 2, LBJL.

85. Briefing Paper, September 15, 1966, National Security Files, NSC Meeting Minutes, box 2, LBJL.

86. National Policy Paper—South Africa, (Secret), January 18, 1965, RG 59, S/P Files: Lot 72 D 139, NARA.

87. "Liberation Movements in Southern Africa," November 24, 1967, National Security Files, National Intelligence Estimates, South and East Africa File, box 8, LBJL.

88. Intelligence Memorandum, "Some Aspects of Subversion in Africa," October 19, 1967, 10/66–9-68, National Security Files, South Africa, box 78, LBJL.

89. Rostow to Katzenbach, December 20, 1967, RG 59, Central Files, DEF 12-5 South Africa, NARA.

90. For documentary overview of the United Kingdom's stance toward the South Africa arms embargo, see PREM 13/2400, 13/3498, FCO 45/283, FCO 45/284, NA.

91. Rostow to Katzenbach, December 20, 1967, RG 59, Central Files, DEF 12-5 South Africa, NARA.

92. Collins, "The Economic Crisis of 1968,'" 396–422.

93. For an excellent overview of U.S.-South Africa relations in this period, see Borstelmann, *Apartheid's Reluctant Uncle*.

94. Memorandum to the President, July 17, 1968; Memorandum to the President, September 28, 1968; Memorandum to the President, October 4, 1968, all in National Security Files, South Africa, Memos and Misc., box 78, LBJL.

95. For analysis see Intelligence Memo: "South Africa, Prospects for the Gold Industry," April 1968; Intelligence Memo: "Competition for South African Gold," no date; Intelligence Memo: "Prospects for Resumption of South African Gold Sales," June 1968, all in National Security Files, South Africa, Memos and Misc, box 78, LBJL.

96. National Policy Paper—Southern Africa, November 20, 1968, RG 59, S/S Files: Lot 70D263, NARA.

97. "Summary of Discussion and Decisions at the 47th Senior Interdepartmental Group Meeting," December 3, 1968, RG59, S/S Files: Lot 70D263, NARA.

98. Ibid.

99. Ibid.

100. Memorandum, Joint Chiefs of Staff to Secretary of Defense McNamara, December 12, 1968, *FRUS, 1964–1968*, 24: 412.

Chapter 6

1. "Final Report of Cyrus Vance Special Assistant to the Secretary of Defense Concerning the Detroit Riots," July 23 through August 2, 1967, LBJ Library and Museum, www.lbjlib. utexas.edu/johnson/archives.hom/oralhistory.hom/Vance-C/DetroitReport.asp, accessed September 25, 2009.

2. Handwritten note, July 31, 1967, BTS, 1/33/3, vol. 8, ASAMFA.

3. "Call to Revolution, A Message from O. R. Tambo," *Sechaba* 2:1 (January 1968).

4. Joe Slovo, "South Africa: No Middle Road," in *Southern Africa*, ed. Basil Davidson (Harmondsworth, 1976), 194.

5. Jeremi Suri, *Power and Protest* (Cambridge, MA, 2003), 258–59; Samuel Moyn, *Last Utopia* (Cambridge, MA, 2010).

6. "Tragedy in South Africa," *South Africa Digest* 13:13, 1–2.

7. Beinart, *Twentieth-Century South Africa*, 126.

8. "Prosperity Blueprint for SA's Future," *South Africa Digest* 13:14, 1.

9. "World Reaction to S.A. Election," *South Africa Digest* 13:14, 2.

10. "Verwoerd's Victory," *Financial Times*, March 20, 1966, 6A.

11. See Louw, *The Rise, Fall, and Legacy of Apartheid*; Beinart, *Twentieth-Century South Africa*; Beinart and Saul DuBow, *Segregation and Apartheid* (London, 1995); Giliomee, *The Afrikaners*; F. A. van Jaarsveld, *Die Evolusie van Apartheid* (Cape Town, 1979).

12. Hendrik Verwoerd, no title, July 21, 1966, BTS 1/18/15/3 (62), vol. 4, ASAMFA.

13. "Survey of Domestic Press," July 29, 1966, BTS 1/18/15/3 (62), vol. 9, ASAMFA.

14. Ibid.

15. Ibid.

16. John D'Oliveira, *Vorster—The Man* (Johannesburg, 1977), 130.

17. Quoted in ibid., 137.

18. Ibid., 156–62.

19. John Barber and John Barratt, *South Africa's Foreign Policy* (New York, 1990), 107–17.

20. James Sanders, *Apartheid's Friends* (London, 2006). See also Gordon Winter, *Inside BOSS* (Harmondsworth, 1981).

21. D'Oliveira, *Vorster—The Man*, 232–33.

22. Ibid., 233–34.

23. Quoted in Gail-Maryse Cockram, *Vorster's Foreign Policy* (Pretoria, 1970), 124.

24. Interview with Prime Minister, May 3, 1971, BTS 1/99/19, vol. 10, ASAMFA.

25. "Vorster and the World," *Star*, February 17, 1967.

26. "Sud Afrika Vershoolk," *Die Burger*, March 6, 1967.

27. Ockert Geyser, ed., *Select Speeches* (Bloemfontein, 1977), 80–88.

28. Quoted in Beinart, *Twentieth-Century South Africa*, 199.

29. Barber and Barratt, *South Africa's Foreign Policy*, 128.

30. Ibid., 130–33.

31. "Decision on South Africa Defended," *Star*, September 11, 1967, BTS 1/99/19, vol. 8, ASAMFA.

32. "South Africa's Forward Policy," October 1970, BTS 1/99/19, vol. 12, ASAMFA.

33. Hilgard Muller, "South Africa's Relations with African States," September 1967, BTS 1/99/19, vol. 8, ASAMFA.

34. Interview with Prime Minister, May 3, 1971, BTS 1/99/19, vol. 10, ASAMFA.

35. Sue Onslow, "A Question of Timing: South Africa and Rhodesia's Unilateral Declaration of Independence, 1964–65," *Cold War History* 5:2 (May 2005): 129.

36. See Ken Flower, *Serving Secretly* (London, 1987), 157.

37. Barber and Barratt, *South Africa's Foreign Policy*, 139.

38. Vorster to Kaunda, May 2, 1968, *Dear Mr Vorster . . . : Details of exchanges between President Kaunda of Zambia and Prime Minister Vorster of South Africa* (Lusaka, 1972), 4.

39. Kaunda to Vorster, August 15, 1968, ibid., 7.

40. Vorster to Kaunda, August 29, 1968, ibid., 7–8.

41. *The Lusaka Manifesto on Southern Africa, April 14–16, 1969* (Lusaka, 1972), 6.

42. Hilgard Muller, "Address to House of Assembly," May 7, 1969, BTS 1/33/3, vol. 13, ASAMFA.

43. It is important to underscore that South African officials never embraced Kaunda fully. As the Zambian president began working to bolster his country's political profile among Third World nations in the 1970s—in part to position himself to succeed Egypt's Gamal Abdel Nasser as secretary-general of the Nonaligned Movement—Vorster grew increasingly frustrated with his counterpart's supposed "double-dealing," and, in early 1971, exposed South Africa's private dealings with Lusaka in a transparent effort to embarrass the Zambian president. See "Minister's Discussion with Mr Rogers, Secretary of State," October 3, 1969, BTS 1/33/3, vol. 13, ASAMFA; "Vorster Aims to Split Africans," April 25, 1971, BTS 1/99/19, vol. 10, ASAMFA.

44. "Conference de Presse de S. Ex. Monsier le President Felix Houphouet-Boigny, President de la Republique de Cote D'Ivoire," Avril 28, 1971, BTS 1/99/19, vol. 12, ASAMFA; Malawi to Pretoria, December 22, 1970, BTS 1/99/19, vol. 10, ASAMFA.

45. Dialogue, May 14, 1971, BTS 1/99/19, vol. 11, ASAMFA.

46. Dialogue, May 15, 1971, BTS 1/99/19, vol. 11, ASAMFA.

47. Dialogue, April 29, 1971, BTS 1/99/19, vol. 10, ASAMFA.

48. "South Africa's Forward Policy," no date, BTS 1/99/19, vol. 12, ASAMFA.

49. "Dialogue and Divisions," *African Confidential*, May 14, 1971, BTS 1/99/19, vol. 11, ASAMFA.

50. "Interview with Prime Minister," May 3, 1971, BTS 1/99/19, vol. 10, ASAMFA.

51. Memo to Director of Information (Secret), August 4, 1966, BTS 1/33/3, vol. 7a, ASAMFA.

52. "South West Africa Interview with Mr. Ball," (Secret) August 19, 1966, BTS 1/18/15/3 (62), vol. 9, ASAMFA.

53. "Interview between Dr. Muller and Mr. Rusk at the United States Mission," October 7, 1967, BTS 1/33/3, vol. 8, ASAMFA.

54. M. D. Banghart, Memorandum, November 3, 1966, BTS 1/33/3, vol. 7, ASAMFA.

55. Richard Hull, *American Enterprise in South Africa* (New York, 1990), 242–95.

56. "Discussions with Senator Mansfield," September 29, 1966, BTS 1/33/3, vol. 7, ASAMFA.

57. "Summary of Situation Concerning O'Hare Hearings," BTS 1/33/3, vol. 7, ASAMFA, emphasis in original.

58. Quoted in Barber and Barratt, *South Africa's Foreign Policy*, 114.

59. *South West Africa Survey 1967* (Pretoria, 1967).

60. "South Africa and the U.S.—A Basis for Understanding (Top Secret)," BTS 1/33/3/1, vol. 2, ASAMFA. See also Ryan Irwin, "Wind of Change? White Redoubt and the Postcolonial Moment," *Diplomatic History* 33:5 (November 2009): 897–935.

61. "Riots in the City of the Angels," August 24, 1966, BTS 1/33/10, vol. 6, ASAMFA.

62. "Addressing the Students," December 10, 1968, BTS 1/33/3, vol. 10, ASAMFA.

63. Sole to Taswell, December 13, 1968, BTS 1/33/3, vol. 10, ASAMFA.
64. "Some Good News at Last," February 7, 1969, BTS 1/33/3, vol. 11, ASAMFA.
65. "Interview with Mr. William Rogers, Secretary of State," March 20, 1969, BTS 1/33/3, vol. 11, ASAMFA.
66. "US Policy on South Africa," September 19, 1969, BTS 1/33/3, vol. 13, ASAMFA.
67. The Chappaquiddick incident refers to the circumstances surrounding the death of Mary Jo Kopechne on July 19, 1969. An informal acquaintance of Edward Kennedy, Kopechne drowned after the senator drove his car off a bridge while returning her to a hotel following a late night party on Chappaquiddick Island. Circumstantial evidence suggests he was intoxicated. The event and Kennedy's subsequent failure to report Kopechne's death significantly damaged the senator's reputation, curtailing the possibility that he would run for president in 1972.
68. "US Policy on South Africa," September 19, 1969, BTS 1/33/3, vol. 13, ASAMFA.
69. Morris to Kissinger, April 23, 1969, *FRUS, 1969–1976*, vol. E-5, Documents on Africa, 1969–1972, 3; Morris to Kissinger, May 13, 1969, *FRUS, 1969–1976*, vol. E-5, Documents on Africa, 1969–1972, 4.
70. Kissinger to Nixon, Tab B: South Africa, January 2, 1970, Richard Nixon Presidential Materials (hereafter RNPM), National Security Files, box 744, NARA.
71. Kissinger to Nixon, Tab C: South West Africa, January 2, 1970, RNPM, National Security Files, box 744, NARA.
72. Anthony Lake, *The "Tar Baby" Option* (New York, 1976), 124–27.
73. "Black African Manifesto on Southern Africa," May 15, 1969, RNPM, National Security Files, box 747, NARA.
74. Kennedy to Rodman, March 30, 1970, RNPM, National Security Files, box 747, NARA.
75. Kissinger to Nixon, February 4, 1971, RNPM, National Security Files, box 744, NARA.
76. "Minister's Discussion with Mr. Rogers, Secretary of State," October 3, 1969, BTS 1/33/3, vol. 13, ASAMFA.
77. For foundational texts, see Steve Fraser and Gary Gerstle, eds., *The Rise and Fall of the New Deal Order, 1930–1980* (Princeton, 1989); Thomas Sugrue, *The Origins of the Urban Crisis* (Princeton, 1996); Lizabeth Cohen, *A Consumer's Republic* (New York, 2003). For an influential recent interpretation of Nixon, see Rick Perlstein, *Nixonland* (New York, 2008). For perhaps the most comprehensive overview of the postwar period, see James Patterson, *Grand Expectations* (New York, 1996).
78. Lake, *The "Tar Baby" Option*, 122–69.
79. "U. S. Foreign Policy for the 1970's: A New Strategy for Peace: A Report to the Congress by Richard Nixon, President of the United States," Washington, February 18, 1970, p. 7; "U. S. Foreign Policy for the 1970's: Building for Peace: A Report to the Congress by Richard Nixon, President of the United States," Washington, February 25, 1971, p. 14; "U. S. Foreign Policy for the 1970's: Building for Peace: A Report to the Congress by Richard Nixon, President of the United States," Washington, February 9, 1971, p. 18, all in *FRUS, 1969–1976*, volume E-5, Documents on Africa, 1969–1972; Marshall Wright to Kissinger, September 15, 1970, RNPM, National Security Files, box 747, NARA.
80. Memorandum, President Nixon to the President's Assistants (Haldeman), (Ehrlichman) and (Kissinger), Washington, March 2, 1970, *FRUS, 1969–1976*, vol. E-5, Documents on Africa, 1969–1972, 10.
81. Jussi Hanhimäki, "An Elusive Grand Design," in *Nixon in the World*, ed. Fredrik Logevall and Andrew Preston (New York, 2008), 25–26. See also Jussi Hanhimäki, *The Flawed Architect* (New York, 2004); as well as Richard Dallek, *Nixon and Kissinger* (New York, 2007).
82. Ibid.
83. Jeremi Suri, "Henry Kissinger and American Grand Strategy," in *Nixon in the World*, ed. Logevall and Preston, 70. See also Jeremi Suri, *Power and Protest*; Jeremi Suri, *The Global Revolutions of 1968* (New York, 2007); and Jeremi Suri, *Henry Kissinger and the American Century* (Cambridge, MA, 2007).

84. "Address by Richard M. Nixon to the Bohemian Club," July 29, 1967, *FRUS, 1969–1972*, vol. 1, 2.

85. Ibid.

86. For useful works, see Leffler, *Preponderance of Power*; Leffler, *For the Soul of Mankind*; Gaddis, *Strategies of Containment*; Hogan, *The Marshall Plan*; Louis, *Imperialism at Bay*; Lawrence, *Assuming the Burden*; Maier, *Among Empires*; Trachtenberg, *A Constructed Peace*; Westad, *The Global Cold War*; and Borgwardt, *A New Deal for the World*.

87. Essay by Henry A. Kissinger, *FRUS, 1969–1972*, vol. 1, 4.

88. Cooper, *Colonialism in Question*, 197.

89. See Hull, *American Enterprise in South Africa*; Anna-Mart van Wyk, "The USA and Apartheid South Africa's Nuclear Aspirations, 1949–1980," in *Cold War in Southern Africa*, ed. Sue Onslow (London, 2009).

90. Gleijeses, *Conflicting Missions*.

91. A. G. Hopkins, introduction to *Globalization in World History*, ed. A. G. Hopkins (New York, 2002).

92. PAC Memorandum, Submitted to Six-Member Sub-Committee of the Special Committee on Policies of Apartheid of the Government of the Republic of South Africa, Visiting Dar es Salaam, Tanzania, August 20 to August 23, 1969, PAC, 1969, box 17, E. S. Reddy Collection, YUMA; "Recommendation Submitted by the African National Congress of South Africa to the Meeting of the Special Sub-Committee on Apartheid held in Lusaka on August 18, 1969," PAC, 1969, box 17, E. S. Reddy Collection, YUMA.

93. "Meeting with A.N.C. in Lusaka," August 18, 1969, PAC, 1969, box 17, E.CS. Reddy Collection, YUMA.

94. Minutes, Meeting of the Sub-Committee of the Special Committee on Apartheid with Representatives of the South West Africa People's Organization in Dar es Salaam, August 21, 1969, folder: 1968–1969, box 27, E. S. Reddy Collection, YUMA.

95. Westad, *The Global Cold War*, 207.

96. Thomas Karis and Gail Gerhart, *From Protest to Challenge*, vol. 5 (Bloomington, 1997), 46–50.

97. Nkoana to Leballo, December 2, 1966; and Notes by Charles Lakaje, February 1970, both in *Pan Africanist Congress of South Africa: Material from the Collection of Gail M. Gerhart*, microfilm MF—6030, PAC, *Collections and Documents*.

98. Memorandum, Submitted by the Pan Africanist Congress of South Africa to the 5th Summit Conference of the O.A.U. Meeting in Algiers from the September 13th–16th, 1968; Report by Treasurer-General to Commission of Inquiry Set Up by Moshi Meeting (September 19–21, 1967) of the National Executive Committee of the Pan Africanist Congress of South Africa (Azania); "A Statement Concerning the Dispute Within the Pan-Africanist Congress (S.A.) to the African Liberation Committee," all in *The Pan Africanist Congress of South Africa*, reel 4, microfilm MF—6030, PAC, *Collections and Documents*.

99. Sifiso Mxolisi Ndlovu, "The ANC in Exile, 1960–1970," in *The Road to Democracy*.

100. Karis and Gerhart, *From Protest to Challenge*, vol. 5, 6–17.

101. Ndlovu, "The ANC in Exile, 1960–1970," in *The Road to Democracy*, 443–44.

102. Tambo to Matthews, March 2, 1966, ANC Morogoro Papers, box 11, UFH.

103. Quoted in Ndlovu, "The ANC in Exile, 1960–1970," in *The Road to Democracy*, 443.

104. Callinicos, *Oliver Tambo*, 14–15.

105. Ndlovu, "The ANC in Exile, 1960–1970," in *The Road to Democracy*, 446–47.

106. "Directive Concerning the Nature of the Forthcoming ANC Consultative Conference in Morogoro, March 1969," www.anc.org.za/, accessed February 24, 2009.

107. Ndlovu, "The ANC in Exile, 1960–1970," in *The Road to Democracy*, 445–51.

108. Vladimir Shubin, *ANC* (Sunnyside, 2008), 47–59.

109. Ibid., 47–59.

110. "The South African Revolution and Our Tasks," 1969, ANC Lusaka Papers, box 52-part 2, folder 1, UFH.

111. Karis and Gerhart, *From Protest to Challenge*, vol. 5, 6–17.
112. For an overview of Morogoro conference, see Nhlanhla Ndebele and Noor Nieftagodien, "The Morogoro Conference: A Moment of Self-Reflection," in *The Road to Democracy*, 573–600.
113. "Strategic Problems in the Struggle for the Liberation of Southern Africa," ANC Lusaka Papers, box 52-part 2, folder 1, UFH, emphasis added.
114. "Report of the Secretariat on External Affairs," ANC Lusaka Papers, box 52-part 2, folder 1, UFH.
115. "On Our Perspective and Meager Funds," ANC Lusaka Papers, box 52-part 2, folder 1, UFH.
116. Lectures, ANC Lusaka Papers, box 52-part 2, folder 2, UFH.
117. "Education as an Instrument of Liberation," ANC Lusaka Papers, box 52-part 2, folder 2, UFH.
118. "Discussion Guide: Our Struggle," 1969, ANC Lusaka Papers, box 52-part 2, folder 2, UFH.
119. Ibid.
120. Aydin, *The Politics of Anti-Westernism in Asia*.
121. "Discussion Guide: Congress Alliance," 1969, ANC Lusaka Papers, box 52-part 2, folder 2, UFH.
122. Ibid.
123. "Forward to Freedom," 1973, www.anc.org.za/, accessed February 17, 2009.
124. "The South African Revolution and Our Tasks," 1969, ANC Lusaka Papers, box 52-part 2, folder 1, UFH. See also Connelly, *A Diplomatic Revolution*.
125. "Report on the International Situation," 1973, ANC Lusaka Papers, box 52-part 2, folder 1, UFH.
126. Notes, ANC Lusaka Papers, box 52-part 2, folder 2, UFH.
127. "Close Ranks," *Sechaba* 3:7 (July 7, 1969): 3–4 (microfilm).
128. "Discussion Paper: External Solidarity Work," ANC Lusaka Papers, box 52-part 2, folder 2, UFH.
129. "Fund Raising Projects," no date, ANC Lusaka Papers, box 52-part 2, folder 1, UFH.
130. Ibid., 342–43.
131. Håkan Thörn, *Anti-Apartheid and the Emergence of a Global Civil Society* (London, 2009); Callinicos, *Oliver Tambo*, 340.
132. "Discussion Paper: Foreign Relations," 1969, ANC Lusaka Papers, box 52-part 2, folder 1, UFH.
133. "South Africa Sells Her Image Abroad: The Propaganda Machine of the South African Government," *Sechaba* 1:4 (April 1967): 12–18.
134. "Discussion Paper: Foreign Relations," 1969, ANC Lusaka Papers, box 52-part 2, folder 1, UFH.

Conclusion

1. Mandela, *Long Walk to Freedom*, 563.
2. For a reflection on these changes, see Akira Iriye, *Global Community*; and Niall Ferguson et al., *The Shock of the Global*.
3. Mandela, *Long Walk to Freedom*, 584.
4. Nelson Mandela, "Speech at Rally in Cuba," July 26, 1991, http://db.nelsonmandela.org/speeches/pub_view.asp?pg=item&ItemID=NMS1526&txtstr=Dates:%201990%20-%201991; Mandela, "Address to the Joint Session of the House of Congress of the USA," June 26, 1990, http://db.nelsonmandela.org/speeches/pub_view.asp?pg=item&ItemID=NMS040&txtstr=Dates:%201990%20-%201991, accessed December 10, 2011.
5. Mandela, "Address to the Swedish Parliament," March 13, 1990, http://db.nelsonmandela.org/speeches/pub_view.asp?pg=item&ItemID=NMS024&txtstr=Dates:%201990%20-%201991, accessed December 10, 2011.

6. Lodge, *Sharpeville*, 249.
7. Ibid., 279.
8. Roger Fieldhouse, *Anti-Apartheid* (London, 2005), 428; cited in Lodge, *Sharpeville*, 245–46.
9. For an overview, see Sellström, *Sweden and National Liberation in Southern Africa*.
10. Quoted in episode five of Connie Field's seven-part documentary film, *Have You Heard From Johannesburg: From Selma to Soweto* (Berkeley: Clarity Films, 2010). For short overviews of the U.S. anti-apartheid movement, see Culverson, *Contesting Apartheid*; and Love, *The U.S. Anti-Apartheid Movement*.

BIBLIOGRAPHY

Manuscripts and Archives

GREAT BRITAIN

National Archives of Great Britain, Kew
Cabinet Office Records
Commonwealth Records
Foreign Office Records
Prime Minister's Office Records
Rhodes House Library, Oxford University
Papers of Anti-Apartheid Movement

SOUTH AFRICA

Archives of the South African Ministry of Foreign Affairs, Pretoria
Ministry of Foreign Affairs Records
Liberation Movement Archives, University of Fort Hare
African National Congress Papers
Pan-Africanist Congress of Azania Papers
Nelson Mandela Papers
E. S. Reddy Papers
Robert Sobukwe Papers
Oliver Tambo Papers
Mayibuye Archives, University of Western Cape, Robben Island
African National Congress Papers
Afro-Asian Solidarity Committee Papers
MA Naidoo Papers
Yusuf Dadoo Papers
Govan Mbeki Papers
Neville Naidoo Papers
National Archives of South Africa, Pretoria
Department of Co-operation and Development Records
Ministry of Foreign Affairs Records
Ministry of Information Records

UNITED STATES

John F. Kennedy Library, Boston, Massachusetts
John F. Kennedy Papers
National Security Files
President's Office Files
Country Series
Special Series

Library of Congress, Washington, DC
Averill Harriman Papers
NAACP Papers

Lyndon B. Johnson Library, Austin, Texas
Lyndon B. Johnson Papers
National Security Files
President's Office Files
Special Files
Oral Histories
Mennen Williams
Andrew Young, Jr.

Moorland-Springarn Research Center, Howard University, Washington, DC
Dabu Gizenga Collection on Kwame Nkrumah

National Archives and Records Administration (II), College Park, Maryland
Record Group 59, Records of the Department of State
G. Mennen Williams

Personal Papers
Chester Bowles, New Haven, Connecticut
E.S. Reddy, New Haven, Connecticut
Adlai Stevenson, Princeton, New Jersey
G. Mennen Williams, Ann Arbor, Michigan

Richard Nixon Presidential Materials, College Park, Maryland
White House Special Files
President's Office Files
President's Personal Files
Egil M. Krogh
White House Central Files—Subject Files
Country Files
Commission on Civil Rights Files

United Nations Archives and Records Management, New York
Office of the Secretary General
U.N. Chef de Cabinet

Sources

Abdul-Raheem, Tajudeen, ed. *Pan Africanism: Politics, Economy, and Social Change in the Twenty-First Century.* New York: New York University Press, 1996.

Abraham, Willie E. *The Mind of Africa.* Chicago: University of Chicago Press, 1962.

Adam, Heribert. *Modernizing Racial Domination: The Dynamics of South African Politics.* Berkeley: University of California Press, 1978.

Adam, Heribert, and Hermann Giliomee. *Ethnic Power Mobilized: Can South Africa Change?* New Haven, CT: Yale University Press, 1983.

Adebajo, Adekeye, ed. *From Global Apartheid to Global Village: Africa and the United Nations.* Scottsville, South Africa: University of KwaZulu-Natal Press, 2009.

Adi, Hakim, and Marika Sherwood, eds. *Pan-African History: Political Figures from African and the Diaspora Since 1787.* London: Routledge, 2003.

African National Congress. *African National Congress Collection, 1928–1962.* Johannesburg, 1963. Microfilm.

African National Congress. *Sechaba,* vol. 1-24. Dar-es-Salaam, Tanzanzia: African National Congress of South Africa, 1967. Microfilm.

———. *South Africa Freedom News, 1963–1966.* Cairo: African National Congress. Microfilm. Reels 1–6, 17–39.

Alexander, Peter, and Richard Halpern, eds. *Beyond White Supremacy: Towards a New Agenda for the Comparative Histories of South Africa and the United States.* London, 1997.

———. "Introduction: Comparing Race and Labour in South Africa and the United States." *Journal of Southern African Studies.* Special Issue, *Race and Class in South Africa and the United States* 30: 1 (March 2004): 5–18.

Ali, Sheikh. *Southern Africa: An American Enigma.* New York: Praeger, 1987.

Anderson, Benedict. *Imagined Communities: Reflections on the Origins and Spread of Nationalism.* New York: Verso, 1983.

Anderson, Carol. *Eyes Off the Prize: The U.N. and the African American Struggle for Human Rights, 1944–1955.* Cambridge: Cambridge University Press, 2003.

———. "International Conscience, the Cold War, and Apartheid: The NAACP's Alliance with the Reverend Michael Scott for South West Africa's Liberation, 1946–1952." *Journal of World History* 19:3 (September 2008): 297–326.

Anzovin, Steven, ed. *South Africa: Apartheid and Divestiture.* New York: H. W. Wilson, 1987.

Appiah, Kwame. *In My Father's House: Africa in the Philosophy of Culture.* New York: Oxford University Press, 1992.

Arnesen, Eric. "Whiteness and the Historians' Imagination." *International Labor and Working-Class History,* 60 (Fall 2001): 3–27.

Aronowitz, Stanley. "The Double Bind." *Transition,* 69 (1996): 222–35.

Asante, Molefi Kete. *The Afrocentric Idea.* Philadelphia: Temple University Press, 1987.

Aydin, Cemil. *The Politics of Anti-Westernism in Asia: Visions of World Order in Pan- Islamic and Pan-Asian Thought.* New York: Columbia University Press, 2007.

Azikiwe, Nnamdi. *My Odyssey: An Autobiography.* New York: Praeger, 1971.

———. *Renascent Africa.* London: Cass, 1968.

Badie, Bertrand. *The Imported State: The Westernization of the Political Order.* Stanford, CA: Stanford University Press, 2000.

Baldwin, Lewis V. *Toward the Beloved Community: Martin Luther King Jr. and South Africa.* Cleveland, OH: Pilgrim, 1995.

Ball, George. *The Discipline of Power: Essentials of a Modern World Structure.* Boston: Little, Brown, 1968.

Barber, John, and John Barratt. *South Africa's Foreign Policy: The Search for Status and Security, 1945–1988.* Cambridge: Cambridge University Press, 1990.

Bayly, C. A., Sven Beckert, Matthew Connelly, Isabel Hofmeyr, Wendy Kozol, and Patricia Seed. "AHR Conversation: On Transnational History." *American Historical Review* 111:5 (December 2006): 1441–64.

Beinart, William. *Hidden Struggles in Rural South Africa: Politics and Popular Movements in the Transkei and Eastern Cape, 1890-1930.* London: J. Currey, 1987.

———. *The Political Economy of Pondoland, 1860–1930.* Cambridge: Cambridge University Press, 1982.

———. *Twentieth Century South Africa.* Oxford: Oxford University Press, 2001.

Beinart, William, and Peter Coates. *Environment and History: The Taming of Nature in the U.S.A and South Africa.* London: Routledge, 1995.

Beinart, William, Peter Delius, and Stanley Trapido, eds. *Putting a Plough to the Ground: Accumulation and Dispossession in Rural South Africa, 1850–1930.* Johannesburg: Ravan Press, 1986.

Beinart, William, and Saul DuBow, eds. *Segregation and Apartheid in Twentieth Century South Africa.* London: Routledge, 1995.

Bender, Thomas, ed. *Rethinking American History in a Global Age.* Berkeley: University of California Press, 2002.

Beusekom, Monica M. Van. *Negotiating Development: African Farmers and Colonial Experts at the Office du Niger, 1920–1960.* Portsmouth, NH: Heinemann, 2002.

Bhabha, Homi. *The Location of Culture.* New York: Routledge, 1994.

Birmingham, David. *Kwame Nkrumah: The Father of African Nationalism.* Athens: Ohio University Press, 1998.

Bissell, Richard E. *South Africa and the United States: The Erosion of an Influence Relationship.* New York: Praeger, 1982.

Bjornson, Richard. *The African Quest for Freedom and Identity: Cameroonian Writing and the National Experience.* Bloomington: Indiana University Press, 1991.

Boahen, A. Adu. *General History of Africa: Africa Under Colonial Domination, 1880–1935.* Berkeley: University of California Press, 1985.

Bonner, Philip. *Kathorus: A History.* Cape Town: Longman, 2001.

Bonner, Philip, Peter Delius, and Deborah Posel. *Apartheid's Genesis, 1935–1962.* Johannesburg: Ravan Press, 1993.

Bonner, Philip, Isabel Hofmeyr, Deborah James, and Tom Lodge, eds. *Holding Their Ground: Class, Locality and Culture in 19th and 20th Century South Africa.* Johannesburg: Witwatersrand University Press, 1989.

Bonnett, Alastair. *White Identities: Historical and International Perspectives.* Harlow, UK: Longman, 2000.

Borgwardt, Elizabeth. *A New Deal for the World: America's Vision for Human Rights.* Cambridge, MA: Harvard University Press, 2005.

Borstelmann, Thomas. *Apartheid's Reluctant Uncle: The United States and Southern Africa in the Early Cold War.* New York: Oxford University Press, 1993.

———. *Cold War and the Color Line: American Race Relations in the Global Arena.* Cambridge, MA: Harvard University Press, 2001.

Bosco, David. *Five to Rule Them All: The UN Security Council and the Making of the Modern World.* New York: Oxford University Press, 2009.

Bowman, Larry. *South Africa's Outward Strategy: A Foreign Policy Dilemma for the United States.* Athens, OH: Center for International Studies, 1973.

Bozzoli, Belinda, ed. *Class Community and Conflict: South African Perspectives.* Johannesburg: Ravan Press, 1987.

———. *Town and Countryside in the Transvaal: Capitalist Penetration and Popular Response.* Johannesburg: Ravan Press, 1983.

Bradford, Helen. *A Taste of Freedom: The ICU in Rural South Africa, 1924–1930.* Johannesburg: Ravan Press, 1988.

Brigham, Robert. *Guerrilla Diplomacy: The NLF's Foreign Relations and the Viet Nam War.* Ithaca, NY: Cornell University Press, 1999.

Burton, Antoinette, ed. *After the Imperial Turn: Thinking With and Through the Nation.* Durham, NC: Duke University Press, 2003.

Butts, Kent H. *The Geopolitics of Southern Africa: South Africa as Regional Superpower.* Boulder, CO: Westview Press, 1986.

Callinicos, Luli. *Oliver Tambo: Beyond the Engeli Mountains.* Cape Town: David Philip, 2004.

Campbell, James T. *Songs of Zion: The African Methodist Episcopal Church in the United States and South Africa.* New York: Oxford University Press, 1995.

Carter, Gwendolen M. *American Policy and the Search for Justice and Reconciliation in South Africa.* Racine, WI: The Johnson Foundation, 1976.

Cell, John W. *The Highest Stage of White Supremacy: The Origins of Segregation in South Africa and the American South.* Cambridge: Cambridge University Press, 1982.

Chakrabarty, Dipesh. *Provincializing Europe: Postcolonial Thought and Historical Difference.* Princeton, NJ: Princeton University Press, 2000.

———. *Rethinking Working-Class History.* Princeton, NJ: Princeton University Press, 1989.

Chatterjee, Partha. *The Nation and Its Fragments: Colonial and Postcolonial Histories.* Princeton, NJ: Princeton University Press, 1993.

———. *Nationalist Thought and the Colonial World: A Derivative Discourse.* Tokyo: Zed Books, 1986.

Clark, Nancy, and William Worger. *South Africa: The Rise and Fall of Apartheid.* New York: Pearson, 2004.

Clarke, James, ed. *Like It Was: The Star 100 Years in Johannesburg*. Johannesburg: Keartland Press, 1987.

Cockram, Gail-Maryse. *Vorster's Foreign Policy*. Pretoria: Academica, 1970.

Cohen, Warren, and Nancy Tucker, eds. *Lyndon Johnson Confronts the World: American Foreign Policy, 1963–1968*. Cambridge: Cambridge University Press, 1995.

Coker, Christopher. *The United States and South Africa, 1968–1985: Constructive Engagement and Its Critics*. Durham, NC: Duke University Press, 1986.

Coleman, James Smoot. *Nigeria: Background to Nationalism*. Berkeley: University of California Press, 1958.

Collins, Robert. "The Economic Crisis of 1968 and the Waning of the 'American Century.'" *American Historical Review* 101:2 (April 1996): 396–422.

Connelly, Matthew. *A Diplomatic Revolution: Algeria's Fight for Independence and the Origins of the Post-Cold War World*. New York: Oxford University Press, 2001.

———. *Fatal Misconception: The Struggle to Control World Population*. Cambridge, MA: Harvard University Press, 2008.

———. "Taking Off the Cold War Lens: Visions of North-South Conflict during the Algerian War for Independence." *American Historical Review* 105:3 (June 2000): 739–69.

Cooper, Frederick. *Africa Since 1940: The Past of the Present*. Cambridge: Cambridge University Press, 2002.

———. "Africa's Pasts and Africa's Historians." *Canadian Journal of African Studies/Revue Canadienne des Éstudes Africaines* 34:2 (2000): 298–336.

———. *Colonialism in Question: Theory, Knowledge, History*. Berkeley: University of California Press, 2005.

———. "Conflict and Connection: Rethinking Colonial African History." *American Historical Review* 99:5 (December 1994): 1516–45.

———. *Decolonization and African Society: The Labor Question in French and British Africa*. Cambridge: Cambridge University Press, 1996.

———. "Race, Ideology, and the Perils of Comparative History." *American Historical Review* 101:4 (October 1996): 1135–36.

Cooper, Frederick, and Randall Packard, eds. *International Development and the Social Sciences: Essays on the History and Politics of Knowledge*. Berkeley: University of California Press, 1997.

Cooper, Frederick, and Ann Laura Stoler, eds. *Tensions of Empire: Colonial Cultures in a Bourgeois World*. Berkeley: University of California Press, 1997.

Cope, Nicholas. *To Bind the Nation: Solomon kaDinuzulu and Zulu Nationalism, 1913–1933*. Pietermaritzburg, South Africa: University of Natal Press, 1993.

Crawford, James, and Tom Grant. "International Court of Justice." In *The Oxford Handbook to the United Nations*, ed. Thomas Weiss and Sam Daws. New York: Oxford University Press, 2008.

Crocker, Chester. *High Noon in Southern Africa: Making Peace in a Rough Neighborhood*. New York: W.W. Norton, 1992.

Cronje, Geoffrey. *In Tuiste vir die Nageslag: Die blywende Oplossing van Suid-Afrika se Rasse-Vraagstukke*. Johannesburg: Publicite, 1945.

Crummey, Donald, ed. *Banditry, Rebellion and Social Protest in South Africa*. Johannesburg: James Currey, 1986.

Crush, Jonathan, Alan Jeeves, and David Yudelman. *South Africa's Labour Empire: A History of Black Migrancy to the Gold Mines*. New York: Westview Press, 1991.

Cullather, Nick. *The Hungry World: America's Cold War Battle Against Poverty in Asia*. Cambridge, MA: Harvard University Press, 2010.

Culverson, Donald. *Contesting Apartheid: U.S. Activism, 1960–1987*. Boulder, CO: Westview Press, 1999.

Cumings, Bruce. *The Origins of the Korean War*. Vols. 1–2. Princeton, NJ: Princeton University Press, 1981, 1990.

Dallek, Richard. *Nixon and Kissinger: Partners in Power*. New York: Harper, 2007.

Danaher, Kevin. *In Whose Interest?: A Guide to U.S.-South Africa Relations.* Washington, DC: Institute for Policy Studies, 1984.

———. *The Political Economy of U.S. Policy toward South Africa.* Boulder, CO: Westview Press, 1985.

Davenport, Rodney, and Christopher Saunders. *South Africa: A Modern History.* 5th ed. New York: Macmillan Press, 2000.

Dear Mr. Vorster: Exchanges between President Kaunda and Mr. Vorster. Lusaka: Zambian Information Services, 1971.

DeConde, Alexander. *Ethnicity, Race, and American Foreign Policy.* Boston: Northwestern University Press, 1992.

Delius, Peter. *A Lion Amongst Cattle: Reconstruction and Resistance in Northern Transvaal.* Cape Town: University of Cape Town Press, 1997.

Deroche, Andy. *Andrew Young: Civil Rights Ambassador.* Wilmington, DE: SR Books, 2003.

———. *Black, White, and Chrome: The United States and Zimbabwe, 1953–1998.* New York: Africa World Press, 2001.

Diederichs, Nico. *Nasionalisme as Lewensbeskouing en sy Verhouding tot Internasionalisme.* Bloemfontein, South Africa: Nasionale Pers, 1936.

D'Oliveira, John. *Vorster—The Man.* Johannesburg: Ernest Stanton Publishers, 1977.

Drew, Allison, ed. *South Africa's Radical Tradition: A Documentary History,* vol. 2. Cape Town: Banchu Books, 1997.

Duara, Prasenjit, ed. *Decolonization: Perspectives from Now and Then.* New York: Routledge, 2004.

Dubow, Saul. *Scientific Racism in Modern South Africa.* Cambridge: Cambridge University Press, 1995.

Dudziak, Mary L. *Cold War Civil Rights: Race and the Image of American Democracy.* Princeton, NJ: Princeton University Press, 2000.

———. *Exporting American Dreams: Thurgood Marshall's African Journey.* New York: Oxford University Press, 2008.

Dugard, John, ed. *The South West Africa/Namibia Dispute: Documents and Scholarly Writings on the Controversy Between South Africa and the United Nations.* Berkeley: University of California Press, 1973.

Duignan, Peter, and L. H. Gann. *The United States and Africa: A History.* Cambridge: Cambridge University Press, 1984.

Dunn, Ross, ed. *The New World History.* New York: Bedford St. Martin's, 1999.

Du Toit, P. *Verslag van die Volkskongres oor die Armblankevraagstuk.* Cape Town: Nasionale Pers Beperk, 1935.

Dyer, Richard. *White.* London: Routledge, 1997.

Ekbladh, David. *The Great American Mission: Modernization & the Construction of an American World Order.* Princeton, NJ: Princeton University Press, 2010.

Elphick, Richard. "A Comparative History of White Supremacy." *Journal of Interdisciplinary History* 13:3 (Winter 1983): 503–13.

Enwezor, Okwui, ed. *Under Siege: Four African Cities, Freetown, Johannesburg, Kinshasa, Lagos.* Ostfildern-Ruit: Hatje Cantz, 2002.

Erasmus, Zimitri, ed. *Coloured by History, Shaped by Place: New Perspectives on Coloured Identities in Cape Town.* Colorado Springs: International Academic Publishers, 2001.

Ethiopia and Liberia v. South Africa: The South West Africa Cases, Occasional Papers No. 5. Los Angeles: University of California Press, 1968.

Eyffinger, Arthur. *The International Court of Justice, 1946–1996.* Boston: Kluwer Law International, 1996.

Eze, Emmanuel Chukwudi, ed. *African Philosophy: An Anthology.* Oxford: Blackwell Publishers, 1998.

Falola, Toyin. *Nationalism and African Intellectuals.* Rochester, NY: University of Rochester Press, 2001.

Fanon, Frantz. *Black Skin, White Masks.* New York: Grove Press, 1967.

──────. *The Wretched of the Earth*. New York: Grove Press, 1962.

Ferguson, James. *Global Shadows: Africa in the Neoliberal World Order*. Durham, NC: Duke University Press, 2006.

Ferguson, Niall, Charlies S. Maier, Erez Manela, and Daniel J. Sargent, eds. *The Shock of the Global: The 1970s in Perspective*. Cambridge, MA: Harvard University Press, 2010.

Fieldhouse, Roger. *Anti-Apartheid: A History of the Movement in Britain*. London: Merlin, 2004.

First, Ruth, Jonathan Steele, and Chestabel Gurney. *The South African Connection: Western Investment in Apartheid*. London: Temple Smith, 1972.

Flower, Ken. *Serving Secretly: An Intelligence Chief on Record, Rhodesia into Zimbabwe 1964–1981*. London: John Murray, 1987.

Fogg-Davis, Hawley. "The Racial Retreat of Contemporary Political Theory." *Perspectives on Politics* 1:3 (September 2003): 555–64.

Foot, Rosemary. *Substitute for Victory: The Politics of Peacemaking at the Korean Armistice Talks*. Ithaca, NY: Cornell University Press, 1990.

Franck, Thomas. *Judging the World Court*. New York: Priority Press Publications, 1986.

Franklin, John Hope. *The Color Line: Legacy for the Twenty-First Century*. Columbia: University of Missouri Press, 1993.

Fraser, Steve, and Gary Gerstle, eds. *The Rise and Fall of the New Deal Order, 1930–1980*. Princeton, NJ: Princeton University Press, 1989.

Fredrickson, George M. *Black Liberation: A Comparative History of Black Ideologies in the United States and South Africa*. Oxford: Oxford University Press, 1995.

──────. *White Supremacy: A Comparative Study of American and South African History*. Oxford: Oxford University Press, 1981.

Freund, Bill. *The Making of Contemporary Africa: The Development of African Society Since 1800*. 2nd ed. Boulder, CO: Lynne Rienner, 1998.

Gaddis, John Lewis. *The Cold War: A New History*. New York: Penguin Books, 2005.

──────. *Strategies of Containment: A Critical Appraisal of Postwar American National Security*. 2nd ed. New York: Oxford University Press, 2005.

──────. *We Now Know: Rethinking Cold War History*. New York: Oxford University Press, 1997.

Gaines, Kevin K. *American Africans in Ghana: Black Expatriates and the Civil Rights Era*. Chapel Hill: University of North Carolina Press, 2006.

Gandhi, Leela, ed. *Postcolonial Theory: A Critical Introduction*. New York: Columbia University Press, 1998.

Geiss, Imanuel. *The Pan-African Movement: A History of Pan-Africanism in America, Europe, and Africa*. London: Africana Publishing Company, 1974.

Gerhart, Gail M. *Black Power in South Africa: The Evolution of an Ideology*. Berkeley: University of California Press, 1979.

──────. *Gail M. Gerhart Collection, 1944–1979*. Chicago: Cooperative Africana Microfilm Project, 1979. Microfilm, Reels 1–11.

Gershenhorn, Jerry. *Melville J. Herskovits and the Racial Politics of Knowledge*. Lincoln: University of Nebraska Press, 2004.

Gerstle, Gary. *American Crucible: Race and Nation in the Twentieth Century*. Princeton, NJ: Princeton University Press, 2002.

Geyser, Ockert, ed. *Select Speeches*. Bloemfontein, South Africa: Institute of Contemporary History, 1977.

Gienow-Hecht, Jessica. "Cultural Transfer." In *Explaining the History of American Foreign Relations*. Edited by Michael J. Hogan and Thomas G. Paterson. Cambridge: Cambridge University Press, 2004.

Giliomee, Hermann. *The Afrikaners: A Biography of a People*. Charlottesville: University of Virginia, 2003.

Gilroy, Paul. *The Black Atlantic: Modernity and Double Consciousness*. Cambridge, MA: Harvard University Press, 1993.

————. "Nationalism, History and Ethnic Absolutism." *History Workshop* 30 (Autumn 1990): 114–20.

Gleijeses, Piero. *Conflicting Missions: Havana, Washington, and Africa, 1959–1976.* Chapel Hill: University of North Carolina Press, 2002.

Glendon, Mary Ann. *A World Made New: Eleanor Roosevelt and the Universal Declaration of Human Rights.* New York: Random House, 2002.

Goldin, Ian. *Making Race: The Politics and Economics of Coloured Identity.* Essex, UK: Longman, 1987.

Goudge, Paulette. *The Whiteness of Power: Racism in Third World Development and Aid.* London: Lawrence and Wishart, 2003.

Greenberg, Stanley. *Race and State in Capitalist Development: Comparative Perspectives.* New Haven, CT: Yale University Press, 1980.

Greenstein, Ran, ed. *Comparative Perspectives on South Africa.* Basingstoke, South Africa: Palgrave 1998.

Gregg, Robert. *Inside Out, Outside In: Essays in Comparative History.* Basingstoke, South Africa: Palgrave, 2000.

Grobler, Jackie. *A Decisive Clash? A Short History of Black Protest in South Africa, 1875–1976.* Pretoria: Acacia Books, 1988.

Gross, Ernest. *The Reminiscences of Ernest Gross.* New York: Columbia Center for Oral History. Microfilm, Reels 1–10.

————. *The United Nations: Structure for Peace.* New York: Harper, 1962.

Grubbs, Larry. *Secular Missionaries: American and African Development in the 1960s.* Amherst: University of Massachusetts, 2011.

Guelke, Adrian. *Rethinking the Rise and Fall of Apartheid: South Africa and World Politics.* New York: Palgrave Macmillan, 2005.

Gump, James. *The Dust Rose Like Smoke: The Subjugation of the Zulu and Sioux.* Lincoln: University of Nebraska Press, 1994.

Gurney, Christabel. "'A Great Cause': The Origins of the Anti-Apartheid Movement, June 1959–1960." *Journal of South African Studies* 26:1 (March 2000): 213–244.

Hance, William A. *Southern Africa and the United States.* New York: Columbia University Press, 1968.

Hanhimäki, Jussi. *The Flawed Architect: Henry Kissinger and American Foreign Policy.* New York: Oxford University Press, 2004.

Hanlon, Joseph. *Apartheid's Second Front: South Africa's War Against its Neighbors.* New York: Viking Penguin, 1986.

Hardt, Michael, and Antonio Negri. *Empire.* Cambridge, MA: Harvard University Press, 2000.

Hargreaves, James D. *Decolonization in Africa.* London: Longman, 1988.

Haslam, Jonathan. *Russia's Cold War: From the October Revolution to the Fall of the Wall.* New Haven, CT: Yale University Press, 2011.

Headlam, Cecil, ed. *The Milner Papers.* London: Cassell & Company, 1931, 1933.

Hepple, Alex. *South Africa: A Political and Economic History.* New York: Praeger, 1966.

Herbstein, Denis. *White Lies: Canon Collins and The Secret War Against Apartheid.* Cape Town: HSRC Press, 2004.

Hickey, Dennis, and Kenneth Wylie. *An Enchanting Darkness: The American Vision of Africa in the Twentieth Century.* East Lansing: Michigan State University Press, 1993.

Hilderbrand, Robert. *Dumbarton Oaks: The Origins of the United Nations and the Search for Postwar Security.* Chapel Hill: University of North Carolina Press, 1990.

Hill, Adelaide, and Martin Kilson, eds. *Apropos of Africa: Sentiments of Negro America Leaders on Africa from the 1800s to the 1950s.* London: Frank Cass, 1969.

Hindson, Douglas. *Pass Controls and the Urban African Proletariat.* Johannesburg: Ravan Press, 1987.

Hine, Darlene Clark, and Jacqueline McLeod, eds. *Crossing Boundaries: Comparative History of Black People in Diaspora.* Bloomington: University of Indiana Press, 1999.

Hobsbawm, E. J. *Nations and Nationalism since 1780: Programme, Myth, Reality.* Cambridge: Cambridge University Press, 1990.

Hodgkin, Thomas. *Nationalism in Colonial Africa*. New York: New York University Press, 1957.

Hogan, Michael J., ed. *America in the World: The Historiography of American Foreign Relations since 1941*. Cambridge: Cambridge University Press, 1996.

———. *The Marshall Plan: America, Britain, and the Reconstruction of Europe, 1947–1952*. Cambridge: Cambridge University Press, 1989.

Holt, Thomas. *The Problem of Race in the Twenty-First Century*. Cambridge, MA: Harvard University Press, 2000.

Hopkins, A. G. *Globalization in World History*. New York: W. W. Norton, 2002.

Horne, Gerald. *From the Barrel of a Gun: The United States and the War Against Zimbabwe, 1965–1980*. Chapel Hill: University of North Carolina Press, 2001.

Horwitz, Ralph. *The Political Economy of South Africa*. New York: Praeger, 1967.

Houser, George. *No One Can Stop the Train: Glimpses of Africa's Liberation Struggle*. New York: Pilgrim, 1989.

Hovet, Thomas, Jr. *Africa in the United Nations*. Chicago: Northwestern University Press, 1963.

Hull, Richard. *American Enterprise in South Africa: Historical Dimensions of Engagement and Disengagement*. New York. New York University Press, 1990.

Hurd, Ian. *After Anarchy: Legitimacy & Power in the United Nations Security Council*. Princeton, NJ: Princeton University Press, 2007.

Hyam, Ronald, and Peter Henshaw. *The Lion and the Springbok: Britain and South Africa since the Boer War*. Cambridge: Cambridge University Press, 2003.

Ikenberry, G. John. *After Victory: Institutions, Strategic Restraint, and the Rebuilding of Order After Major Wars*. Princeton, NJ: Princeton University Press, 2001.

———. *Liberal Leviathan: The Origins, Triumph, Crisis, and Transformation of the American World Order*. Princeton, NJ: Princeton University Press, 2011.

———. *Liberal Order and Imperial Ambition: Essays on American Power and International Order*. London: Polity Press, 2006.

International Court of Justice. *South West Africa Cases (Ethiopia and Liberia v. South Africa)*. Reports of Judgments, Advisory Opinions, and Orders. The Hague. Vols. 1–12.

Iriye, Akira. *Global Community: The Role of International Organizations in the Making of the Contemporary World*. Berkeley: University of California Press, 2002.

Jackson, Henry. *From the Congo to Soweto: U.S. Foreign Policy toward Africa since 1960*. New York: W. Morrow, 1982.

Jackson, Robert H. *Quasi-states: Sovereignty, International Relations and the Third World*. Cambridge: Cambridge University Press, 1990.

Jacobson, Matthew Frye. *Whiteness of a Different Color: European Immigrants and the Alchemy of Race*. Cambridge, MA: Harvard University Press, 1998.

Jansen, G. H. *Afro-Asia and Non-Alignment*. London: Faber & Faber, 1966.

Jian, Chen. *China's Road to the Korean War: The Making of the Sino-American Confrontation*. New York: Columbia University Press, 1994.

———. *Mao's China and the Cold War*. Chapel Hill: University of North Carolina Press, 2001.

Johnson, John C. DeGraft. *African Glory: The Story of Vanished Negro Kingdoms*. London: Watts, 1954.

July, Robert W., and Peter Benson, eds. *African Culture and Intellectual Leaders and the Development of the New African Nations*. New York: Rockefeller Foundation, 1982.

Kahin, George McTurnan. *The Asian-African Conference: Bandung, Indonesia, 1955*. Ithaca, NY: Cornell University Press, 1956.

Kallaway, Peter, ed. *Apartheid and Education: The Education of Black Africans*. Johannesburg: Ravan Press, 1984.

Karis, Thomas, and Gwendolen M. Carter, eds. *From Protest to Challenge: A Documentary History of African Politics in South Africa, 1953–1964*. Vol. 3. Stanford, CA: Hoover Institution Press, 1977.

Katzen, Leo. *Gold and the South African Economy: The Influence of the Goldmining Industry on Business Cycles and Economic Growth in South Africa, 1886–1961.* Cape Town: Gothic Printing, 1964.

Kaunda, Kenneth. *Zambia: Independence and Beyond—The Speeches of Kenneth Kaunda.* London: Thomas Nelson and Sons, 1966.

Kay, David. *The New Nations in the United Nations, 1960–1967.* New York: Columbia University Press, 1970.

Kitchen, Helen. *The United States and South Africa: Realities and Red Herrings.* Washington, DC: Center for Strategic and International Studies, Georgetown University, 1984.

Klerk, Willem de. *The Puritans of Africa: A History of Afrikanerdom.* Harmondsworth, UK: Penguin, 1976.

Kline, Benjamin. *Profit, Principle and Apartheid, 1948–1994: The Conflict of Economic and Moral Issues in the United States-South African Relations.* Lewiston, NY: Edwin Mellen Press, 1997.

Klotz, Audie. *Norms in International Relations: The Struggle against Apartheid.* Ithaca, NY: Cornell University Press, 1995.

Kolchin, Peter. "Whiteness Studies: The New History of Race in America." *Journal of American History* 89:1 (June 2002): 154–73.

Krenn, Michael. *Black Diplomacy: African Americans and the State Department, 1945–1969.* Armonk, NY: Sharpe, 1999.

Kunz, Diane. *Diplomacy of the Crucial Decade: American Foreign Relations During the 1960s.* New York: Columbia University Press, 1994.

Lake, Anthony. *The "Tar Baby" Option: American Policy toward Southern Rhodesia.* New York: Columbia University Press, 1976.

Lake, Marilyn, and Henry Reynolds. *Drawing the Global Colour Line: White Men's Countries and the International Challenge of Racial Equality.* Cambridge: Cambridge University Press, 2008.

Lamar, Howard, and Leonard Thompson, eds. *The Frontier in History: North America and Southern Africa Compared.* New Haven, CT: Yale University Press, 1981.

Latham, Michael E. *Modernization as Ideology: American Social Science and National Building in the Kennedy Era.* Chapel Hill: University of North Carolina Press, 2000.

———. *The Right Kind of Revolution: Modernization, Development, and U.S. Foreign Policy from the Cold War to the Present.* Ithaca, NY: Cornell University Press, 2011.

Lauren, Paul Gordon. *The Evolution of International Human Rights: Visions Seen.* Philadelphia: University of Pennsylvania Press, 2003.

———. *Power and Prejudice: The Politics and Diplomacy of Racial Discrimination.* Boulder, CO: Westview Press, 1988.

Lawrence, Mark Atwood. *Assuming the Burden: Europe and the American Commitment to War in Vietnam.* Berkeley: University of California Press, 2005.

Layton, Azza Salama. *International Politics and Civil Rights Politics in the United States.* Cambridge: Cambridge University Press, 2000.

Lee, Christopher J., ed. *Making a World after Empire: The Bandung Moment and Its Political Afterlives.* Athens: Ohio University Press, 2010.

Leffler, Melvyn P. *For the Soul of Mankind: The United States, the Soviet Union, and the Cold War.* New York: Hill and Wang, 2007.

———. *A Preponderance of Power: National Security, the Truman Administration, and the Cold War.* Stanford: Stanford University Press, 1991.

Legum, Colin. *Pan-Africanism: A Short Political Guide.* New York: Praeger, 1962.

Lemon, Anthony, ed. *Homes Apart: South Africa's Segregated Cities.* Bloomington: Indiana University Press, 1991.

Lerner, Mitchell, ed. *Looking Back at LBJ: White House Politics in a New Light.* Lawrence: University Press of Kansas, 2005.

Le Sueur, James D., ed. *The Decolonization Reader.* New York: Routledge, 2003.

Lewis, Martin, and Karen Wigen. *The Myth of Continents: A Critique of Metageography.* Berkeley: University of California Press, 1997.

Libby, Ronald T. *The Politics of Economic Power in Southern Africa.* Princeton, NJ: Princeton University Press, 1987.

Lochner, J. *Taal en Hegemony: Die Ontwikkeling van Afrikaans as Uitsaaitaal, 1923–1948.* Johannesburg: Potchefstroom, 2002.

Lodge, Tom. *Black Politics in South Africa since 1945.* London: Longman, 1983.

———. *Sharpeville: An Apartheid Massacre and Its Consequences.* New York: Oxford University Press, 2011.

Logevall, Fredrik. *Choosing War: The Lost Chance for Peace and the Escalation of War in Vietnam.* Berkeley: University of California Press, 1999.

Loney, Martin. *Rhodesia: White Racism and Imperial Response.* Harmondsworth, UK: Penguin, 1975.

Loomba, Ania, Suvir Kaul, Matti Bunzl, Antoinette Burton, and Jed Esty, eds. *Postcolonial Studies and Beyond.* Durham, NC: Duke University Press, 2005.

Lopez, Alfred, ed. *Postcolonial Whiteness: A Critical Reader on Race and Empire.* Albany: SUNY University Press, 2005.

Louis, Wm. Roger. *Ends of British Imperialism: The Scramble for Empire, Suez and Decolonization.* New York: I. B. Taurus, 2006.

———. *Imperialism at Bay: The United States and the Decolonization of the British Empire, 1941–1945.* New York: Oxford University Press, 1978.

Louw, P. Eric. *The Rise, Fall, and Legacy of Apartheid.* New York: Praeger, 2004.

Love, Janice. *The U.S. Anti-Apartheid Movement: Local Activism in Global Politics.* New York: Praeger, 1985.

Lundestad, Geir. "Empire by Invitation? The United States and Western Europe, 1945–1952." *Journal of Peace Research* 23:3 (September 1986): 263–77.

The Lusaka Manifesto On Southern Africa, 5th Summit of East and Central African States. Lusaka: Zambian Information Services, 1969.

Luthi, Lorenz M. *The Sino-Soviet Split: Cold War in the Communist World.* Princeton, NJ: Princeton University Press, 2008.

Mackler, Ian. *Pattern for Profit in Southern Africa.* London: Lexington Books, 1972.

MacShane, Denis, Martin Plaut, and David Ward. *Power! Black Workers, Their Unions, and the Struggle for Freedom in South Africa.* Nottingham, UK: Spokeman, 1984.

Magubane, Bernard Makhosezwe. *The Political Economy of Race and Class in South Africa.* New York: Monthly Review Press, 1979.

———. *The Ties That Bind: African-American Consciousness of Africa.* Trenton, NJ: Africa World Press, 1987.

Mahoney, Richard. *JFK: Ordeal in Africa.* Oxford: Oxford University Press, 1983.

Maier, Charles S. *Among Empires: American Ascendancy and its Predecessors.* Cambridge, MA: Harvard University Press, 2006.

———. "Consigning the Twentieth Century to History: Alternative Narratives for the Modern Era." *American Historical Review* 105:3 (2000): 807–31.

Makgetla, Neva, and Ann Seidman. *Outposts of Monopoly Capitalism: Southern African in the Changing Global Economy.* Westport, CT: Lawrence Hill, 1980.

Mamdani, Mahmood. *Citizen and Subject: Contemporary Africa and the Legacy of Late Colonialism.* Princeton, NJ: Princeton University Press, 1996.

Manela, Erez. *The Wilsonian Moment: Self-Determination and the International Origins of Anticolonial Nationalism.* New York: Oxford University Press, 2007.

———. "Writing Disease Control into Cold War History." *Diplomatic History* 34:2 (April 2010): 299–323.

Manning, Patrick. *Navigating World History: Historians Create a Global Past.* New York: Palgrave Macmillan, 2003.

Mansergh, Nicholas, ed. *Documents and Speeches on Commonwealth Affairs, 1952–1962.* Oxford: Oxford University Press, 1963.

Marks, Shula. *The Ambiguities of Dependence in South Africa: Class, Nationalism, and the State in Twentieth-Century.* Johannesburg: Ravan Press, 1986.

Marks, Shula, and Stanley Trapido, eds. *The Politics of Race, Class, and Nationalism in Twentieth Century South Africa.* Essex, UK: Longman, 1987.

Marx, Anthony. *Making Race and Nation: A Comparison of South Africa, the United States and Brazil.* Cambridge: Cambridge University Press, 1998.

Massie, Robert Kinloch. *Losing the Bonds: The United States and South Africa in the Apartheid Years.* New York: Nan A. Talese, 1997.

Mazower, Mark. *No Enchanted Palace: The End of Empire and the Ideological Origins of the United Nations.* Princeton, NJ: Princeton University Press, 2009.

Mazrui, Ali. *Towards a Pax Africana.* London: Littlehampton Book Services, 1967.

Mbembe, Achille. *On the Postcolony.* Berkeley: University of California Press, 2001.

McCormick, Thomas. *America's Half-Century: United States Foreign Policy in the Cold War and After.* 2nd ed. Baltimore: John Hopkins University Press, 1995.

McMahon, Robert. *The Cold War on the Periphery: The United States, India, and Pakistan.* New York: Columbia University Press, 1994.

———. *Colonialism and Cold War: The United States and the Struggle for Indonesian Independence, 1945–1949.* Ithaca, NY: Cornell University Press, 1981.

Memmi, Albert. *The Colonizer and the Colonized.* Boston: Beacon Press, 1965.

Meredith, Martin. *In the Name of Apartheid: South African in the Postwar Period.* London: Hamish Hamilton, 1988.

Meriwether, James H. *Proudly We Can Be Africans: Black Americans and Africa, 1935–1961.* Chapel Hill: University of North Carolina Press, 2002.

Milner, Alfred. *Nation and the Empire; Being a Collection of Speeches and Addresses.* London: Constable and Company, 1913.

Minter, William. *King Soloman's Mines Revisited: Western Interests and the Burdened History of Southern Africa.* New York: Basic Books, 1986.

Mokoena, Kenneth, ed. *South Africa and the United States: The Declassified History.* New York: W. W. Norton, 1993.

Moodie, T. Dunbar. *The Rise of Afrikanerdom: Power, Apartheid, and Afrikaner Civil Religion.* Berkeley: University of California Press, 1975.

Moodie, T. Dunbar, and Vivienne Ndatshe. *Going for Gold: Men, Mines, and Migration.* Berkeley: University of California Press, 1994.

Mostern, Kenneth. "Social Marginality/Blackness: Subjects of Postmodernity." *MELUS* 23:4 (Winter 1998): 167–87.

Moyn, Samuel. *Last Utopia: Human Rights in History.* Cambridge, MA: Harvard University Press, 2010.

Mtshali, B. Vulindlela. *Rhodesia: Background to Conflict.* New York: Hawthorn Books, 1967.

Muehlenbeck, Philip E. *Betting on the Africans: John F. Kennedy's Courting of African Nationalist Leaders.* New York: Oxford University Press, 2012.

Nattrass, Jill. *The South African Economy: Its Growth and Change.* Oxford: Oxford University Press, 1981.

Nesbitt, Francis Njubi. *Race for Sanctions: African Americans against Apartheid, 1946–1994.* Bloomington: Indiana University Press, 2004.

Ngai, Mai M. *Impossible Subjects: Illegal Aliens and the Making of Modern America.* Princeton, NJ: Princeton University Press, 2004.

Nimocks, Walter. *Milner's Young Men: The Kindergarten in Edwardian Imperial Affairs.* Durham, NC: Duke University Press, 1968.

Nixon, Rob. *Homelands, Harlem and Hollywood: South African Culture and the World Beyond.* New York: Routledge, 1994.

Nkrumah, Kwame. *Africa Must Unite.* London: Heinemann, 1963.

———. *Ghana: The Autobiography of Kwame Nkrumah.* New York: International Publishers, 1957.

———. *Towards Colonial Freedom: Africa in the Struggle Against World Imperialism.* London: Heinemann, 1962.

Noer, Thomas J. *Cold War and Black Liberation: The United States and White Rule in Africa, 1948–1967.* Columbia: University of Missouri Press, 1985.

———. *Soapy: A Biography of G. Mennen Williams*. Ann Arbor: University of Michigan Press, 2005.

Norval, Morgan. *Inside the ANC: The Evolution of a Terrorist Organization*. Washington, DC: Selous Foundation Press, 1990.

Nye, Joseph S. Jr. *Soft Power: The Means to Success in World Politics*. New York, Public Affairs, 2004.

Odendaal, Andr. *Vukani Bantu! The Beginnings of Black Protest Politics in South Africa to 1912*. Cape Town: David Phillip, 1984.

Offenburger, Andrew, Scott Rosenberg, and Christopher Saunders, eds. *A South African and American Comparative Reader: The Best of Safundi and Other Selected Articles*. New York: Safundi, 2002.

O'Meara, Dan. *Volkskapitalisme: Class, Capital and Ideology in the Development of Afrikaner Nationalism*. Johannesburg: Ravan Press, 1983.

Omi, Michael, and Howard Winant. *Racial Formation in the United States: From the 1960s to the 1990s*. 2nd ed. New York: Routledge, 1994.

Onslow, Sue, ed. *Cold War in Southern Africa: White Power, Black Liberation*. London: Routledge, 2009.

Padmore, George. *Pan-Africanism or Communism? The Coming Struggle for Africa*. New York: Doubleday, 1956.

Pakenham, Thomas. *The Boer War*. New York: Random House, 1979.

Pan Africanist Congress. *The Africanist*. Maseru, Lesotho: Department of Publicity and Information, 1968. Microfilm, Reel 1.

Pan Africanist Congress Collections and Documents. York, England: University of York Photographic Unit by the Southern African Documentation Project of the Centre for Southern African Studies, 1976. Microfilm, Reel 1.

Parker, Jason C. *Brother's Keeper: The United States, Race, and Empire in the British Caribbean, 1937–1962*. New York: Oxford University Press, 2008.

Patterson, James. *Grand Expectations: The United State, 1945–1974*. New York: Oxford University Press, 1996.

Perlstein, Rick. *Nixonland: The Rise of a President and the Fracturing of America*. New York: Scribner, 2008.

Pfister, Roger. *Apartheid South Africa and Africa States: From Pariah to Middle Power, 1992–1994*. London: Tauris Academic Studies, 2005.

Plummer, Brenda Gayle. *Orientalism*. New York: Vintage, 1979.

———. *Rising Wind: Black Americans and U.S. Foreign Affairs, 1935–1960*. Chapel Hill: University of North Carolina Press, 1996.

———, ed. *Window on Freedom: Race, Civil Rights and Foreign Affairs, 1945–1988*. Chapel Hill: University of North Carolina Press, 2003.

Pomeroy, William J. *Apartheid, Imperialism, and African Freedom*. New York: International Publishers, 1986.

Posel, Deborah. *The Making of Apartheid, 1948–1961: Conflict and Compromise*. Oxford: Oxford University Press, 1991.

Prashad, Vijay. *The Darker Nations: A People's History of the Third World*. New York: The New Press, 2007.

Précis of the Reports of the Commissions Appointed to Enquire into the Events Occurring on March 21, 1960 at Sharpeville and Langa. Johannesburg: South African Institute of Race Relations, 1961.

Preston, Andrew. *The War Council: McGeorge Bundy, the NSC, and Vietnam*. Cambridge, MA: Harvard University Press, 2006.

Quaison-Sackey, Alex. *African Unbound: Reflections of an African Statesman*. New York: Praeger, 1963.

Ralinala, Rendani Moses. *Urban Apartheid and African Response*. Cape Town: University of Cape Town Press, 2002.

Rathbone, Richard. *Nkrumah & the Chiefs: Politics of Chieftaincy in Ghana, 1951–1960*. Athens: Ohio University Press, 2000.

Razis, Vincent. *The American Connection: The Influence of United States Business on South Africa.* New York: St. Martin's Press, 1986.

Reddy, Enuga S., ed. *Oliver Tambo: Apartheid and the International Community, Addresses to the United Nations Committees and Conferences.* New Delhi: Sterling, 1991.

The Road to Democracy in South Africa: Volume I (1960–1970). Compiled by South African Democracy Education Trust. Paarl: Zebra Press, 2004.

Romulo, Carlos. *The Meaning of Bandung.* Chapel Hill: University of North Carolina Press, 1966.

Rosenberg, Emily S. "Considering Borders." In *Explaining the History of Foreign Relations.* Edited by Michael J. Hogan and Thomas G. Paterson. Cambridge: Cambridge University Press, 2005.

Rosenne, Shabtai. *The World Court: What It Is and How It Works.* Leiden: Martinus Nijhoff Publishers, 2003.

Rusk, Dean. *As I Saw It: As Told to Richard Rusk.* New York: Penguin Books, 1990.

Sachs, Bernard. *The Road to Sharpeville.* New York: Liberty Book Club, 1961.

Said, Edward W. *Culture and Imperialism.* London: Chatto and Windus, 1993.

Sanders, James. *Apartheid's Friends: The Rise and Fall of South Africa's Secret Service.* London: John Murray, 2006.

Schulzinger, Robert D. A., ed. *A Companion to American Foreign Relations.* Oxford: Wiley-Blackwell, 2003.

———. *Time for War: The United States and Vietnam, 1941–1975.* New York: Oxford University Press, 1997.

Scott, David. *Conscripts of Modernity: The Tragedy of Colonial Enlightenment.* Durham, NC: Duke University Press, 2004.

Scott, James C. *Domination and the Arts of Resistance: Hidden Transcripts.* New Haven, CT: Yale University Press, 1990.

Seidman, Ann. *South Africa and U.S. Multinational Corporations.* Westport, CT: Lawrence Hill, 1977.

Sellström, Tor. *Sweden and National Liberation: Southern Africa.* Stockholm: Nordiska Afrikainstitet, 1999.

Serfontein, J. H. P. *Brotherhood of Power: Exposé of the Secret Afrikaner Broederbond.* London: Rex Collings, 1979.

Shepard, Todd. *The Invention of Decolonization: The Algerian War and the Remaking of France.* Ithaca, NY: Cornell University Press, 2006.

Shepherd, Jr., George. *Anti-Apartheid: Transnational Conflict and Western Policy in the Liberation of South Africa.* Westport, CT: Greenwood, 1977.

Shipway, Martin. *Decolonization and Its Impact: A Comparative Approach to the End of Colonial Empires.* Oxford: Blackwell, 2008.

Shubin, Vladmir. *ANC: The View from Moscow,* 2nd revised ed. Sunnyside, South Africa: Jacana Media, 2008.

———. *The Hot "Cold War": The USSR in Southern Africa.* London: Pluto Press, 2008.

Singh, Nagendra. *The Role and Record of the International Court of Justice.* Boston: Martinus Nijhoff Publishers, 1989.

Singh, Nikhil Pal. *Black Is a Country: Race and the Unfinished Struggle for Democracy.* Cambridge, MA: Harvard University Press, 2004.

Skinner, Rob. *The Foundations of Anti-Apartheid: Liberal Humanitarians and Transnational Activists in Britain and the United States, c.1919–64.* London: Palgrave Macmillan, 2010.

Skocpol, Theda, and Margaret Somers. "The Uses of Comparative History in Macrosocial Inquiry." *Comparative Studies in Society and History* 22:2 (1980): 174–97.

Slonim, Soloman. *South West Africa and the United Nations: An International Mandate in Dispute.* Baltimore: John Hopkins University Press, 1972.

Smith, Ian. *The Great Betrayal: The Memoirs of Ian Douglas Smith.* London: Blake Publishing, 1997.

Smith, Tony. "New Bottles for New Wine: A Pericentric Framework for the Study of the Cold War." *Diplomatic History* 24:4 (December 2002): 567–91.

Snyder, Sarah B. *Human Rights Activism and the End of the Cold War: A Transnational History of the Helsinki Network*. Cambridge: Cambridge University Press, 2011.

———. *Report of Ordinary General Meeting of Stockholders*. Johannesburg: Cape Times Limited, 1956–1970.

South African Reserve Bank. *Annual Economic Report*. Pretoria: Hayne & Gibson, 1962–1972.

South West Africa Survey 1967. Pretoria: Department of Foreign Affairs, 1967.

Staniland, Martin. *American Intellectuals and African Nationalists, 1951–1970*. New Haven, CT: Yale University Press, 1971.

Staples, Amy. *The Birth of Development: How the World Bank, Food and Agricultural Organization, and World Health Organization Change the World, 1945–1965*. Kent, OH: Kent State University Press, 2006.

Stebenne, David. *Arthur J. Goldberg: New Deal Liberal*. New York: Oxford University Press, 1996.

Stoler, Ann Laura. *Carnal Knowledge and Imperial Power: Race and the Intimate in Colonial Rule*. Berkeley: University of California Press, 2002.

———, ed. *Haunted by Empire: Geographies of the Intimate in North American History*. Durham, NC: Duke University Press, 2006.

Stueck, William. *The Korean War: An International History*. Princeton, NJ: Princeton University Press, 1995.

Sugrue, Thomas. *The Origins of the Urban Crisis: Race and Inequality in Postwar Detroit*. Princeton, NJ: Princeton University Press, 1996.

Suri, Jeremi. *The Global Revolutions of 1968*. New York: W. W. Norton, 2007.

———. *Henry Kissinger and the American Century*. Cambridge, MA: Harvard University Press, 2007.

———. *Power and Protest: Global Revolution and the Rise of Détente*. Cambridge, MA: Harvard University Press, 2003.

Tan, See Seng, and Amitav Acharya, ed. *Bandung Revisited: The Legacy of the 1955 Asian-African Conference for International Order*. Singapore: NUS Press, 2008.

Thiongo, Ngugi Wa. *Decolonizing the Mind: The Politics of Language in African Literature*. Portsmouth, NH: Heinemann, 1986.

Thomas, A. M. *The American Predicament: Apartheid and United States Foreign Policy*. Brookfield, VT: Ashgate, 1997.

Thomas, Scott M. *The Diplomacy of Liberation: The Foreign Relations of the African National Congress Since 1960*. London: I. B. Taurus, 1996.

Thompson, Leonard. *A History of South Africa*. 3rd ed. New Haven, CT: Yale University Press, 2000.

———. *The Political Mythology of Apartheid*. New Haven, CT: Yale University Press, 1985.

———. "The Study of South African History in the United States." *International Journal of African Historical Studies* 25:1 (1992): 25–37.

Thomson, Alex. *Incomplete Engagement: U.S. Foreign Policy towards the Republic of South Africa, 1981–1988*. Brookfield, VT: Ashgate, 1996.

Thörn, Håkan. *Anti-Apartheid and the Emergence of a Global Civil Society*. London: Palgrave, 2009.

Tignor, Robert L. *Capitalism and Nationalism at the End of Empire: State and Business in Decolonizing Egypt, Nigeria, and Kenya, 1945–1963*. Princeton, NJ: Princeton University Press, 1998.

Tilley, Alvin B. *Between Homeland and Motherland: Africa, U.S. Foreign Policy, and Black Leadership in America*. Ithaca, NY: Cornell University Press, 2011.

Trachtenberg, Marc. *A Constructed Peace: The Making of the European Settlement, 1945–1963*. Princeton, NJ: Princeton University Press, 1999.

U.N. *General Assembly Official Records*. New York: U.N. Office of Information.

U.N. *Security Council Official Records*. New York: U.N. Office of Information.

U.N. *The United Nations and Apartheid, 1948–1994*. New York: U.N. Office of Information, 1994.

U.N. *Yearbook of the United Nations*. New York: U.N. Office of Information.

U.S. Central Intelligence Agency. *CIA Research Reports: Africa, 1946–1976.* Frederick, MD: University Publications of America, 1983. Microfilm, Reels 1–3.

U.S. Congress, House. *Hearings Before the Subcommittee on Africa of the Committee on Foreign Affairs.* Parts 1–3. 89th Cong. (1966).

U.S. Department of State. *South Africa: Internal Affairs and Foreign Affairs, Confidential U.S. State Department Central Files.* Frederick, MD: University Publications of America, 1985. Microfilm. Reels 28–37.

U.S. Department of State. Office of the Historian. *Foreign Relations of the United States: Foundations of Foreign Policy, 1958–1960, vol. 14: Africa.* Washington, DC: GPO.

U.S. Department of State. Office of the Historian. *Foreign Relations of the United States: Foundations of Foreign Policy, 1961–1963, vol. 21: Africa, vol. 24: United Nations.* Washington, DC: GPO.

U.S. Department of State. Office of the Historian. *Foreign Relations of the United States: Foundations of Foreign Policy, 1964–1968, vol. 24: Africa, vol. 33: United Nations.* Washington, DC: GPO.

U.S. Department of State. Office of the Historian. *Foreign Relations of the United States: Foundations of Foreign Policy, 1969–1972, vol. 1: Foundations, vol. 5: United Nations, vol. E-5: Sub-Saharan Africa.* Washington, DC: GPO.

Van Jaarsveld, Floris Albertus. *The Awakening of Afrikaner Nationalism, 1868–1881.* Cape Town: Human and Rousseau, 1961.

Villiers, Les de. *In Sight of Surrender: The U.S. Sanctions Campaign against South Africa, 1946–1993.* New York: Praeger, 1995.

Von Eschen, Penny. *Race Against Empire: Black Americans and Anticolonialism, 1937–1957.* Ithaca, NY: Cornell University Press, 1997.

Wallerstein, Immanuel. *Africa and the Modern World.* Trenton, NJ: Africa World Press, 1986.

———. *Africa: The Politics of Independence and Unity.* Lincoln: University of Nebraska Press, 2005.

———. *The Essential Wallerstein.* New York: The New Press, 2000.

Walshe, Peter. *The Rise of African Nationalism in South Africa: The African National Congress, 1912–1952.* London: C. Hurst, 1970.

Warwick, Peter, ed. *The South African War: The Anglo-Boer War, 1899–1902.* London: Longmans, 1980.

Waters, Ronald. *Pan Africanism in the African Diaspora: An Analysis of Modern Afrocentric Political Movements.* Detroit: Wayne State University Press, 1993.

Weitz, Eric. "From Vienna to the Paris System." *American Historical Review,* 113:5 (2008): 1313–43.

Welensky, Roy. *Welensky's 4000 Days: The Life and Death of the Federation of Rhodesia and Nyasaland.* London: Collins, 1964.

Westad, Odd Arne, ed. *Brothers in Arms: The Rise and Fall of the Sino-Soviet Alliance, 1945–1963.* Stanford: Stanford University Press, 1998.

———. *The Global Cold War: Third World Interventions and the Making of our Times.* Cambridge: Cambridge University Press, 2005.

White, George. *Holding the Line: Race, Racism, and American Foreign Policy toward Africa, 1953–1961.* Lanham, MD: Rowman and Littlefield, 2005.

Wilcox, Francis. *UN and the Nonaligned Nations.* New York: Foreign Policy Association, 1962.

Willetts, Peter. *The Non-Aligned Movement: The Origins of a Third World Alliance.* London: Frances Printer, 1978.

Wilson, Francis. *Labour in the South African Gold Mines, 1911–1969.* Cambridge: Cambridge University Press, 1972.

Wilson, Henry S. *Origins of West African Nationalism.* London: Macmillan, 1969.

Winant, Howard. *The World Is a Ghetto: Race and Democracy since World War II.* New York: Basic Books, 2001.

Windrich, Elaine. *Britain and the Politics of Rhodesian Independence.* New York: Africana Publishing Company, 1978.

Winter, Gordon. *Inside BOSS: South Africa's Secret Police.* Harmondsworth, UK: Penguin, 1981.

Woods, Randall B. *LBJ: Architect of American Ambition.* Cambridge, MA: Harvard University Press, 2007.

Worger, William H. *South Africa's City of Diamonds: Mine Workers and Monopoly Capitalism in Kimberly, 1867–1895*. New Haven, CT: Yale University Press, 1987.

Wright, Richard. *Black Power: Three Books From Exile*. New York: Harper Perennial, 2008.

Young, Kenneth. *Rhodesia and Independence: A Study in British Colonial Policy*. London: Eyre and Spottiswoode, 1967.

Young, Marilyn B. *The Vietnam Wars, 1945–1990*. New York: Harper Perennial, 1991.

Young, Robert J. C. *Postcolonialism: An Historical Introduction*. London: Blackwell, 2001.

Zacklin, Ralph. *The United Nations and Rhodesia: A Study in International Law*. New York: Praeger, 1974.

Zubok, Vladislav M. *A Failed Empire: The Soviet Union in the Cold War from Stalin to Gorbachev*. Chapel Hill: University of North Carolina Press, 2008.

———. *Inside the Kremlin's Cold War: From Stalin to Krushchev*. Cambridge, MA: Harvard University Press, 1997.

Bibliography

INDEX